PRAISE FOR
BILLY JOEL

"[A] funny and revealing account of one of the most popular songwriters of our time."

—*New York Daily News*

"[*Billy Joel: The Definitive Biography*] not only lives up to its subtitle, but has the strengths of both an autobiography and biography. . . . [It] will likely end up as the most complete tome on the bard of Long Island, with the most access to its subject."

—*Houston Press*

"Schruers clearly realizes he has gold in his interviews with Joel, his friends, paramours, and confidants. . . . [He delivers] insights on individual songs that will surprise even the most studied Joel fan . . . [and] has given us the most complete look at Joel's life and career to date."

—*Dallas Morning News*

"Schruers's account of Joel's 1970s rise is fantastic, rich in anecdotes about the origins of different songs."

—*Billboard*

"[T]he rollicking story of a Hicksville boy made good."

—Maura Johnston, *Newsday*

"Schruers uses interviews to great effect, allowing to emerge the everyman persona that resonates with Joel's fans. . . . a fair, thorough assessment of Joel's celebrity."

—*Publishers Weekly*

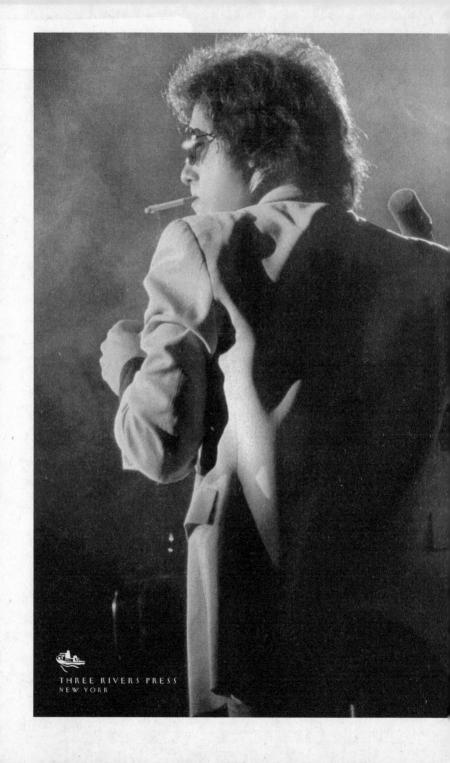

THREE RIVERS PRESS
NEW YORK

BILLY JOEL

THE DEFINITIVE BIOGRAPHY

FRED SCHRUERS

Photography credits can be found on page 371.
Grateful acknowledgments is made to Newsday LLC for permission to
reprint excerpts from "Look What Grew on Our Lawns" by Harvey Aronson
(October 28, 1967), copyright © 1967 Newsday LLC, and "Joel, Wife
Splitting Up" by Glenn Gamboa (June 18, 2009), copyright © 2009 Newsday
LLC. All rights reserved. Reprinted by permission of Newsday LLC.

Library of Congress Cataloging-in-Publication Data
Schruers, Fred.
Billy Joel / Fred Schruers. — First edition.
Includes bibliographical references and index.
1. Joel, Billy. 2. Rock musicians—United States—Biography. I. Title.
ML420.J72S34 2014
782.42166092—dc23
[B]
2014034084

ISBN 978-0-8041-4021-8
eBook ISBN 978-0-8041-4020-1

PRINTED IN THE UNITED STATES OF AMERICA

Book design by Elizabeth Rendfleisch
Cover design by Michael Morris
Cover photograph © Todd Kaplan/AtlasIcons.com

10 9 8 7 6 5 4 3 2 1

First Paperback Edition

CONTENTS

BILLY JOEL

PROLOGUE

I t's five o'clock on a Monday, and the regular crowd shuffles in ... to the chilly, unpopulated great hall of Madison Square Garden, where a crew is still slapping down chairs on the big slabs of decking that cover the hockey rink.

Toting guitars, drumsticks, horns, and earpieces, Billy Joel's band arrays itself for a sound check, and now up a metal staircase comes the man himself. You could say he's shuffling as well; both hips were replaced in mid-2010, and now, January 27, 2014, he's fully mended—but not likely to be doing the backflips off the piano that, he'll occasionally speculate, led to that operation.

As he perches on his compact stool, checking settings on the hybrid acoustic/synthesized piano he uses, the band looks up expectantly. He's notoriously bored by sound checks, which means there'll be plenty of japes about his age, certain band peccadillos, or the world situation, all delivered with ready wit. But at the same time, all hands had better be "on the one" when he delivers a casual instruction, because the message won't come twice.

From time to time, as in an open-air-arena sound check in Perth in December 2008, he'll get a wild hair and lead the band through pretty much an entire classic album. In that case, it was *Disraeli Gears* by Cream—at least until the constables put a stop to it after a volley of noise complaints from the neighborhood.

Billy, warmed by a plain black watch cap and a wool sports coat, plinks out a few exploratory notes as the others tune up around him. He gazes about—"I don't hear the room as well I used to hear it."

Tonight will be his forty-seventh show at what's pretty much the most storied concert venue in the world. You get here just the way you get to Carnegie Hall—"Practice"—but it really helps if you sell tens of millions of albums. In his case the figure is 110 million or so, and that's part of the reason he's playing this inaugural gig to kick off an open-ended "residency," a series of monthly Garden dates that will continue, as he said in a recent press conference, "as long as there's demand."

A blogger for *Forbes* computed that, based on rapid sellouts, the strength of the Joel catalog, and what demographers might call his enormous local and worldwide fan base, something approaching forty shows might match that demand.

No one's expecting him to do that many, of course, but you never know.

Billy's still eyeballing the arena's distant reaches, somewhat obscured by new carpeted catwalks leading to bunkerlike luxury suites. He's wondering why the sound waves seem muted: "Either I'm going deaf or the room is different. Is there a big sponge up there?" He waits a beat, as the band, knowing his timing, remains at parade rest—"Ah, I guess it's the hair in my ears."

At sixty-four, he's allowed to kvetch a bit. Three hours from now, a few songs into his set, when the packed house has already marched in place to the epic sweep of "Miami 2017," bounced in rhythm (the Garden is on massive, pulsating springs) to "Pressure," crooned along to the enchanting soliloquy that is "Summer, Highland Falls," and ditty-bopped and doo-wopped to "The Longest Time," he pauses: "Good evening, New York City . . ." A roar like a gut punch breaks over the stage. "I have no idea how long this is gonna go."

The alert eyes, somehow made more magnetic by the bald pate

above, swivel around the room as he takes a sip of water. The guys in the crowd give their dates a knowing look—*You think it's really water?* "This year is my fiftieth year in show business." A subtle resettling of his spine—as in, *We're practicing our trade here.* Another beat. "What was I thinking?" Now he turns to peer at the image of his head and torso, many times life-size. "I didn't think I was gonna end up looking like that in 1964."

The big banks of speakers are putting out their crisp, almost sub-liminal exhalations as the crowd noise modulates down—the fans are thinking what fifty years means to Billy, and to them. They're hoping to hear "Movin' Out (Anthony's Song)," "New York State of Mind," and "River of Dreams," which are all but a certainty, as well as "Piano Man," which *is* a certainty, and the set list sites have hinted they'll be sent out into the night after a four-song encore capped by a tub-thumping, horn-washed take of "Only the Good Die Young."

There's time enough for the key anthems, and time, too, for some "deep cuts" like "Where's the Orchestra?" But first Billy's got one more observation about the doo-wop moment: "It sounds better in the men's room," as he and his bandmates demonstrated, bouncing "The Longest Time" off dingy tiles in the song's 1984 video. "We used to sneak out at night and sing it on the street corner—and people would throw shit at us!"

Well, clearly that was then. And tonight, when he's sixty-four, they still need him, too, to borrow a phrase from a song. Mike DelGuidice, new utility player in the band, centerpiece of his own Joel tribute band called Big Shot, and maybe the number one fan in the room, will sum it up later in the bar where the band gathers. "He's just the guy. That is *the guy.* He's more loved than anyone on he planet, musically." Mike has just come down from the hotel room he hurried to after the gig to take a family phone call. When he sat on the bed and started to think about having just played opening night alongside Billy in the Garden, he "wept like a baby for a good five minutes."

That Billy's even here in this sacramental spot, soon to be filled with eighteen thousand faithful fans, goes against the steepest of odds. If a harbormaster in Havana hadn't let his father's family disembark to find refuge from the Nazis; if his mom hadn't found that piano teacher; if he hadn't drilled into his own alienation to write his saga as that piano man; and if some label bosses hadn't stuck by him after his first two albums tanked, he might be sitting down to the keys at a very different spot on the map.

There's a particular moment in almost every one of his shows when, a song or two in, while listening to that odd sonic tumult of roaring approval, hollered song titles, and proprietary shout-outs of his first name, he leans left and forward on his piano stool and searches the faces of the crowd in his periphery. There's usually a tentative grin, but there's also a jigger of uncertainty—and therefore vulnerability—that stops short of neediness but is still somehow in touch with it. Tonight it will come before "Summer, Highland Falls," with its telling lyric: "And as we stand upon the ledges of our lives / With our respective similarities / It's either sadness or euphoria."

On a different day, in a different city, in what his intimates still think of as the bad, sad old days of 2009, he grew reflective on a hotel balcony: "Obviously I have plenty of regrets. Whenever I hurt somebody, whether it was inadvertently or rashly, I still regret that to this day. I've never wanted to ever hurt anybody, and those are regrets I'll take with me to the grave. But I don't think you've lived unless you have regrets. I don't think you've had that experience without them, where you can say honestly, when you're ready to kick, hey, I *lived*. Good Lord, man, what a life I've lived.

"I think I'm going to do that. That may take some of the sting out of dying—to say, I did it all."

THE BALLAD OF BILLY THE KID

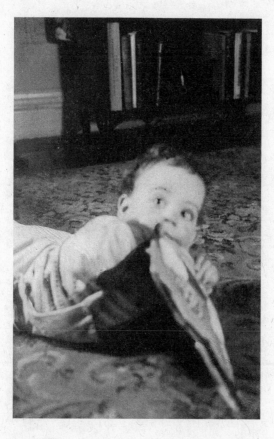

CHAPTER I

LIVING HERE IN LEVITTOWN

Asmokestack rises from a hulking brick factory. Along its flank, large descending letters read "JOEL." It is a grainy black-and-white image, part of a documentary called *The Joel Files* that was made about Billy Joel's family and their struggles to survive—and escape—the rise of the Nazis in Germany. In a striking film portrait of war's aftermath, Billy and his half-brother Alex meet the family of the Nazi industrialist who usurped the Joel family fortune—and went on to be a highly regarded member of the German commercial elite in the post-war years. The shot of the factory was taken in Nuremberg during the height of the family's textile operation in the late 1930s. There's no trace of the factory now, but there is a small family cemetery where some of Billy's relatives are buried.

As a student of history, Billy knows that the odds his father beat in getting out of wartime Europe were long. Only when he visited that graveyard in Nuremberg did he fully realize how many of his family members—uncles, aunts, granduncles, grave marker upon grave marker of Joels—were less fortunate. And there's also the knowledge of those who were never brought back, whose bodies are gone forever. Billy grew up hearing the names of the lost sporadically in family conversations, but only in recent years has a fuller picture of his family history emerged.

Of course Billy Joel's stature as a celebrity, as well as the existence of a body of work that has touched so many lives and even transformed a few, does not make the Joel family's Holocaust saga any more tragic than millions of obscure ones. In fact, Billy's very existence is the result of a rare happy ending. But over time, that happy ending has not been his alone. It's filtered out into the broad swath of people to whom Billy's music has meant so much. Along with his peers Bruce Springsteen and John Mellencamp, he has addressed both the hopes and the heartbreaks at the center of the American dream—the one his forebears, he has learned, traveled far and struggled hard to experience.

THE JOEL FAMILY'S tumultuous journey to America began with Billy's paternal grandfather, Karl Amson Joel, who came from a family in Coburg, in Bavarian Franconia, in Germany's scenic southeast. The patriarch was a man named Faustus Joel, whose son Julius became a tailor and eventually began the small textile business Billy's grandfather expanded into Waschenmanufakturer Joel. Karl married Meta Fleischmann, and their only child and Billy's father, Helmut (later anglicized to Howard), was born in 1923. By the time Karl was thirty-nine, in 1927, he had enough savings to start a business in household linens, the Karl Joel Linen Goods Company, which grew from a four-room apartment foothold into a substantial line of mail-order clothing. By the early 1930s, the family had moved into an imposing villa in a prosperous section of Nuremberg.

But Hitler and the Nazis were steadily seizing power in 1933, bolstered by an influx of money from the major industrialists, who were hoping to collect favors later—and would do so, in one particular case, to the Joel family's detriment. The family firm had grown prosperous during the 1920s, despite the post–World War I woes of hyperinflation and the communist uprisings it triggered. At one stage before the currency was revalued in the mid-1920s, inflation in Germany ran so rampant that Reichsmarks were virtually worthless. Billy recalls hearing the story that at that time, "You needed a wheelbarrow of bills to pay for a loaf of bread." Still, Hitler's ominous Munich (or "Beer Hall") Putsch of 1923 failed. But later in the decade, as government cutbacks accompanying deflation mixed with fears of a worldwide financial crisis—the American stock market crashed in 1929—the national mood was bleak. Says Billy, "everybody started looking to the Nazis for salvation." Young Helmut was part of the Jewish population that would be caught up in the building nationalistic fervor.

"I've read a lot of this history, and because it affected my own up-bringing, it's hard not to take it personally," Billy says. "I think anti-Semitism was always kind of innate in those Middle European cultures anyway. In Germany, Austria, and even France, to an extent, there's a long history of anti-Semitism that was simmering for generations. Hit-ler tapped into it. He knew how to exploit popular prejudice."

Billy still wonders how his grandfather Karl, who was supposed to be sharp-witted, couldn't see what was coming until Kristallnacht in November 1938. Even then Karl, loath to sacrifice what he had built through decades of hard work, was still trying to make a deal with his connections to get the proceeds from selling his business to German entrepreneur Josef Neckermann.

Neckermann was a Catholic conservative who joined the Nazi Party when he saw the advantage in it. Using a Nazi innovation known as Aryanization—by which the General State Prosecutor's Office of the State Court of Berlin would put citizens on "trial" for being Jewish, homosexual, or "asocial"—he made the Joel family his first sizable tar-get. In the United States Holocaust Memorial Museum database titled "Index of Jews Whose German Nationality was Annulled by Nazi Re-gime, 1935–1944," Karl is listed as being accused of *Devisenvergehen* (monetary or currency offenses) in records of two separate "trials" in the 1930s. Says Billy, "After taking part in the making of *The Joel Files*, I realized what the film's director, Beate Thalberg, had discovered: My relatives were hounded out of the country and forced to sell the largest business of its kind in Germany at an absurd price—a paradigm of the economic casualties during the Nazi takeover."

The Nazi takeover rumbled up from below, as Karl and his lifelong best friend, Rudi Weber (actually not Jewish and later drafted into the German army) would experience. In Steffen Radlmaier's German-language book on the Joel family history, Karl recalls the two boys passing a glass display case with a newspaper bearing the headline, "The Jews Are Our Misfortune." The headline was the work of a Hitler acolyte (so much so he was dubbed "The Franconian Führer") named Julius Streicher. Streicher's *Der Stürmer,* a propaganda sheet of a newspaper that he had founded as the hounding of Jews caught fire, was waging a vendetta against Billy's grandfather Karl.

In May 1933 *Der Stürmer* ran a front-page article calling Karl a "Yid" and accusing him of underpaying and sexually harassing his workers. Just months before, the Joel family had epitomized comfortable normalcy, moving into a bosky section of the city where their sizable two-story home boasted a telephone and a gramophone, with a chauffeured sedan in the driveway. But as the Nazis rose in power, the party established a parade ground in the park near the Joel home. The commands, songs, and rallying cries of the brownshirts became the sound track for lives governed more and more by fear and a growing helplessness.

The Joel family's situation was soon barely tenable. Radlmaier describes how on April 1, 1933, the "systematic persecution" of the Jews began with leaflets falling from the sky, and as part of the campaign admonishing the populace "Don't buy from Jews!" the lingerie shop owned by Karl's brother Leon in nearby Ansbach was listed as off limits to any not wishing to be marked as "traitors to the Fatherland."

Helmut was one of four Jews in his Nuremberg classroom; they were directed to sit apart from their classmates. While the city's Jews still had access to the zoo, where Helmut enjoyed the elephants and talking parrots, they could no longer use the public swimming pool.

"My grandfather thought he might still ride out the crisis," says Billy. Karl traveled to Berlin, a five-hour train ride north, in early 1934 and sought supposedly neutral advice from a textile manufacturer named Fritz Tillmann, the Nazis' "economic town counselor." Later

Tillmann would lead efforts to round up the city's Jewish population and ship them to the death camps.

Under the nominally more lenient administration in the capital, Karl would be permitted to move and reopen his business there, and he announced as much in mid-May to his employees. (Three-fourths of them would join him; he was in fact a well-liked boss.)

Seven articles appeared that year denouncing "Jew Joel, the bloodsucker and oppressor," and after the massive Nuremberg Rally, where crowds roared for Hitler in the swastika-bedecked streets, Karl Joel was arrested three times in short order—and freed each time upon word from Tillmann, who had plans for the family business.

While Karl was optimistically reestablishing his business under the strict new regulations, installing German-made machinery and putting up a mandatory sign declaring that the business was Jewish-owned, he took the precaution of shipping Helmut to an elite boarding school in St. Gall, Switzerland. (Helmut would inherit from his father, a great Wagner fan, a deep love of classical music. Thus the photograph, in this book's gallery, of Helmut aged about twelve, playing a piano on the terrace of a resort hotel in the Rhine-side spa town of Flims, Switzerland.)

Even as *Der Stürmer* (loosely, "The Attacker") regularly inveighed against the "Nuremberg Linen-Jew Joel," Helmut would come back to Germany sporadically, including a visit for his bar mitzvah in June 1936. However, any sense of normalcy was giving way to strict new rules for his father—certain suppliers began cutting him off, a German plant manager was installed, and Karl was ordered to stamp all his outgoing packages with a *J.* Then in June 1938, a new law passed, forfeiting all Jewish businesses to Aryan ownership. Karl was visited by Josef Neckermann, who engineered the purchase of the company for some 2.3 million Reichsmarks, then roughly equivalent to a half-million U.S. dollars but less than a fifth of its real value.

Billy's grandfather signed the papers that July. The transaction was overseen by Tillmann, as Karl was forbidden to use his own attorney. . He asked for some assurance that the agreed-upon sum would be paid and was answered with ominous threats that he would be wiser to look after his own security. Neckermann also took possession of the family house, whose inventory included the children's bedroom set that Helmut had used.

Karl and Meta checked into a hotel to await payment, but the prelude to the Nazis' "Final Solution"—propaganda minister Joseph Goebbels had been quoted as saying, "The Jew is a waste product. It is a clinical issue more than a social one"—was ramping up. A great number of Berlin's Jewish population had already been incarcerated in the Gestapo's Moabit district prison, later infamous for the executions committed there, when a warning came to Karl and Meta that the Gestapo planned to arrest them. Karl literally ran out the back door of the hotel where the meeting had been scheduled to take place. "My grandparents fled in the night," Billy says, "and, using fake passports, escaped via the Bahnhof Zoo Station, across the Swiss border to Zurich. They got in touch with my father at his school and told him that they had left Germany for good and planned to stay in Switzerland."

As the family sheltered in a one-room flat in Zurich, the drama took one more twist when Karl Joel was notified by a letter from Josef Neckermann that there had been a problem clearing his payment; the letter advised him to return to Berlin to settle the deal. "That was ambiguous," Billy's father says in *The Joel Files*. "In a way, it was a death threat."

Wary of a trap, Karl nonetheless traveled to Berlin and met surreptitiously in a café with Fritz Tillmann, who asked him for a check for a hundred thousand Reichsmarks for his efforts to straighten things out. Tillmann told Karl, falsely, that Karl couldn't cash the Neckermann payment check himself because the banks had invalidated Jews' accounts. Meanwhile Karl was detained for a week before escaping once again to Switzerland. He had realized that he would never be properly paid for his business, even the reduced amount he had agreed to.

"I think," says Billy, "that's when my grandfather realized that remaining in Europe was simply untenable. Just think of the irony of relocating your business from Nuremburg, the Nazi Party headquarters, to Berlin, only to see Berlin end up as the new Nazi power base."

Karl finally realized he had to take immediate measures to save the family. The account that follows owes much to the expert researchers of the Holocaust Museum. One thing that's certain is that given the rigors of escaping Europe at that moment in history, as well as the difficulty of finding a way into America, the Joel family was among a very small minority of those who successfully evaded the Nazis' clinical, exterminating wrath, if not their depredations.

In *The Joel Files*, Howard cites his gratitude that the family had some cash to spread around to help their escape: "I was lucky because my parents had some money left. That's why I'm still alive." A staffer at the Holocaust Museum agrees: "At the very least, the process would not have been as smooth—relatively speaking—as it was. Certainly people without large sums of money were able to make it out, but the path was much more difficult. Some well-timed bribes may have played a part here and there—there are hundreds of other ways, large and small, where having money would have made an enormous difference. For example, a key part of the immigration process for most individuals at the time involved obtaining affidavits of support from people in the U.S., which often included putting down a financial deposit to help ensure that the immigrants would not become a burden on the state. The country was still reeling from the Great Depression, and fear of immigrants was often driven as much by economic concerns as it was on any ethnic or religious prejudices. Being able to demonstrate that he had the means to support his family would likely have made a big difference in that process, as would being able to call upon his business connections should he need an affidavit."

While most refugees' bank accounts had been completely drained and their property seized by the time they left Nazi Europe, Karl had been able to retain at least a cash residue from his lost fortune. By whatever means, he obtained three visas, and the family headed for England. From there, they secured places on a cruise ship called the

Arandora Star for a January 1939 passage across the Atlantic to Cuba. A 1927 vintage luxury liner with a capacity of four hundred for deluxe voyages and operated by the Blue Star Line, she was known as the "wedding cake" due to her white hull and scarlet trim. A contemporary advertisement listed her winter voyages to Brazil and "Argentine" as featuring "Unsurpassed Comfort ... No emigrants ... No second class"; clearly she epitomized a privilege and frivolity out of joint with the times. Though she would be torpedoed in 1940 in an infamous incident killing eight hundred foreign deportees whom Winston Churchill was shipping to a Canadian prison, in January 1939 England had not yet declared war, and the U-boat wolf packs had not yet begun their deadly campaigns in those waters.

The family must have felt both relief and hope in boarding her for the 4,600-mile passage, which would last about four days. Listed on the "Alien Passenger" manifest as first-class passengers (identified as manufacturer, housewife, and student) "contracted to land" at Havana, the three Joels were also categorized as "intended future permanent" residents of Germany. They of course had no such intention.

Due to the Immigration Act of 1924, pushed through Congress easily in the name of preserving "the ideal of American homogeneity," in part to stem the flow of Jews who had fled Poland and Russia, there were strict quotas in place. For those born in Germany, the quota was only 25,957 immigration slots per year.

As the war erupted in 1939, the would-be emigrants from Germany to the United States greatly outnumbered the available slots, and entry might take years. The Holocaust Museum staff hypothesize that Karl may have applied for a quota number in 1938, when his firm was "Aryanized," and this was likely why the Joels left for Cuba. Many people in their situation who had the means went there rather than waiting in Europe, which by this point was in full-blown war.

Karl Joel's family, having paid the standard fee equivalent to about $500 but feasibly with additional money changing hands, was permitted to disembark in Havana and would reside there for not quite two years.

The same could not be said, however, for Karl Joel's brother Leon, who, along with his wife, Johanna, and son, Gunther, boarded the infamous SS *St. Louis* alongside 934 other passengers traveling to Havana on May 13, 1939. The voyage, later portrayed in the 1976 feature film *Voyage of the Damned*, departed with doomed hopefulness—the passengers little realizing that the Nazi propaganda minister Joseph Goebbels had plans to exploit the seaborne refugees' attempted escape as an example in his endless strivings to make Jews out as problematic. On a Friday morning, five days after arriving in Cuba, the vessel spun up its engines, and the entire group, denied entry and trapped on board, went to the rails to wave to friends and family who bobbed about the harbor in rented boats—Howard's family among them.

Finally, on June 7, after steaming about in the vicinity of Cuba with some forlorn hope of gaining entry to a U.S. port, the ship began a return voyage. Nine days later the disembarkations back in Europe would begin, with the passengers scattered to Holland, Great Britain, Belgium, and France. The Leon Joel family was among 224 in the latter group. Of the original 937 who sailed, 254, as tracked by researchers, would die at the hands of the Nazis, including Leon and Johanna, who, after being moved between various concentrations camps by the collaborationist Vichy government, were killed in the gas chambers at Auschwitz shortly after their arrival in September 1942. Gunther, however, escaped over the mountains to Switzerland and eventually emigrated to the United States, where he would go on to serve in Korea and live on Long Island as Henry Guy Joel until his death in 2009.

"I am eternally grateful," says Billy today, "that my father's family was finally allowed to enter Cuba—that the Cuban authorities allowed Jews to find asylum in their country was probably my salvation." In fact, Howard Joel, turning seventeen and attending the University of Havana at roughly the same time as Fidel Castro, would even find himself returning to some of the casual joys of growing up. ""It was great," he would recall to Tim White. "There were lots of girls."

Finally word came down that the family could be admitted to the

United States. They boarded the SS *Oriente* (typically transporting tourists to "Gay, Carefree Havana" on all-inclusive six-day cruises for $75) on September 18, 1942, listing their new address as 200 Nineti-eth Street, New York City. They had very little savings and minimal prospects, and Howard's war was far from over. But for now, the family was safe.

THE WORST FEARS were clearly in the past for Karl and Meta Joel when they stepped onto a Hudson River pier in early 1942. What possi-ble terrors could the New World hold after what they had been through in the old one?

They found an apartment on Bogardus Place in the Washington Heights section of New York, overlooking Fort Tryon Park near the Cloisters. Karl started a business in downtown Manhattan at 395 Broadway (a commercial fifteen-story limestone building at White Street) making headbands, ribbons, and hair clips for five-and-dime stores, and Howard helped make the deliveries.

One of the odd synchronicities of Billy Joel's life in music is that not only did his maternal grandparents, Philip and Rebecca Nyman, meet thanks to a Gilbert and Sullivan production (in their case, at London's Royal Albert Hall), his parents, Howard and wife-to-be Rosalind, did as well—in 1942, while performing in a City College of New York Glee Club production of *The Pirates of Penzance*. They were also both in *The Mikado*, conducted by the well-known maestro Julius Rudel, who'd fled Vienna in 1938. "I'd like to think the musical DNA in our family is largely responsible for my parents getting together," says Billy.

By contrast to the (once-)prosperous Joels of upscale Nuremberg, the ancestral Nymans were denizens of the notorious Whitechapel dis-trict in London's East End. Known for the tanneries, ironworks, and breweries that fouled the air, it attracted workers in those trades and those who could abide their effluvium. Billy's grandfather Philip—who was to be the real and frequently acknowledged hero of his life—was born there as the son of Jacob and Leah, both originally from Kiev, in November 1889, the year before Jack the Ripper began preying on the neighborhood prostitutes. Wife Rebecca was from Polish stock, born in London in 1896. (Both her region of origin and her husband's would see violent anti-Jewish pogroms as the century turned, perhaps explaining their parents' relocation to London, and if so, giving Billy two lines of forebears with refugee histories.)

Rosalind (Roz, as she was known for short) Nyman arrived—as the third of three daughters born to Philip and Rebecca—in 1922, in the Coney Island neighborhood of Brooklyn, where the family had migrated after leaving England in 1914, at the outbreak of the First World War. "Her father didn't want to get conscripted into the English army," relates Billy, "which was a pretty smart thing to avoid."

Roz and her parents, along with her elder sisters Muriel (born 1918) and Bertha (1920), settled in the Flatbush district of Brooklyn, on Ditmas Avenue. Billy would visit there and remember their home as a pile of dingy bricks, "dark and small," a turn-of-the-century row house in a Jewish neighborhood, with kosher butchers all around. His mother's parents would live there the rest of their lives.

Philip Nyman had an antiauthoritarian streak that ran deep. As a young man, he fought with the Republicans in Spain against Franco and would be under suspicion in America for his leftist leanings—but he also had a kind of elegance in his bearing, Billy recalls: "He didn't have a lot of money—as far as I could tell, the family never did—but he would sneak us into the Brooklyn Academy of Music, by slipping the usher a pack of Luckies, to see recitals and other classical music performances."

The newlyweds who had been united by Gilbert and Sullivan had families more appropriate to Shakespeare's famous lovers: "two households, both alike in dignity," with very little use for each other. "Despite my parents' love for each other," says Billy, "their two families weren't compatible at all. Karl was a German Jew, rightly or wrongly self-styled as the aristocrat of the tribe, and my mother's people were English and

Russian Jews whom the Germans would have viewed as the lower, *untermenschen* class."

The courtship faced a still greater obstacle when Howard Joel was drafted into the U.S. Army in July 1943. He wasn't yet twenty-one, but his ability to speak fluent German earned him a quick ticket to the European theater.

Howard Joel was part of the Fifth Army, originally in the legendarily savage Italian campaign with Gen. Mark Clark. From September 1943 through the war's end, the region's battles would result in 300,000 Allied casualties, about a fifth of that number deaths, mostly from the army's slog up the boot of Italy through the mountains. Clark had an agenda to get to Rome, and he led terrible duels of attrition, such as the Battle of Monte Cassino, to capture Rome by whatever means necessary. And on June 5, 1944, he did. Ironically, that military triumph was completely knocked aside in the headlines by the events of the next morning, June 6, D-Day.

Billy's devotion to military history yielded information about Howard's wartime service, despite his father's general lack of communication about the prelude to it: "My understanding is that just after the Normandy invasion, he and his fellow soldiers were pulled out of Italy and invaded the south of France with Patton's Third Army. The Allies were bombing heavily, and the Reich was pretty tattered as Patton's troops mopped up." Howard's battalion would be part of the liberation of Dachau, near Munich, in April 1945—he wouldn't yet know of relatives he lost at Auschwitz.

Says Billy, "I remember him talking to me about that—what it felt like to be in your own hometown of Nuremberg with the U.S. Army overrunning the place. He recalled not wanting to shoot any of his old friends who might be there—his pal Rudy [who served with Herman Göring's Panzer tank division] or the kids he went to school with. He may have been an American, but he still had strong ties to the town; he had friendships; it was his childhood. I didn't really understand how, after being disenfranchised and treated so badly, he could want to show any mercy. But that reveals the compassionate side of my father. At one point he ended up behind the wheel of a Jeep in Nuremberg, driving past his family's bombed-out factory, but the smokestack was still standing amid the rubble."

After the war, Josef Neckermann would pay a certain price. Goaded into action by pressure from the Nazis' conquerors, the military government would sentence him to one year in a military prison in his hometown of Würzburg. Five years later, facing simultaneous lawsuits from Karl Joel (whose postwar attempt to solicit repayment from Neckermann in a meeting at a Four Seasons Hotel in Berlin had yielded nothing), from another victimized businessman named Siegmund Ruschewitz, and from the military government (this time it charged that he'd violated regulations by returning to business immediately after the armistice), he would face paying restitutions—plus four years for the state charges. The court finally decreed that he would avoid prison if he agreed to the two-million-Deutschmark Joel settlement. He had dodged a bigger payment by claiming that the war's disruption had destroyed a special account he'd set aside for safekeeping to pay Joel. Days after the deal was struck, paperwork emerged proving that to be a lie, but no money was added to the restitution.

Despite it all, the expropriated mail-order business that had risen from the ashes of the war under its new owner's name burgeoned, and Neckermann would become the poster boy for the German "Economic Miracle." In 1960 *Time* magazine dubbed him "The Mail Order King," and his business—with a disruptive sprawl that perhaps compares only to present-day Amazon.com—sent out 3.5 million catalogs each year, offering some 5,500 items at prices 40 percent lower than retail competitors. With 40,000 orders a day, the firm moved into a massive steel and concrete headquarters.

Beginning in 1960, destined to be known as perhaps the richest Olympic athlete ever, Neckermann began his run of netting six medals as a dressage horseman, in the 1960, 1964, 1968, and 1972 games. Yet ultimately, after a rough run spurred by inept price-cutting, he sold the failing company.

Karl and Meta used the long-awaited settlement to travel the world extensively before returning to New York to shut down their business in 1970. They then repatriated to Germany, where Meta died in Nuremberg in 1971. Karl, alone and still embittered from his troubles, passed away eleven years later in Berlin. He and Meta are buried in the Jewish cemetery in Berlin; in *The Joel Files*, Alex Joel is seen on the site, using a stiff, soapy brush to clean the mottled headstone above the grave of Karl and Leon's father, where below the added names of the vanished Leon and Rebecca lie. The subtitles translate the legend beneath the names: *"Deported to and died in a concentration camp."*

Upon Howard's return from the war in 1946, he and Roz married and moved into an apartment on Strong Street in the Bronx. Howard took jobs first with the Dumont television manufacturing company, then with RCA, and eventually with General Electric. His work for them would, over time, take him more and more frequently out of the country, to Latin America and Europe. But by the late summer of 1948, a child was on the way.

WILLIAM MARTIN "BILLY" JOEL was born May 9, 1949, in the Bronx. According to Billy, "I don't have any particular nostalgia for the Bronx. We would move away in 1950, and I never really saw that neighborhood again once we left for Long Island. So my earliest childhood memories are of being a little kid in our house in Hicksville." Soon after the family moved to Long Island, they were joined there by his cousin Judy, who was two years older and taken in as an act of kindness by his mom when his mother's older sister Muriel died.

The two forged a deep bond that would later emerge in "Why Judy Why" from 1971's *Cold Spring Harbor*, in which Billy forthrightly sings, "Of all the people in the world that I know / You're the best place to go when I cry." Says Billy: "Judy and I have always remained in close touch. She was raised like my sister, and I have always thought of her in that way. Together, back then, she and I were allies in the difficult life we all shared on Meeting Lane."

Judy was twelve years old before Roz finally related to her just how dismal the circumstances of her adoption were. The news was delivered on the day Marilyn Monroe died—August 5, 1962—an occasion Billy and Judy perceived as having some odd significance for Roz, who apparently saw in the troubled Hollywood star a kindred spirit.

The story is grim enough. After Judy's birth in 1947, Muriel—known to the family as Moochie and described by one relation as "a bookworm . . . shy, funny, and a good cook"—suffered from crushing postpartum depression. She'd married her husband, Max, an accountant, in the Brooklyn Town Hall when she was nineteen, with the wedding breakfast in Chinatown. Over the next eight years of married life, Max was said by some to lack empathy and already had one foot out the door. One day when Judy was eight weeks old, and her sister, Susie, four, was out with Muriel's mom, Rebecca, Muriel placed the infant Judy on the bed in a back bedroom of their Flatbush apartment, cracked a window to supply some fresh air, and surrounded Judy with a row of chairs so she wouldn't roll off the bed. Then she moved to the kitchen, fastened a wool Army blanket across the doorway, opened the oven door, and turned on the gas. According to Rebecca Gehrkin, Judy's daughter, Muriel placed a note in plain view: "Dear Mom, Pop and Max, I know that I have cancer and I do not want to be a burden to the family so I have taken this way out. Please forgive me. Love, Mooch."

Judy recounts what came next: "My grandparents came home to it. She was just lying flat on the ground. A little while later came Roz and my other sister from those biological parents, Susan. Roz jumped on top of Moochie, calling her name, and tried to resuscitate her. It was useless, but she just wouldn't get off her."

The family was so shattered that only Muriel's husband, Max, attended the funeral. He then went off to his new life, taking Susie with him and remarrying within a year. He left Judy, the infant he barely knew, with Billy's grandparents Phillip and Rebecca Nyman in Brooklyn. "Eventually," says Billy, "when Judy was about four, they bundled her out to Hicksville, where I found myself with a new sister I barely knew." Though Billy will speak fondly of Roz and her efforts at keeping the family fed, clothed, and at last occasionally happy during the coming years, Judy has a different memory and carries considerable bitterness: "Roz would do—not nice things. At one point when we were very young, she left us alone for three days."

That episode led to an extended family dispute over the care of the offspring, but as much as Judy tangled with the emotional vagaries exhibited by Roz, she little enjoyed the visits to the Joel side of the family in upper Manhattan: "They were ice cold—what they say, typical Germans."

The difficulties between Roz and Judy, who was formally adopted in 1955, continued. "Judy was willing to have only limited contact with our mother in the decades that followed," says Billy. "There was too much conflict, too many misadventures over the years.

"It didn't take me long to realize that my family was noticeably different from those around us. For starters, I don't recall my father being around our home much. I'd see him, of course, but he was never really a fixture in the house, never a regular part of the household. I remember it being just my mother, my sister, and me. And I remember thinking that we were the family that didn't have a dad, and were being perceived that way by the neighbors. We weren't ostracized, but we certainly were looked at somewhat differently. Money was tight, so the small home improvements other families were making weren't available to us. They were little things, but also conspicuous—we weren't able to put in a driveway, or install a dormer upstairs, or do all the fixing-up our neighbors appeared to be doing."

Then there was the neighbors' perception of Roz, who Judy says damaged the family bank account with erratic behavior sometimes exacerbated by what Judy recalls as helpings of "brown liquor" and spates of refusing to eat: "One day I walked in and Billy's sitting on top of her and he's shoving ice cream down her throat, thinking she's going to die."

The mood inside the compact house was not improved by the social climate just outside the door. On the somewhat windswept stretch that was Meeting Lane (not much shrubbery had yet had the chance to grow in the postwar tract, formerly acres of potato fields), harsh judgments were levied, says Judy: "We were the only Jews, we were the only family without a driveway—we had a carport. People made fun of us."

"In the 1950s, an attractive woman in a neighborhood of married people was viewed with a certain amount of suspicion," says Billy. "Our area was heavily Catholic, which added to the sense that we weren't like everyone else. The little girl across the street once actually said as much to me, very matter-of-factly, when I was about six years old: 'You're going to grow horns because you're a Jew.' And I honestly remember going to bed at night feeling my head to see if the horns were coming in. I didn't understand anything about anti-Semitism. I didn't even really know what a Jew was, except for the bits and pieces of information I would pick up from other kids. You have to remember, this is long before the era of political correctness. Back then, people would use ugly ethnic and racial slurs such as *polack*, *mick*, *spic*, *kike*, and especially the N-word—and it was all right out there, in the open. Nobody thought of it as racism; it was just how people talked. If there was any upside to all of this bigotry, it's that you could see it coming at you from a mile away. Now it's a lot more subtle, but I still think it's there."

If America was a "melting pot"—the phrase was popularized by a 1906 play portraying a survivor of Russian pogroms trying to assimilate—Meeting Lane was a specimen of the pain that came from the heat beneath. Perhaps Howard Joel's increasingly frequent absences came in part from questioning what he had fought for in Europe, whom he had lost, and whether he had escaped the bias that fueled that cataclysm. He seldom missed a chance to scorn the materialist, know-nothing culture he was enmeshed in ("He hated America," says Billy, who in later years would exasperatedly rebut the tirades), helping to deliver plastic ware to America's own robust postwar economy. Billy remembers, "In those rare times when my father was around, he was always a dark presence. People later said they believed the war had changed him. Something I've never forgotten was when I was about six years old, he said to me, 'Life is a cesspool.' I don't remember him saying much, but I remember that. I didn't fully understand what he meant at the time. Years later it occurred to me that it was a pretty rough thing to say to a kid."

The unforgettable—one might almost say unforgivable—"cesspool" remark, says Billy, "gave me some insight into the darkness my father carried around inside him. He would go into the room where the upright piano was and play Chopin and Beethoven and Debussy. I thought it was pretty great; I would get stoned just from listening to it. But when he finished, he was always in a really bad mood. I guess because it made him feel frustrated and angry that he wasn't a virtuoso pianist. But what would put him in a bad mood would put me in a great mood. I thought, *If I could do that, I'd be a really happy guy.* Not my father, though. He was very sad man."

What helped make up for Howard's emotional absence was the presence of Philip Nyman, who, even as he made the rounds of the concert halls with his palmed packs of unfiltered smokes, would deliver disquisitions on the great books and musical works. Closer to home turf, different dodges were needed. "I was always going to the movies at the Hicksville Theater," says Billy. "In the early sixties the price for adults was a buck and a quarter; kids under a certain age got in for thirty-five cents. I remember one time I went to the movies with my grandfather and I was thirteen. The sign said that children under ten got in at a discounted price. My grandfather walked up to the ticket window and casually told the cashier that I was nine. I was really infuriated, because that's a time in your life when you want to be older. 'No, I'm not,' I started to protest, but by then my grandfather was clasping his hand over my mouth. Years later I came to understand that my mom's side of my family didn't have much money, so that's the way they got along."

As his parents grew apart, Billy saw Roz's helplessness to fix the union: "I know my mother was very sad about it. They were such completely different personalities. She was overly communicative, and my father could barely express his emotions. When they argued, she would yell, and he would just sit there in silence. And of course that would make her even madder. So even as a little kid, I knew that these two people weren't cut out to be together. I was kind of relieved when they got divorced, actually. I just didn't know that I wouldn't see him for many years to come."

Rosalind may have realized the finality of the break, but still would come the times around dusk when the Buicks and Chevy Impalas and Plymouth Valiants arrived home from the island's electronics firms and metal shops and the Hicksville train station, six minutes' drive north. The dads in their high-waisted slacks would knock the car door shut with their knee and cross the lawn with a hug for the kids and a kiss for the wife—what Billy would later call the "Donna Reed" world. Billy would see his mom staring out the kitchen window and ask what she was looking at. And sometimes, as he told Tim White for *Billboard* three decades later, she would say—consciously or unconsciously distributing the pain—"Just looking out the window. Maybe your father's coming home."

Asked by White what he got from Howard as a father, Billy responded, effectively, naught: "As a dad, it's too late. I'm thirty-one. I met him when I was twenty-four . . . it was too late already, I was already me." However, characteristically, he was able to find some redemption in the situation: "I knew a lot of kids when I was growing up who were afraid of their fathers, fathers who beat them up, were bastards, creeps. I was brought up by women . . . a nice upbringing. The worst my mother did was grab hangers off the rack and whip me over the shoulders . . . which hurts."

Minus a father, Billy was also spared some of the patriarchal baggage that others knew. Howard Joel had become an engineering student at his father's insistence, despite his deep love for music, "because in those days you did what your old man told you to do." In his son's case, "I probably would never have been able to consider being a professional musician, certainly a rock musician, if my father had been around when I was growing up. He just wouldn't have allowed it—too impractical. Whereas my mom said, 'Go ahead'; she encouraged me. So I was lucky in that way, even though I missed having a father, and as I came of age, I found myself trying to replace him as the provider and head of the family.

"I became the father, whether I liked it or not, but without my own father around, I was constantly searching for my own identity. Who am I? I don't know anything about myself because I don't have a father to let me know what I'm supposed to be like.

"In some ways, this can free you up—you can be anything you want, go in any direction. But in other ways, you may not feel that you ever have a center."

ANOTHER ACCIDENT OF Billy's upbringing that could have been a pedestrian detail but would prove a major theme in his life was simply being a Long Islander. In late 2008 Bruce Springsteen, no minor local hero himself, and Billy united for their Obama fund-raiser at Hammerstein Ballroom in Manhattan—where Bruce had good reason to declare the evening "a summit meeting." As surely as Springsteen was the bard of New Jersey, from the swamps to the northern reaches of Highway 9, Billy has for decades been the poet who punches out insights on and evocations of and ultimately, despite its many complications, the essence of Long Island: "I don't speak about the Island with the condescension you so often hear even from people raised there. I'm an Islander. No one is prouder to come from Long Island than I am, and I've always been a booster for the place. Long Island is separated from Manhattan Island by bridges, but it's part of an archipelago that includes Manhattan and Staten Island, Fire Island, Shelter Island—dozens of islands floating off the mainland." Much as Billy's parents did in their turn, "over the course of the history of New York City, hundreds of thousands of

New Yorkers have fled the city for those suburbs of Long Island. And of course when you're a kid, you can't wait to get back into the city."

The man generally credited for speeding this eastern migration of New Yorkers is the legendary urban planner Robert Moses, a civic czar back in the days when a czar could get a lot done. Beginning in the 1930s and all the way into the 1970s, Moses built the parkways and bridges of New York, developed the beaches, and installed infrastructure. He once lobbied for and nearly succeeded in commanding the construction of a bridge from Rye, New York, across Long Island Sound to Oyster Bay, which would have flung eight lanes of traffic right through Billy's charming little adopted hamlet.

One of the landmark projects that an accessible island permitted was the vision of real estate developer Abraham Levitt and his sons Albert and William Levitt, who created Billy's boyhood street of Meeting Lane very near the center of Levittown—a sprawling housing development spurred by the demand for housing from the local contingent of some sixteen million veterans returning after the war. The cheaply built homes (the Levitts owned their own forest land to supply timber and made their own nails) demanded minimal down payments. Most of the tracts clustered near the new freeways on Long Island. The $7,000 homes, in five variations of a basic Cape Cod style, sat on sixty-by-one-hundred-foot plots. Hicksville, where the Joels settled, was a pop-up patch of small-town, Main Street America. It was also a rail junction, which brought growth and restless, resettling city dwellers.

When a blight struck the sprawling acres of potato farms, the farmers started selling off big swaths of land, and Levittown—the name given to these cascades of homes that epitomized the "Little Boxes" of a 1963 folk song—spread out from Hicksville, down to East Meadow and Uniondale and into Westbury. The total area covered half a dozen towns. "I was from Hicksville, the village," says Billy, "but I was also from Levittown, the area. Still, when you say Levittown, you're talking about a particular suburban way of life at a particular time.

"But even though my friends and I were living in the suburbs—that basically became the theme of my *Nylon Curtain* album—we played city games, stickball and stoopball, Ringolevio and Johnny on the Pony, and plenty of chicken fights. After all, these were New York City people who thought they were in the country. Of course, we kids knew we weren't really in the country; this was a suburb where every house looked the same, and we were bored out of our skulls. As people my age grew older, we went into the city every chance we got, because that was our Disneyland; that was Oz. We couldn't wait to get the hell *out* of the suburbs."

Something Billy's Hicksville neighborhood shared with less sophisticated outposts of small-town America was a lack of diversity in its population. Recalls Billy, "The real estate agents quietly made sure to keep it that way. They didn't sell to black families." In fact, Clause 25 of the initial standard lease for Levitt houses read that the home "could not be used or occupied by any person other than members of the Caucasian race." The clause was scrapped after a Supreme Court decision on a similar case, but the 1990 census still showed the populace as 97.37 percent white. "I don't remember seeing a black man in our town until I glimpsed some of the migrant workers on the nearby farm in the early fifties. And as we would soon discover—ironically, considering what the world had just gone through to defeat Nazism—the area wasn't necessarily welcoming to Jews either." As the *New York Times* stated in 1997, William J. Levitt, "although he was the grandson of a rabbi . . . built housing on Long Island that excluded Jews."

During Billy's formative years, the combination of an absent father, a sometimes enveloping if loyal mother, and the blatant biases of the surrounding neighborhood enforced a singularity in the youngster's developing personality. Colleagues who have been in close contact with him for two, three, four, even five decades are generally eager to attest to his wit, his unsentimental warmth, and an overall considerateness. At the same time, there's a kind of self-sufficiency to him, a toughness that communicates that—short of the rare special circumstances when he's had a romantic breakup or has fears that someone in his family, notably daughter Alexa Ray, has been hurt in any way—he's not looking for a shoulder to cry on.

Year in and year out, Billy Joel doesn't do "pathetic," doesn't do "needy," doesn't do "poor me." What some might see as a shortfall in his capacity for intimacy is recognized by longtime friends as an unwillingness to show vulnerability. The more he's the center of attention—say, in a backstage production office a couple hours before a show—the more he seems to have one foot out the door. But what verges on introversion is more than compensated for by an often-wicked sense of humor that's sharpest when he's being self-deprecating. There was enough solitude and self-determination in his upbringing to set him up to, as the expression goes, row his own little boat.

Those stalwart companions who might lay claim to being inside his psyche are the first to warn you of the complexities within. His is anything but an unexamined life, but much of what he's discovered remains private. Still, when he talks about his boyhood years, he isn't averse to using his considerable self-awareness that developed early: "As a teen, I had absolutely no fear of authority types. Even though I was looking for a father figure—which I found in my mother's father, Philip, or in men such as our chorus teacher, Chuck Arnold—I probably came off as a little insular, a bit remote.

"I was developing a sense of how I might make my way in the world. Recently, someone wrote me a letter about one of their kids, who'd been diagnosed with autism, but then it turned out the kid was just extremely shy. I wrote back and said, 'Listen, believe it or not, I was excruciatingly shy when I was a kid, up until my midteens. That's when I realized that I could make my piano talk for me. The piano spoke what I was feeling.'

"Part of why I looked for answers in boxing was practical: I used to get brutally picked on when I went to piano lessons. And I got tired of it." If he was to be an aesthete, like his grandfather Philip Nyman, he could also emulate Philip's more masculine pursuits as a boxer. "Also, not only was I a smaller kid, but my piano teacher happened to teach ballet as well, so when I walked down the street with my piano books, I'd get these kids shouting, 'Billy, where's your tutu?' They'd knock the books out of my hand and smack me around. So I took up boxing, and I got pretty good at it." Of his twenty-six bouts, Billy lost two by judges' decisions, two more by knockouts, and had twenty-two wins. "And one day, when the usual pack of teenagers up the block taunted me on the street again, I picked the biggest guy in the bunch, and I decked him.

"It felt great. I remember looking around, just eyeballing each of them as if to say, *All right, does anybody else want some of that?* After that, everybody left me alone. Being able to defend myself gave me a certain level of self-confidence, but I was never really a violent guy.

"After all, there's always somebody tougher and stronger, no matter how good a boxer you are. The last fight I had, one that was actually in a ring, was with a guy who was a terrible boxer. He had no defense, no footwork. There was no science at all to what he was doing. He just had a head made out of rubber. I hit him and I hit him and I hit him, but he wouldn't go down. I was outscoring him on points like crazy. Finally, when I got close enough, he tagged me. He broke my nose, and I went down. That's when I realized that no matter how 'bad' I think I am, there's always somebody badder."

Part of the distinctiveness of Billy's features is the slightly askew and bulbous nose, the outcome of an amateur resetting of smashed cartilage by a fellow pugilist. Add in his slightly snaggle-toothed incisors (he'd get them realigned decades later), he might have fit in with '40s cinema's Dead End Kids.

"Boxing got me in the best shape of my life, and it required much the same discipline as piano playing—you have to put in the work. But I also think you have to have a killer instinct to excel at it, and I didn't have that. I just wanted to take care of myself.

"I can't even watch the sport anymore. I used to be a boxing fan, and now I can't stand the violence of it. Because I know what it feels like to get hit.

"But I also know what it takes to get back up."

CHAPTER 2

PIANO KID

Whatever his shortcomings as a father, Howard Joel passed on his love of music to Billy at an early age: "We had a piano in the house. It wasn't a grand piano, or even a good one—it was an old, beat-up Lester upright, and it was terrible. Every fifth key didn't work. But I would go over and 'play' it every day when I was a little boy. I'd go, *bang, bang, bang*, here's the thunder, *bing, bing, bing*, here's the lightning. And after a few years of that, my mother finally said, 'Enough of the storm song. You're gonna have to learn how to play right,' and she dragged me down the street to the piano teacher, Frances Neiman." Twelve years of childhood piano lessons followed, sometimes more at his mother's urgings than due to Billy's eagerness. "Sometimes felt like drudgery, but I've continued to rely on that training every day of my musical life.

"After a few lessons with Miss Frances, I was able to pick out pieces by ear, and that's when I truly fell in love with music. It wasn't so much from reading the flyspecks in the Mozart sheet music; it was when I discovered that I could figure that stuff out in my head. *I love this*, I thought. There was wizardry to it, a kind of sorcery to the manipulation of sound. I was just a little guy, and I wasn't a real social butterfly, but wherever I went, if there was a piano, I'd wander over and play it. And it enchanted people. As I got older and started liking girls, I realized that the piano was better than a sports car. I'd be playing and I'd look up, and, *Wow, there's a girl!* And I'd play a little more, and, *Man, there's another girl!* I thought, *This is great.*"

Like many kids in the late 1950s, Billy was fascinated by Elvis, and his first experience trying to channel him would prove a revelation. "I was in third grade and I did my best Elvis impersonation—I performed 'Hound Dog' as the scheduled entertainment at lunch break—and the girls in the fourth grade started screaming. That's when I recognized that there's a lot of power in this music stuff. I'm in third grade, and the fourth-grade girls are screaming? And I wasn't even into girls at that point. That routine ended when I got pulled off the stage for wiggling my hips. You don't even *have* hips in the third grade, but the teachers were all in an uproar. I thought it was the coolest thing in the world. Man, did I make trouble or what? *That must be a cool thing to do. Rock star, hmmm.*"

IF MODERN PARENTS are obsessed with keeping their children off various screens, Billy says his parents had little need to worry. "Our television broke when I was about two years old"—many Levitt houses had an Admiral twelve-inch set built into the staircase—"and after that I didn't have a TV again until I was in my twenties. I read a lot and listened to the radio, and my mom would play albums on our little Magnavox record player. We didn't have that large a musical library, but we had all sorts of genres—Broadway, classical, jazz, country, folk, opera, rock, and whatever records my father brought home. There was also the pop music on the radio from New York City—all kinds of music, and I liked all of it."

Billy would not be the first classically trained kid to embrace rock and roll as his music of first resort: "By the time of the British Invasion, I'd be defining my musical personality *against* rather than within classical music. You know, 'Roll over Beethoven, and tell Tchaikovsky the news.'"

In 1966 John Lennon set off a controversy by mildly observing that the Beatles were more popular than Jesus. But what many people don't remember is that, years before, he had said that "Elvis was bigger than religion in [John's] mind." At the time, he was apologizing for ceding some of his loyalty from Elvis to Little Richard because of the latter's new single, "Tutti Frutti." Again, in a typical aspiring rocker's experience, Billy was in part guided into black music by young Brits who, underneath their pop radio hits, made albums that were suffused with their love of American rhythm and blues, including Chuck Berry songs (especially Johnnie Johnson's revved-up piano) and Isley Brothers tunes like "Twist and Shout."

In October 1963, at age fourteen, Billy got a taste of what soul music was really about, up close, when he ventured into Harlem with a friend and saw James Brown play the Apollo. A famous live recording—financed by "The Godfather of Soul" himself when his label showed reluctance to do so—came out of one of these Apollo shows. "His footwork alone was amazing," Billy recalls, "but that great soulful rasp, all his the ferocity mixed with the precision of the band, and the unabashed showmanship of the man made an indelible impression on me."

A more universal cultural moment came with the assassination of John F. Kennedy the following month. Like anyone from his generation, Billy has his own personal recollection of the event. "What I strongly recall is walking down to the corner drugstore, which rented TVs, and bringing one home on the cart that was included in the deal, tugging it down Meeting Lane on four wobbly wheels. Not long after we turned it on in our living room, we saw Jack Ruby shoot Lee Harvey Oswald."

Many years later the moment was still reverberating for Billy, as listeners would hear in his bellowing summation halfway through 1989's "We Didn't Start the Fire": "J.F.K. blown away, what else do I have to say?"

Contemporaneous with the tragic intrusion of the president's assassination was the ongoing influence of pop music on the radio—Ray Charles doing "Busted," the Kingsmen grinding through "Louie Louie," the Beach Boys displaying California's earnest naïveté with "Be True to Your School," Dion DiMucci epitomizing the hitter-with-heart with "Donna the Prima Donna" and "Drip Drop," and the Ronettes doing "Be My Baby" as Phil Spector's seemingly unstoppable rise neared its peak.

By the time the British Invasion fully kicked in the following year, says Billy, "thanks to that magical era in radio, even beyond Elvis, what was really striking to a fledgling rock piano player like me was how Little Richard had completely upset the convention that the piano was a secondary, static element in rock music. And you turn and look at Jerry Lee Lewis and Fats Domino, it was plain to see that the insurgent energy of rock was well represented by guys pounding on keyboards. After all, it's a percussion instrument—you *strike* the keys, literally pounding the instrument. It was meant to be played hard, like the drums."

In addition to those piano gods, Ray Charles, with his statelier style that mingled soul with country, piled up hits like "Georgia on My Mind" and "Hit the Road Jack" (1960), "I Can't Stop Loving You" (1962), and "Crying Time" (1965), and served as another touchstone for Billy: "From the moment I first heard him, I wanted to sing like him. There's something going on inside the larynx with Ray that creates almost the sound you'd get out of a speaker if you hooked up a Leslie Tone cabinet to a Hammond B3 organ: he's got a slow swirl that sounds growly but always so *musical*." As Billy would write in *Rolling Stone*'s coverage of the 100 Greatest Singers (where Ray was second only to Aretha Franklin), Ray's was a unique voice in popular music: "It was clear he was getting such a kick out of what he was doing, and his joy was infectious. . . . He took the yelp, the whoop, the grunt, the groan and made them music." Billy adds, "Ray also produced all these different sounds—*huh-hey!*—as if he were tickled by the noise he'd just made. He would sing a phrase and respond to himself with an *oh, all right!*

"The soulfulness that shone through him was harder to place. I'd sit there just marveling, *How the hell does he do that?* Is it because he beat himself up so much? Was it the black experience, coming up in the Jim

Crow South? Was it the church thing? Was it the drugs? Hard living? I just thought, *Man, I want to sound like that.*"

Ray Charles was the antithesis of life in Levittown, and listening to his 1962 LP *Modern Sounds in Country and Western Music,* Billy heard "a black man giving you the whitest possible music in the blackest possible way, while all hell is breaking loose in the civil rights movement. When he sang, 'You Don't Know Me,' I thought, *He isn't just singing the lyrics. He's saying, 'You don't know me, get to know me.'* . . . He shows you his humanity. The spontaneity is evident." The eventual experience of working with Ray (in 1986) was "an evangelical event. He was the minister and I was the congregation," he wrote.

"To think that he and I would one day perform a duet together," says Billy, "a song I'd written for him, 'Baby Grand'—that would have been beyond imagining for me back in the sixties. For starters, I've never thought I had a good voice. I can be objective about it. I like it better now that it's thickened out more at the bottom end than when I was younger, but I don't compare it to those naturally compelling voices I came up listening to. I can sing in key; I can sing in pitch. I can growl it up or rock it up or soul it up, but my natural voice, to me, is sort of like a kid singing in church.

"I wasn't the only one chirping onstage to have that complaint about his own voice. We were all studying at the feet of titans. Then along came these guys who seemed to make it all more accessible—the Beatles were mining classic American rock and R&B, making that music their own.

"John Lennon had full awareness of the musical history. He had studied it all, and said early on that you can do a whole lot in a two- or three-minute rock song, that it was an art form in its own right. I agree—I think you have to have a good amount of innocence, ambition, and also confidence in your craft to be able to say, 'We can tie all this up in three minutes.'"

It's instructive, for anyone wondering why Billy all but ceased writing pop songs after 1993's *River of Dreams*, to hear his thoughts on the ineluctable diminishing of the bravado that energized his work back then: "It's the innocence that goes first—at least it did for me—and then the confidence." Few musicians, or artists in any field, have made so much out of the slaphappy enthusiasms of youth. While Billy was embarking on what would become a three-decade run when he began composing in the 1960s, today, he says, "to write the same kind of songs now, at this age, I don't think I'd even be able to try it. I didn't know any better then."

THE STUDY IN Billy Joel's Centre Island home is a kind of inviting gentleman's den of mahogany and nautical charts and sweeping views of the water surrounding his property, with bookshelves stacked to the ceiling with history, fiction, biography—books that have received much attention in his many years as an autodidact. Anyone who's not at the PhD level of study in domestic and world history, especially military history, is unlikely to match his chapter-and-verse knowledge of those disciplines. He has no trace of defensiveness about being a high school dropout who never seriously contemplated higher education: "By junior high, I remember everybody talking about what college they wanted to attend. I had no desire to go to college. From the age of fourteen on, I had focused on being a musician. *That's what I'm going to do. I'm not going to go to college. It's pointless.* I had no ambitions in that direction at all, though I did want to get the high school diploma—for my mom."

At Hicksville High School, there were more than a thousand kids in the class of '67, but by Billy's senior year, his likeliest affinity group—the hood-punk-greaser kids—was starting to fade in prominence. In their place emerged the folky, prepsychedelic, earnestly bohemian crowd who preferred turtlenecks and black-framed glasses to varsity jackets. "Pot had started coming in," Billy recalls, "but I didn't want to do it. I guess I was scared. But I wasn't scared when I was with the jocks drinking beer, and I wasn't scared hanging out with the hoods who were sniffing glue and drinking Tango or Ripple. Still, by the time I hit high school, I had crossed over from the junior high die-hard greaser type to being a bit of a hippie—because I was in a band. I grew my hair long and started wearing jeans. I also made a point of knowing the collegiate crowd, because a lot of the cute girls were the rah-rah college types—blond, athletic surfer-style girls with nicely developed chests. I managed to get along with everybody."

Still, there were the usual teen romantic pitfalls. Despite being named in the paean to young love that is "Only the Good Die Young," the real life Virginia "was all in my imagination, never consummated; she was the fantasy love girl." Thus Billy widened the playing field. He "madly crushed" for Carol Mulally in eighth grade, "such a beautiful creature," until she wrote a note about him to her girlfriend Dina—"The creep has been staring at me all day." He cultivated dating "wallflower girls," names he can still tick off like Cathy, Lorraine, and Glenna, nicknamed Glenna Glide "because she walked like she was on skates." Most of these passing fancies amounted to what he terms "shiksa madness," as he sought the less obvious targets. "I kind of prided myself on picking out these blossoming beauties that no one else recognized. The other guys would go, 'Where'd you find that one?' I'm not a breast man—I fall in love with the face."

One face, though, seemed to eclipse the others: "The one girl who made the strongest impression on me was Patti Lee Berridge, who lived a couple of miles away, in Bethpage. We spotted each other one night in 1968, when she was in the audience at a bar in Plainview called My House and I was onstage with my band, the Hassles. She was my age, eighteen, and she looked like Ann-Margret." Billy couldn't have missed her: a cascade of red hair, features that were somewhere between model-chiseled and girl next door, and in her eyes, a clear zest for living.

It's a time-honored showbiz staple to pick out someone in the audience to sing to, and that night, spotting Patti Lee made it easy for him: "Patti Lee was *the* girl, for some years—really, until she went off to college and I started up with Elizabeth." For years to come, Billy would admit she had a kind of ownership of him: "If not the *one* that got away, she was the *first* one that got away—and always in the background of my thoughts romantically, even when I was married. I don't know if I'm ashamed to say it, but I'm surprised to hear myself say it." While years later, in "Keeping the Faith," Billy would claim, "My past is something that never got in my way," he wasn't always as ebullient as that 1983 song's narrator:

> I thought I was the Duke of Earl
> When I made it with a red-haired girl
> In a Chevrolet.

When asked, Patti Lee Berridge says, "I think that is about me, yes—I was probably a senior in high school when we got romantically involved." She remembers the first time their eyes locked as well as Billy does: "It was a total flirtation. He took a liking to me right away, and he would like, talk to me when he was onstage. It wasn't verbal—he'd make gestures at me, and he would like, carry on a conversation with me. I knew he was talking to me, but nobody else did."

Patti Lee would be in Billy's life for the next decade, but the early days of snuggling on the Joel family couch trading hickeys in the company of Whitey, a shepherd/lab mix, and Cupcake, Roz's cat—once Patti Lee hid *under* the couch when Roz came home unexpectedly—gave way to the breakup as she prepared to go to college upstate.

Billy remembers, "When we broke up, I was pointing out, 'Our relationship really means a lot to me. After all, Patti Lee, we've had sex together.' This was like 1967 or so. And she answered me back with, 'So?' She was like the *guy*, and I was being the girl. She's like, 'Yeah? And so what?' And it was a real splash of cold water in the face that a woman would say that to a man. She was completely at ease with her sexuality, her intellect, and her femininity before that was even a political hot potato."

"I went to college," Patti Lee recalls, "and Billy was very—he asked me to marry him. And I said, 'Are you kidding me? I'm way too young for that.'"

Patti Lee would go off to college in Buffalo, return for chiropractic school on Long Island, and later study chiropractic in California, hanging out with Billy and his first wife, Elizabeth Weber (whom she befriended and later grew estranged from). She was steadily—and platonically—in Billy's life, but also a bittersweet reminder that romantically, "Billy and I were always one beat off. Always friends, but always one beat off."

To Billy, the breakup back in the Hicksville days was a lesson in humility and a kind of life lesson. In Eric Rohmer's film *Claire's Knee,* the befuddled protagonist Jerome thinks he's owed something due to his obsession with the enchanting young woman of the title: "The turmoil she arouses in me gives me a sort of right over her." Much as Jerome would settle for a brief touch of Claire's besotting knee, Billy would remember that infatuation, however deep, has to be reciprocated. She turned him down, the first but most important beat they would miss, "and I learned a lot from that. Oh, she was my muse for years. There are probably songs that I can say, yeah, that's probably about Elizabeth—but quite possibly more about Patti Lee."

Perhaps the conversation that undid another potential marriage is the one that sums up the thwarted quest. "Billy and I were having dinner one time," Patti Lee says, "and he was talking about a girlfriend at the time—I think it was Carolyn [Beegan, a romance going strong in 2000–2], and he said, 'I'm pretty much in love with her.' I said, 'Let me tell you something, Billy. She has your heart but I have your soul.' He was like, 'Whoa, I should write that down.'

"I told him, she's not the one for you. I think I'm one of the reasons why he broke up with her. I asked him, 'Are you going to marry her?' And he said no. I said, 'You're stringing her on through some really good years of hers. You shouldn't do that. If you're going to marry her, fine. If you're not, let her go.'"

"It wasn't really territorial," says Billy. "There was a sweetness to how she said it." Patti Lee was the challenging introductory course in his education about women: "Do they feel the same things we feel? She taught me that they not only did, they surpassed us in some ways, and could take us or leave us. Wow. 'But we had sex, Patti.' 'So? So what? Get over it, you sissy.' I'm supposed to be known for these love songs, these ballads, or these crooner type of tunes. And I suppose I should explore where does that shit come from—'An Innocent Man,' 'She's Got a Way,' 'Just the Way You Are,' 'You're My Home,' some of them frigging wimpoid. Well, where they come from is, I've been madly in love with women all my life."

IF ONE OF the takeaways from the 1960s, as enunciated by Billy in "Keeping the Faith," was "You can linger too long / In your dreams," young romance was inextricable from simple rock-and-roll exuberance:

> Oh, I'm going to listen to my 45s
> Ain't it wonderful to be alive
> When the rock 'n' roll plays, yeah.

And that excitement was incrementally being moved onstage in Billy's early garage-rocking days: "Despite our mostly marginal musical virtues, being in any sort of rock band at the dawn of that era was heady. Our original band name, when we were formed by my high school friend Jim Bosse, was the Echoes."

Jim—along with Billy's childhood friend Bill Zampino—was to become "James" of the 1976 song from *Turnstiles* that had a life on FM radio (and was a hit in the Netherlands). It was about how their paths had diverged, from one friend to another but unsparing in its candor:

> I went on the road
> You pursued an education . . .
> Do you like your life

Can you find release
And will you ever change
When will you write your masterpiece?
Do what's good for you
Or you're not good for anybody . . .

Billy was recruited as a bit of an unknown quantity, recalls Bosse: "My impression of him right off the bat was that he was somewhat of a loner, not just with us but in general. But he had an inner self-confidence that was unusual. We were fourteen, fifteen years old at the time. And his skills on piano were head and shoulders above where we were at that moment. He could play classical music, but rock and roll had just been invented, so we were learning it on our own."

The Parkway Green gang that both were part of, a gaggle of young men living in the vicinity of one of Levittown's designed public spaces, was not likely about to be mistaken for the local scout troop, Bosse recalls. They indulged in a fair amount of booze, glue-huffing, vandalism, and casual juvenile delinquency: "A lot of the members of that original crowd are deceased; a lot of them got pruned off rather early because of drugs, alcohol, and just hard living."

Billy recalls, "We were playing small local gigs at first, mostly at the Holy Family Church, with Billy Zampino as the drummer for a while. Then someone pointed out that a 1950s-era band who had a hit with 'Baby Blue' was called the Echoes, so [after a brief incarnation as Billy Joe and the Hydros] we became the Lost Souls, which of course wasn't exactly a great fit for the Holy Family Church."

The band entered a statewide band competition, easily cakewalked through the local rounds, and emerged as Long Island's champs. In October '65, they played a final round up against three other bands at the New York State Pavilion of the World's Fair, coming in second to the Rockin' Angels of North Woodmere. In order to play clubs where alcohol was served, the band needed IDs, a problem soon solved by one of incoming drummer Dave Boglioli's acquaintances, who plunked down a trunk of stolen wallets that had been emptied of cash but still had licenses that might do the trick.

The Lost Souls found a manager named Dick Ryan who had a connection with Mercury Records, and after an audition, the group signed with them. But soon they had to change the name once more, as there was already an English band called the Lost Souls. "This time we were really bummed," says Billy, "because we loved the name. Then the head of the record company, Frank Mooney, came to us and said, 'Here's a name for you guys: the Commandos.' We looked at him, thinking, *That sucks.* Even if Vietnam was not yet quite as unpopular a war as it would soon become, being tagged with that name was hardly an asset. But who were we to object? Just this bunch of stupid rock-and-roll guys, young kids, and they, the music executives, had the power to do what they wanted. So we became the Commandos—truly hating the name. That lasted less than a year, because the record company dropped us, thank God, after a couple of failed singles.

"We stumbled ahead as the Lost Souls again, though we briefly became U.S. Male, I suppose as some misguided tribute to the cornpone Elvis song of that same name. Another lousy moniker for a band.

"At that point, I was resolved to leave the group anyway, even before it became evident that the Hassles were looking for a keyboardist. The other guys in the Lost Souls, except for Jim Bosse, who'd become an accomplished guitar player, didn't seem really serious about pursuing a career in music."

Recognizing the futility of trying for music stardom—especially with Billy leaving the band—Jim Bosse indeed headed forth to pursue an education, as depicted in "James." He enrolled in a two-year college, then Hofstra University, before heading to Philadelphia for a postgrad optometry degree. Though his wife-to-be was renting an apartment that Roz had set up in the Meeting Lane house to bring in some revenue, he saw Billy only rarely. Billy, meanwhile, was on a very different course, pursuing his rock-and-roll future with the Hassles: "You have to remember, by this time I had already cut off most of my other options, because I was on my way to not being allowed to graduate from Hicksville High School."

Jim was in his final year of undergrad school as a bio major when Billy came by and sat at a piano in Jim's apartment to play the songs that would become cuts on the *Cold Spring Harbor* album. As Bosse recollects, "I was saying, 'Wow, this is great stuff.' 'Jim,' he said, 'I want you to come to the studio and play the guitar parts on it.'"

Bosse hadn't played guitar in a year and was a week from his final exams. "I said, 'Billy, I can't. Number one, I'm real rusty. Secondly, if I go into the studio and miss my final, I waste a semester.' So I passed. One of the major regrets of my life."

After relocating to Denver, Jim would sporadically see Billy on tour dates there, and then on a visit back east, Jim played Billy an arrangement of "James" transposed to classical guitar: "I think that's when he first started to formulate his own classical pieces."

Did Bosse ever feel that the song was a bit too tough on him? "It's a complex song—I took it as advice from an old friend, because Billy truly believed I was going down the wrong path, based on that meeting where he came to my apartment and played his pieces, and I turned down being the guitarist on the album. For Billy it's always been music and that's it. If he couldn't do music, he'd just as soon die. He was not going to do anything else with his life, so he couldn't imagine how I could change streams and give up music.

"That fire in his belly was burning too strong, and so he was giving me his really heartfelt opinion. And of course once you start writing a song, at some point what inspired the song becomes secondary to making the song really good. So the lyrics can become a little more biting and a little more critical, but that's not necessarily how I interpreted the song."

Regardless, the result is probably not being used in career counseling in high schools. "Yeah," says Bosse, "you're going to criticize a guy for becoming a doctor? Come on. But that's Billy's take on the world. Billy is the American dream—rags to riches. But under his own terms."

IN 1966, DURING his junior year at Hicksville High, Billy joined the rest of his class in filling out a questionnaire called "Idea Associations." It listed about forty items for which the students were supposed to state what response the phrases evoked. A few of Billy's responses, in retrospect, are intriguing:

I LIKE: good music, New York City, pretty girls, Chinese food
I HATE: loud-voiced people, phony people, prejudiced people
THE BEST: singer of popular music was Nat King Cole
I SUFFER: from a lack of taking things seriously
I WANT TO KNOW: why Negroes are persecuted
A MOTHER: is indispensable
I NEED: a good shot of confidence
A BROTHER: never had one
MY FATHER: left when I was younger

"I probably sound like sixteen going on clinically depressed," says Billy now, "but my childhood hadn't exactly been all noodle salad and laughs. And I was already beginning to feel a certain determination to find what David Copperfield called 'the hero of my own life.' Because I didn't see anyone else likely to fill that role."

For kids like Billy, who weren't sons of privilege, the examples weren't the All-American golden boys but rather the tough guys of the working class. A couple of notable boxers were among them. One was Barney Ross, the game welterweight who was raised in Chicago's Maxwell Street Jewish ghetto and became a symbol of his tribe's toughness. Known for his indomitability in winning seventy-four of his eighty-one bouts and earning a Silver Star in a Guadalcanal firefight, he ended up wounded and addicted to opiates. (He would also fight Hollywood when he felt they'd stolen his life story with the film *Monkey on My Back*.)

Another was Rocky Graziano, a New York slum kid who came out of poverty and prison to be a middleweight legend, and the tattered hero—as portrayed by Paul Newman—of the 1956 film *Somebody Up There Likes Me*. And of course there was the ultimate antihero Terry Malloy in *On the Waterfront*. As played by Marlon Brando, Terry discovers that it's a short step from fixing fights to fixing the justice system. Put 'simply, he learns that you go astray when you don't pursue what you know in your heart is right. By the time he told his brother, "You shoulda taken care of me, just a little bit, so I wouldn't have to take them dives for the short-end money," it was too late for redemption. He'd already entered the gallery of stubborn American heroes that the Greatest Generation passed on, by oral legend, to kids like Billy.

The high school word-association exercise continued:

I AM SORRY: that I got in with the wrong crowd
THE ONLY TROUBLE IS: what's done is done
PEOPLE: make you or break you
I AM MOST AFRAID OF: ruining someone's life
I WISH: I had a million dollars
MY GREATEST WORRY IS: what my family thinks of me
. I SUFFER: when my family is angry with me
I FAILED: to enter the Golden Gloves because of my wrist

Despite constant fatigue from staying up nights to play in bands, Billy did some of his coursework and straggled all the way to the end of the school year with the class of '67. But about a week before graduation, he was told he didn't have enough credits to get a diploma and would have to go to summer school.

That wasn't going to happen. "I was eighteen years old, I had already been in a band for four years, and I knew what I wanted to do. It was very clear: *I'm going to be a musician. And I don't want to have any further schooling.* I felt I knew enough. I was very well read. I'd taught myself a lot of what I knew, all from books. Besides, with no TV in the house, all I did was read: history, science, literature—in a pinch, even textbooks. Throughout my childhood, my mother was always going to the library and bringing home stacks of books. It was like candy for me. It sounds arrogant, but I knew more than some of the teachers. And the kids who were graduating—okay, they had their credits, but they weren't all that smart as far as I was concerned; they knew enough to pass a test. So I'd effectively dropped out a long time before I actually wasn't allowed to graduate."

Billy had mixed feelings about forsaking the diploma, because he knew his mother's heart would be broken. She knew he was a smart kid and wanted him to go to college. To fail to graduate was an aberration in middle-class Hicksville. She worried about his future.

Billy says, "I knew that it would hurt her, and she'd had a tough enough time as it was, because she was a single mother. She couldn't get good jobs. We were the poor family on the block. But I didn't give a rat's ass. I even said, 'I'm not going to go to Columbia University. I'm going to Columbia Records. I don't need any more of this. Summer school? I'm not going to put one more day into this penal institution, because I hate it.'"

Once Billy was in a working band, an irrevocable life change occurred: "I knew I was going to be a musician. I didn't exactly know how I was going to make a living at it, whether it was writing, playing, recording, being a session guy, or being part of the band, I didn't know, but that's what I was going to do.

"I remember one night on a road trip in 1986, in some hotel room, I was moved to write my mom about what her loyalty and persistence and inspiration had meant to me. A few days later came the first of two letters in which she returned the sentiments. I was really touched by them."

"God," Roz wrote, "I enjoyed being your mother. I was so lucky. I had a ray of sunshine living right in my own house." The letter continued:

And it didn't take anything big to "turn you on." You were so appreciative of the smallest things. A new map for your room— "Wow!" A new plaid shirt. "Gee—neato!" Books brought home from the library. "Hey, great!" A plate of spaghetti—"Hot dog." We never had any money, but we communicated, we laughed, we cried, we celebrated holidays, birthdays, picnics, shows, concerts, friends, grandpas, grandmas, aunts. We were a family who were there for each other when times were good or bad. And your laughter and your music and your enthusiasm brought so much life to that little house in Hicksville. Between you and Judy and me and our pets, it was a home, and no money in the world could buy that pleasure I had from knowing the joy of living in that home with those fabulous kids. The quiet was deafening when you left.

She went on, relating a story he had heard before, but that was moving in the mere repetition of it, about what it meant that her sacrifice at the time ended up paying dividends:

Did I ever tell you how we came to have our piano? Howie didn't want any more children. One month I was "late." He was petrified. God—he was upset. I said, "I'll tell you what. I'll go for a test at the doctor's. If I'm not pregnant, we get a secondhand piano. I want a piano. You can play—how can we not have a piano? I need real music in this house." I wasn't pregnant. (Too bad, I adored kids.) The piano cost $75—and the transportation (from New York City) cost $125.00. What a lot of money that was in those days. But he didn't welsh on the promise. And that's when it all began. I was soooo happy with that piano. It was painted so many different colors. And remember putting tacks in the felt tape to make it sound like honky tonk? Remember the *Fireside Book of Songs* with all the pretty country peasant-type songs? I wonder if you remember that. Life was simpler then, cornier, sweeter. Feels cruel and cold and kind of heartless these days.

Not long before Roz passed away in July of 2014, at ninety-three, Billy said, "We're in much closer touch now, as my mom hangs in her early nineties. And I'd like to make certain, in the time she has left, that she never has that cold feeling again."

CHAPTER 3

TOMORROW IS TODAY

In the late 1960s, as the British Invasion led to an expanding galaxy of stateside rock groups, Billy and his chronically unnameable band ended up being dropped from Mercury Records but played the Plainview, Long Island, nightclub My House frequently. The Island was aswarm with fledgling bands. Billy had often watched My House's resident band, the Hassles, who were relied upon, if hardly coddled, by club owner and sometime restaurateur Danny Mazur. Danny—recalled by Billy as "a typical Long Island club owner, kind of a tough, older Jewish guy, pinky ring, very heavyset, kind of gruff"—sometimes kept company with some beefy types Billy surmised were wiseguys. Working alongside him—and as the Hassles' manager—was his son Irwin. Though Irwin would later, via Danny's connections, be briefly employed by industry legend Morris "Moishe" Levy (of whom Irwin freely says, "He was Jewish Mafia"), at this time he was helping Danny audition and book bands. He had returned to Long Island for that purpose from Philadelphia, where he was studying dentistry at University of Pennsylvania.

The Hassles were drawing big crowds at the time. "We could draw a thousand people a night to a place," recalls drummer Jon Small, already a cover-band veteran when he formed the group. "We were very, very popular." They had a keyboard player named Harry Weber, and Small was married to Harry's sister Elizabeth and had a son by her, Sean, born in April 1967. Billy would never know Harry well—he recalls the infamously dissolute musician had a "lot of issues"—but of course he would come to know Elizabeth very well indeed.

Finally one night Harry and Jon had a serious set-to triggered by Harry's deepening immersion in glue-sniffing, even onstage, where he'd catch half-hidden snorts from a poly bag while crouched on the low bench behind his keyboard. Harry finally exploded backstage after being rebuked one last time. As Small describes it: "He had his feet on my shoulders and was pulling my hair out. What it came down to was either him leaving or me leaving. And the other guys stuck with me."

Harry, as part of a gaggle of Weber siblings who were raised in tony Syosset but lived a cursed history that most would associate with a less privileged lifestyle, would not land happily. A few years after being discharged from the band, he was found dead on a railroad track, the reported victim of an overdose.

In what Small smilingly calls "a very crafty" maneuver, he put an ad in the local paper in the spring of 1966 saying My House was seeking a second house band. "What they"—the Echoes, the key auditioning band that included Billy—"didn't know was that I was sitting there looking to steal their keyboard player." As Small sat in the otherwise empty club with Elizabeth, Hassles guitarist Richie McKenna, lead singer "Little John" Dizek, and Irwin, the Echoes—with Billy on Farfisa organ—performed a few songs. Small remembers, "I instantly loved this keyboard player. He wore a little bebop hat, and he actually got down on one knee and sang 'Soul and Inspiration,' the Righteous Brothers song.

"So I convinced the other guys that this is the guy, and I went to Billy and sat him in the room and said, 'The reason you're here is—how would you like to join the Hassles?' And he looked at me and said, 'Nope, not interested.'

"So I had to use another tactic. I knew these guys—nobody had any money. I had to bribe him is what it really came down to. I said, 'So what is it going to take for you to get in the band?' He said, 'Look, I'm loyal to my band, I've been with these guys, grew up with these guys.' I said, 'Well, I have a Hammond B3 organ.' That's what everybody wanted. 'You join the band, it's yours.'

"It didn't take more than a glimmer in his eye to think about it, and he said, 'Okay, I'll come in the band. But you have to take the bass player from my band, Howie Blauvelt.'"

Billy didn't want to be responsible, as Weber had been, for playing the bass line on the Hammond's bass pedals. "The Hassles were only a four-piece band," says Small. "But I thought, *Okay, why not? We'll just branch out, we'll be a five-piece band*. So Billy and Howie joined."

The Hassles offered Billy $250 a week, which in 1967—when the minimum hourly wage was a little more than two dollars—was good money, especially given the added benefit of being drafted into a top local band. "You're working fifty-two weeks a year if you want," Mazur added to Jon Small's pitch, "guaranteed." For someone who had worked in an inking factory blacking typewriter ribbons; and had worked winter mornings on the wet, greasy deck of an oyster dredge; and had even written a few rock reviews for *Changes* magazine for the twenty-five-dollar fee they earned him, it all sounded quite satisfactory.

"Nobody was worried about having a real job then," recalls Billy. "I was happy just to be a musician with enough money to buy some food and have my own place."

As for that Hammond B3 Jon said they'd give Billy? They'd be deducting fifty dollars a month from his pay to cover the cost.

What his new bandmates soon found out was that their new keyboardist—still singing backgrounds while the band worked the crowd with a raspy-voiced and marginally talented (but very Mick Jagger–like) front man, Little John—was interested in little else but the music. "What was important to Billy besides music was smoking cigarettes," says Small. "He smoked cigarettes like a chimney, and I hated smoke—and he didn't have a driver's license. Billy didn't even have a wallet. He was this funny guy. You could tell he was very smart, but the thing young guys craved was to have their first car—but he had no craving to have one. So I became the chauffeur."

As Little John was slowly being edged out, Small and Billy bonded over music, cruising the Island clubs, drinking in the emerging local bands like the Pigeons, who would become Vanilla Fudge, and the Vagrants featuring Leslie West, later of Mountain—both signed to the Atco label. The slate of local groups included the Good Rats, the Illusion, and the Rich Kids. But to Billy, the defining band of that moment was the Young Rascals, led by organ virtuoso Felix Cavaliere: "Anybody who played covers in bars for a living had to know their Rascals. They were out of northern New Jersey, but they were cool with the Long Island fans, as well as great musicians in that hybrid genre that was known as 'blue-eyed soul.'"

There were forays into Manhattan and, conveniently close, the borough of Queens: "I'll never forget sneaking into the Jimi Hendrix gig at the Singer Bowl, which is now the Louis Armstrong Stadium," Billy says. "We did the same at Randall's Island Stadium," now Carl Icahn Stadium.

Jon Small remembers regularly teaming with Billy—who used his gift for mimicry to sound British—to sneak into Carnegie Hall shows for the likes of Led Zeppelin and Jethro Tull, until they were exposed and all but literally booted out of the hall by notoriously thuggy British manager (and Sharon Osbourne's dad) Don Arden. When the Beatles played Shea Stadium in August 1965, the Hassles even had the delirious notion of jumping onstage as an uninvited warm-up act. With manager Irwin Mazur's connivance, they gave one of the Hassles' roadies a dark suit and a skipper's cap belonging to Irwin's dad, Danny, and arrived in Danny's Cadillac Fleetwood Brougham. Promoter Sid Bernstein sniffed out the ruse—though the band lore insists he was leaning toward allowing it until Beatles manager Brian Epstein vetoed them for not having the needed membership in the musicians' union—but the scheme got them as far as privileged seats in the dugout. (Of course in 2008,

Paul McCartney would jump onto Billy's stage there by invitation, as recorded in the *Last Play at Shea* film.)

During 1965 and 1966 the Hassles honed their live chops via steady gigging at My House and, during the summer of 1966, a series of dates at a Hamptons club called the Eye. "We played all summer long," recalled Blauvelt in an interview for the Great East Coast Bands website two decades later. "We used to play five sets a night. That got the band really tight." Some two years of steady live work led to recording sessions in May 1967.

Billy considers the two albums he made with the Hassles unmemorable other than their role as part of his education in the music business. The Hassles were signed by United Artists, which had been formed as a label to put out sound tracks for the film side of the company and ended up with a few notable acts, including Traffic. In fact, the Hassles' self-titled 1967 debut had a cover of "Coloured Rain," which Stevie Winwood and his bandmates in Traffic had sent to UA as a demo track and would soon record, but which label mates the Hassles were also given a crack at. The lyrics were full of adolescent yearning: "Yesterday I was a young boy, searchin' for my way / Not knowing what I wanted, living life from day to day."

"Stevie was an early hero," says Billy, "a multi-instrumentalist especially good on the Hammond organ, and about a decade later I persuaded him to be a guest player on my [1986] album *The Bridge*." Billy had his own Hammond sound, much in evidence in a Hassles love song collected on the 2005 *My Lives* box set, called "Every Step I Take (Every Move I Make)," a brew of Rascals and Zombies influences. (The similarly titled and musically kindred Police song quite innocently resembled it—and was the best-selling single of 1983.) The two producers of that first Hassles album, Tony Michaels and Vinny Gorman, took two-thirds of the copyright and publishing credits for the songs Billy had written—his first taste of larceny in the music business.

Billy and the band also recorded one of their live favorites, Sam and Dave's "You Got Me Hummin,'" which labored its way to number 112 on the *Billboard* "Bubbling Under the Hot 100" singles chart (and reached number 71 in *Record World*). It was an energetic stab at blue-eyed soul and the original's gospel-rooted, highly improvisational Stax studio sound, but in Billy's words, "it wasn't going to make Sam *or* Dave quit the business."

ON OCTOBER 28, 1967, about eight months after the first single had hit and as the band was completing their debut album, the leading Long Island daily *Newsday* published staffer Harvey Aronson's "Look What Grew on Our Lawns," a three-page celebration—leavened with some wry asides about suburbia—of the Hassles and their homegrown success. Occupying much of the opening spread was a sprawling group shot of the band clutching their instruments in front of the Dizek family's Syosset home. Framed in the foreground were the impatiently squinting Danny and Irwin Mazur, who sported suits and ties. Arrayed behind were friends and family, all on "the neatly clipped lawn in front of a split level." Text and photo worked the same conceit, as summed up in a pull quote—"The Hassles are all heart and all suburban. And they stand for the universality of rock 'n' roll"—and further text: "A group of sprouts native to Long Island has blossomed into one of the area's hottest rock 'n' roll combos, feeding on fees of $1,000 a night. With a little more care—and a hit record or two—the Hassles could begin to resemble a high-rising money tree."

Portrayed as working twenty-hour days roaming between the Island and Manhattan clubs (including Steve Paul's the Scene, where Jim Morrison and Jimi Hendrix actually once got on stage together with the Young Rascals), and even needing a police escort from an unnamed Queens venue, the group was said to have sold ten thousand copies of "You Got Me Hummin'" in the first week in such cities as New York, Baltimore, Philadelphia, Providence, and Pittsburgh. The single is described as "a glorious mélange of wham-bam-boom with lots of moans and a sensational scream," though whether Aronson was aware of the Sam & Dave original seems dubious. The writer notes that "Irwin talks in terms of The Hassles' grossing $250,000 this year," but today Irwin recalls that he had to stretch his own finances to provide $30,000 (presumably less Billy's fifty dollars per week for the B3) to buy the band's equipment.

The piece recounts the band's reaction to hearing their song on the radio. "I was in the back of the truck," says Richie ("a phlegmatic kid who gets animated when he talks about the record"), ". . . It's the best feeling there is to ride in a car and hear the record on the radio. Everybody started screaming and banging on the walls. . . . We almost hit another car."

The band member whom the article calls "Billy Joe" and equips with an erroneous added name (which dogged him for years), "William Martin Joseph Joel," is correctly depicted as age eighteen and from Hicksville. He's described as lead singer (though Dizek is cited as "front man" and, per Irwin, "the group's sex symbol") as well as piano and organ player, and as the group's "most learned musician . . . He likes Beethoven and Rachmaninoff, but they don't pay off for longhairs anymore."

In a sentiment he would echo throughout his career, Billy advised the reporter that "playing rock 'n' roll isn't hard; getting new ideas is the hard thing." Most of the current rock songs, he conceded, would be unsung and unremembered a generation hence, unlike—and apparently these are Billy's examples—"White Christmas" and "I'm in the Mood for Love." The point that "we squares should try to grasp," wrote Aronson, teeing Billy up for some hipster jargon, is that (Billy declared) "our music is all part of the today scene—we're not trying to add anything to posterity."

Things would work out a little differently, but who could have said so then?

As Irwin and Danny estimated for the piece, since they'd auditioned the Hassles in August 1966, Long Island had come to boast more than four hundred "discotheques" (a term that embraced rock clubs as well as dance venues) and one thousand groups. Despite the long odds, the Mazurs had sold My House in July 1967, annexed the first album's producers (Michaels, twenty-six, and Gorman, twenty-one) as part of Mazur Enterprises, and added two road managers. A UA spokesman said of the Hassles, "We're going all out with them. We're giving them a lot of promotion, we're getting them as many TV shows as possible."

In fact, their breakout hit, "You Got Me Hummin'," would be squandered as a commercial point of entry. Irwin told Aronson that he wanted to send the boys to drama school and "make them bigger than the Monkees." And yet he almost seemed to foresee problems with the dysfunction that was built into the band—front man Little John had the moves, but Billy, hidden behind his Hammond, had the voice. Irwin knew, he said, that "it has to happen with a record—if not this one, the next one." The article included a round of parents' musings. "I always knew he would be in show business," said Billy's mom. "He sang before he could talk."

Finally, Aronson describes their appearance on *The Clay Cole Show*, a dance show starring the local rock-on-TV bellwether—who'd once hosted a pairing of the Beatles and Stones—that typically featured lip-synching bands and a cast of regular dancers à la Dick Clark's national counterpart, *American Bandstand*. Cole would quit in January 1968, simply walking away from a scene that he—a self-described "black-tie, tuxedo guy . . . adrift . . . in 'the quicksand of psychedelic acid rock'"—felt alienated from. Virtually all the shows are lost to pop history, erased so the tape could be reused. With "Billy Joe sporting an Indian shawl" and Little John in a paisley print shirt, the Hassles may have spooked Cole with what Aronson called the "flying hair and the flying hips, and the big-beat stridence that makes young people of today jump, scream, and spend money." Aronson concluded with "Make it? Why not? And just think—it all happened right here on our lawns."

Perhaps the article was a jinx in its own right. In any event, the Hassles' slide into obscurity—or at best, to getting the occasional nod as one of Billy's early bands—was already quietly awaiting.

* * *

THE BAND'S SECOND album, *Hour of the Wolf*, was made with an underground legend named Thomas Jefferson Kaye, who had disputably claimed to have produced Question Mark and the Mysterians' 1966 classic "96 Tears," and who later worked with Steely Dan. As much as Billy would be a fan of the latter group, the eccentric Kaye was probably not the best producer for the Hassles.

Billy and the band set up the sessions in the old Skitch Henderson studio in New York and spent months recording. Some of the bunch were smoking hash, but Jon and Billy abstained. "The drug-addled process went on endlessly," Billy recalls, and Small remembers being aggravated when an inebriated Judy Garland, apparently an acquaintance of Kaye's, sat slumped on the sofa in the control room batting out mumbled queries. "Everybody was tripping," Billy would recall, "and we spent six months in this crazy little studio until we got so psychedelic we didn't know what we were doing anymore." Despite it all, the musicianship was capable and generally a cut above the lyrics of the title track (cowritten by Billy and Little John):

> *Death*
> *Has come alive within a creature*
> *With the eyes of burning fire*
> *There is a tingling in your brain*
> *You want to run but you remain*
> *It is the hour of the wolf.*

The title song shared a title (and, by coincidence, a theme of dawning madness) with the Ingmar Bergman movie of a year earlier, and amid its grandiose twelve minutes, featured wolf noises from the band.

Ultimately the Hassles' *Hour of the Wolf*, with an acid-expressionistic cover centered on a wolf's skull in lurid colors, was released in January 1969 and disappeared immediately.

Around that point, John Dizek decided he'd had enough. Years later, for the liner notes to a reissue of the band's work, he groused that the Mazurs were out for their own interests: "They used us to support themselves ... [and] kept us at My House during the most crucial time. . . . We should have been touring to support our album."

Billy took over lead vocals. Also left in the band were the untamed Howie Blauvelt and guitar player Richie McKenna, always viewed by Billy as difficult. Howie had been a steady friend of Billy's for years, from their early days in Hicksville and the Parkway Green gang through their shared discoveries of rock music's magic. However, Billy eventually grew apart from him, largely due to Howie's experiments with different intoxicants. (Unexceptionally, if unluckily for the era, Blauvelt had been arrested in January 1966 at age nineteen, charged with possession of marijuana as a felony with eight other minors, in a pot bust at a Hicksville motel; the disposition of the case is unknown.) Another bad sign came when Howie fell off the stage one night, midperformance. Given the kinds of clubs they were playing, where there was barely room for a couple of small risers onstage, it was hazardous enough up there without being in an altered state.

So Jon and Billy inevitably became a clique of two and would simply leave the Hassles and their only too appropriate moniker behind. (Howie would go on to brief notoriety in the local band Ram Jam, and died in 1993.) To them, the group's 1960s soul-pop had begun to pale beside a new influence like Led Zeppelin. "We wanted to be a heavy band and decided we were going to get heavy. Somehow." At that moment in rock, *heavy* signified intense, stoney, even psychedelic workouts— though soon enough, *heavy* would be connected with *metal* and turn away from its blues-influenced roots toward faster, head-banging, Judas Priest–style fare. In any event, Billy—unlike, say, John Lennon—had never actually taken acid.

It was during this apprenticeship that Billy had a couple one-off gigs that gave him a minor stake in the pop ethos that preceded the hippie 1960s. One was a session gig playing keyboards behind Chubby

Checker, he of "The Twist" (a monumental 1960 remake of the Hank Ballard original) and other dance hits in a string that petered out around 1965. Also around then Billy went to a Long Island studio to assist minor legend Shadow Morton in producing some tracks. Whether Billy is heard on the demo or the master recording for producers Ellie Greenwich and Jeff Barry's "Walking in the Sand" has been discussed in certain obscure pop history circles for years. Billy to this day can't swear if he is or isn't in the mix on that great anthem of teenage love and loss.

After a few more desultory gigs, Jon and Billy split from the Hassles and began their quest for musical heft—in the basement of Jon's parents' wallpaper store in Syosset. They were encouraged when they quickly snared a sponsorship deal with an outfit called Plush Amplifiers, whose amp cases were lined in rolled and tucked black vinyl padding but, more crucially, were capable of shoving out torrents of noise. By trial and error—Jon took some painful voltage while holding stripped wire from the organ to contacts on an amplifier—the duo figured out how to wire Billy's gear for a maximum raunch-rock noise, and it produced an ear-splitting, distorted sound. Now they felt, Billy recalls, "unstoppable."

"Although I missed Jimi Hendrix at Woodstock—I went up for one day, realized I didn't really care for mud, rain, or acid, and hitchhiked home—he was the nexus of what was becoming the fuzz and feedback era," Billy says. "I got a wah-wah pedal so I could wow-wow-ee-ow like Jimi, and added a distortion pedal, which I figured would double the mangled noise we already were making. Then we just pinned the volume to the wall."

The year was 1969, and rock's insurgent energy was still shrouded under such radio hits as Tommy Roe's "Dizzy" and the Archies' "Sugar Sugar" (though Billy's role models, Rod Argent's Zombies, had a hit with "Time of the Season" and the Brits made a raucous statement with the Rolling Stones' "Honky Tonk Women" and the Beatles' "Get Back").

Billy wrote a bunch of heavy metal songs, which were somewhat indecipherable onstage or on tape, and Irwin Mazur, who continued to manage him and Jon post-Hassles, thought the result was "the worst crap I ever heard in my life, but I got them a deal with Epic Records"— with a fifty-thousand-dollar advance. Some of that money went toward investing in some real rock "threads": goofy Carnaby Street–style outfits they bought at an East Village store called Granny Takes a Trip.

Soon afterward Billy and Jon set out to make their self-titled album for Epic under the moniker Attila. The name, which Billy chose, was in tribute to Jack Palance, who had slashed Romans and smooched a princess as Attila the Hun in Douglas Sirk's 1954 *Sign of the Pagan*.

"If you're going to assault the rock world and crush it under ten Marshall amps, wouldn't Attila the Hun, who plundered Italy and Gaul and slaughtered quite a few innocents along the way, work as a role model?" thought Billy. "I was nineteen, and at that age, if you're loving your heavy metal, it's all about thrash, kill, metal, slash, burn, pillage, repeat." Unfortunately, the art director at Epic took this inspiration a bit too literally and set up an album cover photo shoot in a meat locker, with Billy and Jon in fur-and-breastplate barbarian getups and surrounded by giant, marbled carcasses of beef.

It was a moment in Billy's career when absurdity ruled. A video from the era—a snippet of it appears in the documentary *The Last Play at Shea*—shows Jon and Billy on the famous Cyclone roller coaster at Coney Island. Back then, the park had a little person from one of the nearby freak shows zapping people with a cattle prod when they got off the ride, which seemed to suit the outré tendencies of the *Attila* album as it marched to oblivion. For most of the songs on the record, Billy deployed a small keyboard beside his left hand that could supply the bass line, and with his right hand he played his chords and leads— screaming the lyrics at the top of his lungs. Jon played drums feverishly all the way though every song. Ultimately, Billy was relieved that the band wasn't a success, realizing that he would have had to scream like that every night for years: "I was trying to sing like Robert Plant, and I was no Robert Plant."

Inevitably, they didn't sell many albums and got dropped by their label quickly. Jon didn't recall much *tsuris* about it. "Irwin was making all the deals; we were just the dopey musicians in the basement of my parents' wallpaper store."

After all these years, Jon and Billy are still in agreement that *Attila* "sucked." As Jon admits, "We sucked in the studio, and in the six or so gigs we ever played live. But the bond that grew between us as we were going through the low points probably equipped us for a friendship that would stand the test of time."

Time was far from the only test the friendship would see. The signal challenge for the comradeship would see the two men sharing an ex-wife, Harry Weber's sister Elizabeth. Jon and Elizabeth had married abruptly not long into their relationship, shortly before Billy joined the Hassles, when she became pregnant with their son Sean. (Sean can be seen, at age nine, on the cover of 1976's *Turnstiles*, at Billy's elbow amid various crowded-in extras.)

The history of the love triangle emerges straightforwardly, in the present day, from the two male principals. In fact, the two men, insiders say, still compare notes on their shared ex—*Did you have to go through this too?* But at the time when the partners were changed, and in several tumultuous years afterward, the relationship would be wrenchingly emotional.

Jon remembers one crucial twist. "This is the part where it gets a little squirrely for me," he says. "We were a bunch of hippies. That's what we really were. And [in 1970] we moved into one house together, in Dix Hills. It was all stone and cement, so we'd end up naming it the Rock House. And it was me, Elizabeth, and Billy." Prior to that, the trio had been living in the Fairhaven Apartments near Billy's old street in Hicksville—Jon and Elizabeth in one apartment, with Billy across the hall.

At the same time, Jon ranged about Long Island's clubs seeking out gigs, while Billy worked occasional odd jobs. Says Jon: "What happened is real simple—he just fell in love with my wife. That's it. And when I found out, our friendship was over." In fact, the bond between Billy and Jon would ultimately survive. But Billy's fascination with Elizabeth was inescapable, partly based on her indefinability: "She was—different. She wasn't like a lot of the other girls I knew at that time who had taken home ec and cooking classes. She was a very bright woman, and she wasn't afraid to show how smart she was. I suppose that made her kind of exotic. Intelligent and not afraid to speak her mind, but could also be seductive. Almost like a European type—not a typical American girl."

The situation reached its breaking point one day when Billy and Jon were doing one of the rare gigs they played as Attila—two shows, both sold out, at a club in Amityville. "So we played the first set," remembers Jon, and "and we went over great.

"Billy never perspired, but when I'd go in the dressing room, I'd be soaking wet. I used to use an Electrolux vacuum cleaner to blow-dry my hair, because there were no blow dryers back then. So I had this big vacuum cleaner going, holding it up. I'm looking out the window, and there are Elizabeth and Billy talking.

"The next thing I see is that Billy's getting in the car with her and leaving. But we still have another show to do. I get dressed as fast as I can, jump in my car, and I know they're going back to the Rock House . . . and there they were."

Whether Jon's anger was purely a late wave of jealousy and resentment, or partly derived from his bandmate skipping out on a gig Jon had set up, he reacted blindly: "Billy was sitting playing piano, Elizabeth was there, and her sister was there.

"I walked in, I was in a rage. I threw her younger sister, Josephine, through the screen door; she went right through the screen and broke the glass. And then Elizabeth ran out, and I punched Billy."

Billy describes the turn of events as unexpected: "I remember that I was turning toward Jon—and I got hit. There was blood coming out of my nose. I was just kind of startled, even though I had been punched many times when I used to box. This was just a punch I hadn't seen coming. But let's face it, I deserved it."

Before that night, Billy believed that Elizabeth had already talked to Jon about them; in his mind, the long-alienated married couple were already separated—at least emotionally—and headed for a clean break. Making matters worse, the two men hadn't discussed the couple's issues—or the budding romance between Elizabeth and Billy that was becoming obvious from body language, muted exchanges, and not-quite-stolen glances. Billy attributes the silence to a typically male mix of sensitivity and yet also not wanting to overly share. (Long Island guys with a foot still in the working class simply don't share on most subjects deeper than the Mets.)

"Up until that moment when Jon clocked me, I don't remember feeling particularly guilty, because I thought it was all out in the open, what was going on," says Billy. "But Jon didn't know [the whole truth] about Elizabeth and me. When I realized that Jon didn't know, I was filled with crippling guilt."

After that scene and the realization that he'd been *deeply* deceiving Jon, Billy felt like everything was crumbling at once. Attila had been a failure. He didn't have any bank account to speak of. And now he felt that he was causing his best friend's divorce. Then, to top it all off, rather than divorcing Jon to be with Billy, Elizabeth disappeared. "That's when I started feeling suicidal," says Billy.

"Billy called me up at one in the morning—he's got to talk to me. And I meet him at the Jericho Diner," recalls Irwin Mazur. "He tells me he's having an affair with Elizabeth. And he doesn't know what to do."

For a few months leading up to the blowup, Billy had been keeping a small apartment in the Fairhaven—where he slept under an American flag—even as Jon anchored the Rock House and Elizabeth increasingly spent time in the Weber family home in Syosset. But with Elizabeth absenting herself from both men for a time and Jon in a kind of exile, Billy was adrift, lacking the money for rent, without a car or license, and occasionally crashing at Irwin Mazur's home.

"So Billy's staying in our apartment one night," Irwin says, "and I get up in the morning, and I go in the dining room, and there's a loose-leaf page Billy left there with what are obviously lyrics to a song. And I read it, and the title of the song is 'Tomorrow Is Today.' I think his state of mind would be pretty well summed up in his song. It was a suicide note."

> *I've been livin' for the moment*
> *But I just can't have my way*
> *And I'm afraid to go to sleep*
> *'Cause tomorrow is today . . .*
>
> *I don't care to know the hour*
> *'Cause it's passing anyway*
> *I don't have to see tomorrow*
> *'Cause I saw it yesterday . . .*
>
> *Oh, my, I'm goin' to the river*
> *Gonna take a ride and the Lord will deliver me*
> *Make my bed, now I'm gonna lie in it*
> *If you don't come, I'm sure gonna die in it*
> *Too late, too much givin'*
> *I've seen a lot of life and I'm damn sick of livin' it*
> *I keep hopin' that you will pass my way.*

"It was 1970. I'd reached the age of twenty-one and still had no money," says Billy. "I had no place to live. I was out of the Rock House, crashing at my mom's place again, which is abject failure, when you have to go back to your parents' house. To avoid that, I'd been roaming about like a homeless person—crashing on friends' couches, sometimes in a car I'd find unlocked, in the warmth of a Laundromat, back and forth in the subways in Queens, even in the woods."

Jon Small remembers one day—as communication between himself and Billy slowly resumed, with Elizabeth's reclusiveness easing the state of détente—saying to Billy, " 'Come on, we're going to go out and go hang out at the bar, bring some girls or whatever, we'll figure it out.' And he was just lying there, couldn't even talk. And he said to me, 'I think I'm going to commit suicide or something.' And I said to him, 'Well, go ahead. Go ahead. Kill yourself. Get it over with. Because this is not doing you any good.' So I left him there and I went out. And when I came back, he was on the floor."

"I was still feeling so down," Billy says. "A well-intentioned friend of mine had gotten me some pills—Nembutal—to try to help me to cope with this terrible guilt and anxiety I was having. I was at my mom's house in Hicksville, and I thought to myself, *Well, I've got these pills, I might as well take them.*"

The way Billy's sister, Judy, tells the story, Billy called up Jon to apologize for the transgressions that, despite the seeming reconciliation, still left him feeling remorseful, and Jon came and found Billy passed out. Jon and Billy's mother called the ambulance, and Billy was taken to the hospital. "The next thing I remember, I woke up in the hospital and learned that they had pumped my stomach," says Billy. "I thought to myself, *Oh, great, I couldn't even do this right.* It was just another failure."

Billy was released, but he'd be back in a hospital within a few weeks.

"I was still having all these feelings of guilt and despair and hopelessness, and in the closet at home I saw there were two bottles that bore a skull and crossbones warning," remembers Billy. "The bleach didn't look too palatable. So I drank the Old English Scratch Cover [Not, as often has been cited, Lemon Pledge].

"After I drank it, I remember sitting in a chair waiting to die. I thought, *I'll sit in this chair, and I'll die here.* I ended up sitting there, polishing my mother's furniture by farting a lot. Judy's husband, Frank Molinari, got the job of taking me off to the hospital. Even as we were traveling there, I was saying to myself, *This is stupid. This is ridiculous. I need help.* I was coherent enough to check myself in to an observation ward at what was then called Meadowbrook Hospital."

Billy would remain in the hospital three weeks. He later remembered the hospital as being just like the one in *One Flew Over the Cuckoo's Nest*: "You go to the nurses' station, they give you your little cup of pills, and they look at your chart. I remember going up to the nurses at the station and saying, 'Hey, I'm okay. They're crazy. But I'm okay.' And the nurses would just look at me, with my long hair and moustache looking like Louis the Fourteenth, and say, 'Yes, Mr. Joel. Here are your pills.'

"I just couldn't wait to get out of there. We all slept in one big community room, on cots, right next to one another. The next guy over would be moaning all night, and another guy would be screaming. It was like Bedlam, a very scary place." At the end of three weeks, after Billy had talked to a battery of doctors and they were satisfied that they could release him, Billy was free to leave.

"I walked out. I remember this, because they had an electric door with bars on it, and it made a big noise—*schlank!*—like a prison door. And I remember walking down Carmen Avenue, where the Nassau County Jail was, right down the street, and thinking, *Don't look back.* I hitched a ride to my mom's house."

Billy's time in the hospital proved to be a lesson in reality and a life-long guard against self-pity: "To be in that observation ward with all those profoundly disturbed patients—I realized that my situation was nothing compared to that of the others.

"For the most part, the people I was locked up with were never going to be able to overcome their problems, whereas mine were all self-made. *I can fix this*, I thought. All things considered, it was probably one of the best things I've ever done, because I learned not to get so hung up on self-pity that I couldn't think straight. I'd like to think I shed the rock star skin at that point."

Irwin Mazur confronted Billy sometime after he was released from the hospital: "I asked him, 'What the hell did you do?' and Billy says, 'I drank furniture polish.' And he says, 'Listen, I can't take this music business anymore.' I said, 'Have you been writing songs?' And Billy says, 'Yeah, I have.' And there was 'She's Got a Way' and 'Why Judy

Why' and 'Everybody Loves You Now.' He played me those. So he says, 'Listen, I'm ready.'"

Billy was determined to get one of his songs covered soon, ideally by an artist he admired, or he'd find some alternative path through life, some other means of self-support. "Look," he warned Irwin, "I'm going to go to the Midwest. I'll be a bartender. I've had enough of this. If it doesn't happen soon, I'm not hanging on anymore."

II. BREAKING THROUGH

THEY SAY THERE'S
A HEAVEN FOR
THOSE WHO
WILL WAIT

CHAPTER 4

SAY HELLO TO HOLLYWOOD

As Billy Joel gave one last push for a music career in the early 1970s, he did so in the era of the singer-songwriter—a period that saw the rise of Joni Mitchell, Carole King, James Taylor, and other sensitive balladeers. It was a turning point when folk-rock began to emphasize highly personalized emotions and shrug off the more generic conventions of its folk origins—though Billy, as he tuned in to these new voices, would always remain fond of the full-throated, throwback style of Gordon Lightfoot. Along with more rock-oriented figures like Neil Young and Jackson Browne, the lyrics-centered balladeers were the most influential musicians of the day—certainly to the ears of one newly solo performer. "Well, I'd like to do that," Billy recalls musing as he grew familiar with the postfolk types, but he wasn't overeager to showcase himself. "I don't want to be a 'rock-and-roll star' anymore," he thought. "I want to write songs for other people." But Irwin Mazur made it clear to his neophyte charge: "All the people I've talked to in the music industry say if you want to get your songs heard, you should make your own recording."

At that point, as his work would later chronicle, Billy was living in Oyster Bay, Long Island, and writing productively—if in impatient obscurity. He recorded some demos that would become part of *Cold Spring Harbor*. He also wrote a few that ended up on *Piano Man* three years later—songs like "Captain Jack," part of "The Ballad of Billy the Kid," and the beginnings of "Scenes from an Italian Restaurant." The lyric that became "Things are okay with me these days," in fact, was originally "Things are okay in Oyster Bay."

Soon "things" actually started looking up. Irwin got Billy an advance, based on two or three songs, from Woodstock impresario Michael Lang—a minor irony, given Billy's dislike of his trip to that festival—who had a company called Just Sunshine. Lang had a production deal at a Gulf + Western subsidiary called Paramount Records, and he recorded a demo with Billy in a conference room at Paramount. However, Lang wasn't fully invested in Billy's music; he was concentrating on a Jimi Hendrix wannabe named Velvert Turner. But Lang felt he might have just the guy for Billy, a mildly notorious music business character named Artie Ripp. Together Ripp and Lang would each add a piece to their respective legends—in part because they'd each also take a piece of much of Billy's future earnings.

"I WAS ENJOYING an evening with Michael Lang, who had an office next door to me at Paramount Music," remembers Artie Ripp. "It was maybe midnight. He says, 'I got a tape. I don't get it, maybe you will.' And he plays me the tape—piano, vocal, a demo. I said, 'The guy that's singing and playing, that's his words, his music?' He says, 'Yeah. And what you're hearing got turned down by every record company in New York City.' I said, 'Oh really? I think the guy's terrific. What's his name?'"

" 'Billy Joel,' he says.

"I said, 'Okay, give me the manager's name and number.' And I pick up the phone. And at that point, I don't know, it's four-thirty, five o'clock in the morning in New York. I say, 'Michael Lang just played me a tape of your artist Billy Joel. I think he's wonderful. And I'd like to sign him. What do you want?'"

Irwin Mazur would have been well aware of Ripp's close professional relations with Irwin's mentor-of-sorts, Morris Levy; eventually Ripp's Family Productions would funnel several artists to Levy's Tiger Lily label, which, due to the practice of regularly dumping hopelessly unsalable albums into the marketplace, was investigated by the authorities as part of an alleged tax scam. (In fact, when he died at sixty-two in 1990, Levy was due to surrender for a ten-year sentence in a federal prison for extortion.)

While Irwin was far from naïve about the music business's underbelly of alleged racketeers, his first thought when Ripp called was to make haste because Billy was on the point of giving up. As Lang recalls, "In that first meeting, Irwin said he had to get fifteen thousand dollars, 'cause Billy was considering suicide." It was an exaggeration by now, if a useful one. "So we met, and the next day Billy came in and sat down and sang me a dozen songs, and then we talked for a while. And I didn't get the suicide thing that day, but Irwin was adamant." When he saw Billy perform his songs in person, using his virtuoso piano skills to re-create a range of effects indicating where other instruments would chime in, Lang was "blown away" by Billy's talent: "I knew I'd sign him, [but] you could see that there was always this possibility of an accident waiting to happen. This train wreck that was potentially around the corner."

If Lang saw a certain instability in the artist, Billy himself was relieved to be on *any* label; he'd had enough rebuffs to be hungry for any deal he might latch onto. Aptly enough, Artie's Family Productions logo was derived from the classic Etruscan sculpture showing Romulus and Remus, the mythological twins who founded Rome after being suckled in their infancy by a she-wolf. A history buff from early on—it was Romans, of course, that Attila had warred against—Billy knew that legend. The tale goes that the twins were rescued after being cast into the Tiber River. Perhaps his salvation was at hand.

If this was the start of his journey, though, as a practical matter it was to be transcontinental. Ripp was based in Los Angeles, and Billy was told that Artie was going to get him out there, and they'd make the album.

* * *

THE PRESENT-DAY MODEL for emerging artists in the music business is building an audience by slow accretion, using readily accessible and inexpensive electronic tools to get a few songs online, then diligently touring to support them. (In many ways it resembles the cost-conscious late-1950s–early-1960s model of trying to break a one-off hit single and proceed from there.) But the business Billy stepped into in the late 1960s mandated that aspirants find a label with pockets deep enough to make an entire "long-playing record," then stoke the market with promotion and tour support. With the right combination of talent, luck, and radio play, both artist and label could make plenty of money just by selling albums.

In 1967 the best-selling album was *More of the Monkees*, *Billboard*'s first pop/rock number one, with the Neil Diamond composition "I'm a Believer" played by session men. At a then-staggering five million copies sold, it eclipsed competing albums from the Beatles and Rolling Stones. The numbers would ascend the following year, with the Beatles' *White Album* on top. Soon the medium would become accustomed to sporadic buying frenzies as artists from the Bee Gees to Michael Jackson to Peter Frampton headed toward the twenty-million-copies mark.

Billy could hardly have compared himself to those Olympian figures as he debuted in the late 1960s, and yet in 1979 his *52nd Street*, released the previous October, would be the year's best seller. And these days, comfortably and profitably filling any arena of his choice with sellout crowds often approaching twenty thousand fans, he doesn't have to care that the megaselling album days are over for all but a few acts: "People forget that those numbers were part of that 1970s album-oriented label-and-radio machinery for selling albums—not singles, and God knows, not downloads you could steal off the Internet. That whole formula is shot to hell now.

"I don't want to sound like the old guy yelling at the kids to get off my lawn, but back in the early days of rock and roll—back when, say,

Elvis recorded 'Heartbreak Hotel'—somebody in your family got you the Elvis album as a Christmas gift. And even though kids didn't run out and buy albums, they still bought 45s. The girls would spin them on their little record players. That's how the rock-and-roll era in the record business took off."

As an early and ardent admirer of the Beatles' 1965 *Rubber Soul,* Billy was attuned to how the British had led the way in energizing the album as an artistic format. The long-playing record had been created by Billy's label-to-be, Columbia, in 1948, in part to showcase star conductor Bruno Walter's symphonies uninterruptedly. (Toscanini, distributed on 78s by RCA, soon forced his label to follow suit.) The format thrived with show recordings like *South Pacific,* the ubiquitous must-own for anyone with a turntable circa 1958, and through the era of Sinatra and Tony Bennett. As Billy recalls, the adult ethos of the time was, "Put on an LP, stir up some martinis, and maybe start making out with your wife."

Though "concept" albums emerged sporadically from such forerunners as Woody Guthrie and Johnny Cash with their populist-themed collections, Billy's awareness of what Sinatra was up to on 1955's *In the Wee Small Hours,* with its hymns to loneliness, is bone-deep in his artistic makeup. He would compose one of his exceedingly rare post-1993 songs, 2007's "All My Life," as a ballad squarely in the only-the-lonely Frank tradition—right down to the making-of video in a cavernous studio, wearing the fedora and loosened tie.

But as the 1960s turned to the 1970s, the Beatles were the most reverberant presence in music. "It's hard to separate the simple youthful exuberance the Beatles represented from the musical trailblazing they accomplished," recalls Billy. "They arrived as a singles band and erased all sorts of records for selling forty-fives. But their real accomplishment was what they did with the LP. By the time I was trying to catch up with them, they'd taken that three-minute-length limit for songs and moved it to a more conceptual level."

That process fascinated Billy, even though, given the arduousness of composing just a single song, it tormented him. Having grown up in the era of concept albums, he would stick by the ethic of linking songs to a theme, however understated, throughout his recording career: "When I was writing music, there was that opportunity—sometimes it felt like a burden—to have a coherent feel and message across nine or ten cuts. Right through *River of Dreams*, that was the discipline."

Thus, even as the Beatles stamped out further templates like 1966's *Revolver* and 1967's *Sgt. Pepper's Lonely Hearts Club Band* (third and first, respectively, on *Rolling Stone*'s list of the 500 Greatest Albums of All Time; *Rubber Soul* is fifth), it was clear to Billy that "not just the Beatles but other people got really good at it: Cream, the Who, Hendrix, Traffic—lots of great bands. And I got good at it. But think about how far these songwriters and these bands had to stretch themselves to come up with an album's worth of material. Essentially they were usually a guitar player and a drummer and a bass player, and they had to have a really good songwriter—or two—for the album to stand up to its competitors."

If the album cleared that bar, not just the poppier tracks got played, thanks to the then-deejay-friendly freedom of FM radio. It was a moment in rock music both unprecedented and never to be matched. "And the people who liked the last album you did were going to buy this one," Billy says. "If they didn't like your last album, if there were some weak cuts because you hurried things or didn't live up to your concept, they were going to buy somebody else's."

To be embarking on a solo career in this commercial and artistic climate, as Billy was in 1970, meant entering a heat with top-charting records that included the blues-stoked bombast of Led Zeppelin's "Whole Lotta Love," the propulsive rasp of Creedence Clearwater Revival's "Fortunate Son," the hypersensitive poeticizing of Simon and Garfunkel's "Bridge over Troubled Water," and James Taylor's "Sweet Baby James." Those nearly irresistible hits lifted off the long-playing records and into a whole generation's rock canon. And that's before you got around to certain wildly popular holdover hits from 1969, like the Beatles' *Abbey Road* with

George Harrison's lilting balladry ("Something") and the cosmic—in the vernacular of the day—Lennon crunchiness of "Come Together" and "I Want You (She's So Heavy)." Throw in Joe Cocker, Crosby, Stills, Nash & Young, and various other acts who were not just rock stars but cultural heroes, and the depth of the challenge to be heard was clear.

BILLY'S MANAGERIAL GUIDE into this proving ground was not the new-model, laid-back-hipster L.A. impresario like Lou Adler (of both the Monkees and the Mamas and Papas) or Elliot Roberts (Neil Young and Joni Mitchell), but a rough-edged Bronxite: "When I got to L.A., my first impression of Artie Ripp was that he was more than a little theatrical—he had a deep voice, the ponytail, and there was a lot of gesturing, a lot of hand movements," recounts Billy. "I guess you could say he came across as gangstery."

Nonetheless, Artie sounded like he knew what he was talking about: "He gave me this great spiel that he had worked with the Lovin' Spoonful and all these labels—Roulette and Chess and Red Bird—with all the girl groups, and Kama Sutra. He threw a lot of names around, musicians I'd heard of, and so I figured, okay, I guess this guy knows what he's doing. He knows how to make an album."

So Billy went along with Artie's program, at least initially, as he began to record *Cold Spring Harbor*—named for a favorite picturesque hamlet near Oyster Bay—in July 1971 at the Record Plant in L.A. What sticks in Billy's memory is that the studio was furnished with lawn furniture. Artie must have been the decorator, Billy thought, because it was his taste: "After all, in the office he had in his house, there was a chair that looked like an oversize hand. That should have been a dead giveaway: you were literally sitting in the palm of his hand."

Billy hated the recording process. "I should have sung the tunes two, three, four times at most, with very simple arrangements, no orchestration, no bells and whistles, just get in and get out. Other singer-songwriters were doing that, very simple folk-oriented stuff."

But as Billy remembers, Artie would call for fifteen or twenty takes: "It was like pulling teeth. *This time can you do it with more feeling?* I hated the strings. I didn't want the session players. The whole thing was completely overproduced."

Billy had a youthful, vigorous vocal instrument to deploy, a high, full baritone that could readily shade into tenor and even access a falsetto, but he lost all sense of perspective on how to sing the songs naturally because of the multiple takes Artie was having him do. "I didn't even know how I should sing anymore," he said. "I couldn't wait to get it over with. It was sterile, it was cold, and I felt Artie was thoroughly incompetent in the studio."

The infamous error Ripp would make was in the mixing. Billy would never know precisely how it happened. "All I know is that the master got sped up during the process—at that point, unbeknownst to me—and Artie had run out of money to fix it."

Artie remembers the album sounding strange when they were mixing it, though he sounded no alert to Billy, and indeed he seems untroubled by any particular remorse over the snafu: "On one of the playbacks, I knew there was something wrong. And we had mixed to a machine, a two-track that was running slow. So let's say it was running at fourteen point seven inches per second. When you put it on the standard fifteen-i.p.s. machine, it now speeded up."

The first time Billy heard the test pressing Artie sent him, he was back in his little apartment in Oyster Bay with a group that included his tour manager, Bob Romaine (a Vietnam vet later portrayed in song as the "Angry Young Man"); his sound mixer, Brian Ruggles; a buddy from the Parkway Green gang, Bob Coilisanti; and some girls they knew. It was going to be an album-listening party; everybody had a few drinks, and they dropped the needle on the record.

"I was humiliated," recalls Billy. "Bob Romaine started laughing first. 'It sounds like Alvin and the Chipmunks,' he said. And then Brian started laughing. I was so bent out of shape, I just whipped the thing off the turntable and ran outside and threw it down the street. It took a couple of skips and then it shattered, because it was acetate. And that was the end of that. I wanted to crawl inside my piano and close the lid. I called Artie immediately—'What the fuck happened?'

"Good God, it had already been a torturous process making the album, and misery working with Artie. Then after deciding just to go with it, that maybe he was right, that all our hard work would end up creating a great album, to have it be this horrible-sounding thing—it was so depressing."

Irwin Mazur was supposedly delegated to help fix the album, but perhaps because of the lack of funds—which may have been part of Ripp's reluctance to remedy the error—Billy recalls the situation as "all kind of turning into mush after that." It was then that he realized, despite the résumé that reached back to Artie's days with a white doo-wop group called the Four Temptations, he was living out a fantasy that was a bit beyond his grasp: "I believe that Artie saw me as his opportunity to be a musical impresario, some sort of studio wizard and not just a cigar-chomping producer," says Billy. "I was going to be his instrument."

Still, despite these snafus, Billy gives Artie credit: "After all the people in the industry who passed on me, Artie Ripp was the guy who wanted me to be his artist. Nobody else heard it, nobody else wanted to sign me, nobody else was making me a deal. Artie made me a deal. He heard something. Was what he heard what I wanted to be as an artist? No. Was it my vision of what the record should be? No. Was it a good deal? No, it was a horrible deal. But he's the guy who got me on the radar screen."

Regardless of the recording and technical issues, the music that emerged from the session showed early signs of the artist to come. Billy's musical style, which would prove to be perhaps the most broadly eclectic of any major pop star inhabiting the half-century he was working in, was still emerging. Even now he will speak of preferring to be simply "a guy in a band"—his recording career was coming at him faster than he was prepared for. Neither the schooling in cover bands—even the original songs on the Hassles albums were greatly derivative, if not covers—nor the feverish psychedelia of Attila had begun to forge the songwriter and live performer he was to become.

Largely because Billy had been writing songs that he hoped his more folk-oriented role models would cover, *Cold Spring Harbor* centered on Billy's deft work on piano, organ, harpsichord, and harmonica, leaning toward midtempo tunes that ran from 2:42 to 6:05 in length. It was a doleful set of songs, with "Why Judy Why" showing the singer pleading for emotional succor from a woman with, not coincidentally, Billy's adoptive sister's name.

Some of the lyrics were essentially lovelorn plaints emerging from the uncertainty that had dogged his romance with Elizabeth ever since the topsy-turvy scene at the Rock House. But by the time he was actually singing the songs in the studio, he and Elizabeth were committed anew to trying to stay together. Out of the relationship's confusion, at least one gem came to the fore. "She's Got a Way" would lead off the album, a more than sensible choice given its virtues—a now-surging, now-relenting melody; a stately accompaniment on Billy's piano; and four verses of plainspoken, never-quite-corny adoration of a loved one. When Billy aims to plumb his lover's "way of pleasin'," he can't quite do so: "I don't know what it is / But there doesn't have to be a reason anyway."

The last word hangs in the air, completing the thought but also trailing off, disrupting the tempo and seemingly giving in to the emotion, to the state somewhere between heart and hormones sometimes known as being in love with love.

To dissect it is almost to spoil the subliminal impact, because Joel isn't trying for cleverness so much as what John Donne was seeking in his sonnets: an exploration of his own passion. Although Billy would give his fans a new, live version on 1981's *Songs in the Attic*—a technically better performance much more in a chest register—it can't quite trump the poignancy of that 1970 session. It's a tremulous but precisely enunciated reading, the vocal growing more resolute, then almost fainting away before the final verse and its recall of that crucial word: "anyway."

If Billy would aver on the live album's notes a decade later that the song was "written in 1970, [but] I still feel the same way," the album's other standout, "Everybody Loves You Now," is the flip side of a relationship apparently fallen on hard times. Stoked by hammering, almost barrelhousing piano chords, it's both a rebuke and confession of tangled desire:

> Ah they all want your white body
> And they await your reply
> Ah, but between you and me and the Staten Island Ferry
> So do I

It's a thrumming march reminding its target, "You have lost your innocence somehow," while sometimes finding itself interrupted by asides at a conversational pace: "Ah, but you ain't got the time / To go to Cold Spring Harbor no more."

By the time he revisited it in a live version on *Songs in the Attic*, he'd call it "a macho rationale for being rejected. Her? Leave me? She must be a self-possessed bitch! Anyway, everybody didn't really love her. I just thought they did."

Though he'd be divorced from Elizabeth two years after those liner notes were set down, Billy stops short of attributing all the song's invective, whether it sounds forth in 1970 or a decade later, to that relationship: "It's kind of a sour grapes, unrequited love song, inspired in part by Bob Dylan's kind of alienation—'This is what you wanted, ain't you proud / 'Cause ev'rybody loves you now.' I still love to do that song." He says the vituperative performance under Ripp's command was in part a reaction to being fed up with the sessions and even with the songs he'd been repeatedly asked to perform as the producer sought better takes. But yes, in some part it must be attributed to the agonies of picking up the pieces of a troubled love triangle: "Because of the traumatic life experience I had just been through, I thought this was fertile ground to write about."

DESPITE THE RECORDING disaster, Billy went on a multicity promotional tour for *Cold Spring Harbor* in late 1971, with the album's drummer, Rhys Clark, anchoring his road band. Artie Ripp tried to pitch in via the old-school means he knew best. He began by slathering on some promotional perks. Small squads of girls were showing up for the shows in various towns along the tour, and Billy and his bandmates couldn't figure out where they were coming from. "They were kind of like college girls, but they seemed more like marketing types," Billy recalled. At first he suspected that they were the sort of swimsuit-clad models who typically stood next to cars at the big auto shows of the era. "And then we finally figured it out—they were hookers whom Artie had hired to convince the local deejays to play my album."

The deejays of the era lived in relatively high style, and Artie was just the man to encourage that: "I'm not gonna say that I was some sort of a goody-two-shoes," he says. "I was the guy who would fill up a hotel floor and put chicks in every room for the disk jockeys and say, 'You finish the redhead, now you got to get to the blonde. But I don't know if you're man enough to be able to deal with the blonde.'"

Possibly because airplay showed no noticeable spike, though not without causing a stir in a few diners and truck stops, the band kiboshed the caravansary. Says Billy: "We told them to get lost."

After some time playing in clubs, showcases, and music conventions, Billy and the band were headed for a debut international tour. One key date was an April 1971 appearance at the Mar y Sol Festival, Puerto Rico's answer to Woodstock (complete with rain), and the island's first international festival. There were prestigious names on the bill, including Dave Brubeck, a jazz eminence Billy was almost tongue-tied to meet. But when relative unknown Billy took the stage, the soggy mud flats just in front of the stage were all but empty of concertgoers.

Irwin Mazur claims that he hissed to Billy to do "The Letter"—not just the Box Tops' number one hit but Billy's expert, full-on mimicry of the Joe Cocker cover version, complete with gesticulations and rasp. Soon a steady stream of fans who thought Joe himself was onstage began to arrive, and the resultant outbreak of enthusiasm permitted Billy to not only do his set but throw in a few more impersonations.

Don Heckman of the *New York Times* would say much of the festival "droned on" as the food and sanitary facilities "continued to deteriorate," but he found something to praise in Billy's set: "The first real excitement was generated by Billy Joel's gospel-tinged rock band. . . . [They] brought some life to what had been a generally dispirited environment."

An apocryphal tale has it that Clive Davis, supposedly in attendance, caught the show and set his sights on signing Billy. However, in Davis's autobiography, he recounts that Billy came to his attention "through a Columbia promotion man named Herb 'The Babe' Gordon, who had heard a live version of 'Captain Jack' on the radio in Philadelphia."

The partnership with Clive was only about a year away, but first Billy had the tour to complete—a passel of European dates that, much like the previous swings across America, produced virtually no income for the band. Returning home to Long Island, painfully aware he'd barely sold any albums, Billy wrote the whole tour off as a waste of time and effort.

At that point, Artie was still paying the rent on the place in Hampton Bays where Billy and Elizabeth were living. But with even the paltry tour receipts now spent, there came a day in the summer of 1972 when the rent check didn't go out; some days later, the landlord came looking for it.

Embarrassed and not a little disgusted by the situation with Ripp, Billy sat Elizabeth down and told her, "I've got to get out of this." "I remember very clearly. I had just seen the movie *The Godfather*, in March 1972, and it had had a profound impact on me, as it had with most guys," says Billy. "We quoted it like it was Shakespeare. How you have to take care of your family, and you have to do whatever it takes. Al Pacino goes through the complete transformation from being this nice guy, Marine hero, to becoming a Mafia chieftain. So I said to myself, *I have to do whatever I have to do. We're going to get out of here; we're going to go back to the West Coast. I'm going to get an attorney. I'm going to get a whole new team of people to help me with this situation. I'm going to do whatever I have to do to make this right.*"

There were two immediate impediments. The chief one was Elizabeth's five-year-old son, Sean, from her marriage to Jon Small. She wanted to bring him along to the West Coast, but she feared that his father would never consent to it. Once again there would be a miscommunication between Elizabeth and Billy. Billy assumed that she and Jon had worked out the arrangement "and that he'd agreed to our taking Sean with them." He was soon to find out this was not the case.

The smaller problem was that he didn't have a driver's license. (He'd finally get one in 1973.) Though Billy had been driving motorcycles for years, he had no liking for four-wheelers. (A much-repeated motif of his younger days is that friends, or girlfriends, almost always drove the car.) Elizabeth owned a compact, manual-shift green Datsun station wagon, so they loaded it up, with Sean in the backseat, and Elizabeth drove the three of them across the country. The licensed-driver problem was solved—but the Jon Small issue remained.

They planned to stop in Albuquerque, where Elizabeth's sister Josephine lived. "There's a line in the song 'Worse Comes to Worst' on *Piano Man*: . . . 'it doesn't matter which direction though / I know a woman in New Mexico / Oh worse comes to worse, I'll get along.' That's what that whole song is about," says Billy. "I didn't know what the future was going to hold. I didn't know how we were going to make ends meet. We had no prospects. Everything felt so uncertain. I was trying to make the best out of a bad situation. This meant going into hiding, and there were all kinds of legal and contractual complications." Would Artie come after Billy for some unfulfilled tenet of their deal? And an angry Jon on his heels? The getaway was to be done covertly, but neither of the escapees had the kind of spycraft to really get off the grid. What were they going to live on? "Worse Comes to Worst" starts with the lyric: "Today I'm livin' like a rich man's son / Tomorrow mornin' I could be a bum."

Elizabeth drove a few hundred miles a day. As the eastern states dropped away in the rearview, for moments at a time, the two felt free. They had no plan and crashed in whatever motel they got to at day's end. A song he'd write soon afterward, "You're My Home," would surface on *Piano Man* and later on *Songs in the Attic*. He describes it this way in the liner notes: "Corny but true; I was broke at the time ('73) so I wrote this for my wife as a Valentine's day gift."

> *Home can be the Pennsylvania Turnpike*
> *Indiana early morning too*
> *High up in the hills of California*
> *Home is just another word for you*

About a week after departing, Billy, Elizabeth, and Sean arrived in L.A. a little bleary. Billy had wanted to leave the East Coast and the misadventures with the music business behind—"to drop off the face of the earth." But he really hadn't managed that—at least not as far as Jon Small was concerned.

"ONE DAY I went to see my son Sean, and he wasn't around," says Jon. "And I'm calling everybody, looking for them. Nobody knows where they are. On the same day, I get a call back from Billy. 'Hey, I heard you're looking for me.' I go, 'Yeah, hey, where are you?' He goes, 'Well, I'm in California.' I go, 'Oh. Well, it's funny—Elizabeth's gone and Sean's gone, too. I don't know where they are.'"

After a few uncomfortable moments, it became clear that Elizabeth hadn't told Jon the trio was decamping for L.A.

An angry Jon didn't linger on the call. "As soon as I hung up that phone," he says, "I got on the plane and flew to L.A., rented a car. I drove up La Cienega, because he'd told me he was playing at the Troubadour. The club wouldn't tell me where he was, but the next day, I'm on Santa Monica Boulevard, calling my mom. And I look at the Tropicana Hotel, and there's Billy coming out of the office. A second later I see Elizabeth and Sean coming down the stairs, and I say, 'I got them, I got them, Ma'—and I run across the street as they're getting into the car, and I go right up and bang on the hood and go, 'I got you.'"

Despite all that had gone on, including something one might describe as a kidnapping, the sheer tomfoolery of the absurd moment struck them all at the same time. Says Jon, "We went back to the hotel, and within twenty minutes we were all laughing because we all realized how much we missed each other. All of a sudden I felt great. There I was with my buddy, and even though I didn't like what Elizabeth had done, I still liked Elizabeth. They were my two best friends. And we all were having a good time. And there was Sean—everything was great."

As night fell, some deeper consideration began for Jon: "Elizabeth told me she'd go home to New York the next day with me. We'd fly back. So now we're in there, and it was funny: Billy and Liz went to the bedroom, and now I'm going to be out in this living room with Sean, going to sleep. And I call my mom. I go, 'Mom, I'm here,' and my mother says, 'We're sending detectives.' I said, 'No, it's all set.' She and my dad go, 'No, no. Don't trust him. They'll be there around three o'clock in the morning. Be ready to go.'"

Sleepless, brooding, turned around by what seemed to be the grave concerns of his parents, Jon was counting minutes. "So I was waiting. I figured that these hired guys would come; I'd take Sean—we'd just slip out. Billy and Elizabeth would be sound asleep; we'd catch that first plane, they wouldn't even know we were gone. Well, these bozos come, and they knock on the door, and this little guy comes in: 'We want to see her.' And they wake Elizabeth up, and Billy, but she's now not going to let Sean go. But they convince her that he's got to go; they're like scaring her. So it's the two guys, me, Elizabeth, and Sean. And she's so pissed at me—we're in the backseat of this car trying to get to LAX. They're asking Elizabeth for directions—'How do you get to the airport?' She goes, 'Fuck you.'

"We finally got to the airport. Soon as we stepped out, there was a policeman walking. Elizabeth went up and said, 'They're trying to abduct me.' And the guy [with her] said, 'Well, we're private detectives from New York,' and the cop said, 'You have no jurisdiction here, goodbye.' So they left, and I went back with Elizabeth, and when we drove back to the Tropicana, there was Billy standing in the middle of the parking lot, devastated. And here we are back forty minutes later. And then the next day we three—her, me, Sean—all went back. Billy stayed."

According to Jon, "It was a very heartbreaking thing, not just for me but for him, too. And I'm sure Elizabeth as well. If I was going to say one thing about it—love is really strong. When you love somebody, you step over anything else to get there. And Billy's pretty much a romantic. I knew it hurt him, and it hurt me and—look, I know that even today it still bothers him."

"All I remember about that night," says Billy, "were the two private investigators who said, 'We're taking Sean back to New York. You have illegally taken him, blah blah blah.'"

Billy didn't think he was ever in any physical danger, but he didn't know what the legality of the situation was. "They seemed to have the law on their side," he says of the investigators, "so Elizabeth left with them. I didn't know anything about this." What would eventually turn into mistrust and alienation between Billy and Elizabeth may have almost subconsciously commenced then.

"It was pretty heavy. Now all of a sudden I was on my own at the Tropicana: no girlfriend and no kid. Everybody was gone."

CHAPTER 5

SING US A SONG

If Billy was spiritually bereft, standing in the Tropicana parking lot effectively alone in the world, he also had little to cheer him professionally. In an effort to extricate himself from his deal with Artie Ripp, he executed on a blunt strategy to mark time, earn nothing, and force Ripp to free him from his contract. While Billy waited, any music he made would have to be made clandestinely. Los Angeles was the geographical center of the singer-songwriter movement—and yet he was living there in forced obscurity.

After their brief stay in the Tropicana, on the promise that Elizabeth would be returning with Sean once she'd made a cleaner break with the East Coast and her dissolved marriage, Billy found an apartment in North Hollywood—a decent, cheap roost in a two-story building with a swimming pool in the middle of the communal courtyard. Now he needed to find a gig.

What he found was a place called Corky's, on Van Nuys Boulevard in "the Valley." Corky's was, in his words, "a big cafeteria-style restaurant that had a terrible piano and 'entertainment.' I played there for just a few weeks. They auditioned somebody else while I was working there—a girl with a big set of bongos; she also played guitar—and they shit-canned me right before Christmas, which I thought really sucked.

One night after I got fired, I remember throwing a rock through their window."

The unceremonious exit from Corky's—the rock-tossing would be mirrored on the *Glass Houses* cover many years later—spurred Billy to find a talent agency in Hollywood that booked what he soon perceived to be D-list acts for bars, clubs, and parties. The agency got Billy an audition at a spot called the Executive Room, on Wilshire Boulevard near its junction with Western Avenue in Koreatown. He was hired and played long evenings at the lounge, a gig that lasted six months—or, looked at in another way, it became the definitive employment of his life and a landmark in American popular song. As piano bar crooner Bill Martin, he was taking a detour that, thanks to its enduring musical rendering in "Piano Man," turned out to be a signature moment of his career. It paid a union-scale wage, and Billy made steady money and tips—and got free drinks. He would work from after the dinner hour until two in the morning, six days a week, playing five or six thirty-minute sets a night.

When Billy spoke with Tim White for a November 1978 *Crawdaddy* cover story and described how he "just disappeared," the ever-meticulous White interviewed Angelique Norton, who owned the bar with her husband, Russell. "There'd been so many piano players coming and going," she said, "but he stood out . . . and he had a following. On slow nights I'd ask him to play some of the classics, like a polonaise by Chopin, and he'd do them. But he used to tell me he didn't like playing requests for people. Sometimes customers would start singing along, and he definitely didn't like that, either."

Billy would pick up the story in the transcript: "It was all right. . . . I took on this whole alternate identity, totally make-believe. I was like Buddy Greco, wearing my shirt with the collar turned up, unbuttoned halfway down. The characters that Steve Martin or Bill Murray do as a goof, I was doing, too, but people didn't know I was kidding. They thought, *Wow, this guy is really hip.* They would say [in a drunken slur],

'Play thish shthong.' . . . I never knew the song, so I played a lot of major-seventh chords [which were strewn through all genres of pop and would be shared by later rock songs, from Lennon's "Imagine" to the Red Hot Chili Peppers' "Under the Bridge"], and they'd go, 'Yeah—that's it!'"

Making his exile from the music business a lot more palatable was Elizabeth's impending return. "I had a sense of mission, but at first there was a real loneliness to the entire enterprise," says Billy. Finally, Elizabeth, who had been studying business at Long Island's Adelphi University, rejoined Billy in L.A., where, with Sean in tow, she picked up her business studies at UCLA.

Soon she, too, began working nights at the Executive Room, wait-ressing. They each brought home about two hundred dollars a night. Their closest friends during that period were John and Sandy Gibson, whom they'd met at Family Productions. Sandy edited a newsletter and handled press there, and soon thereafter she was working at the indus-try trade paper *Cashbox*. John was a *Hollywood Reporter* staffer. Later they'd both move to Atlantic Records in New York. (Eventually John left the music business to became a personality on Fox News.)

When their Atlantic staff jobs took them east, John and Sandy were happy to have Elizabeth and Billy move in as house-sitters for their place on remote Scheuren Road, up Las Flores Canyon in the hills of Malibu, where the rent was just $219 a month. They bunkered in, essentially waiting for Artie to lose interest. "My hope was that by going under-ground, he'd lose track of me and be persuaded, sometime in the near future, to let me out of the onerous deal I'd made," says Billy. (A few years later Bruce Springsteen would similarly go silent while disentan-gling himself from a bad management deal with Mike Appel.) "Mean-while, Artie had no idea where I was. I was calling myself Bill Martin professionally. How were they going to find me in this big sprawling city, hiding in plain sight at a piano bar? I had dropped off the face of the earth."

During the Malibu encampment, Billy laid eyes on his father for the first time in many years. The international label Phonogram, European distributor of Artie Ripp's label, sought out Howard Joel (mistakenly, at first, in Germany rather than Austria) as part of their PR strategy. Although Billy was in Milan when he got the news, the easiest course was to fly Howard to Los Angeles soon afterward.

At LAX, Billy met Howard upon arrival outside customs. Despite the nearly two decades that had passed, he spotted him at once, based on shared genes: "the same bug eyes." Over several days of catching up, Billy would learn of Howard's remarriage to an Austrian woman, Audrey, and also that he had a half-brother, Alex. Although there was no glad-handing, given Howard's saturnine personality, and the older man seemed more bemused than impressed by Billy's career, the reconnection solved at least part of the puzzle that had been Billy's childhood.

AS BILLY KILLED time playing the Executive Room, he considered what his next step would be, if he could indeed break free from Ripp's control. Fortunately, the market for even a damaged talent—as he was after *Cold Spring Harbor*'s underwhelming performance—was quite robust as the decade turned. The two important music labels in the early 1970s were Warner Elektra Atlantic Records (known as WEA) and Columbia. The Atlantic fiefdom had the hippest cachet, thanks to bellwether groups like Cream and Led Zeppelin dominating rock alongside such great holdovers from the soul era as Sam and Dave, Ray Charles, and a wide territory in between that included the Rascals and Crosby, Stills and Nash.

Columbia was the bigger label, with a more corporate image. It made Blood, Sweat, and Tears very radio-friendly, and even Janis Joplin came out a little less raunchy (and authentic) than she actually was. But above all, Columbia was the label of Bob Dylan.

For that reason alone Columbia appealed to Billy: "Here was this raspy singer who got no radio play, had no hit singles, had nothing going for him except that he was Bob Dylan—and they had the sense to see what that meant. They stayed with him and put out those records, and he's ended up being the most important solo artist of our time. To this day, Dylan is still at Columbia Records. What that said to me was, *This is a career-oriented label*."

Over time Columbia would end up being the right choice for Billy. They stuck with him through five albums that weren't hits. Even *Piano Man,* which was perceived to be successful, barely dented the charts at first. *The Stranger,* in 1977, would be his first commercially impressive album.

Not that he could have walked into any label's office ready to sign on. Beyond the strictures of his deal with Ripp, he was stigmatized by the very fact that a bottom-feeder such as Artie had discovered him.

Artie was the classic jack-of-all-trades, master only of working the seams in between. Billy needed a different setup altogether, far from the Runyonesque world of Artie's Broadway connections. He wanted to be independent, but needed help from a West Coast lawyer, a West Coast accountant, and a record company that had a strong presence there, where the real heat in the industry was at the time. Thus in that familiar and more often than not futile way of Tinseltown wannabes, Billy and Elizabeth would live by their wits for a while to see what they could make happen in their parallel careers.

At the time, Billy had an aide-de-camp named Jon Troy, a gruff but mostly likable character who'd been a bartender, worked alongside powerful Top 40 radio programmer Bill Drake, and finally came into Billy's orbit by contacting Artie while between jobs as indie record promo man. He'd heard *Cold Spring Harbor* as a demo that Drake had forwarded—"By the third track I said, 'Whoa, this guy's great.'" Troy made a pilgrimage from New York to Philly to see Billy open for Taj Mahal, "and he just blew me away, ten times better than even the record. I went backstage and visited. Next thing I know we're on the road together.'"

With an organizational vacuum already forming due to Billy's alienation from Mazur and Ripp, Troy stepped into a role as a sort of ad hoc manager, part gofer. One task he recalls, from the early days on Billy's

Cold Spring Harbor tour, was hounding Artie Ripp to wire money to their hotel. Artie had neglected to pay for the band's stay, and the hotel had locked them out—they were waiting to get into the rooms.

Jon Troy was also handy when club owners tried to stiff the band: "I'm an Irish New Yorker—I'd get in there and make sure they got paid, one way or the other." He and Billy had a rapport, partly, Jon felt, because each had lost consciousness from a suicide attempt earlier in life. They had discussed the odd moment of coming back to awareness. "I woke up," Troy remembers. "I had been in a coma for three days, and my mother was standing over me. I said, 'Oh, shit, I'm still here.'"

As Jon recalls, "I remember at one point Billy was saying how fed up he was with it all and how long he had been at it and nothing was happening. Artie was definitely jerking him around. And Billy just felt like chucking it all and going back to clamming or whatever it was he did out there on Long Island. And I said to him, 'I'll kill you if you do that. You've got a God-given talent.' His quick remark back to me, which I've never forgotten, was 'Fuck you, Troy—the only time I am playing with God is at a piano. But *you* can go out and write marketing plans, you can run a restaurant, you can talk to people, deal with executives or radio people. I can't do any of that shit.'

"He humbled me, he really did, with that statement,"

Perhaps because Billy sensed that he possessed just one financially rewarding skill in life, he renewed his commitment to the course he'd set out on: "I was not going to take another job. I was going to be a musician—that's my work. I recognized how corrupt and decadent, how larcenous, this business was, but I just had to try to find the most straight-up people I could."

Artie had proven to be anything but that, so Billy set up a meeting with an attorney named Lee Colton, who Jon Troy had heard was a robust negotiator with real record-business savvy. He also hired veteran accountant Ralph Goldman's firm. Now the troika was in place to rejigger the deal with Artie and take the accompanying step of finding a new contract with a real record company.

Lee Colton carried himself casually, but Billy would come to find out that he could take on the industry sharks. He was an Angeleno who reliably wore a dark suit and conservative tie. (He would strongly hint that Billy go onstage with his own version of that outfit, which became his practice.) Lee was also a strapping figure, a former football player at the inner city's Los Angeles High School and a boxer of sorts, like Billy. He'd attended UCLA law school and gone into the then slightly disreputable trade of lawyering in the record business. "I guess it's not exactly a ticket to respectability even now," remarks Billy, "which may be why he always behaved impeccably."

Over time Lee would represent such acts as Blood, Sweat, and Tears and Sly Stone, who found success as Billy's eventual label mates. This was when Walter Yetnikoff ran things at Columbia after taking over in 1974, in the wake of Clive Davis's departure.

Lee's gutsy lawyering is best summed up in an anecdote from a couple years later. Lee was still fairly new to the music business game when, a couple of albums into Billy's Columbia contract, he went to visit Yetnikoff at the Beverly Hills Hotel. His unannounced agenda was to win a boost in Billy's royalty rate from Columbia.

Yetnikoff saw it coming. Opening the door to what he presumably thought would be just another elegantly attired Beverly Hills suit, Yetnikoff greeted Colton with a volley of epithets to the effect that if he was there to seek a bump-up in royalties, there was *no fucking way* he was going to get it. He then fixed a gimlet eye on the lawyer to see the result.

"You cocksucker," Lee replied. "Who do you think you're talking to?"

Then he sat down, and they talked.

Lee's self-assurance had already begun to show itself in 1972, when he set out to free Billy from his burdensome deal with Artie Ripp in order to clear a path for the Columbia signing. One point of leverage in Billy's favor was that Artie and his Family Productions label were handcuffed to the disadvantageous deal at Paramount and its umbrella corporation, Gulf + Western (or Engulf + Devour, as the Hollywood business wags dubbed it). Artie would see little profit in holding Billy to the label deal already in place—he has frequently referred to it as "a platinum coffin with diamond studs"—because, despite various perks the label offered in terms of payouts, it was too dysfunctional to do the kind of marketing and promotion that would trigger really profitable album sales. Fed up with his "coffin," Artie needed to cut his losses and walk away from Paramount; even if he could control Billy, it would do him little good to do so at a label so ill equipped to bring profits to artist *or* manager.

Lee Colton intended to make very certain that Artie no longer considered Billy one of his ongoing assets. Together he and Billy resolved to continue waiting Artie out. It was a cruel set of handcuffs for an eager young artist, but in cases like Billy's, where a manager has little else going for him, it can be effective.

Meanwhile, "Captain Jack" was gaining a growing buzz, as the premier FM radio station in Philadelphia, WMMR, had a live version of the song in heavy rotation. The track was destined for the next, unnamed album (it would be *Piano Man*) and was a popular part of the band's live show.

The live track was part of a wide-ranging studio show that took place on April 15, 1972, two weeks after Billy's performance in the downpour at Mar y Sol and about a year before he would be signed to Columbia. The concert was spurred by the enthusiasm of local FM deejay and music writer Jonathan Takiff, who had been playing a couple of *Cold Spring Harbor* tracks even before he saw Billy open for Taj Mahal—the same show that so excited Jon Troy at Philly's Main Point club. Takiff's favorite song was "Captain Jack," which he'd describe as "yer classic youth wasted on (not enough) sex, drugs, and rock-and-roll narrative. And it was told with a searing, pitiless tone, unique suburban twist, and a chorus so dynamic it could 'get you high tonight' on its lonesome."

Takiff must have sounded just as fevered when he talked the boss at WMMR into featuring Billy live on the air. The twelve-song set (subsequently released by Columbia/LEGACY as a bonus CD on a 2010

Piano Man reissue) became a turning point as Billy's career gained traction that would never quit. After Takiff duped the live tape and aired it a few times on his late-night weekend show, "Captain Jack" created a groundswell, and soon it was the most requested song in the station's history.

Given the sudden serendipitous airplay in one of the nation's most music-loving constituencies, the good reception Billy and his backing band were getting as the opening act for a string of college concerts they were playing, and insider chatter about the minor sensation Billy had caused at the at the Mar y Sol Festival, Irwin Mazur wasn't surprised to get a call in early 1973 from Kip Cohen, head of Artists and Repertoire (A&R) at Columbia. Kip had worked in the shadow of Clive Davis, who became head of the label largely thanks to his own A&R prowess. Whether or not Cohen was aware of an imminent deal Ripp was discussing with Atlantic, Davis wanted to meet with Billy at the earliest opportunity. Irwin met with Davis and Kip Cohen on his own, but Elizabeth and Billy made a clandestine trip to the Beverly Hills Hotel, in early May 1973, to meet with him in his bungalow. That was when the crucial handshake took place.

During the meeting, Davis, never one to stint on revealing his accomplishments, made a point of mentioning having signed such artists as Janis Joplin. In his memoir Clive would mention that Artie Ripp added a certain spice: "[He was] an extremely colorful record industry personality with whom Billy would dramatically fall out. At the time, however, Ripp was tireless in his promotion of Billy in ways that suggested the stereotypical music biz character. . . . Artie insisted I go to see Billy in a club, and needless to say, he tore the place apart. . . . He was clearly a triple threat—a gifted singer-songwriter, a torrid piano player, and a sensational live performer. I had to sign him."

Simultaneously, Artie, despite Columbia's urgency, was following up on the competing interest from Atlantic Records. The connection dated back to a year before, when Billy and Elizabeth's friend from her days in Artie's employ, Sandy Gibson, made a zealous pitch for Billy to label head Ahmet Ertegun, her employer at Atlantic. Another legend in the business and a figure Billy respected, Ertegun had presided over some of Billy's favorite R&B greats, from Ray Charles to Sam and Dave.

In 1972 Ertegun brought his two key execs to Artie's home in the Hollywood Hills. The visitors were Jerry Greenberg, whom they called in the business "a good records man," and Jerry Wexler, a writer-turned-R&B-producer-turned-impresario and legend almost on the scale of Ertegun.

Billy sat at the Steinway and launched into the strongest songs in his repertoire, several of which, like "Travelin' Prayer," "You're My Home," "Piano Man," and "Captain Jack," would end up on his second album. Aiming to replicate as closely as he could the arrangements the full band would perform, Billy played his fingers numb for the people in the room.

Then Jerry Wexler piped up: "You play too much. Stop playing so much." This wasn't, in Billy's mind, a good sign: "I'd been doing this job for pay for nearly a decade, and for better or worse, what they were hearing was my style."

Wexler also had an opinion on "Piano Man." To him, it sounded too much like the 1968 Jerry Jeff Walker song "Mr. Bojangles," which had become a top-ten hit for the Nitty Gritty Dirt Band in 1971. "Jerry, God rest his soul," says Ripp, "was a person, like Ahmet, with a sense of humor. And Jerry makes a remark like, 'If 'Bojangles' wasn't written, maybe you would not have written that song.' Okay, now Billy didn't like what he heard." Billy pointed out that despite a similar structure and chord progression, the song was his own and had come out of a personal experience.

The meeting was cordial enough and, recalls Artie, "at the end of the day, Ahmet and I negotiated a deal for Billy to be an Atlantic artist.

"And then all of a sudden, out of the blue, Clive Davis comes into the picture."

What was a surprise to Artie had of course been engineered by Irwin, Billy, and Elizabeth. Whether because Billy wanted a chance to be on Dylan's label (which Davis would later say was the clincher) or perhaps because Billy felt sideswiped by Wexler's comment, Columbia would win the day.

When Artie was informed that Billy and his inner circle had already agreed to the deal with Clive, he moaned, "You can't go with Columbia Records. You said you wanted to be with Atlantic. Ahmet and I, we shook hands. It's done."

But Billy's meeting with Clive had only confirmed his resolve, and Irwin was still the manager of record. "Now," says Artie, "there's a whole new game there. So, without being involved with Billy—'cause Billy and I are not talking to one another, okay?—I said, at the end of the day, 'I don't really care. What I care about is his talent, his genius, doesn't get flushed down the toilet.' Clive and his team of people go and look at my contract every which way to go see whether in fact there's a hole in my contract. And they find out there ain't no hole in it, other than the loose-leaf binder hole. That's the only hole in it."

So the deal was made, with Lang, who still held the contractual rights to a cut of Billy's output, tugging Artie into the deal, as a kind of finder's fee, for an even bigger share than Lang would get. In a fairly typical arrangement, each had a percentage of the retail price of albums Billy would sell—Artie's was said to be four percent, or about twenty-eight cents per album sold, and Lang, benefiting at two percent, would make half that. A "sunset" clause limited their participation to Billy's first ten albums. It wasn't the most advantageous deal for the artist, but in any event, Billy's long-ago boast to his mom that he'd be headed not to Columbia University but to Columbia Records was finally fulfilled.

Billy didn't know that Clive was in jeopardy from an internal investigation for alleged misuse of company funds (Davis has an alternative version of events) to renovate his apartment and stage his son's bar mitzvah. Clive would later write in his memoir that while he and Billy were having their meeting at the Beverly Hills Hotel, he had had to push the company investigation out of his mind.

"I'll never forget hearing," says Billy, "on the Monday after the Memorial Day weekend in 1973, that Clive had gotten the ax from Columbia. He was very important to me at the time, as a storied talent scout and a believer in what I might become. He was very much a song guy; that was his reputation. Bruce [Springsteen] and I had signed with Columbia at about the same time, and there were a lot of parallels early on; this was very important to us. So when Clive was ousted, we were a little bit hesitant to go ahead."

But Kip Cohen, who'd survived the shakeup, assured Billy and the band that Columbia would support his efforts, that they were committed to making him a major artist, and that Clive's replacement, a veteran TV exec named Irwin Segelstein, would work in concert with Billy and Goddard Lieberson, a cultivated and artist-friendly head man who oversaw all the record labels.

Now that Billy had got his wish, Columbia needed an album. In terms of material, he was off to a good start based on the reception "Captain Jack" had already received. He also had "Piano Man," which had come to him in a rush of creativity and had already been rated as a must-listen by those who'd heard it. "Travelin' Prayer" had been written almost two years before, as had "The Ballad of Billy the Kid." Clearly that bunch of songs, the core of the album, was inspired by his move to Los Angeles with Elizabeth (and what followed).

The theme of escape can be heard in snippets all through the album. You don't have to probe too far to see some of Elizabeth in "Stop in Nevada":

She tried for years to be a good wife
It never quite got off the ground
And all those stories of the good life
Convinced her not to hang around.

And of course "Worse Comes to Worst" contained a nod to the cross-country road trip and its legendary stopgap job:

I'll do my writing on my road guitar
And make a living at a piano bar.

Given Billy's desire to be part of the California scene that then featured singer-songwriters incorporating country and western and folk-rock, Columbia assigned Michael Stewart, who was fresh from producing an album by his brother (and sometime Kingston Trio stalwart) John, called *Lonesome Picker Rides Again.* Recruiting a band similar to that album's countrified L.A. session pros, led by guitar virtuoso Larry Carlton, with his sweet Gibson ES 355 stylings, Stewart would even embrace bluegrass influences.

Kicking off the album with "Travelin' Prayer"—with its skipping locomotive rhythm, its hurrying mouth harp, and a fleet banjo solo from Eric Weissberg, of "Dueling Banjos" fame—definitely set the tone. "In retrospect, leading off with 'Travelin' Prayer' might have confounded some people's expectations," says Billy. "Wasn't I supposed to be some sort of ivory-tickling city boy?"

If so, "Piano Man" had its say as the second cut. It was perhaps already guaranteed its primacy in his body of work—the indispensable, inescapable, signature song. "After all these years," says Billy, "after all the bills it's paid and the concerts it's closed, and with the realization that the song and I are forever and inextricably linked, it's hard to know what to say about it. To me, it's really just a waltz. Back in Vienna, the waltz was at first viewed as somewhat scandalous—the European courts, who supported classical musicians, were too prudish to accept a dance made for couples virtually embracing, face to face."

But, of course, in Billy's waltz, the lyrics are about anything but romantic happiness:

And the waitress is practicing politics
As the businessmen slowly get stoned
Yes they're sharing a drink they call loneliness
But it's better than drinkin' alone.

Not many twenty-one-year-olds are capable of writing and singing words as world-weary as Billy's opening stanza:

> *It's nine o'clock on a Saturday*
> *The regular crowd shuffles in*
> *There's an old man sitting next to me*
> *Making love to his tonic and gin*

If the scene seems almost out of one of Charles Bukowski's tattered memoirs (or imaginably *about* him, as he lived just three miles up Normandie Avenue from the Wilshire Boulevard location of the Executive Room), there's an empathy and a universality to the observations made. In the song's eight verses (interspersed three times by the refrain), there's no wasted motion and, despite some sharply observed character portraits that seem recognizable as types, no clichés.

Just as "John at the bar" was at some level inveterate bartender Jon Troy, the barkeep's pathos is acute:

> *He says, "Bill, I believe this is killing me"*
> *As a smile ran away from his face.*

Our narrator has a name, but whether that makes the song more or less personal is open to question. The use of "Bill" without the diminutive is the songwriter's prerogative—the song never promised straight autobiography, and after all, the Executive Room's actual signage proffered entertainment by "Bill Martin." But it's worth noting that the shorter version is the name many of his intimates use more regularly than "Billy."

Eventually, the song's point of view slides all the way around, and we focus on the singer. The manager gives him a smile, "'Cause he knows it's me they've been coming to see / To forget about life for a while."

On a website that purported to provide song lyrics, an interpretation of the penultimate verse reads, "And the piano smells like a carnivore," which greatly amused Billy, who has called the instrument "the beast with eighty-eight teeth." The singer has been getting his drinks for free, and the following line—"And the microphone smells like a beer"— is a reminder that those who have just been described to us are indeed not "drinking alone." We are arriving at the memorable place where both the rhyme and the revelation have been heading:

> *And they sit at the bar and put bread in my jar*
> *And say, "Man, what are you doing here?"*

The beauty part, as one might say around the Parkway Green, is that Bill of the song and Billy the record-biz-entrapped singer-songwriter come together in that line. What indeed is Billy Joel, superstar-to-be, doing in this embarrassing scenario?

And finally, the refrain that's been played to—and sung by—so many crowds on so many nights:

> *Sing us a song, you're the piano man*
> *Sing us a song tonight*
> *Well we're all in the mood for a melody*
> *And you've got us feeling all right.*

The waitress, according to Billy, was Elizabeth, who, when she was younger, "somewhat resembled the actress from *Gigi*, Leslie Caron." The couple were relying on the kindness of strangers, to some extent, but they were making the rent. "These were the days of, if not wine and roses, then rye and high hopes for us," says Billy.

Their relationship back then, before Elizabeth moved into managing Billy, was already subject to plenty of strain. Billy had been, and would continue to be, on the road a lot. But Elizabeth made it clear she wanted to make the romantic partnership official, as soon as possible— something Billy perhaps resisted a bit too diplomatically.

One day in September 1973, she entered the room where Billy was sitting and simply said, "We're getting married today."

Billy answered, "We are?"

She told him that she had the marriage all set up, and that if he didn't marry her, she was leaving. She was from a Catholic family, and it was important to her that she and Billy weren't "living in sin."

Elizabeth had been very supportive, but as much as he loved her, Billy didn't think he should marry her. With road trips and myriad career business going on, he just didn't feel it was the right time. Plus, they were still very young. He was only twenty-four years old—too young, he felt, to get married. And yet rather than risk a deep rift in the relationship and face her well-known obduracy, he agreed.

"Elizabeth had it all planned out," says Billy. The two lived in Malibu at the time, and they went to the local courthouse. "I remember our getting married by the justice of the peace, and the witness was a sheriff's deputy with a Smokey the Bear hat. I thought to myself, *What's wrong with this picture? This looks like I'm getting booked.*"

Right after the wedding ceremony, the newlyweds drove up to Point Dume, in Malibu, and visited a little bar called the Dume Room (described in a local blog years later as "borderline dangerous in the best dive tradition ... Steve McQueen and John Wayne drank here"). "I didn't miss the linguistic irony of that spot," says Billy. "I ordered a Zombie. I was kind of in a daze about it all, and while I didn't think it was the right thing for me to do, I thought it was the right thing to do by her."

As *Piano Man* found its way into the marketplace, it headed for number twenty-five on the *Billboard* Hot 100 chart, and ultimately it ranked fourth on the Adult Contemporary chart. The band's inevitable tour started in late February 1974 in a New York hot spot, Max's Kansas City, home to the Warhol crowd. The *New York Times* pop music critic John Rockwell showed gratifying enthusiasm, saying, "Mr. Joel is fast developing into an important artist." He found Billy's piano playing virtuosic (although some of his arrangements he deemed "bombastic"). Three months later, when Billy played Carnegie Hall (opening for Jesse Colin Young), Rockwell wrote of Billy, "One knew this artist was fulfilling all of his promise as a musician and a star." (Billy was still working the college circuit as well, and a live pairing that occurred at Rutgers University in mid-1974—and would have later echoes—came when Billy invited local boy Bruce Springsteen onstage to do "Twist and Shout.")

Amid all these positive reactions to *Piano Man*, Elizabeth and Billy were still sitting at the kitchen table wondering how to make ends meet. Not only did Billy's earnings barely trickle in—he had made less than $8,000 on the album by a 1978 accounting—they also struggled to shake money loose from Columbia for promotion and touring. Billy and Elizabeth were coming to realize that Jon Troy just didn't have enough power within the music industry to make things happen fast enough.

In Billy's mind, his best selling point wasn't the recordings; it was the live shows. "I kept insisting on this—I was beating my head against the wall. But Jon really didn't have a lot of leverage with Columbia and couldn't convince them," recalls Billy. "Although Jon empathized with me and liked the band, and we all got along with him, he tended to defer to the company's wishes. What you really want in a manager is somebody who's willing to take the recording company head on and say, 'This is not the best thing for my artist.'"

The ultimate realization of how little clout Jon had with Columbia came with Billy's next album, *Streetlife Serenade*. For the label, this was its chance to put out a *Piano Man II*, a fully realized set of songs, but in fact Columbia rushed the album out less than a year after the first album was released, in October 1974.

Then as now, if you had a successful debut album—and *Piano Man* was regarded as a debut, even though it had been preceded by *Cold Spring Harbor* and the earlier releases with the Hassles and Attila—you would be under great pressure to get the second one out quickly. "This is why people talk about the sophomore slump," says Billy. "You spend your youth building up material, crafting that bildungsroman that tells your story, and then, in the middle of abruptly finding success and crashing in Holiday Inns, of being a bandleader and wondering when the checks will arrive, you have a couple months to write ten or twelve heartfelt new songs. By the way, remember, the songs about how much the road sucks have already been done, and nobody wants to hear them."

Nonetheless, Billy had one song in that vein, and it's probably the only song on *Streetlife Serenade* that he would always regard somewhat fondly: "The Entertainer." That song was ready to add in when, shortly after they concluded the *Piano Man* tour in Cincinnati in early May 1974, Billy found himself back at Devonshire Studios in North Hollywood cutting tracks.

Says Billy, " 'The Entertainer' came partly out of the experience of seeing 'Piano Man' downsized from the original six-minute album cut to a three-minute single."

> *I am the entertainer, I've come to do my show*
> *You've heard my latest record, it's been on the radio*
> *It took me years to write it, they were the best years of my life*
> *It was a beautiful song but it ran too long*
> *If you're gonna have a hit you gotta make it fit*
> *So they cut it down to 3:05.*

"I don't suppose that little aside did me that much good with the Columbia brass," says Billy, but the rest of the song's lyrics constituted a broadside against the entire apparatus of pop stardom—"Got to get those fees to the agencies"—and a summary of the education any performer receives:

> *I am the entertainer and I've had to pay my price*
> *The things I did not know at first I learned by doing twice*
> *But still they come to haunt me, still they want their say*
> *So I've learned to dance with a hand in my pants, I let 'em rub my neck*
> *And I write 'em a check, and they go their merry way.*

When Billy performed this song before an audience, he would often point out that the narrator wasn't, strictly speaking, him: "I wouldn't want to be heard complaining about the 'rough' life of a singer-songwriter—'I've played all kinds of palaces and laid all kinds of girls'—by, say, a group of all-night truckers or machine shop guys."

Even the relationship that stars have with their fans wasn't excluded from the song. "In retrospect," says Billy, "the stanza concerning that was the product of inexperience, because, without wanting to sound corny, I've been rewarded over the years with a touchingly dedicated army of fans." But back then the guy in the song was definitely hedging his bets:

> Today I am your champion, I may have won your hearts,
> But I know the game, you'll forget my name,
> And I won't be here in another year
> If I don't stay on the charts.

The *Streetlife* of the album title is clearly Los Angeles, with the mention of "Shoppin' center heroes" on "Streetlife Serenader" and Billy's best attempt to sketch a portrait of the city amid the hip-swinging rhythms of "Los Angelenos":

> Hiding up in the mountains
> Laying low in the canyons
> Goin' nowhere on the streets
> With the Spanish names.

As a lifelong student of piano, if Billy was ever going to do a ragtime cut, 1974—right after the movie *The Sting* briefly propelled the music of Scott Joplin and the entire ragtime genre back into vogue—was the time. "I've shown the song 'Root Beer Rag' some loyalty over the years, tossing it into set lists as a kind of instrumental palate cleanser," says Billy. "It requires my full attention as the notes spill out."

To record the *Streetlife* album, Michael Stewart once again recruited an all-star lineup of session men, though Billy was still hungering to work with his road band and make use of the wordless communication they had acquired from gigging night after night. Tight as the ensemble was, Billy couldn't resist what he later called "dribbling" another sonic layer on top: He was going through a period of enchantment with the stinging sounds of the Moog synthesizer; "And I felt the jagged stabs of sound it lent to a song like 'The Entertainer' helped make my point," he adds.

"Overall, though, to be honest, I have a very low regard for that particular album. The rush to record it left me with less than my strongest material. In general, the album seemed directionless."

It would turn out that Billy wasn't alone in that assessment of the release. "Desiccated of ideas" was hardly the unkindest phrase from a pan in *Rolling Stone*. Other critical dismissals were soon followed by disappointing sales figures. "The Entertainer" barely clicked as a single, and when it stalled at number thirty-four, the album ground to a halt at thirty-five. It would have been a likely time for Billy to reassess where he stood in his career. But Jon Troy was getting pressure from Columbia to schedule recording dates for yet another album.

It wasn't hard to read in the label's attitude that they considered the album to be a complete bomb. Somehow Billy persuaded them to stop the bleeding and not release it in what had been a promising market in Australia. Says Billy, "I'm actually convinced that my success in Australia was due to the fact that *Streetlife* was held back there." Instead, *Piano Man* was followed up two years later, down under, by the *Turnstiles* album, and that kept radio play and critical acceptance in Australia at a high level for him.

"Over the years," says Billy, "my opinion of that album has persisted. *Streetlife,* to quote one of its lyrics, should be 'put in the back in the discount rack like another can of beans.'"

CHAPTER 6

GOODBYE TO HOLLYWOOD

In mid-1975 Billy sensed a restlessness in Elizabeth, seemingly the result of varied pressures she was feeling. She and Jon Small looked after Sean on a rotating basis, and the boy flew, often solo, west to east and back again. During Sean's L.A. stays, since Billy was often on the road or simply too busy to stand in as the boy's father figure, she took on most of the caretaking responsibility herself.

At the same time, Billy had his own set of pressures, the key one being an urgent need to build a body of songs that could serve him better in the studio than the last bunch had. Meanwhile, his unsettled management situation only added to the career instability he felt. He was sensing that he probably had kept Jon Troy on as manager longer than he should have. Billy had gleaned from those around him that they all liked Jon—he understood record promotion and was road smart; he also knew plenty of people in the music business, knew about radio, knew about retail. But Troy had filled the role more as a road-dog comrade-in-arms than as a plugged-in pro. He had no credentials as a manager.

Troy believes that Elizabeth had targeted him early on as an impediment to her own aims: "She was a very ambitious woman, and it was obvious she was hitching her wagon to a star and positioning herself to learn as much from me as she could. It didn't take me long to realize,

She's in training for my job. The frustration was, it didn't matter. I could talk to Billy all day, but she had him every night in bed. Only Billy saw the beauty and the love. Nobody else could."

Billy's original drummer in his solo launch, Rhys Clark, felt concern over the pair: "He was very obsessed with her and wrote songs accordingly. . . . They had some difficulty with Jon when they first came out here; they had Sean with them. And Elizabeth would kinda cry on [Rhys's wife] Marilyn's shoulder about Billy and the road and so forth. He did tell us one time about when he came home to the house on Mulholland, the occasion was Valentine's or something, and she put on the gear in terms of the garter belt and everything—made a night of it. He loved it."

Whatever happened later, Billy would never discount the role Elizabeth played in that period, "how much hard work she did on my behalf, and the real love that existed between us." As he said in "You're My Home,'" she saw "the crazy gypsy in my soul" as no one else could.

When the time came to let Jon Troy go, Billy did so with remorse. Ultimately, all he could offer had already been written down in "Say Goodbye to Hollywood" with (especially in the live version on *Songs in the Attic*) its mocking castanets; terse, declamatory sax breaks (each following the baleful reminder, "Forever"); punchingly relentless drums; and, most of all, the impassioned vocal—derived from the throb of the Ronettes' Ronnie Spector and done by her to good effect with the E Street Band in 1977, as well as by Bette Midler the same year. (As the song fades, Billy can be heard hollering to his band as they depart the studio.)

As an apology for what came to pass, the song has a bit of rhino skin on it, a refusal to give all the way in to sentiment:

> *So many faces in and out of my life*
> *Some will last*
> *Some will be just now and then*
> *Life is a series of hellos and goodbyes*
> *I'm afraid it's time for goodbye again.*

The two men would see each other over the years, and Troy remembers a dinner in New Orleans, where he was bartending at the time, as a kind of warm summing-up moment. Billy's ultimate take on the split was delivered as a benediction, not a taunt, says Troy. "Yeah, that was it. He told me a few years later, 'Your problem was you were in it for the music.' And he said, 'Well, you got a song.'"

After Jon's death in 2009, a music business friend would note that no one had expected a long life for him: "Jon's idea of a good breakfast was vodka and amphetamines." But he lives on as Johnny in "Say Goodbye to Hollywood," in Billy's guilt-tinged depiction of how their arrangement would end under pressure from later handlers:

> Johnny's takin' care of things for a while
> And his style is so right for troubadours
> They got him sitting with his back to the door
> Now he won't be my fast gun anymore.

"'Johnny's taking care of things for a while / and his style is so right for troubadours' is of course about Jon Troy," says Billy. "Jon was a good man, he loved music, and he really loved what I was doing. The 'they' in 'they got him sitting with his back to the door' refers to my attorney, my accountant, and me. We all agreed we couldn't move forward effectively with Jon in. It all had a kind of Wild West theme. The legend was, Wild Bill Hickok never liked sitting with his back to the door, and indeed doing so one day is what killed him. And like Wild Bill, Jon just didn't see the bullets coming."

THE DENOUEMENT OF the Jon Troy chapter would happen by degrees, as whatever Elizabeth's aspirations, she was busy with her academic studies (later curtailed by her move back East) at the UCLA Anderson School of Management. She was perhaps wary, then, that combining the roles of wife and manager would put undue strain on a less-than-perfect relationship. Meanwhile she began looking about for a seasoned manager who could bring experience, contacts, and aggressive energy to the party.

Lee Colton, having capably renegotiated the terms of the Artie Ripp deal, suggested a new full-service team, Caribou Management, to take over. It initially made sense to both Elizabeth and Billy. From his legal work with Blood, Sweat, and Tears, Lee knew Caribou's Jimmy Guercio, who had produced their Grammy-winning second album. Jimmy's partner was Larry Fitzgerald, the manager of Chicago and the Beach Boys. They added up to a powerhouse in the music industry, and in 1971, after Guercio grew weary of paying union scale at studios on either coast, they had built a deluxe recording retreat called Caribou Ranch in the remote mountains outside Boulder, Colorado. In fact, Elton John, with his 1974 *Caribou* album coming out of sessions there, was beginning a string of three albums on the site. Billy and the band prepared to put their career in Caribou's hands. It seemed like an appealing package deal—a well-connected management team who also had their own creative outpost to shelter the artist during the process of making a crucial album.

The managers were already making noises about using Elton's band, who were familiar with the facility, to play on Billy's record. But pushing in from an opposite angle was Billy's road band, including mainstays Rhys Clark on drums and Doug Stegmeyer on bass, who were avid to play on his recording sessions. It would be a good row of paydays for the band. They also knew that Billy believed in the powerful machine that the group could be onstage, and that he wanted that same feel in the studio. On *Streetlife Serenade*, Michael Stewart had brought in highly able session guys, but for Billy, the vibe just wasn't there. Still, Michael hadn't wanted to work with Billy's musicians. "This was frustrating the guys," says Billy. "Little by little, the band's camaraderie and joy in playing on the road were starting to fall apart."

Rhys had been on the road with Billy since *Cold Spring Harbor*, and he and the others wondered, *When are we going to get to make a record?* It was getting hard for Billy to pull the guys together. Nobody, including Billy, was getting paid a whole lot of money, and his well-honed road band was starting to fray.

The record company finally relented, and the band attempted some live recordings at the Great American Music Hall in San Francisco. Those sessions were scrapped, though, which only increased the frustration.

By the time the several weeks allocated to record *Turnstiles* rolled around in January 1976, Billy was feeling chastened from watching *Streetlife* tank. So knowing the label was in favor of a change, he started out with Guercio as producer. It looked good on paper; he had made big records with various best-selling artists. Wearing the twin hats of manager and producer, he indeed insisted—in spite of Billy's concerns—on using Elton John's band, saying, "Well, you're a piano player. Let's get Elton's guys." Billy thought, *What's the point of that, exactly? That's already Elton's band—I want my own band.*

It was immediately clear to Billy that this creative arrangement wouldn't work. "I played a little bit with Elton's guys, Dee Murray and Nigel Olsson," says Billy, "and they were really nice guys, but it sounded like Elton's band. There was a real myopia to that move by Caribou—I was already sick of being called 'the American Elton John.' It was such a misstep that I already was sure I wouldn't go much further with Caribou.

"So I fired Jimmy Guercio as the producer. Now at this point, this was my third album with Columbia. You have to imagine the executives up there going, 'He fired Jimmy Guercio? He's not big enough to fire Jimmy Guercio.' And then I was about to officially install Elizabeth to be the manager at that point. It just wasn't working out with Caribou; it was just not the right company for me at all. It was too big, too West Coast oriented."

At the same time, in addition to their romantic partnership, Elizabeth and Billy formally entered into a professional partnership, and she began to show the kind of business prowess that would stand her in good stead as Billy's manager. Michael Lang had seen the change coming all the way back in the Irwin Mazur days. "I liked Irwin," Lang recalls, "but I thought he was inept and wasn't furthering Billy's career. Artie had him body and soul, as they say. So I didn't think Billy had a champion in a situation where he needed one at the time. . . . I think Elizabeth was just sort of formulating the idea, *I could do this.* I think I could see that building in her."

According to Billy, "Elizabeth had good instincts, and she was also protective—she *was* my wife. She saw me kind of getting screwed around by people like Artie Ripp, and then she thought Jon Troy wasn't doing a very good job. Then with Caribou, it was the arrogance of those guys and just their whole way of doing things was just so corporate and not me at all. And I turned to her when I was going to leave Caribou. I said, 'Why don't you do it? You've been watching this stuff. You're pretty smart. You always have something very insightful to say about what's going on. Why don't you handle it?' She thought, *Great.* I think she was just waiting for me to give her the go-ahead."

The change was immediate. Billy still had one foot on the West Coast, but Elizabeth moved their home and operation to New York, to a townhouse on East Ninety-second Street, near Central Park. The day after they agreed on it, she turned one floor into Home Run Systems Corp., filling it with desks, telephones, assistants, and stationery, and "boom—it was *on.*"

Their energetic friend Dennis Arfa—they had met when he managed a band that opened for the Hassles—set up shop as the in-house booking agent. The move spelled the end of savvy booker Chip Rachlin's tenure. In another move that ran counter to the conventional wisdom, they agreed with Dennis that they wanted to play headlining gigs only, rather than some of the illogical—and in some cases absurd—pairings they'd been subjected to. "Nothing against Olivia Newton-John, but we were hardly a natural fit as a co-billed concert attraction," says Billy. Also coming on board as road manager was Jeff Schock, who would grow into a role guiding marketing and promotion for Billy.

Howard Kaufman, for decades an influential music business operative who was part of the Caribou team back then, insists that Elizabeth's role in Billy's ascent has been consistently undersold: "Because she had the drive and Billy trusted her, and she took over his management— that's why he's successful today. That's my opinion. No one else could have managed him, because he wasn't going to listen to anyone else. She got him out from behind the piano; she got him to make the kind of records he could make, to do the things he needed to do to be a star. We were never going to get him to do them."

At that moment, however, Billy's split from Caribou left an unsettled, unpromising career crossroads in its wake. As he remembers: "I was already headed back to New York and I said, 'Okay, my wife's going to manage me.' So I imagine little red check marks went by my name up at Columbia Records: his wife's managing him, he hasn't had a hit, his album stiffed, he fired Jimmy Guercio. And the other thing was, I had passed on hiring George Martin to produce, which was another strike."

The George Martin episode still hurts: "That was 'seventy-three, and George Martin was looked on by the music industry as the state-of-the-art producer, the Beatles' guy. If you could get George Martin, then you must be pretty damn good. He was interested, but when we had a conversation, he said, 'I've seen you play, I like your stuff. I don't like your band. I want you to work with the studio musicians.' It was a crucial moment because here I had the opportunity to work with George Martin, a producer of the band I admired most in the world, the Beatles, and he didn't want to work with my band. I said, 'What do I do?' It was a real dilemma. And I kept trying to convince him to try the guys out, just let them try. We'd been on the road, and that was what I wanted. I didn't want smooth."

In fact, Billy himself was full of jagged energy, both musically and lyrically. As a songwriter, he would respond to news-making events in the world around him—often getting his updates via the New York tabloids he would seek out at the newsstands of whatever town he was in. The jolt that drove him back to New York, after three years out west, was the famous *Daily News* headline of October 29, 1975: "Ford to City: Drop Dead." New York was going to default, and the city, as it begged for federal help, was going bankrupt.

"I wrote a song, which ended up on *Turnstiles,* called 'Miami 2017,' based on the idea of what would happen if New York actually went down," says Billy. "The answer I came up with was: the apocalypse would happen. That's what everybody was predicting. The cops wouldn't be there. The firemen wouldn't be there. The city would burn. There'd be riots, all kinds of terrible things. So I pictured myself being an old Jewish guy living in Miami Beach in the year 2017, telling my grandchildren that I was there—'Seen the lights go out on Broadway / I saw the Empire State laid low.' "

The song was also Billy's reaction to the casually voiced anti–New York sentiment from people in L.A., a steady gnawing at his hometown loyalty: "I didn't move out to California assuming I was going to stay there forever. I was there temporarily, and when I left, it wasn't so much because of a bad experience in Los Angeles; living there was actually quite pleasant at that time. The music business was centered there. I had a nice house up on Mulholland Drive. The California lifestyle was very easy, and I was still coasting a bit on the success of *Piano Man,* though *Streetlife* had come out and . . . dropped dead. But when I experienced any kind of anti–New York feeling, I actually felt angry. 'Miami 2017' came out of that. It was a kind of science fiction song. More personally, it was a challenging premise about going home, which is where 'New York State of Mind' came from as well."

Billy never assumed "New York State of Mind" would be a hit. He saw it as more of a standard, a 1940s- or 1950s-style blues song, in the manner of "Georgia on My Mind." The song was never even released as a single. It got FM play and a certain amount of airplay on New York pop stations. But when Barbra Streisand recorded it on her hit *Streisand Superman* album, it got a lot of attention. (Says Billy, "Certainly my mom looked at me with fresh eyes—finally, a *real* singer had picked up on her errant son's efforts.") A number of other artists, including Mose

Allison, covered "New York State of Mind" because it was known as a great singer's song. But to Billy's mind, it didn't become truly iconic until after 9/11: "It took on a whole other meaning then, because it was a song about coming back to New York, and how much this place means to someone who's had to leave it for a while."

The songs for *Turnstiles*—the title evoked not just the subway entrances in his beloved city but the access points to certain music venues—were emerging with Billy's return to the East Coast in 1975 going into 1976. The move had its roots in a day about a year before, as he and Elizabeth drove from upstate New York across the Connecticut border on Route 84. "Driving that road, you cross the Newburgh-Beacon Bridge," remembers Billy. "It was the fall and just beautiful, the Hudson Valley in full fall-foliage glory, and I said, 'Good God, this is gorgeous. I never realized that we had this kind of stuff, and I miss New York.'"

"I want to find a house up here," he told Elizabeth. "I don't want to move back to the city. I want to move just outside of town and kind of work my way back into the city."

Elizabeth found a house for rent in Highland Falls, a small community just south of West Point on the Hudson River. The house, once the carriage house for J. P. Morgan's estate, was in a daffodil-strewn retreat overlooking the river. The compact Georgian structure wasn't grand, but it was picturesque.

Billy finished a tour, flew in from the final gig, got on a Greyhound bus headed to West Point, and took a seat by the window. "On that ride I started writing the song that became 'New York State of Mind,' thinking, *This is where I'm going to end up. I'm back*," says Billy.

"It really was intended to reflect a New York *state* of mind, not a New York *city* of mind, but I wanted to include the city in it," he explains. "I was so glad to be back home again, feeling, *This is where I belong*. And that song was a celebration of that."

"Say Goodbye to Hollywood" overlapped the theme: "It was all about putting L.A. behind me—*Okay, thank you, you've been great, it's been fun, but I'm leaving, say goodbye.* A lot of the *Turnstiles* album was really that dynamic of coming home."

When Billy saw his new lodgings for the first time—the house they rented would later be reconfigured by hoteliers as a bed and breakfast, themed to the couple's stay there—he gave Elizabeth a hug and a kiss and blurted, "Do we have a piano here?" Hearing they did, he rushed upstairs to it and finished composing the song in a matter of minutes, as the Hudson rolled past outside the window.

TO BILLY, THOSE days with Elizabeth were a period of ambivalence, notably in his marriage. In "Summer, Highland Falls," the songwriter's state is described as swinging between "sadness or euphoria," but it's much more subtle than that: "I still get a lot of people telling me that 'Summer, Highland Falls' is a favorite song for them. It will always have a place for me as a kind of veiled autobiographical account of perhaps the last really good season—although it was in the summer of 1976, still six years before our divorce—that Elizabeth and I would share."

There's more than a hint of the long fade-out of their romance in the song:

> *Now, I have seen that sad surrender in my lover's eyes*
> *And I can only stand apart and sympathize*
> *For we are always what our situations hand us*
> *It's either sadness or euphoria.*

Billy would always find the "spilling your guts" aspect of songwriting challenging, but he was benefiting from a greater sense of what its crucial tools were. "Melody is a sensual thing, just as the sounds of a child's laughter or a marching band, a church hymn or someone in sexual transport, are highly evocative," he says. "As I was composing 'Summer, Highland Falls,' I found a pattern with my left hand that was up-and-down, both in terms of the keyboard and the mood that it created. I knew I had something, but it lacked an element. Then I began knocking out a fast, arpeggiated pattern of 'straight eights' with my right hand, almost like something out of Bach. I was trying to communicate that sometimes frantic, scurrying side of how we live our lives, and how we think about them. Between the up-and-down and fast-and-slow elements, I had the music to match my mood; the emotion of the language was already encoded in the music. And the words came with relative ease. I call it an ode to manic depression."

When he was working that way, he'd push the "record" button on his little Sony cassette deck. In this case the process was happening upstairs in the location that lent its name to the song, at a Baldwin baby grand that Elizabeth had arranged for. The rollingly melodic opening couple of lines—"They say that these are not the best of times / But they're the only times I've ever known"—of course echo Dickens at the start of *A Tale of Two Cities*. "I suppose at some level I was writing about a certain sadness I felt on behalf of Elizabeth and myself as the relationship began to show cracks," Billy says. "You try to address your times. There's some inspiration in a figure like Beethoven—of course he had magical talent, and the opportunity to work on a much larger canvas. He began by calling his third symphony the 'Bonaparte Symphony,' inspired by Napoleon and the revolutionary energy coursing through Europe. When he felt Napoleon had broken faith with the movement, he tore the title page up and retitled it 'Eroica.'"

A hallmark of Billy's work has been his ability to take his own deeply rooted emotions and universalize them, and "Summer, Highland Falls" finds its lovers as they "stand upon the ledges of our lives." After spending much of 1976 in the Highland Falls house, they'd soon be back in the city, grinding through the continuing effort to break through with a hit song and album but increasingly alienated. That very effort would damage the relationship, which would finally crash in 1980. As would happen often in a career that was inseparable from his life, Billy, pugilist that he was, would stay on his feet, hoping the next round could win the day.

IRONICALLY, THE ROAD band that had been such a point of contention due to Billy's loyalty was about to be reshuffled. Billy had met Doug Stegmeyer, the bass player for *Streetlife Serenade* and the subsequent tour dates, years before in the Long Island bar band scene. A Syosset native, whose dad was a professional horn player, Stegmeyer had been part of a high school band that included rhythm guitarist Russell Javors and drummer Liberty DeVitto. Eventually they became the group Topper, featuring Javors's songs. Along with lead guitarist and longtime friend Howie Emerson, who had backed eminent folkie Eric Andersen, the four formed a tight unit.

They were in the right place at the right time to team with Billy, who was still finding his way back into the New York scene. After all the stress and confusion of the producer search, says Billy, "I ended up producing *Turnstiles* myself, back in New York, with a few overdubs at Caribou. I don't know how to produce to save my ass. I know what I'm going for, and as time went on, I learned more and more and more. I didn't know how to translate it into the technology. I didn't know what was available. I didn't know how to get a drum sound. I don't know how to EQ [equalize, or boost sound levels on certain instrumental or vocal recorded tracks] anything."

Engineer John Bradley, who had done some work on *Cold Spring Harbor*, was recruited to help with the technical side. The sessions took place at the UltraSonic Studios in Hempstead, which given its location about fifteen minutes southwest of Oyster Bay provided a comfort zone. (The studio had been the site of a row of Tuesday-night radio concerts featuring acts from Lou Reed to Little Feat and had proved to be a congenial setting for Billy's November 1971 four-song set in that series.)

Billy recorded *Turnstiles*'s basic tracks with Doug and Liberty, with sound man Brian Ruggles kibitzing. When it came time to add guitars, he took the advice of his rhythm section and simply moved Javors and Emerson into place, and with Richie Cannata joining in on sax, keyboards, and vocals, he effectively formed his new recording and road band. They would stay together for more than a decade to come.

The eight tracks of *Turnstiles*, at 34:18, made for a pretty lean piece of product. (*Streetlife* had come in at 37:41, thanks only to two instrumentals of genre fare totaling 6:36.) But most of the eight songs are keepers, half of them concert staples. An argument can and has been made that this album is an indispensable time capsule not just of Billy in the mid-1970s but of that moment in pop music. The octet of songs insightfully evokes life at a time when America's leisure class and those who aspired to it somehow turned inward. (Tom Wolfe's landmark essay "The Me Decade" would come out three months almost to the day after *Turnstiles*'s May 1976 release.) As "I've Loved These Days" would put it, over one of Billy's more Sinatra-esque vocal monologues:

We drown our doubts in dry champagne
And soothe our souls with fine cocaine
I don't know why I even care
We get so high and get nowhere
We'll have to change our jaded ways
But I've loved these days.

Aware they had goods worth handling with care, Billy and the bandmates involved flew to Denver and headed off into the mountains to complete the album overdubs and mixing. Months before, when the experiment with Elton's sidemen didn't take, Billy had departed quickly from Caribou Ranch, but the recording complex was still state-of-the-art and would serve their purpose now. (The Ranch would eventually spawn albums that sold many millions of copies for various artists.) Howard Kaufman describes it as "a beautiful, 4,000-acre ranch with state-of-the-art studio in the barn, bungalows all around, a fishing hole,

London, about a century ago. Billy Joel's great-uncle Harry Nyman (standing) was an amateur boxer like Billy. Seated next to him is Billy's grandfather Phillip Nyman.

Billy Joel's paternal grandfather, Karl Joel.

Billy's dad, Helmut (later Howard) Julius Joel, born in June 1923, was sent by his parents to a private school in northeastern Switzerland, as Hitler was coming to power in their native Germany.

Billy's mom, Roz Nyman, and dad, sometime around their marriage in 1942.

Billy and his sister, Judy, at the family upright piano on Meeting Lane, Hicksville.

Billy with Roz and Judy behind their house at 20 Meeting Lane, Hicksville, circa 1952.

Billy in his band uniform, holding the French horn, circa 1958.

LEFT: The Lost Souls in 1965 (they played the New York World's Fair in September): clockwise, Billy, Ken Recher, Jim Bosse, Howie Blauvelt, and Billy Zampino. Jim and Bill were the inspiration for Billy's song "James." RIGHT: Hicksville High School yearbook photo, 1967.

The Hassles at a local Long Island club, 1968. John Dizek, with the tambourine, had Jagger's moves—but Billy's superior singing and deft playing, here on the Hammond B3 organ, soon made him the band's focus.

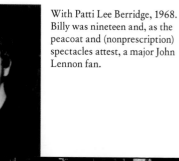

With Patti Lee Berridge, 1968. Billy was nineteen and, as the peacoat and (nonprescription) spectacles attest, a major John Lennon fan.

An outtake from the photo shoot for the self-titled 1970 Attila album.

Jon Small, Sean Weber-Small, and Billy, circa 1970.

Irwin Mazur's duties as manager on the tour to promote the *Cold Spring Harbor* album included such expertise as tire changing (left to right: Billy making a snowball, guitarist Al Hertzberg, bassist Larry Russell, and Elizabeth Weber).

First post-signing performance for the label, 1973, at a ritual known as the singles meeting, in a CBS conference room.

The attention from *Cashbox* was encouraging— Billy hadn't had a hit album or single yet, just a too-long-for-mainstream-radio waltz called "Piano Man."

Another Holiday Inn on the *Piano Man* tour.

Backstage at Academy of Music in Philadelphia, 1974, with Bruce Springsteen, noted local deejay Ed Sciaky, and Janis Ian.

On the road, or at least on the shoulder—left to right, Russell Javors, Richie Cannata, Billy Joel, Doug Stegmeyer, Brian Ruggles, and Liberty DeVitto. Guitarist Howie Emerson would have taken this shot.

The 1977 Home Run office party at the Copacabana—Billy with Dennis Arfa, Elizabeth, and of course, Santa.

Soundman Brian Ruggles, left, and lighting designer Steve Cohen, right, had already been with Billy on several tours when this photo was taken at a Columbia Records party in 1978. As part of the road cadre once known as the Mean Brothers, they're now in their fifth decade as leaders in the Joel brain trust.

Cuba, March of 1979, as Billy and the band visited for the Havana Jam '79 show that guitarist Russell Javors called "The Bay of Gigs."

Billy and Elizabeth, on the shoreline at Cold Spring Harbor in 1979, awaiting a seaplane lift.

Billy, thirty-five, and Christie, thirty-one, on board the yacht that served
as the setting for their wedding and part of the subsequent celebration as it toured
New York Harbor, March 1985. INSET: Christie's handcrafted invitation to the wedding.

and a full staff—eight or ten beautiful women. [Billy] probably would have been happier without his wife there, but people paid a lot of money to record up at Caribou."

Billy recalls the climbing drive to the ranch through the foothills around Boulder: "You go past these sleepy little hamlets with the last of the hippies sitting on the porch of the general store with their dogs asleep on the sidewalk. I remember how, on our way, we kept winding up the mountain road until the Woody-Allen-city-boy-lost-in-the-woods aspect of me came out. And that air—it was so thin." (The story goes that Freddy King went up there to record when he weighed about three hundred pounds, and he stepped out of his bus and said, "Yeah, I'm gonna need the oxygen mask right away.")

"It's said you can hit high notes up there you can't hit at sea level, but if you're a singer or a horn player, you may not have the wind to get to them." Ironically, horns were a key element of these latter sessions there.

At a time when an album's reception by the popular press could do considerable good or harm, *Turnstiles*'s reviews were mixed. In a lengthy 1994 feature in the record collector's magazine *Goldmine*, William Ruhlmann quoted from the downbeat critical consensus on the album at the time. Robert Christgau's *Village Voice* summary was a "C+": "As Joel's craft improves . . . he becomes more obnoxious." In the same pages Stephen Holden called him "boring as hell" but called the album "extraordinarily ambitious . . . in some ways the most impressive record Billy Joel has ever made." He made an apt comparison to F. Scott Fitzgerald's precedent: " 'I've Loved These Days,' with its beautiful melody and its lyrics that incriminate the singer, has a brilliantly Gatsby-like tone that is emotionally intricate—the wealthy, as they go down, are as aware as anyone of their immorality . . . but they can't help raising a last toast."

If *Turnstiles* was in some ways Billy's "Eroica"—a big, self-produced canvas with a thundering farewell to Hollywood and the apocalyptic, crashing chords of "Miami 2017"—it also had "I've Loved These Days," at times as ethereal as an oboe solo. The crowded cover photograph—with the giddy couple illustrating the latter song, and young Sean Weber-Small peering sullenly up from a supposed grandmother's grasp—felt challenging. Perhaps that was part of the reason why the record, following two earlier LPs for the label that had cracked the Top 40, got no higher than 122 on the *Billboard* Hot 200 chart. "Say Goodbye to Hollywood" got a good deal of FM radio play, but that song and "Summer, Highland Falls" tanked as attempted hit singles.

His career still lacked a champion, but emerging as the most Napoleonic figure in Billy's human landscape at the time was the increasingly active Elizabeth. The troublesome state of Billy's career in 1976 is made evident by an interview she did with *Forbes* magazine in 1978 (in a sidebar called "They Were Mauling Her Man" that accompanied a record-biz story): "When we started to live together, I wasn't even sure if Billy was talented. I thought I might have to support him. I was in love."

She went on to depict how she spent three years extricating Billy from the old contracts ("The person in the middle"—between Bill and Columbia, in other words, Artie Ripp, who was disempowered but still taking his cut—"seemed to be making all the money") and how she'd fall asleep over the payroll books at four-thirty A.M.

She blamed the Caribou Management hangover for the failure of *Turnstiles* and implied she'd more than merely rooted for it to die to prove a point: "Everything that was done on the *Turnstiles* album . . . I watched it go down the tubes [only 200,000 albums sold at the time, so-so for that era] and I guess I did it on purpose." She adds, "I was sick of having Billy's lawyers call and ask for advice at midnight and then hearing it be their idea the next day."

One might ask, if consigning an album to cut-out bins was a good plan, what was the bad one? She points out she solved her issues with the concert policies the Caribou team had put in place. After getting a call from Billy's original booking agent to have him open for the Beach Boys at Nassau Coliseum for a mere $2,000, "I told the guy, 'Go to hell, you're fired.'" An upcoming tour, she added, was predicted to gross $3 million.

Her concluding remarks are out of a Scorsese-film voiceover. "This is a business," she asserts. "People never expected me to be as smart as I was, and they would be totally frank because they didn't realize I was building my empire. They taught me that money is the bottom line of everything. It's an actual, factual scale of how to see things."

One might wonder if in the tetchy, male-dominated environment of the music business, feminism was being advanced or reversed by such representations, but her success helped lay the groundwork for what was soon to arrive.

"*Streetlife Serenade* in 1974 and *Turnstiles* in 1976 turned out to be disappointments, both to me and the label," says Billy. "Jon Troy never could have ridden that out, but Elizabeth had just the right mix of finesse, manipulation, and the odd surprise move going for her." Possibly the most advantageous thing that happened with Elizabeth in her role as manager was that she developed a relationship with the new head of Columbia Records, Walter Yetnikoff.

"At the time," says Billy, "it was real important for us. We were just running out of money, just barely making ends meet on tour, and I had a band to pay. I had a road crew. We were becoming pretty well set as an organization, and we needed help from the record company, about eighty grand at the time."

Elizabeth insisted Walter attend a New York–area show, and as he recalls: "My habit then as now is, I watch the audience. I know what the artist sounds like, I don't have to watch him. I watch the audience. And they were really jiving and shucking and bubbling. Something was going on here. And I saw Elizabeth afterward and I said, 'You've got to keep this show on the road. There's something going on here.' And she says, 'We can't—we're out of money.' I said, 'So ask.' She said, 'I asked.' I said, 'Who did you ask?' She said, 'I asked business affairs.' 'What did you ask for?' She asked for eighty grand. I said, 'That's it?' She said, 'Yeah, they said no.' I said, 'Call them tomorrow, they'll say yes.'"

Billy recalls, "There was all this 'bubbling under' stuff that was going on, excitement that I don't think the record company had been aware of. We were getting a lot of support from college radio, progressive FM radio, live audiences. Even the press was good. There was a lot of praise in the press in those days because they like to discover you *before* you're successful.

"Elizabeth was telling Walter, 'He needs this, that, and the other thing.' And she looked after me. She would get Yetnikoff to get the company behind me for *The Stranger* album. I know there was a renegotiation with Artie Ripp on his percentage—he still stayed in the picture, but Walter got back my publishing rights."

The passage of time may have enhanced the story, but Walter Yetnikoff relates his version, which can be heard in the *Last Play at Shea* documentary: "I said, 'I want Billy Joel's publishing back'—because it included 'Piano Man' and stuff. And he said, 'It's worth a fortune.' I said, 'I'm going to pay you, I'll give you four hundred grand.' He said, 'No, no, it's far more. I'm not selling the publishing.' And I grabbed him, and I said, 'I'll fuckin' kill you. I'm a guy from Brooklyn. You can't start with me.' I said, 'Let me explain something to you. Even if I can't put your head through the wall, you think you're going to succeed in this business when I'm the great exec and I'm going to be pissed at you? Anyone that talks to you can't talk to me. I represent CBS.' I said, 'Anyone who talks to you can't talk to Columbia, Epic, or anything else. You think you're going to live with that very long?' As I recall, we bought it back, and I gave his copyrights to Billy as a birthday present."

"Now, a lot of people might tell you that the kind of faith it took for me to hire my wife as my manager was delusional in some ways," Billy says. "We were in love at one time, but you change a lot in your twenties. We wanted to have a kid around that time, not long before she started managing me, but it didn't work out that way."

Billy admitted to being fairly oblivious to the business side of his career, but he did start to notice how Elizabeth was representing him—and that she was not doing things in the firm but courteous way he preferred. The reports filtered in that Elizabeth was upbraiding business contacts, pulling no punches. Though Billy knew that a manager was supposed to play hardball sometimes, it wasn't his style of doing business. He told her, at various points, "Please, don't treat people like that. Don't fuck people over."

The business arrangement certainly didn't help the marriage. Beyond the stresses of her dispensing the orders, Billy was on the road a lot—and only in his midtwenties. Inevitably, the two spent a great deal of time apart. She developed her own social circle, while Billy hung out with his gang, the band.

Things also became strained between the couple because, while Billy struggled not to act like a rock star, Elizabeth embraced that life immediately. It became apparent that she felt she was entitled to her full share of the fame, the credit, and the money. "She played the game. She loved moving in circles with celebrities and the record company executives like a big shot," says Billy. "I just wasn't comfortable with it."

Another thing Billy grew to be uncomfortable with was the math. The couple had married for richer and for poorer, so she had every chance of ultimately sharing his assets fifty-fifty, depending on what deals he had signed on to as his own, sole entitlements. But then Elizabeth started taking a management commission on top of that, so she was picking up not only half the money but a further chunk of the gross proceeds. Whatever tussles the divorce lawyers would later have, a goodly amount of cash was flowing into the shared kitty.

At the same time, Billy respected her effectiveness and her robust dialogue with the label. "It probably didn't hurt that she got friendly with Walter Yetnikoff," says Billy. The rumors afoot that Elizabeth had gotten more than casually friendly with the exec could probably be ascribed to the casual sexism of the music business, which only made them more persistent. "But Walter always denied it," says Billy, "and since he's the most shockingly honest person I know, I believe him."

They didn't call Walter Velvel, or "The Wolf," for nothing. Yetnikoff wrote in his memoir of getting a birthday greeting from Billy, which his girlfriend Boom Boom stashed in a male stripper's jock strap and fished out with her teeth: "Happy 50th birthday, Walter," it read, "You redefine insanity."

That said, Yetnikoff's denial is clear. "Nothing ever happened," he says. "I didn't think she was that attractive, number one. Number two, I'm really gutsy and ballsy, but you think I'm going to start with a major artist's wife? I'm not *that* gutsy. I'm not that crazy. And I always stayed away from trying to entangle personal and business. We'd get friendly and everything, but at one time Elizabeth's brother Frank, when he took over from her, asked me to invest with him. He said, 'We're going to make a ton of money; we'll buy real estate.' And I said, 'I'm not going to do it.' He said, 'Why? You afraid to lose money? We'll guarantee it.' I said, 'That's not the reason. If it's a successful investment, now what do I do? I owe the artist a favor. Do I give him an extra royalty point? If it's an unsuccessful investment, what do I do? Throw him off the label? I lose no matter what I do. So I'm not going to invest with him.' I'm also not going to fuck his wife. As crazy as I may be."

Yetnikoff remembers one night saying to Billy, just so he knew where they stood, "She's your wife *and* your manager. This is not my personal friend. I'll tell you what, fire her, and I'll never go out [to business meetings] with her again."

As the label head recalls, Elizabeth was not averse to stoking jealousy on Billy's part. "She would tell people, 'Walter has a very nice apartment.' She was talking about leaving him at that time. Billy said, 'So why is she telling me this?' I said, 'She's looking to piss you off for whatever reason. She wants to get even for something, real or imagined. And I'm the one guy you really can't have a fight with—nor me with you. So therefore she's telling you it's me, and setting up this whole thing. So she's pulling your chain, I have no idea why.'" Yetnikoff remembers, "She had a little bit of a sadistic thing. . . . Emotionally, Elizabeth took advantage of him . . . a little cold. I remember once he said, 'My feet are hurting . . . Elizabeth made me wear these shoes.'"

However complex the triad of manager, artist, and executive, and however discouraging the results from Billy's first two Columbia albums, Yetnikoff believed that his initial feelings about Billy, as refreshed by the energetic live date he saw, would bring talent and good fortune together. The turning point would come in 1977, when he first heard what would become the title cut of Billy's album—"The Stranger": "That sort of just went click! It hit me right away, you know—this guy's got it—it's a done deal."

CHAPTER 7

JUST THE WAY I AM

Songwriting has always been an obsessive—sometimes joyous, sometimes torturous—part of Billy Joel's life. It probably hasn't helped that his method is the inverse of that of most writers: "I start with a melody, a chord pattern, and a rhythm, and then I try to decode what's in the music. What is it saying? What was my motivation for writing it? What's the emotion?

"It's really the backward way to write songs; most songwriters begin with words, lyrics, poetry, and then set it to music. Over the years, I've marveled watching Elton John write songs. Here's how Elton typically works: [longtime collaborator] Bernie Taupin will send him a bunch of lyrics, and then Elton will sit down at the piano and bang out a melody. I always say to him, 'How the hell do you do that?' Because I do it the other way around. The music is there and then I jam the words on top of it. It may be more difficult, but that's the way I've always worked."

Similarly, Billy has always listened to songs with the music as the essential tableau and has tended to discover the words more gradually. "I actually discussed this once with Keith Richards when we found ourselves sitting together at some music industry function. He talked about the discovery he'd made that he called 'Vowel Movements.' You need to find a good vowel to help you round out some of your lines. An example of that is 'Honky Tonk Women': 'I tried to take her upstairs / For a riiiiiiidee . . .'

"I never ignore how much luck and chance can help a song. When I write, I'm not really speculating that a song will resonate with millions of people. I wouldn't even begin to know if a song is going to be a hit—and I certainly don't try to sit down and write one." He also never thought about the record company or the radio when he wrote, or the critics: "And not even the audience. For one thing, I've never viewed the audience as monolithic. They're just individual people who, thankfully, still come to see me in large numbers.

"So, basically, I write for myself—for my own amusement, and with the thought, *What do I want to hear?*" Billy began in the 1970s, largely trying to re-create Beatles music. "When the Beatles broke up, I thought, *Oh, we're not gonna get any of that anymore. Maybe I can try to do something like that.* It might sound selfish, but it was always for me. I'm the only person I know how to please, really. Will that produce hit records? I never know. I certainly didn't see it coming with *The Stranger.*"

During the *Stranger* stage of Billy's life, Elizabeth was Billy's muse. And for better or worse, he adds, "I got a lot of good material.

"When a relationship goes south," says Billy, "and you just sit back and let it happen—hoping maybe it'll get better, maybe things will change, and they aren't going to—you have to ask yourself sometimes, *Do I really like this? Or am I a masochist? Or am I just letting this happen because I don't want to ruffle any feathers?*" He long ago rejected the masochism thesis but adds, "I think sometimes you let things slide because you hope they *will* get better. I was married, and I didn't want it to fail." As he started writing *The Stranger,* the album that would become his breakthrough, he admits, "I was clearly working out a lot of relationship issues in my music."

Among the most famous songs to emerge during this period was "Just the Way You Are." "I think it's a well-written song. It's got a good chord progression, a clever melody, and a great sentiment in the lyric," says Billy. "To this day I still empathize with the song's main feeling: *I love you just the way you are.* Everybody wants to be told that—I always have. You want to be accepted for who you are—not for who you appear to be, or what you present as perhaps a mask to the world, but for exactly who you are. We all want someone to say, 'Don't change for me.' 'Clever conversation' is just a lyric device for saying, 'I don't really want shallow cocktail chatter, superficial chitchat. I want someone I can really talk to, I want a real dialogue, I want real communication.' It's always struck me as odd that some people tend to interpret it as 'He just wants to keep her in her place.'

"I also don't think a love song is effective unless there's an element of anxiety in it, and an undercurrent of darkness. Love is not all glitter and wonderfulness and clouds and happiness forever—there are ups and downs in relationships. There's an element of that anxiety in the bridge of the song: 'What will it take till you believe in me / The way that I believe in you?'

"I think there's always a bit of insecurity in love, if you truly love somebody. If you open yourself up, if you allow yourself to be hurt, there's potential vulnerability. That's real love. Somebody can stomp all over you if you really love them, and you give them your heart anyway."

The first time Billy played "Just the Way You Are" for Elizabeth, they were at a restaurant in Northport on Long Island. He wanted her to know he'd done something special, thinking of her. "I wrote this for your birthday," he told her after he finished playing the song.

"'Do I get the publishing too?'" Billy remembers her replying. ("She might have been half-joking," he says, though his longtime lighting designer and friend Steve Cohen remembers joining her in her white Alfa Romeo in the lot for a smoke as she spat out between inhalations, "Didn't even give me the fucking publishing.") "In retrospect, I probably should have known right then and there that the relationship was doomed. I had written 'Just the Way You Are' for someone who had changed."

When it came time to record the song, Billy and the band didn't like it all that much. "We all thought it was too much of a 'chick song,'" he says, "and that I was going to get tagged as a lounge singer or a wedding singer for doing it."

Billy's new producer, Phil Ramone, suggested a backward samba beat that, in everybody's opinion, sounded much better. Phil had been working with Phoebe Snow, who was spending time in a nearby studio with Linda Ronstadt, and they'd both heard the song. (Phoebe, known for her 1975 hit "Poetry Man," was soon to battle her label and move to Columbia to record a second album with Phil Ramone.)

Phil played the song again for Phoebe in the control room. "Oh, it's a great song," she raved. When Billy and the band told her they didn't like the song, she told them they were crazy. "You have to put that on the record," she said. But Billy still didn't want it on the album, citing it as "too *gushy*."

Then Linda Ronstadt chimed in: "That's one of the greatest songs I've ever heard. You don't want to put it on the album? Are you nuts? That's a hit record."

"All of this shows how much I know about hit records," says Billy. Phoebe and Linda browbeat both Billy and Phil into putting "Just the Way You Are" on the album. "Maybe Phil's way of putting me in a corner was by saying, 'I can't argue with those two. Women know a lot of things better than men do.'"

PHIL RAMONE WAS known to practice the "no bullshit" law: "It's the only way to make music," he says. "If something doesn't quite smell right, or smells slick, those are things that I think the band and Bill and myself always kind of teased each other about—if it crossed that dangerous edge. I think the worry was that 'Just the Way You Are' was going to be categorized as somewhat too 'sweetie pie.' And our standing rule, which I think cemented our relationship, was that you don't want to make a record that you have to apologize for five or ten years later. You don't want to have a song that you're stuck with.

"Jokingly we said, 'Well, you've written a song that may be played many times at weddings.' You make a dumb remark like that and— voilà!—it comes true. But I think the reason Billy seldom plays that song is that it doesn't really do in public what it does on the record. The notes are the same; the playing is done with a certain feel. But it doesn't knock them down like some of the rock-and-roll tunes. So even though it was highly successful, you still can't say we knew from the beginning it was going to put down such a footprint."

"Just the Way You Are" would be one of four tracks from *The Stranger* that charted in 1978. Billy accepted the invitation from *Saturday Night Live* to perform on February 28 of that year—even though, as guest host Chevy Chase pointed out: "The class of 'sixty-seven from Hicksville High out on Long Island is having their reunion tonight, but one alumnus will not be there because he's here. . . . Ladies and gentlemen, Billy Joel."

Despite requests from the producers for Billy not to, Billy chose to launch into his recently released and highly controversial song "Only the Good Die Young," which some decried as anti-Catholic and he described as "pro-lust."

"I suppose sneaking that in is what caused me to bite my thumb a couple times as I exchanged looks with the band afterward," says Billy. "What sticks with me from that night is the squabble [former show mainstay] Chevy Chase got into with Bill Murray, who was essentially his replacement—and at that stage, just making his bones as the *SNL* legend he would become. I was standing in the wings with the band, ready to go on, when they got into it. As I recall, Chase spat out to Murray, 'What's this Second City shit?' and Murray, giving no ground, and mindful that Chase's marital difficulties had recently been made public, suggested Chase go home and do something unprintable to his wife. I think it was John Belushi who stepped in before punches were thrown. When we turned to Lorne Michaels and asked what it was all about, he snapped, 'None of your business.'

"And seconds later we were banging out 'Only the Good Die Young.'"

Billy did make his *twentieth* high school reunion at a local country club. "I noticed two things—the geeky guys from high school were the more successful and well-turned-out ones in the crowd, and even the girls I hadn't made much impression on in the Hicksville High corridors were now quite flirtatious," he remembers.

ANOTHER SONG FROM *The Stranger* that people correctly assume to be about Elizabeth is "She's Always a Woman." "It reflects how she took a lot of heat—because there weren't a lot of women in positions of power in the business at the time," explains Billy. The scuttlebutt on Elizabeth was often—*Oh, she's a bitch, she's a ball buster.* But Billy's attitude was "You can say she's a tough businesswoman, but that isn't my problem, that's *your* problem. She's always a woman to me."

It would remain surprising to Billy that "She's Always a Woman" was, like "Just the Way You Are," misinterpreted as being misogynistic. "I wrote it as a commentary on women in business being persecuted and insulted, talked about as if they were somehow not feminine because of their business acumen," he says. "And my take was 'She can ruin your faith with her casual lies / And she only reveals what she wants you to see'—all second person—but then it comes back to me: 'She's always a woman to me.' Yes, she can be difficult, she can be confounding, she can be impossible, but she's obviously a better businessperson than you are. So give credit where it's due. It was a tribute to Elizabeth.

"I saw it happen with my mom, who got beaten down by the system, unable to get steady, rewarding work. And I saw it happening all over again with Elizabeth. They were giving her a tough time because she was a woman."

That said, Billy would be witness to more than a few of Elizabeth's blowups, sometimes uncomfortably so. With Billy's increasing clout in the business had come the natural corollary: "The people who work with you gain power and an ability to exert more leverage—on the label, on promoters, on media, the gamut." Elizabeth gradually took on more authority and exercised it more blatantly.

Also around this time Elizabeth began to involve her brother Frank.

In 1978, two thieves broke into one of the touring party's hotel rooms in Cincinnati with a shotgun and stole the proceeds of Billy's ticket sales as paid by the promoter. The pair then lay in wait for Billy's sound man, Brian Ruggles, and the tour manager, Rick London. (London was closely tied to Frank; he had married another Weber sister, Mary Sue.)

"We got robbed at gunpoint," says Brian Ruggles. "Shotguns to my head. I was tied and gagged and everything. We'd been bringing a box of shirts and jackets, tour merchandise that I'd offered to help carry up to Rick's room. We walk in the room, and these guys were in there, masks and overcoats. They shoved us down on the floor, and they were yelling at us, 'Where's the money? Where's the drugs?' We were thinking, *Drugs? What drugs?'*

"So Rick said he had some money—he had, like, fifteen thousand in cash, and some checks from the night's receipts. They tied us to the beds, and they gagged and taped us. Meanwhile this whole time I'm thinking, *I'm a dead man*, because the guy had this shotgun right on my neck. Afterward, the mayor, who had been at the gig, asked if there was anything he could do. He said, 'We'll look into it.' Nothing ever happened.

"Anyway, the next night we're playing somewhere else in Ohio, and Billy did 'Just the Way You Are.' And where he'd usually sing, 'Don't go tryin' some new fashion,' he sang, 'Don't go tyin' / Rick and Brian.'

"And then that was the big joke."

In the days following the robbery, Frank was called to come out on the road and lend what help he could (that would later seem ironic, given how his involvement in alleged malfeasances eventually drained the Billy exchequer without deploying a single gun). With another show coming right up, the tour party felt under threat, and though Frank wasn't exactly hired muscle, he had a bumptious edge to him, and the reflex was to get every possible hand on deck as they tightened up security.

Soon afterward Frank was on his way to becoming Billy's new financial steward. Frank would tell author Stan Soocher in *They Fought the Law* that Elizabeth "was sort of secretive" when she invited him and his wife Lucille out to dinner: "She said Billy's business had outgrown her ability to handle it. There were so many people—lawyers and accountants—involved." Frank had virtually no experience in the law or accountancy, but if the experts minding the store took him for a rube, they would find out differently, if too late and much to their regret.

Elizabeth went off to do other projects; she talked about managing Meat Loaf and briefly worked with Phoebe Snow. Meanwhile Frank steadily pointed out all the places where he felt Elizabeth had made wrong business decisions. "He kept saying 'She missed this, she missed that.' 'She didn't do this, she didn't do that.' Frank was making himself look like the hero," says Billy. "And I thought, *Man, if this guy is taking my side against his own sister, he must be pretty devoted to my cause.*"

The miserable experience with Elizabeth was, however, a great source of creativity for Billy: "Maybe if people had known just how personal the pain was, they wouldn't have been so quick to accuse me of stereotyping women in certain songs. 'Stiletto'—which I wrote during the same period I was writing *The Stranger* but which ended up on *52nd Street* in 1978—also earned me a bit of a public wrist slap. 'Oh, he's calling a woman a bitch.'

"I said, 'Look, it's more about the guy in the song being an idiot than the woman being horrible.'"

Then she says she needs affection
While she searches for the vein
She's so good with her stiletto
You don't really mind the pain.

"As always, the music led me through the lyrics. I was hearing one of those jazzy beats Steve Winwood and Traffic specialized in—a generation later, that beat got picked up by hip-hop guys.

"I don't think Elizabeth took the sentiment in the song personally—again, it's on the guy: 'You stand there pleadin' / With your insides bleedin' / 'Cause you deep down want some more.'"

So Billy got tagged for misogyny again, "which comes with the territory when people start interpreting your songs," says Billy. "Then again, I think I'm a little bit of an iconoclast. When something becomes too politically correct, I want to go against the grain."

A similar thing happened with "Only the Good Die Young," when the Catholic Church got perturbed by the line "Catholic girls start much too late." "But I'm sure it sold me quite a few records," remarks Billy. "I guess I do like to let the air out of things, to take the piss out of something. There were more than a few ruffled feathers over that song."

Elizabeth would, in a couple years' time, walk away from Billy with a quite generous settlement, with guaranteed future payouts from the continuing sales of the albums created during the marriage. However, the irony of her imminent decision to relinquish her managerial duties was that commercially, the *very* good times were just beginning. Everything clicked when *The Stranger* was released. Even a cut like "Movin' Out (Anthony's Song)," which made it only to number seventeen on the charts, seemed to be ubiquitous for a few weeks. "Time's been good to that one, and also to 'Scenes from an Italian Restaurant.' They share that landscape I grew up in; they delve into the kind of things you hear on the street corner in an old-school neighborhood," says Billy.

The couple at the center of "Scenes," Brenda and Eddie, came to stand in as a sort of iconic duo, capturing a piece of people's high school experience: "With that song, I wanted to explore the eternal question about the anointed kids we all knew: Whatever happened to them? If you peak too early, if you're the hot lick in high school, it's a good bet you're gonna bomb out pretty early. And I had this song started with the title 'The Ballad of Brenda and Eddie.' Then I said to myself, *Okay, I need to set this up better*."

The format of this songwriting was inspired by a chunk of material on the B-side of *Abbey Road*. "Anybody who's familiar with that B-side has probably figured out by now it's a series of song fragments," says Billy. "The Beatles would come into a recording session, and John would go, 'I've got a bit of this,' and Paul would say, 'I've got a piece of this,' and then George Martin would say, 'Well, let's stitch it all together and we can make this work.' It adds up to a sixteen-minute medley, and I thought it was brilliant."

When Billy was working on "Brenda and Eddie," he tried to do something similar: "I had an idea for another fragment that is about a couple that meets after a long time—okay, a bottle of red, a bottle of white. That's it—they're in their old Italian restaurant. Gradually it all came together."

Billy was never quite sure why he subtitled "Movin' Out": "At the time I just pictured some lady yelling out of a house, 'Anthony! Anthony!' and I was thinking about a kid who's been living at home and getting a lot of pressure from his family to do what they want him to do, and this is a guy who wants to go his own way. He isn't buying into the upward mobility thing."

Years later the song continues to resonate with audiences. When Billy and the band perform the song in a venue with any open space down front, the crowd surges toward the footlights. "I guess it's something they're real familiar with," he says.

Billy also gives thanks to Twyla Tharp for popularizing the song. Twenty-five years after *The Stranger* was released, the dancer-choreographer brought Billy's music to the Broadway stage—finding the thread that runs through the songs to effectively mount a musical that tells a story through choreography.

When Twyla first reached out to him, Billy admits, "I was a little dismissive, to be honest, despite knowing she was a real master. I just doubted the premise." However, her gentle provocation was to ask him what happened to Brenda and Eddie in the Italian restaurant, and he didn't have an answer. Nor did he have an answer for her when she asked what happened to Anthony from the grocery store.

It turned out that Twyla had quite a few ideas of her own. "She helped me see the logic of the story, with Vietnam and 'Goodnight Saigon' as a pivot point," he recalls. "She quoted the first line of Homer's *Iliad*, 'Sing to me, muse, of the rage of Achilles.' Ostensibly, I was the muse to that generation of American men who faced the war and represented the rage."

What Twyla created in 2002 was a hit, Tony-winning Broadway musical. Plus, thanks to the involvement of Billy's musical director, Tommy Byrnes, Billy ended up plundering the pit band—the musicians who are typically tucked beneath the stage front playing accompaniments—for musicians who would become some of his best players on the road.

BEYOND THE SONGS that would go on to be major hits, the tracks on *The Stranger* provide deeper insight into Billy's psyche at the time. The album's cover was Freudian in its own right, with Billy posed in suit and tie on an unmade bed in the company of a gaping commedia dell'arte mask and a dangling set of boxing gloves. Several questions in the probing lyrics of "The Stranger" came straight out of Billy and Elizabeth's fraying relationship. The singer asks us directly:

> *Why were you so surprised*
> *That you never saw the stranger*
> *Did you ever let your lover see*
> *The stranger in yourself?*

The woman he comes home to—and there's no use denying how autobiographical the song is, or that the song was the fitting choice for an album title—kicks him "right between the eyes." Perhaps a more painful insight, in this case more prophecy than autobiography, is that these romantic disasters—or with luck, opportunities—will force their way into one's life again:

> Though you drown in good intentions
> You will never quench the fire
> You'll give in to your desire
> When the stranger comes along.

There's an almost startling wistfulness to the whispery-voiced "Everybody Has a Dream," as a gospel-tinged female chorus including Phoebe Snow backs the singer up. His dream, sadly in the context of the album, is "just to be at home / And to be all alone . . . with you."

As *The Stranger* went platinum in 1977, Billy became aware that he'd moved to a different place in the music business. He had hit a level that required him to constantly concentrate on work: "It was all about: What's the next project, what's the next tour, what's going on with the band? I was constantly thinking, *Career, career, career, career.*

"The song 'Big Shot' was about my realization that I derived no real satisfaction from the kind of public profile that had grown all around me. I certainly didn't want to be part of the disco demimonde that was getting all the buzz in New York during that period. I hated that whole coked-out, disco-drenched New York club scene in the late seventies. I never went there. I shouldn't put it down, because I don't really know much about it, but it was very glitzy, and it just seemed trashy, the whole Studio 54 shtick of going into the back room and doing coke, or hanging out with Liza Minnelli and Halston—that scene had nothing to do with rock and roll."

Still, June 1977 would see a moment that is a landmark in any entertainer's book, a three-night stand at Carnegie Hall. The highlights of the first show on June 3 were captured and included in a reissue box of *The Stranger* album in July 2008. Though he'd reluctantly appeared—and stolen the show—as the opener for Jesse Colin Young in the legendary hall in 1974, this stand was all Billy, and featured mostly songs from *Turnstiles* with a couple of cuts from *The Stranger,* still several months from release. "Ev'ry year's a souvenir," sang Billy in the concert closer he relied on at that time, "That slowly fades away." It was odd for a concert audience to be sent along home with the cautionary "Your mementos will turn to dust / But that's the price you pay." His heartfelt rendition of the melody is heard on the recording, producing applause and a few fading huzzahs from the fans.

The final date would be a twenty-sixth birthday and the last gig for Howie Emerson, who despite his elite fingerpicking skills had his guitar parts ordered up note by note by Stegmeyer and hated touring. As he admitted in a job-terminating phone call with the bandleader: "I'm the only one I know of who got fired by Billy himself."

As if to be contrary, Billy looked backward in time with this next album. Its emphasis was that Fifty-second Street was Swing Street, where the old jazz clubs used to reside. (The Cafe Zanzibar, which would get its own song, opened in 1943 at Broadway and Forty-ninth.) Referring again to the Beatles' *Abbey Road,* he decided to title the album *52nd Street.* Says Billy, "We were kind of channeling all this jazz stuff, even though we weren't jazz musicians by any means. We were rock-and-roll guys. But I always felt like an adult when I attempted jazz, like the breakdown in the middle of 'Zanzibar' or the Latin jazz feel of 'Rosalinda's Eyes'":

> Señorita don't be lonely, I will soon be there
> Oh Havana I've been searching for you everywhere
> I've got a chance to make it
> It's time for me to take it
> I'll return before the fire dies
> In Rosalinda's eyes.

Billy thought of the song as a letter that his father, "an uncommunicative guy," should have written to his mother early in their marriage: "It was kind of a romantic notion, and it told the story of a guy who's got music in his hands—*I'll be home, I'll be back, I'm always searching for my Cuban skies.* Because my old man lived in Cuba for a couple of years, I just folded in some bits and pieces of what I knew about my family background and romanticized that situation."

The jazzy piece at the end of the album, called "52nd Street," was an add-on, "a little thematic cakewalk thing."

In the spirit of giving a nod to their jazz predecessors, Billy and the band posed for the album cover outside the wall of the "crappy little luncheonette on the corner of the building where the A&R studios were at Fifty-second Street and Seventh Avenue." Billy leaned against the dirt-stained white brick wall holding a trumpet and giving his best jazz-cat look.

The album was not so relentlessly midtown New York as to leave out a nod to what Billy had left behind in Los Angeles: "The song 'My Life' is based on Tony Lawrence, a guy I knew who had a job on the East Coast but decided to be a comic and move out West to live out his dream: 'Now he gives them a stand-up routine in L.A.' It's essentially about people who are making a transition in their life, who are moving out of a particular rut that they think they're in."

Tony had come into Billy's life as a rock writer friend of the Gibsons and first met Billy after one of the early Troubadour shows. Tony had been recruited by the Gibsons and Artie Ripp for an ad hoc mission to set up a one-off Billy performance in a hotel suite in Kansas City during a record convention there. He'd moved on to a middle-management staff job at Columbia, shortly before Billy signed there. The Gibsons and Billy saw a lot of him—"I had the expense account," Lawrence quips— before he moved along to Warner Bros. in New York. "I left the music business in '77, and I started doing stand-up at [iconic Hollywood club] the Comedy Store," recalls Tony, who went through some scuffling years during and after his stand-up phase and eventually moved on to work more lucratively in reality TV. Just as Tony was making his career transition in 1977, "I was talking to Billy on the phone about it, and he thought it was awesome.

"It was not long after that conversation he said to me, 'Wait till you hear this song I wrote.' He played the piano track and read it to me, and I was very touched by it because it really showed that he was zeroing in on what I was doing, who I was. He saw the independence and the courage it took to try to do that—because I eventually lost everything doing it. I really went bust chasing that dream and ended up at the bottom financially and living in a one-bedroom apartment in Hollywood with a twenty-five-year-old Fiat. So when he wrote that thing, it was very surprising to me that (a) he would even care what I was doing, and (b) he would take it in like that. But I knew he could be such a gifted, brilliant artist.

"Subtle things always reminded me that he wasn't just some guy I knew in the music business. I remember once Jon Troy wanted me to meet Billy's new agent, and we went to Dan Tana's for dinner. We sat down, and Jon introduced me: 'And this is Billy's product manager at the label,' and Billy said, 'No, Tony's my friend.'

"It doesn't get much better than having a song written with you in it, but I just remember him always being accessible. And beyond working at the label, our friendship was based upon a genuine liking of each other as human beings—and me thinking, *God, I hope this guy makes it—he's so deserving.*"

"My Life" didn't exactly express such cheery sentiments—"Ah, but sooner or later you sleep / In your own space"—but somehow it sneaked around the corner to become a hit.

A few years later, in 1982, a wannabe singer-songwriter from Reno, Nevada, named John Powers accused Billy of stealing the song from a demo he'd sent to the record label. Billy felt the claim was absurd, but his lawyers told him the quickest way to make it go away was to pay the guy $42,500, with no admission of liability. They explained to Billy that this kind of nuisance suit was simply the cost of doing business, and you always stood the chance that a misinformed judge or jury would take your musical child, your song, away from you for good. Were that to happen, Billy would also lose the future financial benefits. Comparatively, the money to make Powers go away would be a pittance.

Billy agreed to pay Powers on the promise of a letter from him stating that "My Life" was wholly a Billy Joel song, and that Powers's song was certainly not the same. Billy and his associates never received the letter, and instead of shutting up, Powers started taking out ads repeating his claim, waving the check he'd received before the media.

That year, in a *Playboy* interview, Billy was quoted saying, "I'm going to kill this guy. I want to break his legs with my own hands." He called Powers a creep and a poor little schlump. Of course Powers then sued for emotional distress, which was thrown out by a Nevada judge in 1988. The judge pointed out that Billy had been introduced in the *Playboy* interview as a street kid and "a figure of fiery controversy," fair warning that a guy like Billy might be prone to bursts of "rhetorical hyperbole." To which Billy remarks, "Damn straight."

CHAPTER 8

EVERYBODY'S TALKIN' 'BOUT THE NEW SOUND

As *The Stranger* racked up platinum credentials through 1977—on its way to selling, over time, ten million copies and counting—Billy was running on adrenaline. Realizing that he owed Columbia a sequence of releases within a certain time frame, he was pumping out albums at a pace of nearly one a year—the kind of productivity rate that record companies thrive on.

When Billy set to work on *Glass Houses*, he'd just had back-to-back critical and commercial successes. "Just the Way You Are" won Record of the Year and Song of the Year at the Grammys in 1978, and *52nd Street* won the Grammy for Album of the Year in 1979. Now thirty, Billy was the guy to knock off the pedestal.

This was the era when punk and New Wave were clawing their way into the spotlight and leaving not a few old-school music corpses behind. Billy liked several of the New Wave artists, and at some level he respected punk's raw vitality in the face of an increasingly sluggish medium. But most of the insurgent music didn't viscerally resonate with him: "I always heard it as a reiteration of garage band rock. It reminded me of the Seeds, or Question Mark and the Mysterians, and all those early sixties bands. But everything was being recategorized now, because they needed to define it *against* something. In my neighborhood you didn't call yourself a punk; *other* people called you a punk."

Music critics at the time, searching for ways to contrast what Billy did with the new music, couldn't decide how to pigeonhole his sound. He wasn't fully rock, as capably as he sometimes could bring the noise; and he wasn't really soul. As for his supposed revolutionary opposites, Billy didn't buy the terms *punk* and *New Wave*.

Still, he agreed, "The music business needed a major enema, because you had these big, bloated prog-rock bands such as Emerson, Lake and Palmer and Genesis and Rush—these self-indulgent pseudoclassical rock bands—and also the soulless studio bands like Bread, Toto, and REO Speedwagon, or white-boy disco like KC and the Sunshine Band. And the enema was punk. No wonder it caught people's imagination."

Nonetheless, the *Glass Houses* album wasn't done to co-opt the spittle-flecked energy that was bouncing back and forth between London clubs and the New York scene centered at CBGB's. If anything, it was a return to Billy's roots, to the kind of stuff he played in high school: "I thought I'd do an album of that breed of mid-sixties rock. That was the whole point of it: it was guitar-based, driving, had a lot of punch to it. We had a great guitar player at the time, David Brown."

The defining song of *Glass Houses*—and the first song of Billy's to hit number one on the charts—was "It's Still Rock and Roll to Me," which became a critical lightning rod. "They were saying, 'Oh, he's making fun of the fans.' This was a misinterpretation of the lyric 'aimed at your average teen.' Some people thought I was saying, 'Ain't that your average teen?'—as if I were putting kids down," says Billy. "In fact, I was just pointing out that this supposedly new genre was actually quite familiar, despite the hype in the media." (The song even inspired a parody by Weird Al Yankovic, "It's Still Billy Joel to Me"—which Billy played at a college lecture in 2012.)

Still, Billy felt that he and the band "really rocked out" on that album. "I credited Elizabeth's son, Sean, for 'inspiration,'" he says, "because, at the time, he was tuned in to that kind of disruptive energy that was coming out of punk and New Wave. I shared some of his enthusiasms, like the Cars and Elvis Costello."

Meanwhile Billy and his band were starting to get booked in stadiums and arenas, big places that demanded guitar-driven, hard-rocking energy. On a song like "You May Be Right," which leads off the *Glass Houses* album, says Billy, "You can feel that energy pouring out, and hear it in the crunch of the guitar and the sound of broken glass that precedes the song." Reading between the lines in that song's lyric, he adds, "Perhaps I was wrestling with the differences Elizabeth and I were having":

> *Now think of all the years you tried to*
> *Find someone to satisfy you*
> *I might be as crazy as you say*
> *If I'm crazy then it's true*
> *That it's all because of you*
> *And you wouldn't want me any other way.*

But one composition Joel ranks among his top handful is the dreamily slow "Through the Long Night," with its Beatlesque harmonies and elegiac horns, which he wrote about Elizabeth shortly before they split up. "It was essentially about watching the dying embers burning out":

> *The warm tears*
> *The bad dreams*
> *The soft trembling shoulders . . .*
> *No, I didn't start it*
> *You're broken hearted*
> *From a long, long time ago*

Along with a broken romance, he had reservations about the very success he strove so hard to achieve. ("I ain't yer piano boy," he wrote, then deleted, for a 1981 demo of "The End of the World.") Composing songs that could pound out to the back wall of hockey arenas had not been what he planned when he began as a tunesmith.

"I don't know—if you see a guy standing in front of his own glass house, as I am on that album cover, with a big rock in his hand, you might think that here is a man dealing with high degree of ambivalence about his life and career."

AS THE TOUR for the *52nd Street* album drew to a close, Billy was invited to be part of an April 1979 concert in Cuba. The country was mostly off-limits to Americans at the time, so given Billy's personal history—had his dad's family not been allowed into Cuba, chances are he would not have been born—and an ongoing curiosity about life there, he jumped at the chance. Concert sponsor Columbia called the event Havana Jam and recruited some jazz acts, such as Weather Report and John McLaughlin, along with a folk-rock lineup—Kris Kristofferson, Bonnie Bramlett, and Stephen Stills. "We had some fun in the streets of Havana, checking out spots where Ernest Hemingway had drunk, laughing at the cheerful little kids who were trying to sell us pot," says Billy. "When it came time to perform, I purposely didn't fool around with any speeches. I just said, 'No hablo español,' and got on with my set."

Just prior to that concert in the Karl Marx Theater, Elizabeth, in her capacity as manager, had what would later become a semi-legendary meltdown. Columbia had always planned to record the concert for a video release—and for history's sake—but Billy wasn't entirely comfortable with the commercial aspect of this plan. He was on a journey of discovery, to see where his father had gone as a young boy while fleeing the Holocaust, and he had every intention of performing "Rosalinda's Eyes," the song he had written as a tribute to his parents. He was, as the *New York Times*'s John Rockwell noted, "the only American pop performer here whose career is in full tide [which] lent the proceedings a legitimacy they might otherwise have lacked." Rockwell also wrote that the performance was "stirring . . . and he drew the most fervent response of the entire festival." Partly due to Billy's feelings that he was being exploited as the lead dog for a second-tier roster, Elizabeth flexed her managerial muscle and decreed that the Columbia film crew not shoot Billy's set.

The result would be a damaging report in *Rolling Stone*. In retrospect, Billy would wish the show had been filmed, if only for archival purposes. However, backstage and about to go on, he was in no position to correct that situation. Elizabeth may well have felt she was doing what Billy preferred; no deal had been signed yet. In any event, Elizabeth reportedly went in and said, "Pull the plug. Don't you put that damn camera on him."

Afterward there were some hard feelings about the way Elizabeth had handled everything. Many viewed her action as nasty, and Billy wasn't comfortable being represented that way: "I know controlling situations as they emerge is what managers do, but there's a way to do it diplomatically. You don't throw your power around and use me as the leverage. I didn't like being used like that."

Rolling Stone's Chet Flippo wrote about the incident in his piece in the May 1979 issue called "Rocking Havana: 'Yanqui Musicians Find Rebels, Repression and Bad Cigars.'" Using the local Spanish speakers' phonetic spelling, he reported that Billy's set was the highlight for the audience: "Billy Yo-el closed out the show with a bang. When he jumped on his piano, the kids in the crowd surged past the guards and really tried to get down. If the Cuban government thought they were keeping rock & roll out of the country, Joel proved them wrong, prompting the American press to dutifully record that he had proved rock & roll can still be subversive."

Flippo also reported that a collection of jazz worthies, including Dexter Gordon and others billed as the "CBS Jazz All-Stars," were "highly pissed off" that Joel was the only musician who refused to allow the network to record and videotape his performance: "That made for some ugly words between [CBS president Bruce Lundvall, who organized the show and planned the recording] and Elizabeth Joel, Billy's wife and manager."

The article cited CBS's $235,000 investment in what they hoped would be a series of albums and a network TV special: "One CBS Jazz All-Star said Joel's decision was 'a slap in the face to the rest of us. We agreed to come down and so did he. Now he becomes a prima donna.'"

In the end, Billy's set at Havana Jam wasn't recorded. Elizabeth, by pulling the plug, had not only superseded Billy's authority, she'd also left no chance to work out the deal down the road or simply quash the footage later. In time, Billy and his team might have found a use for the video, at least as a keepsake of an unusual moment in his history.

After this episode, the relationship between Elizabeth and Billy unraveled quickly. It didn't help that Elizabeth had insisted on making an approach to the Dakota—in 1980, prior to the death of Dakota resident John Lennon—that had been rebuffed: the building board contended that Billy had a history of drug use (based on an admission to *Playboy* magazine about smoking pot). The *New York Times* picked up the *New York Post* account, which incensed Billy; so did a *Times* piece by lead music writer Robert Palmer that acknowledged his success but said, "This listener can't stand him . . . he's the sort of popular artist who makes elitism seem not just defensible but necessary." Billy would rip both articles up onstage in his summer 1980 Madison Square Garden shows.

By August he was equally fed up with a review by Ken Tucker in the *Los Angeles Herald Examiner* that said he had "hopped all over the stage in a self-sustained fit of self-glory. He has always been a megalomaniac." Billy brandished the offending newspaper, tore it up, and hollered, "Fuck you, Ken Tucker!"

Then Tim White pursued Billy to Detroit to do an interview, after *Rolling Stone*'s planned cover for that fortnight fell through. Billy insisted White match him drink for drink from a bottle of Johnnie Walker Red but showed a willingness to reassess his relations with the press: "If I'm considered part of that overhyped, overproduced, overindulgent super group style, then I'm bummed—but I do admit some of my albums had that quality."

Billy took pains (in a passage not quoted in the article) to point out that he wasn't swimming in money, as some thought: "People think I've got this multi-million dollar mansion. It isn't. I paid three hundred thousand dollars. . . . I've got a mortgage. And I just wanted to do a photo of me chucking a rock through the window of the house—through the whole false image. I've been throwing stones my whole life and people have been throwing them at me. . . . So I figured, what the hell, I'm gonna throw a rock at myself—at the whole narrow image people have of me!"

In the piece, published in the September 4, 1980, issue of *Rolling Stone* under the headline "Billy Joel Is Angry," he made the professional if not the personal relationship with his wife quite clear: "Elizabeth no longer manages me. . . . She's got twenty other things going. I said, 'Enough of the strain of being wife and manager, let's just be man and wife.'"

The following spring Billy and the band did an international tour through Europe and Israel. Elizabeth joined them on the road, which Billy, in retrospect, believes was a last effort to reassert her management position. As Billy and Elizabeth traveled about, whether on the plane or in a car or a bus, the tensions were evident. No one felt them more keenly than Billy: "I think that was the last time she was actively involved with anything I did. After that we parted ways, professionally and personally."

Elizabeth ended up living mostly in New York City, while Billy stayed in a place he'd acquired in the rustic harborside village of Lloyd Neck, near Oyster Bay. You can glimpse the setting of the Lloyd Neck place on the back cover of *The Nylon Curtain*, where Billy is sitting with a cup of coffee. "I really loved that house. It was actually a small English Tudor-style cottage, but to me it felt like my first baronial-style waterfront mansion," he remembers.

Aside from the pall cast by the dissolving relationship with Elizabeth, another dynamic influenced *The Nylon Curtain*, one that Billy didn't realize until after he finished the album: how profoundly John Lennon's death in December 1980 had affected him. "I felt a genuine sadness that John was gone, that there were never going to be any other John Lennon recordings. The Beatles were over; we'd all accepted that. But as much as I had loved them and as easy as it was for me to idolize Paul McCartney, I had never realized how much John Lennon meant to me, how much he and Paul were the irreplaceable sweet and sour. It was only later that I realized I was channeling John in a lot of the vocals on that album.

"I wonder if I ever would have written 'Laura'—which had some quirky late-Beatles touches, right down to the *la la*'s and the guitar break—if I hadn't first heard how deep John went with his song 'Mother.'"

"Laura" is emblematic of how seriously Billy took the task of writing his songs. In those lyrics, he put feelings about his mother that had seldom been heard, even among his longtime intimates. While Billy still rarely mentions Roz, her stature as a "mind upsetter" is storied. Their phone conversations tended to be one-sided, with Billy issuing reassurances over worries, real or imagined, that Roz cataloged during the call. Over the course of his career, anytime Billy has started to feel content in his work and life, he always faced the prospect of a late-evening call from a despairing or depressed Roz: "I must have been pretty fed up with some of my own mother's manipulation by the time I wrote the song, as evidenced by the F-word in the lyrics":

> *Here I am feeling like a fucking fool*
> *Do I react the way exactly*
> *She intends me to?*
> *Every time I think I'm off the hook*
> *She makes me lose my cool*
> *I'm her machine*
> *And she can punch all the keys*
> *She can push any button I was programmed through.*

Beyond the issues with Elizabeth and Roz, the *Nylon Curtain* album was a daunting effort for Billy. The United States was in the heart of the Reagan era, and he was aware of America's diminishing horizons. "Things were really changing, and I wanted to tackle the issues that were important then," says Billy. "I didn't want to get up on a soapbox and become a sociopolitical songwriter, but I wanted to talk about people going through hard times. My ethic in writing songs throughout that era was always to be talking about *people*, whether it's a love song, a song about a relationship, or a friend, or a barfly—it's always got to be about a particular person. If you try to write for an audience or to a *concept*, I don't think you're really writing for anybody. But if you're writing for a specific person and a specific situation, a lot of people might be able to identify with that."

That's how "Allentown" became one of the first songs Billy set to work on for the album. He knew that region in eastern Pennsylvania's foundering steel belt, which was where heartland America reached farthest east. Because it was just a bit inland from two of Billy's big audiences, New York and Philly, Billy and the band played the Lehigh Valley over and over again. As Billy recalls, "It was our bread and butter for a while. And I remember that when I started getting big, there was no large venue in Allentown, and some kid came up to me after the show and said, 'You're never coming back here.'

"I asked him why, and he said, 'Because anybody who gets big never comes back here.'

"I was really was touched by that, and at the same time it stirred up a bit of guilt. I thought, *Goddamn it, I'm not going to let that happen.* Yet it did happen. He was right: there was no venue big enough to play in Allentown. So I thought, *How do I write for that kid who told me I'd never be coming back?*"

While Billy was working on the songs for that album, he was reading about what was happening with the steel industry and the economy in those depressed areas: "I had this melody that was originally called

'Levittown,' somewhat in the same way Paul McCartney's 'Scrambled Eggs' became 'Yesterday.'

"But what was there to write about Levittown? That the candy store was understocked? I was thinking about Levittown, and I said, *Wait a minute—Allentown. That sounds like the real America*—which it is. Then when I was writing the song, I wanted to look back and talk about how our fathers had fought the war, and how they had met our mothers in the USO, but also about how the next generation, who thought they'd have a job—a little upward mobility—saw those hopes dashed.

"Look at what happened in that central Pennsylvania world that's portrayed in *The Deer Hunter*: a generation of working-class guys were sent off to fight, and it kind of blew that world apart. Vietnam haunted this album, and you hear that in 'Allentown' ":

> *Well we're waiting here in Allentown*
> *For the Pennsylvania we never found*
> *For the promises our teachers gave*
> *If we worked hard*
> *If we behaved.*

When the bridge kicks in, it changes from regretful to angry:

> *Every child had a pretty good shot*
> *To get at least as far as their old man got*
> *But something happened on the way to that place*
> *They threw an American flag in our face.*

Billy's singing on the last line took Keith Richards's vowel movements to an angry extreme. "I've never regarded myself as qualified to sound off on politics in one of the typical forums that are open to celebrities," says Billy, "but with 'Allentown,' I felt I was presenting a reasonably accurate portrayal of the life lived by that kid who spoke to me after the concert." At that time, the most serious unemployment and blight were in Bethlehem, where the Bethlehem Steel Corporation was headed for oblivion. Mack Truck's big Allentown plant was being taken over by Renault. "I was trying to tell a story that a young fan and the people across the Lehigh Valley could relate to: 'They thought they knew how their lives would go, and it just didn't work out that way.'

"At the time of the Vietnam War draft, my favorite line you'd hear was 'Vietnam is sending the black man to kill the yellow man for the white man who stole the land from the red man.' For a young and rebellious kid like me, it was pretty simple: *Why do I want to go shoot somebody over in Vietnam? I don't feel any threat.*

"But a lot of my friends went, and of course I respected them and what they endured. And over the years, they would say to me, 'Why don't you do a song about it?' And I repeatedly told them that I just didn't feel knowledgeable enough. This led to a series of late-night sessions, some of them very boozy and frank and moving, and I finally felt I could take a stab at inhabiting that world they'd been in, which was how I came to write 'Goodnight Saigon.'"

In Billy's mind, all the soldiers had had was one another: "They fought for our country, and then they didn't get welcomed home. And they did this in the prime of their lives, and to this day, a lot of them are still screwed up over that. You know, no flags, no parades, no brass bands. They were basically told to throw that uniform away and make believe they were never there. 'Grow your hair long and, here, take this pill, you'll be fine.'"

What was being marginalized, in Billy's mind, was the hopeful world of the 1960s—it would be shattered for the people who had fought the war and once staffed the factories. A thread was being broken: "And this was all supposed to be during the time of Reaganomics and God Bless America, the shining city on a hill, aren't we the mighty power!"

Ultimately, Billy and the band went back to Allentown and played a couple of shows. But the city was still having a tough time, not having recovered from the steel recession. "I empathize with people who have difficulty finding work or staying in a job," says Billy. "I know people sometimes think that I don't know what that's like—*He's always been a rich rock star, he doesn't know what people are going through.* The hell I don't. I wasn't born a rock star. I didn't inherit anything. I had to work my whole life, and I consider what I do a job. And there's a lot of actual work involved in it. No, being a musician is not as tough as working in a factory, but I've worked in a factory. Maybe not in a steel mill, but I put in time inking typewriter ribbons in a factory, and my God, it's mind-numbing, a Dickensian existence. To this day I still remember what it feels like to do a meaningless hard day's work for a low wage."

While writing *The Nylon Curtain* in the early 1980s, Billy was still feeling that post-Vietnam seismic shift in the country. The image of a nylon curtain wasn't chosen without some thought. "It had to do with the suburbs, with a certain degradation of our lives as everything went synthetic," explains Billy. "By contrast to the Iron Curtain, a dominant image in Americans' heads from the forties on through the fall of its key physical feature, the Berlin Wall, the nylon curtain is not a clear image. It wavers, it's hazy. Again, I wasn't aiming to send a message as an overt sociopolitical statement, but I wanted to write about people in a different way, and I wanted it to be very richly textured."

In keeping with that, Billy and his team weren't even sure what the record was until the very end of the mixing process. "Rather than writing the songs from the inside out—you start with a basic idea and you build out—I wrote it from the outside in. You take a germ of an idea and you flesh it out. This was done from an aural landscape, working my way into *Well, what's the heart of the song?* And not knowing the answer until the final mix—*Oh, this is what it is.* It's a great way to play the studio as an instrument."

Billy came to the realization that the Beatles had begun using the studio as an instrument around the time of the *Revolver* album. "When they started an album, they weren't always sure what they were going to end up with," he says. "I think of how John Lennon would pick up a French horn, or Paul would play the drums, just messing around with all kinds of stuff. And they ended up in a really cool place.

"I had an idea of the sound I was after, and a certain mood for the album. And with 'Allentown' and 'Goodnight Saigon' in particular, I finished writing the songs using external elements." In the studio, they actually edited in the sounds of a pile driver and, the first noise as the album opens, a factory whistle. Real-life sound effects appear all through that album, such as the jet sounds and the boarding announcement in "Scandinavian Skies," which was an actual airport announcement in Dutch for a flight leaving from Amsterdam to Stockholm. "We had a blast doing all that. It's not just about playing instruments and the right notes; it's also about creating an atmosphere."

The last song on the album, "Where's the Orchestra?" was a summation of all the feelings Billy was having at the time, "that life isn't a Broadway musical, it's a Greek tragedy. Okay, I'm here, my big night at the performance, and this is it? It's a drama."

> Where's the orchestra
> After all
> This is my big night on the town
> My introduction to the theatre crowd
> I assumed that the show would have a song
> So I was wrong.

Twenty years almost to the day after that song was released as the closing cut on *The Nylon Curtain*, Billy would be quoted in Chuck Klosterman's September 2002 *New York Times Magazine* story speaking of it: "'That song still applies to me,' [Joel] says in a weirdly stoic tone. 'I heard it the other day, and it still moved me, because I feel like that today. I've only felt content a few times in my life, and it never lasted. I'm very discontented right now. There are situations in my life that didn't pan out.'"

The *New York Times Magazine* piece had been set up as a kind of curtain opener for the "Movin' Out" Broadway debut about a month later but became a cri de coeur—a bit of a PR backfire. Klosterman had done his homework and knew that the proximate cause of Billy's dour, almost clinically depressed mood was his recent breakup with Long Island television news anchor Trish Bergin.

Billy continued: "I'm like most other human beings. I try and I fail. The whole message of that song is that even though you can enjoy the comedic, ironic elements of what you're experiencing, life will always come up and whap you on the head."

Subsequently, in his 2003 book of essays, *Sex, Drugs and Cocoa Puffs: A Low Culture Manifesto*, Klosterman did something unexpected for a *Spin* magazine emeritus: he wrote a hipster's laudatory critique, "Every Dog Must Have His Day, Every Drunk Must Have His Drink," as an ode to Billy's work, centering on the *Glass Houses* album but also extolling "Where's the Orchestra?" and Klosterman's own personal, even spiritual, relationship to the song. The heart of his thesis can be distilled to "Nobody would ever claim that Billy Joel is *cool* in the conventional sense . . . yet Billy Joel is *great*."

He saw Billy as being "unfairly ghettoized" by listeners who couldn't fit him into a Springsteen-style archetype, but added that by contrast, "it's almost as if Joel's role in the experience is just to create a framework that I can place myself into; some of Raymond Carver's stories do the same thing."

In "Where's the Orchestra?" he writes, "Anyone can figure out Joel is actually discussing the inexplicable emptiness of his own life. . . . It's about having a dark secret, but—once again—not a cool secret." In sum, for Klosterman, the album is really about what he calls the "New Depression," which started around the same time the album came out in mid-1982.

In a later, pamphlet-sized book called *The Billy Joel Essays*, Klosterman notes that his *Times* editor "found it slightly bizarre that I liked Billy Joel, since he was living under the impression that I sat in a bomb shelter listening to Warrant and snorting cocaine off a Ouija board."

Being assigned to write the piece because he liked Billy "proved ironic," he notes in introducing the reprinted piece, "because now Billy Joel hates me."

The *Times* piece indeed kicked up some pushback from Billy's near circle of advisers. While Billy thought, based on the disconsolate interview, that the writer saw him as one of the last romantics, he felt the printed result was maudlin. Billy was quoted in the *New York Post* as complaining that most of the piece was plucked from just a few minutes of their interview. But over time, as Klosterman ascended in the public eye partly on the post-Billy hullabaloo, and as Billy benefited by getting a second look from the kind of rock dweebs who once ignored him, the Klosterman insights have been seen as positive. And he still offers real insight in some of his pronouncements: "[Billy] musically amplifies mainstream depression. He never tried to invent a new way to be sad. Joel's sardonic gloom has been at the vortex of almost all his most visceral work."

The album and the song close together, on a moody note, as Billy finishes singing the final verse (and then, briefly, reprises the theme to "Allentown"):

At least I understand
All the innuendo and the irony
And I appreciate
The roles the actors played
The point the author made
And after the closing lines
And after the curtain calls
The curtain falls
On empty chairs
Where's the orchestra?

"*The Nylon Curtain* was a concept album," says Billy. "Even in the love songs, there are troubles, pressure, surprises, and disappointments. Everybody fails, everybody falls, everybody has something bad happen. It's about how you recover, how you cope with it, how you deal with loss and regret and move on. That's a major, recurring theme in a lot of my lyrics."

Making the album was, at times, in terms of both the work and the mood, an excruciatingly difficult process for him and his band. There's so much going on in the album—so many textures, so many colors, so many instruments, so many vocal parts, and so much production technique. "I was, I guess, trying to create my own *Sgt. Pepper*," says Billy. "I wanted it to be a real statement. I was picturing kids sitting and listening to this album the same way I used to listen to *Sgt. Pepper* under those big padded Koss headphones."

The album, which was released in September 1982, was also made for FM radio, but progressive FM radio had faded in the late 1970s. By 1982 it was all gone. The stations would play "Allentown" only occasionally. "Pressure" and "Goodnight Saigon" got some airplay at college stations, but the album was a commercial failure. For Billy, it was an artistic success, but when he got to the end of it, he reported feeling as if he'd died making the album: "It was so much work and so rich and deep—but not a lot of fun. It was much darker than I had foreseen when I set out to make it."

One revealing track on that album is "Surprises." Even as he recorded it, Billy realized his marriage to Elizabeth was headed for its finale. Says Billy, "There's a line, 'It shouldn't surprise you at all / You know / . . . You were so young and naïve / I know it's hard to believe / But now it shouldn't surprise you at all.'

"Because I kind of knew this all along."

BY EARLY 1980, Elizabeth and Billy lived in different places and had very different lives. The two officially separated that year; Frank Weber had already been guiding Home Run on a day-to-day basis, with Elizabeth as the titular head.

Frank actually took Billy's side in the divorce, causing Billy to feel beholden to him. "People wonder why I hired my brother-in-law to manage my finances after splitting with Elizabeth. But he had put himself in opposition to his sister, his own blood, to take care of my needs at the time," explains Billy. "In hindsight it seems foolish, but at the time, it made perfect sense because Elizabeth really wasn't overseeing business when we parted ways. She was off being more of a rock star than I was. She was living a life of limo rides and hanging with the swells."

While Frank Weber was managing, Elizabeth went to work on other projects. Meanwhile, Frank was pointing out all the places where he felt his sister had made wrong business decisions.

In 1982, however, before the divorce and separation of assets, Elizabeth and Billy made a last attempt to reconcile. During that time, she asked him to buy them a townhouse in Manhattan, and he complied, purchasing a $4 million (very expensive) four-story house in the East Sixties. "I thought, *Well, maybe this will do it. Maybe this will bring us back together*," he remembers.

Elizabeth hired Mario Buatta, the most famous interior designer in Manhattan, to furnish and decorate the townhouse, and wound up spending untold amounts on the home for both figurative and actual chintz. She loved her Alfa Romeo and had assembled an enviable wardrobe. The money was flying out of the kitty. "Finally I figured out the score, and the divorce went ahead full speed," says Billy. "I really felt like I'd been burned this last time, because I didn't feel that she actually had any intention of working on a reconciliation. I think she wanted to get whatever she could get out of me before the shit hit the fan."

Elizabeth, correctly assessing that Billy wouldn't want to stage a fight over the details, persuaded him that the best way to handle the divorce settlement would be to use her own counsel, Texas attorney Ron Williams. Frank signed off on her idea. Along with other assets and shares of the proceeds going forward, Elizabeth ended up with the Upper East Side townhouse as part of the division of marital assets.

Elizabeth's reaction to Billy's serious motorcycle accident on April 15, 1982, would be the lasting proof of the divorce's inevitability.

The accident was horrific. Jim Boyer, longtime sound engineer for Phil Ramone and Billy as they made a string of hit albums, was right behind him on New York Avenue, in Huntington Station, and describes what happened. "I can't tell you how many times people look right at you when you're on a motorcycle and don't see you," he says. "He was on a racer," referring to Billy's favorite breed of bike, a café racer with low-slung handlebars. An elderly local Long Island resident, Cornelia Bynum (who, to add insult to injury, would later sue), "hit him right in the front of the motorcycle, which turned the wheel and jammed his hand between the handlebar and the gas tank. But it knocked him off the bike too."

Billy flew some dozens of feet down the road, in fact. "I got him off the street and sat him down," recalls Boyer. "He was mobile. I made a call, and as soon as they realized who it was, it was a mob scene. We just got him on a helicopter and took him into the city."

"I was surprised," recalls Billy, "that I was able to stand up and stagger over to my bike to see what the damage was. I guess I was in shock, because the pain hadn't hit yet. I sat down on the curb and checked the damage to my hands." The injuries, despite the heavy-duty gloves he'd been wearing, were extensive.

Billy looked up, dazed, at the first cop to arrive, who seemed to be angling for an autograph. "An ambulance ran me over to Huntington Hospital, then into a helicopter, and the next thing I knew, I was in Columbia Presbyterian in Manhattan with both hands in casts, a crushed [left] thumb, and a wrist that had been wrenched out of its socket—just all banged up.

"It's the old joke, right? 'You'll never play the piano again.' I'm sure these expert reconstructive surgeons—and I thank them for what they did for me—had a couple of dark laughs working on my left thumb. It was so crushed, they couldn't save the top bone, the distal phalanx, under the nail."

Billy's hands eventually healed well enough to function, in his opinion, passably. "It still kind of wobbles at the end," says Billy. "Because of the damage to my hand, there's no subtlety in my playing, no real nuance at all. People say I'm a good pianist. I'm not. For rock and roll, I can hold my own, but in classical or jazz terms, I stink. I mostly use two fingers on my left hand; I play octaves. Most people are right-handed, like me, so to be able to manipulate the fingers in your left hand, to do the stuff that greats like Bill Evans could do, is a real gift. Bach teaches you that both hands are equally important, because they're both playing melody. I never really studied enough to emulate that."

One day shortly after the accident, Billy woke up from a "painkiller nap," and Elizabeth was in his hospital room with an attorney. She had a contract she wanted Billy to sign. The contract, as Billy recalls, basically said that he was turning over everything to her and her control. She made the case to Billy that "this is what we should do . . . this would clarify things and there wouldn't be any more battling." "When I finally understood what was in that deal, I said, 'No fucking way—I'm in a hospital bed and you're shedding crocodile tears and bringing me a contract that completely screws me? And I'm supposed to turn over this control to you because you've got an attorney here representing you?'

"I may have acted like an idiot a time or two, but I'm not a complete idiot. I guess she thought I was in a very vulnerable position and that I would have an epiphany—that she knew best and I should turn everything over to her. That really killed it right then and there. You don't do that to somebody in a hospital bed. I was stunned by the whole thing."

Eventually Billy flew to Haiti, accompanied by Frank Weber, and got what has often been termed the "quickie" divorce (with no residency requirement or wait) that local law allowed. "We went to Port-au-Prince, which was a pretty scary place—poor people in the streets, soldiers everywhere; it was nasty—and I remember thinking, *What a poetically perfect place to end this situation. There must be a reason it's not called Love-y.*" After the visit to the Haitian Office du Divorce des Étrangers, he sat with Frank in the airport bar. "Once it was all agreed to, it was a pretty hefty divorce agreement," says Billy.

There were record royalties, publishing rights, copyright royalties, live tour monies, real estate holdings, and more. By 1987, Elizabeth was coming after Billy in New York State court in Manhattan for what she claimed were nonpayments in pension plan funds ($300,000), music earnings ($180,000), and monies ($260,000) that had been held back by Billy's advisers to pay what they saw as her fair share of the taxes due from that period.

No sooner had Billy and Elizabeth settled that out of court than Frank sued his sister; he said she was holding a portion of his share from his 15 percent stake in the income from Billy's music prior to 1981.

Elizabeth turned and sued Frank right back, demanding $7 million for breach of fiduciary duty, breach of contract, and self-dealing in their earlier agreements. Brother and sister would settle in 1993, but the 1987 battle between siblings would come too late as a signal to Billy that Frank might be hoodwinking him. In 1982 he was still sure Frank was his savior—and Elizabeth, quite the opposite. "That's when I said, 'I give up, I surrender. I have no concept as to how this family works,'" remarks Billy. "It was poison from day one. And I really don't know where the blame lies. I hooked up with the Borgias! What a family to pick."

As the seventh cut on *The Nylon Curtain*, "Surprises" helped form the album's emotionally downbeat closing suite. The slow-march-time, Lennonesque ballad, featuring a baleful, hornlike synth accompaniment, would reverberate with a kind of despair—in effect the tearstained letter marking the end of the marriage:

> Break all the records
> Burn the cassettes . . .
> Don't look now but you have changed
> Your best friends wouldn't tell you
> Now it's apparent
> Now it's a fact
> So marshal your forces
> For another attack.

CHAPTER 9

UPTOWN GIRLS

When Billy wrote a lyric like "I said 'I love you' / and that's forever," it was not a stretch for listeners to take him at his word. And when he split from the woman whom the lyric was about, it was, again, not a stretch that people could hold that against him. "I understand that," says Billy. "What I've never understood is where the myth that I dumped Elizabeth for Christie Brinkley came from." The troubled couple had split up long before his chance meeting with Christie in 1983.

The year 1982 had been particularly difficult for Billy. Near the top of the litany of reverses that year was the motorcycle wreck in April, which interrupted the making of *The Nylon Curtain*. (In contrast to Bob Dylan's 1966 motorcycle accident, a moment that led to that artist virtually disappearing for four years, Billy had been faced with little choice but to finish his album.) All told, it had been an exhausting, if rewarding, grind of a year.

Billy's humble beginnings didn't include a family tradition of jetting off to the Caribbean at Christmas. Although he had the money to afford any jaunt, the idea of taking an ultra-posh vacation on St. Bart's—the island where, as the humorist Merrill Markoe says, "lunch costs $3,000"—hadn't occurred to him. It was Paul Simon who put the idea in his head. Paul and Billy had been friends for a few years and shared

Phil Ramone as a producer. They even once lived in the same building on Central Park West.

One day at the end of 1982, Billy sat in on one of Paul's recording sessions and mentioned he was looking for a holiday destination. Paul quickly told him about St. Bart's.

"I told him, 'I don't like going to these privileged enclaves that are beautiful and luxurious but surrounded by rampant poverty and a lot of pissed-off people. I wouldn't be able to relax in St. Bart's,'" says Billy.

"No," Paul said, "it's not a slave-economy island, more like a French settlement. It's really scenic, and the food is great."

Billy had to admit that sounded pretty good. Still, he felt strange about the idea. He approached his sound engineer and motorcycling companion, Jim Boyer, and his girlfriend, Jackie, and told them that he felt kind of funny going to St. Bart's all by himself: "Why don't you guys come with me?"

Getting to the island means that first you fly to St. Martin and take a puddle jumper from there. While waiting in the St. Martin airport for the hop to St. Bart's, Billy spotted Christie for the first time: "She was with a couple of friends. And she totally stunned me.

"I'm not exactly a fashion person, but I certainly knew who Christie Brinkley was and what she looked like," says Billy. She had been on the cover of *Sports Illustrated*'s swimsuit issue and had just finished making *National Lampoon's Vacation* with Chevy Chase. She was the "It Girl" of the moment. "And she was even more of a knockout in person," Billy remembers.

At the airport, "I was doing my best to get noticed, hoping she might recognize me from my album covers—there'd been nine so far, and a couple of them had gone to number one. But my tactic worked *not at all*."

Later, after Billy settled in on the island, he went down to the pool. "After lying by the pool, broiling myself to a kind of lobster-red color, I wandered off on my own." His wanderings led him to a hotel bar called the PLM Club, in St. Jean Village. He noticed a little upright piano in the corner of the bar. "I was in a melancholy mood over the divorce, feeling lonely in this beautiful place," he says. "I recall having a couple drinks, and then I got up to play, just goofing around. I remember playing 'As Time Goes By.'"

Little did Billy know, Christie Brinkley was en route to the bar. "This was St. Bart's back when it was really an untouched little paradise," says Christie. "And on St. Jean beach there was only one hotel, the PLM, where I was staying. I'd gone into the village with a friend of mine, Maury Hopson—I was there on a job, and he was the hairdresser. And suddenly word spread to the town that Billy Joel was at the PLM. Hops was so excited, 'Billy Joel's at the PLM! Let's go back and get a drink at the bar.'

"I said, 'Who? What?' I had missed the Billy Joel thing because I was living in Paris, so I heard the name and thought, *I didn't know Hops was into country music.*

"Well, we get to the bar, and there's this very red man sitting there, and people are maneuvering to be near him but also trying to act casual."

Says the thin red man who was sitting at the piano, "I was just knocking out some tunes, and after a couple minutes I happen to look up, and there, standing on the other side of it, were Elle Macpherson and Christie Brinkley—looking directly at me.

"So I looked back down at the keys and vibed, silently, to the piano, *Thank you. Thank you so much. You did it again. You never let me down.*

"The three of us got to chatting, and then this young girl named Whitney—she must have been about sixteen at the time, cute as a button—came up to tell me she was going to be a singer and wanted me to listen to her. Meanwhile, of course, all I wanted to do was to keep talking with Christie and Elle.

"I hope I was polite to this girl, but I'm sure there was just an edge of *Go away, kid, you're bothering me* to my attitude. I've kicked myself many times since, thinking back to that day on St. Bart's—when I could've discovered Whitney Houston."

"The thing I first noticed was that Billy was so funny," says Christie. "He just kept cracking all these jokes and making funny comments. I'm saying, 'Well, I do sing a little bossa nova,' and he's saying, 'Oh yeah? Let's give it a try.' And Whitney says, 'I can sing!' Meanwhile, Elle's draped herself on the piano like Michelle Pfeiffer [in *The Fabulous Baker Boys*].

"That first night didn't really work," Christie recalls. "But let's face it, he's got this incredible voice, he's got endless talent, and his lyrics show real depth and real heart. When you put it all together, you can see why he's had so many women flock to him."

As it turned out, Christie was otherwise involved with a guy; Billy would learn more about that later. "So . . . not that I was *settling* for Elle. I mean, Elle was six feet tall and absolutely staggeringly beautiful," says Billy. "Elle and I getting together was just the way things naturally worked out. She also had come to St. Bart's—in her case, from Australia—to do a shoot."

"When Billy went to the airport to fly home, Hops and I got these giant palm fronds, and when his plane was taking off, we ran over to the hill where the planes fly out from St. Bart's and we stood there with our palm fronds, waving goodbye," says Christie.

"He and I were really just friends first, and then it sort of progressed. He was really adorable, did really charming, sweet, thoughtful things. He was very modest and a little bit shy. It was so sweet because I came to learn what it really meant that he was 'Billy Joel.' I wasn't sure what to call him, so I just said, 'You look like a Joe to me. I'm gonna call you Joe.' So that's what I did. And I realized that this Joe was really beloved—I mean everywhere we went people were saying, 'Go, Billy!' "

Christie and Billy got to know each other somewhat in St. Bart's, but back in New York, Billy met up with Elle again. Billy had an enviable penthouse apartment at the St. Moritz Hotel, overlooking Central

Park, which he was renting from Allan Carr, the *Grease* producer. It was opulent even for the neighborhood, with a wraparound balcony and ample outdoor space. Elle stayed there with Billy for a brief time.

"I remember somebody got a shot of us walking down a beach at Coney Island—who needs St. Bart's when you can take a girl there?—that ran in the *Daily News*," says Billy. "Elle was so tall that I looked like Bubbles the Chimp next to her, and I realized this was just not going to work. I never really think about how tall a person is, because when you look at someone, if you look in their eyes, you're not thinking, *Boy, look at how big she is.* I'm five seven and never knew I was so height-challenged until I saw those pictures—after that, people just assumed I was a dwarf. Also, it was my first big age-difference relationship. I was in my early thirties, and she was nineteen."

Still, Billy found Elle to be an exceedingly charming girl, who was also very ambitious. Oddly enough, she wasn't sure she'd be able to get magazine covers, because she had brown eyes. "I told her, 'You're going to get a cover very soon.' There was one shot she did wearing glasses. I'm a sucker for a pretty girl in glasses; there's something about taking those glasses off—like in old movies where the guy is always going, 'Why, Miss Jones . . .'"

Once Elle got that first cover, she began to do more modeling in Europe, and Billy thought, *Okay, that's kind of that.* Elle was just starting to go places in her career, and Billy didn't think he'd be seeing much of her anymore. "I actually wrote a song about the experience called 'And So It Goes,'" says Billy. "I did have a strategy for that song—almost every chord had a dissonant note in it, which to me was conveying what's just beneath the words: a kind of pessimism and resignation, because I knew it really wasn't going to work out":

> *In every heart there is a room*
> *A sanctuary safe and strong*
> *To heal the wounds from lovers past*

Until a new one comes along . . .
And every time I've held a rose
It seems I've only felt the thorns
And so it goes, and so it goes
And so will you soon I suppose
But if my silence made you leave
Then that would be my worst mistake
So I will share this room with you
And you can have this heart to break.

After Elle went off to Europe, Billy was having an enjoyable time squiring different women. Newly divorced from Elizabeth, he wasn't, in his words, "a decrepit old rock star at that point, so I had a terrific run." The St. Moritz had a doorman, Nicky, who wore a French gendarme uniform. He eventually became an actor and was cast on *NYPD Blue*, but at this point Nick Turturro was just Nicky to Billy. "He was the guy who'd give me scores, ratings on the women I'd bring back to the place—usually he'd hold up eight, nine, ten fingers," says Billy. Among the women Nick rated was Christie. She got all ten fingers—flashed twice.

"My album *An Innocent Man* was conceived as a tribute to Christie, and the title track describes the early stages of our courtship":

I know you're only protecting yourself
I know you're thinking of somebody else
Someone who hurt you
But I'm not above
Making up for the love
You've been denying you could ever feel.

The lyrics addressed a certain reluctance on her part and Billy's attempt to show her that he understood what it was all about. Like Billy,

Christie had been married and divorced once already, and when they met, she was seriously involved with Olivier Chandon, heir to the Moët et Chandon champagne-producing family's fortune.

Not long after she returned from St. Bart's, however, their relationship cooled. In fact, it was seemingly near its end when disaster struck on March 1, 1983. Accounts from that time say that that day Chandon called Christie to arrange for her to meet him in Palm Beach that evening.

Shortly thereafter he hopped in his powerful Ralt race car for a run on the 2.25-mile West Palm Beach, Florida, track that his team had rented for practice runs. He had gone ten laps when the car, either through his error or a stuck throttle, left the road at around 100 mph, smashing a barrier and catapulting, after an explosion, into a shallow canal about forty yards off the track. He was dead when rescuers removed him from the car, not from burns or injury but apparently by drowning in the overturned racer—his feet had been pinned in the wreckage.

Christie, said to be distraught, remained in California. Teammates escorted Chandon's body home; a service in Paris was followed by burial in a French cemetery in a village near the family holdings.

Christie went into a private period of mourning. As Billy told *Rolling Stone*'s Anthony DeCurtis in a 1986 interview, "I picked up the paper one day, and I saw that Olivier Chandon had been killed. I called her up and said, 'Look, I know you're going through a hard time. If you need someone to talk to, I'm here.'

"I felt for her, and whenever we saw each other after that, I just tried to be a good friend and a good listener," says Billy. He must have succeeded, because she said of Billy later on, "It's his heart and soul that made me want to marry him."

"The fact that we were friends first turned out to be a good thing— and, on one particular night of goddess gridlock at the St. Moritz, [it was] the very thing that saved me," he remembers.

On that particular night, Billy took Christie, still on a just-friends basis, to see the Beach Boys perform. They were old road buddies of

Billy's, so after the concert he and Christie went backstage, and Billy introduced her to the band. It was a fun evening for both, and hoping to continue the night at his place, Billy asked if she wanted to stop by. "It was one of those 'Come on up and see my etchings' moments. Very James Bond," says Billy. "And she actually said, 'Okay.'"

Soon the two were in the lobby of the St. Moritz, waiting for the elevator. "I was trying to act cool," says Billy, "but somewhere inside me the kid from Hicksville was going, *Yesssssss!* Meanwhile I could *feel* Nicky checking us out from his post at the building's entrance, and I didn't dare turn around and make eye contact. Finally the elevator arrived, and we rode it up to the penthouse. The doors opened right onto my foyer, and just beyond it, waiting for us, the perfect view of Central Park and the city beyond, all lit up—except that standing in the foyer, blocking that view, was Elle, back in town with all her luggage and apparently planning to stay the night. Even as part of me thought, *Oh, God, no,* another part of me was going, *Holy crap, if my friends could see me now. Christie Brinkley and Elle Macpherson stacked up at the door of my pad!*"

After some awkward conversation, Christie—who lived nearby, on Central Park West—politely bowed out, and Elle remained. But she wasn't back to stay. She just needed a place to crash.

"The next day I woke up wondering what the hell Christie must think of me," Billy recalls. "When we finally talked a few days later, I said, 'I hope you don't think I'm some kind of playboy.'"

Christie answered, "No, no. I understand." She did, of course, understand. Christie and Elle were colleagues; they knew each other. Whatever complicated shuttling was going on in the supermodel universe—at this point Elle was just getting to the level that Christie had defined—the two women were cordial. "In any event, Christie and I had been seeing each other casually, and she thought there was no harm done," he says.

"Still, I couldn't help thinking that Frank Sinatra would somehow have made a threesome out of that night."

* * *

AS A GUY who'd only recently joined the ranks of the divorced, Billy was dumbstruck to find that there was a world of women out there—even models and actresses—who were actually interested in rock-and-roll guys. And now Billy was swimming in that pool. "But meeting Christie transformed it all from a fun indulgence to wild romance, which is where *An Innocent Man* came from," he explains.

If *The Nylon Curtain* was dark, deep, and deadly serious, Billy now wanted to go 180 degrees in the other direction: "I was feeling like a teenager again, a teenager with a huge happy crush on a girl, so it was only natural to try to capture that feeling with a kind of homage to the music of my teenage years: the Four Seasons, Motown, soul, a cappella, doo-wop, and all those silly, romantic love songs."

But Billy wasn't entirely innocent, of course: "I'd already seen too much of life. So in every song on *An Innocent Man*, there is also that element of anxiety to temper the full-blown, flowers-and-happiness kind of sentimentality. Even in the straight-up doo-wop of 'The Longest Time' there was a little dark corner":

> *Who knows how much further we'll go on*
> *Maybe I'll be sorry when you're gone*
> *I'll take my chances*
> *I forgot how nice romance is*
> *I haven't been there for the longest time.*

"Still, it was a gas to be writing this stuff, and it just kept coming; you don't fight that. I think I wrote the whole album in about eight weeks."

Says Christie, "When I was dating him, I started listening to all of his music and saying, 'Oh wow!' I remember the first time he played 'The Stranger' on the piano. I said, 'I love that song! Who wrote that?' And he said, 'I did.'"

When Christie was living in Paris studying art, she used to stay up at night sketching, and a particular late-night radio show would come on with that song's whistled intro. As a pair, they were night owls, but even bedtime didn't shutter his creativity sometimes.

"His songwriting process was fascinating. Sometimes he would literally dream it, and he'd just like wake up and say, 'Oh!' and he'd have an idea.

"On tour, that whole energy, the audiences were totally into it; they just exuded happiness. That all came off the *Innocent Man* album so strongly, and you'd see the people in the audience with their boyfriend or girlfriend; it was their music together, and you could feel that. It was just wonderful."

At the same time, Christie recalls, there were people in Billy's PR firm who didn't like the idea of him hooking up with her. "They felt that it sort of took this authentic rock-and-roller mystique away and thrust him a little too much in that white-hot spotlight.

"Being Billy and Christie, Christie and Billy, the couple, the item . . . suddenly twice as many people really do recognize you, and it starts becoming a kind of an excitement bubbling around when you enter a room or go anywhere.

"All of that stuff meant cameras, and Billy didn't like cameras. He had this relationship with music critics—he didn't like being critiqued— and photographers were, in his mind, an extension of newspapers—so he was highly suspicious: 'What do they want?' And I'd say, 'Billy, just give them a smile, give them the shot, and then they'll go away.'"

Given Billy's almost giddy absorption in his new romance, smiling for the paparazzi was no great chore, and recording his next album felt almost as natural.

Making *An Innocent Man* fulfilled what had always been Billy's deep-seated desire: to make records as people did in the early, more innocent days of rock. "It was easy to forget," he says, "in these later days, of having to be so relevant and sociopolitically conscious in the face of pressure from the audience and the critics, that once upon a time it was just, *Hey, listen to that record—that's cool, huh?* And you either liked it or you didn't. None of that message stuff."

Pulling *An Innocent Man* together happened so quickly and naturally that the process was a joy for Billy—exactly the opposite of making *The Nylon Curtain*, "which was all turmoil and excruciating, emotional trauma. I wanted to have fun this time, and I did," he remembers. "Artists do get these urges; I related it to John Lennon's oldies album, *Rock 'n' Roll*. But some people think I jumped the shark."

When "Tell Her About It" went to number one, Billy had some misgivings. He wrote it thinking about Diana Ross and the Supremes, but felt it was dangerous to take that song out of the context of the album. "It sounds a little too bubblegum, like Tony Orlando and Dawn," says Billy. The song got a boost from the video, where they simulated an *Ed Sullivan Show* appearance by "B.J. and the Affordables"—a Motown, Jackie Wilson–style throwback.

"Uptown Girl" actually started out as "Uptown Girls"—"Uptown girls, they've been living in their uptown world"—and grew out of Billy's social life before he met Christie. The temporarily plural title paid tribute to the various models Billy was dating, Elle among them, who were living in group apartments—"warrens" as Billy saw them—on the Upper East Side.

When Billy started dating Christie exclusively, he decided to drop the plural; thus "Uptown Girls" became "Uptown Girl." Musically, Billy had created the song as an homage to Frankie Valli and the Four Seasons, but there were those who thought he was trying to sound like them without any irony. "I loved Frankie Valli. But to me, 'Uptown Girl' was the inverse of 'Rag Doll,' in which the singer was the rich guy, she the poor girl."

When Billy put Christie in the video, it was obvious the song was about her. It got incessant rotation on MTV, because it was actually mirroring Billy's life story at the time. "There was gorgeous Christie, and then there was me, the quintessential backstreet guy. People were interested in that stuff; it was almost like replaying the tabloids in a video," says Billy.

The video was shot in New York at a gas station down on the Bowery. It was excruciating for Billy because the producers wanted him to dance: "They wanted me to do these steps with Christie, singing into a wrench, 'Whoa-oh-oh. Cross the legs left, right, left over right.' I was thinking, *Are you kidding me?*"

Jon Small, who produced the video, hired Michael Peters, who designed the dance moves for Michael Jackson's "Beat It" video, as the choreographer. Jon said to Billy, "Here's the deal. We're not going to teach *you* how to dance. We're going to teach the guys *behind* you to do what you do. You just need to get from A to B. You do this every day; you are Elvis onstage."

"Meanwhile, poor Christie is trying to gavotte across the set in hot tar with five hundred people looking on from across the street, with a few mooks shouting stuff like 'Show us your tits!' " remembers Billy.

"I actually worked with a choreographer for those little steps— that's how bad of a dancer I am," says Christie. "Also, it was the hottest night of the summer, a thousand degrees, and the tarmac was so hot my heels would sink right into it. Every time I go to kick my feet, my shoes would just sink in and stay."

Billy had, in fact, despised (and would continue to despise) every video he ever made: "I hated the process, and I was never comfortable in front of the camera. I thought the whole idea was stupid. But I recognized that they were useful promotional tools back when MTV actually showed videos.

"I know I'm not a matinee idol: I don't photograph well, I don't film well," he says. "I've always been aware of that. It's one of the reasons I was comfortable being a musician: I liked the anonymity of being in a studio with a microphone. That's all done behind closed doors, but then when I'd see it on-screen, I would watch the video and say, 'No, no, no, no. That's not what I had in mind at all. That's not what the guy who's singing looks like.' "

When Billy was shooting videos, he would make believe he was Elvis. "But that guy on-screen, *he don't look like Elvis*," says Billy. "It was just wrong. But that was the era.

"The only fun part was roping the band in with me, like in 'The Longest Time.' We start out all looking like old guys with gray hair walking through the halls of our high school the night of our reunion. I could relate in a way to that video because when I was a kid, my friends and I used to sing in the boys' room, sneaking cigarettes and doing a cappella stuff. The acoustics weren't quite as great as in the tunnel at Parking Field Four at Jones Beach, where we'd cut school and sing doo-wop all day, but they were pretty good."

The memory of those oceanside vocal workouts came in handy when Phil Ramone and Billy were recording the vocals for "The Longest Time." They had hired the Persuasions, the top harmony group around. Says Billy, "They came in. They're passing around the cognac, and we had a bass guitar on the track, which meant they had to stay exactly in pitch—and they kept going *flat, flat, flat*. More cognac, *going flatter*."

Phil finally told Billy, "You're going to have do all these parts yourself." So Billy found a technique that worked for him: for the bass singer's part, he imagined he was a very fat black guy, and for the falsetto, he pictured a skinny Italian kid from Newark wearing a wife beater T-shirt. "I did this for the five different harmony parts. Part of making *An Innocent Man* was accepting that, at thirty-four years old, it was time for me to bid farewell to some of those high notes," he says.

> If you said goodbye to me tonight
> There would still be music left to write
> What else could I do
> I'm so inspired by you
> That hasn't happened for the longest time.

> Once I thought my innocence was gone
> Now I know that happiness goes on
> That's where you found me
> When you put your arms around me
> I haven't been there for the longest time.

"*An Innocent Man* is a very special album to me," says Christie. "It was a really special time, because we were falling in love, and the album really reflected that new love and that innocence that sometimes you don't get at that stage in your life—that abandon.

"It's like, you've been hurt before, but you're just going to go for it. I know that reviewers described that album as a valentine, and it really was. I think everybody could kind of feel that love in their own life and relate it to the emotions that he was expressing so openly and so beautifully in that album. And if it's been described as a valentine to me, I think it was also a valentine to some of the musicians that he grew up on and loved and admired."

CHAPTER 10

CHRISTIE LEE

Christie Lee Hudson was born in Michigan and grew up in southern California, the all-American girl. After moving to Los Angeles, her parents eventually divorced, and when Christie's mother remarried Don Brinkley, they left the city smog for the ocean breezes of Malibu. She was educated at Our Lady of Malibu and the Lycée Français, and after graduating, she moved to Paris to study art and began modeling there. Her first husband was a French illustrator named Jean-François Allaux. Her subsequent relationship with Olivier Chandon had its own storybook elements, despite the tragic ending that left her in search of some stability.

When Billy met her, he was looking for steadiness, too, a sentiment he recalls writing around that time in "The Night Is Still Young," although the song was only released on his two-volume *Greatest Hits* collection three years later. "Maybe," he says, "it felt a little too close to home when I first wrote it."

I'd like to settle down
Get married
And maybe have a child someday
I can see a time coming when I'm gonna throw my suitcase out
No more separations

Where you have to say goodnight to a telephone
Baby I've decided that ain't what life is all about.

"There seems to be some wishful thinking in there," says Billy, "about considering quitting the road and this *Death of a Salesman* existence—some admission that even though rock and roll was the only thing I ever gave a damn about, I began to think about what it might be like not to live that life anymore."

As memorable as the courtship was, it would remain a bit of a blur for Billy. The wedding wasn't a celebrity fest—Billy had his regular crew there, and Christie had lots of friends. The event was designed not to play into the hands of the tabloids and paparazzi. Afterward the two got on a cruise boat in New York and tooled around by the Statue of Liberty, then headed back up the East River at twilight to a restaurant called the Water's Edge, in Queens, which looked out on the United Nations. The view from there was of a romantic cityscape, across the East River into Manhattan as the city's lights winked on. Billy and Christie spent their wedding night at the Carlyle Hotel in Manhattan, and reckon that's when their daughter, Alexa, was conceived.

With the start of married life, followed so quickly by the realization that a child was on the way, recording albums lost its priority for Billy: "Whatever your talent, whatever your career, your focus on everything shifts when you have a kid."

Alexa Ray Joel—whose middle name is a tribute to Ray Charles—was born at New York Hospital, at NYU, right before New Year's Eve, on December 29, 1985. Christie and Billy were then living in the Lloyd Neck house, and early that morning Christie started having labor pains and finally said, "Okay, this is it."

"We had thought we'd be ready to go once the moment came," says Billy, "but in reality it was like we were Lucy and Ricky, running into walls while trying to get the right stuff packed." Eventually they made it to the hospital, and for the next fourteen hours Christie was in labor without any pain medication. "I kept begging her, 'Take the epidural, will you?' But she wanted natural childbirth. And it hurt. I could tell it hurt. I had to keep going in and out of the room; I couldn't take it. I thought I was going to faint. I'm pretty sure no guy would be able to take that kind of pain. Seeing that gives you incredible respect for what women are capable of tolerating. If a guy had to go through labor, the second it started, he would say, 'Inject me with painkiller in the eyeballs *right now*.' The doctor took one look at me in the delivery room and told me to stay at the head of the bed.

"When Alexa finally arrived, it was the most joyful moment of my life. We asked a nurse to take a picture, but we didn't know if you were allowed to lift her out of the little bin she was resting in, so the picture is of us holding her like a baby pizza that's just come through the door."

When they left the hospital, they were semidisguised in Groucho Marx glasses—two mustachioed parents with this tiny mustachioed baby, hoping to avoid recognition. The *Daily News* managed to ID their picture anyway.

When they got back home to Lloyd Neck, there were photographers all around the property, trying to get the money shot of Billy and Christie with Alexa. As her parents, they had concerns about ensuring that she would be safe, and now that concern deepened. Making matters worse, Billy received disturbing and deranged letters from different people saying things such as "You'd better watch your kid" or "You'd better watch your wife" or "We're going to get you and we're going to get her." Billy turned the more threatening letters over to the police, but he didn't always tell Christie about them. "I didn't want her to get all freaked out," says Billy. "But those nuts are out there.

"We all know what happened to John Lennon, or about the kidnapping of Frank Sinatra's son, or the Lindbergh baby. There are human time bombs ticking out there. And performers seem to have this totemic weight that brings out the worst instincts in loony people." Eventually the couple let the press take a picture of Alexa, realizing she wasn't going to be recognizable for at least a couple of years.

Billy also credits Alexa's birth with giving him the understanding of unconditional love: "You think you know about love, and then this fierce attachment kicks in, and it's like nothing you've ever experienced before—you feel like what you've been missing all your life is suddenly there. And of course, you never lose that feeling. Before you become a parent, you get bored when people gush on and on about their kids— 'Yeah, yeah, yeah, you and your little brats, who cares?' Then you have one of your own, and you can't shut up. You think, *Oh, my God, I'm a* father. *I have a child. I've brought another human being into the world.* It's very emotional, very moving.

"The thing I remember most about becoming a dad is how my perception of time was completely blown to smithereens. There's this sudden warp in your view of your own mortality. Instead of thinking only in terms of your own lifetime, you start thinking of your child's. Almost immediately you become concerned about the future in a whole different way. You're thinking, *What kind of world is she going to have?* And it really changes you—for the better, I think."

"He was totally in love with Alexa," says Christie. "I remember the two of us just gazing into her little cradle for hours."

"The second you decide to have kids, you just sort of clean up your act, whatever it is that you think needs growing up—you grow up," says Billy. "But as we all know, rock and roll really isn't a business that likes grown-ups too much."

Like all babies, Alexa was easy to pack up and move from place to place, so Billy continued touring. The family traveled around the world many times, as Billy performed in places such as Australia and the Soviet Union, Europe and Japan, and more. Alexa had what her parents termed "a great troupe of gypsies—one big family, all of us raising her and all of us in it together."

Soon there was a group of kids backstage; Liberty DeVitto's daughter and the other kids became Alexa's best friends. "Mary, Lib's wife at the time, and I would hang out, and there were kids and wives and all of that happening backstage," says Christie. "But eventually all the kids needed to start staying home and going to school. And that's when things started to change.

"When you've got a little child at home, it's harder to leave home. Billy's job got a whole lot tougher once he had something so precious and wonderful at home; he just wanted to be there."

AS A STOPGAP while Billy nurtured domesticity, Columbia in June 1985 released *Greatest Hits*, volumes one and two. The twenty-five tracks were spiced by a pair of new songs, the determinedly jaunty anti-suicide message "You're Only Human (Second Wind)" and the lulling, soul-tinged "The Night Is Still Young." Both broke out as hits, reaching number nine and thirty-four, respectively.

At that stage in his life, Billy had to continually remind himself that he had a job. And part of the reason was that he was now financially responsible for another life. (The years of what some would call spectacular album sales would never completely reassure the Hicksville boy within that he was over the financial hump.) Says Billy, "I thought, *Maybe we'll have more kids, and everything's going to change, so I guess I should just keep doing what I'm doing.* But I didn't want to—and I think my next album, *The Bridge*, makes it pretty clear how I was feeling."

Billy didn't want to record *The Bridge* at all and would later express regret over making the album. He knew that whatever he put out, some people would buy it just because they were fans. But he judged the album to be subpar, which made its sales feel like a swindle to him. "At the time I was quietly asking myself, *What are you doing? You're just taking advantage of people liking your old stuff, and the record company's going to market it and hype it—and you know it sucks.* That whole attitude came through on the album."

Noticeably, there are only nine songs on *The Bridge*, which was just enough to make an album. The truth is, Billy barely eked them out.

His dynamic with the band during that period was terrible. In the past the musicians had always weighed in with suggestions, stayed around in the studio, and contributed plenty. None of that happened with *The Bridge*. Liberty DeVitto would play his drum part and leave; Doug Stegmeyer would play his bass part and do the same; and David Brown hung around more because there was some interesting guitar stuff going on. But there was no creative vibe flowing from the band to Billy. Making albums had become a big business for them, and there were rumblings that the musicians weren't happy with their financial deals. Without the connection between them, the situation in the studio was sad.

Meanwhile, Billy's relationship with Phil Ramone, who produced *The Bridge* as well as his previous six Columbia albums, had also changed—and not for the better. The excitement and fun they had had making their earlier albums was gone. Now it was almost drudgery. "The writing process should have warned me," says Billy. "At one stage I cloistered myself in a ten-thousand-square-foot space in the Puck Building in downtown Manhattan—just me with a piano and a notebook in the corner of this sprawling space. There was a lot of pacing back and forth along a span of windows and also out in the surrounding streets, where the espresso bars were. But no matter what, I really didn't like most of the songs. I just didn't think the material was there yet."

Billy asked the label if he could have another year or two, but they wouldn't grant him the extra time. "We've got a lot of pressure and we've got to put it out," they said. And Billy couldn't do anything about it. They owned the recordings and thus could pretty much do whatever they wanted.

Looking at the list of songs on that album, Billy saw what he felt was weak material. "'Running on Ice' is crap," he says. "I was trying to do Sting there, and the lyric is okay, but the words and the music just don't line up. There was kind of a frenetic urban thing to it. I was living in the city and I was feeling the pressure now":

They say this highway's going my way
But I don't know where it's taking me
It's a bad waste, a sad case, a rat race
It's breaking me.

"I was still scooping up things from prior years, for example, 'This Is the Time,' which came out of the realization that Elle Macpherson and I were not meant for the ages":

This is the time to remember
'Cause it will not last forever
These are the days to hold on to
'Cause we won't although we'll want to.

"A Matter of Trust" effectively retraced his courtship of Christie:

I know you're an emotional girl
It took a lot for you to not lose your faith in this world . . .
So break my heart if you must
It's a matter of trust.

Amid the stress of getting the album in the can, Billy got a new jolt of enthusiasm by doing "Baby Grand," with Ray Charles himself playing on it. Because Billy wanted to pay tribute to Charles without simply co-opting his sound, "writing 'Baby Grand' was like a tightrope walk, and the prospect of actually getting to record it with him had me a bit petrified. I was tentative, doing my humble acolyte thing."

Phil, knowing Billy was very practiced at doing a Ray impersonation, told Billy, "You've got to go after him, kid . . . get Ray to sing like *Ray*." And it worked.

Another thrill for Billy was having Stevie Winwood play with them on "Getting Closer." "The lyrics to that song, by the way, should have made Frank Weber paranoid," says Billy. "They were very predictive of the lawsuits to come—as in, 'I don't have all of it worked out yet, but I'm getting there' . . . getting closer":

> I went searching for the truth
> But in my innocence I found
> All the con men and their acrobats
> Who stomped me in the ground . . .
> What was ripped off by professionals
> Is not all that it seems
> While I must live up to contracts
> I did not give up my dreams.

"I think 'Big Man on Mulberry Street' works as a portrait of a nebbish who thinks he's cool, and it is an excursion into a jazz style of singing. From its title, 'Temptation' sounds like it's about a woman, but it's actually about being unable to leave the side of my new baby. 'Code of Silence' was a terrible song and very nearly got scrapped." In fact, Billy wound up enlisting Cyndi Lauper, who was working in the studio next door, to help him finish the song. "She came in and said, with that great Noo Yawk accent, 'I can see ya going through *awl* kinds of *tawment*. Lemme help you write it.'"

"I don't know . . ." Billy replied. But Cyndi insisted. "You just throw out some words," she said, "and I'll help ya *awganize* it." She pushed Billy to finish the song. "She's a funny girl. Great singer, too. I like *her* part of the track, anyway."

The bottom line was that Billy was fed up. He actually thought he was going to retire. But he hadn't released a newly recorded album in three years, and the label had other ideas.

The Bridge was released in July 1986 and soon reached number seven. Billy and the band then started the extensive preparations for a sidetrack from the promotional tour. As the featured event in their travels, they would undertake the first set of American rock concerts in the Soviet Union, which had just introduced its new policy of glasnost.

Despite the news that the IRS was coming after Billy for $5.5 million in unpaid back taxes—his accountants were still figuring that tangle out—he planned to finance the tour and its filming himself.

"I remember the Russian tour very fondly, almost as a series of snapshots," says Billy. "There was Christie with her cargo load of bottled water, to be used for everything from drinking to washing her hair—an outgrowth of her antinuclear activism combined with her fear that Chernobyl's aftereffects might still be poisoning the environment. There was taking Alexa, who wasn't quite two, to Gorky Park and meeting Viktor the clown, who so charmed her that we became pals and I wrote the song 'Leningrad' as a tribute to him. And of course, there was the episode of me getting so pissed off at the film lighting guys for pinning the crowd in their zillion-candle-watt spotlights that I tossed my electric piano off the stage."

It wasn't the first time Billy had done that—on a few U.S. tours it was his standard signal to his piano techs that his keyboards were malfunctioning—but in this context it became the smashed instrument heard 'round the world. "Rockin' Billy's Red Rage" was how one British tabloid billed it.

Billy initiated the trip to the Soviet Union in 1987 because he felt he and the band could make a little history, but it followed an intense string of European dates, so that by the time Billy arrived, his throat was shot and he was bone weary. The recorded performances were, in his opinion, horrible: "I was doing interviews by day and then singing at night in arenas/venues where the PA system was second rate at best. The result was another album that should never have come out."

Another alienating element was the reluctance of some in the band to take a partial cutback on their paychecks. Such a move would have lessened the logistical challenges to mounting a full-on, multi-big-rig tour, transporting tons of steel and personnel across sprawling Russia. To the band—because the producers planned to shoot the stage shows for a concert album and film—it made sense that they should earn more, not less. Phil Ramone backed Billy up on that point, but the band didn't make it easy on him.

"We were asked, because of the production budget, if the guys in the band would do it at a special rate," says Ramone. "At this point in their lives, they could have easily done it—it wasn't going to break them to put a week in at a particular price." Guitar player David Brown had simply gone awol and was replaced. "*Just go along with the rest of the band*," Ramone recalls thinking, "*and say 'We agree.'* It was an opportunity for an American band to be the first top rock-and-roll band to go to Russia."

Frank Weber and his lieutenant, Rick London, both integral to the Russia planning and to overseeing the album and film's release, were executive producers. This would be their peak as Billy's handlers, as they took on the massive task of taking the circus through the crumbling veil that used to be called the Iron Curtain.

The trip to Russia was emotionally uplifting for Billy, as he loved being part of thawing relations between the countries, and day by day he enjoyed seeing that process personalized by connections like the one he and his family made with Viktor the clown (as celebrated in "Leningrad").

That idealistic moment faded rapidly back home, though, as the label's pressure to release the album grew intense. The sixteen-song distillation of Russian performances was entitled *Kohuept* (Concert). "It was hardly our proudest effort," says Billy, "which is why we refer to it to this day as *Kaput*." He felt the label released it almost automatically, "not out of any belief on their part that those Russian shows needed to be documented for posterity—or that the concerts were even good enough as performances to include on an album."

Billy approached the label and asked if they could at least price the record as dirt cheap as possible, telling Frank, "I'll do it if they'll agree to put it out for, say, a buck ninety-nine or something, as a discount item." The label came back with its justification for not lowering the price, which was: *It's a historic event.*

Later, Billy and company would claim in a lawsuit that the then-president of Columbia Records, Al Teller, had been in cahoots with Frank Weber to "wash" money from a pension fund Billy had set up. They also alleged that Frank and Teller had cooked up a deal to ensure that a live album came out of the Soviet trip.

Teller, who was buying a new place in New York, wanted a loan, and Frank agreed to front him the money based on the advance he and Billy got from the record company. "It was all very shady crap," says Billy. "I hated the whole scam. I was so pissed off. This entire period is what really flushed the toilet for me with the music industry."

The Russian tour would mark the end of Doug Stegmeyer's long tenure, stretching back to 1974, with the band. He was the original New York band member whom Brian Ruggles had recruited as Billy was getting ready to move back from L.A.. He had been the key player for twelve years in the highly successful rhythm section. Doug was one of the Mean Brothers, an insiders' clique in the organization consisting of Brian Ruggles, Doug, Steve Cohen, and Billy. The clique had their own jackets made up with Doberman pinschers on the back. They were the senior members of the band and crew, and they hung out with one another all but exclusively. On road trips by car, they had CB radio "handles," Billy's being "Serenader." Doug's was "Dr. No," due to his extremely dark, if often witty, negativity about other musicians, pop music, women, and show-biz excesses in general.

Doug drifted away from the close-knit group when his depression deepened due to heavy drinking. He became more of a loner and eventually stopped interacting with anyone on the road. In the Soviet Union he never left his hotel room. Things got to a point where his enthusiasm for the music dimmed, even as he regularly voiced his resentments over the band's financial arrangements.

Compounding Doug's expanding moodiness was the band's increasing exclusion from input on the recording sessions for *The Bridge*. Moreover, the core of the band was changing. For the next album, 1989's *Storm Front*, Doug was eased out of the bass player role—he simply didn't get the call when it was time to re-form the band—in favor of Schuyler Deale. "I'm still friendly with him," Stegmeyer would tell *Newsday* at the time (October 1989), but added, as did Russell Javors, who was also not invited, that a more personal farewell conversation with Billy would have been appreciated.

Another part of the creative reboot was bringing in Foreigner's Mick Jones after a number of albums with Phil Ramone. Says Jones: "I think Billy just wanted to have some freedom in a way. And maybe some new blood. Doing this album was a new direction for him and I think he wanted to be master of his own ship a bit more."

Stegmeyer opened his own recording studio and did numerous sessions with other artists, and his sure hand as a producer won him an almost cultish following among Long Island musicians. Yet his demons were still very much present. "In 1995, when I heard that he had killed himself with a shotgun, I was completely shocked," says Billy. "I had no idea he was that close to the edge." Subsequently, Liberty DeVitto insinuated that Billy was somehow responsible for Doug's death. However, Billy, along with many of Stegmeyer's friends, had been unable to close the emotional gap between himself and the increasingly isolated musician, as expressed on a 1989 demo, titled "Money or Love," that was clearly about Stegmeyer:

> *Money or love, which one are you doing it for?*
> *Everybody has to make that choice sometime, you know*
> *Something is wrong, I can tell the feeling is gone*
> *Do you still remember when we started long ago?*
> *Wasn't it love that kept us all driving in a rented car?*
> *Who could've known that endless road would ever have come this far?*

"I still miss Doug," says Billy. "He was probably the most solid musician in my band during the years 1976 through 1988 and, in the days before his darkness overrode his humor, a good companion."

The tension of those days wasn't easy for Billy to live with. The external pressure from the record label about money, combined with the internal pressure from the band, sealed it for him—he needed a break.

"Thankfully, life at home was pretty wonderful," says Billy. "Christie has a very witty streak—she's a talented mimic, great with voices." Her politically active streak—centered on environmental causes—happened also to fit neatly into Billy's left-leaning politics.

Christie made fun of her modeling work, but her looks were not lost on her, and she did, reportedly, spend a good deal of time in front of the mirror. "Let's just say it took her a *long* time to get ready," Billy jokes. "I'm probably not the first husband to observe this in a wife. If we had an appointment at eight o'clock, I would tell her that it was at six-thirty—I had to build in a good ninety minutes of prep time.

"No matter what became of our marriage in the future, Christie and I did have a lot of good times," says Billy. "She was very friendly with the guys in the band and, after Elizabeth, a breath of fresh air. When Christie was coming around, I'd let the guys know, and they'd all show up in nice outfits. I got a kick out of that." Before the two got serious, he asked her to visit him in the studio while he was recording, and she invited Dudley Moore to come with her. (This was not long after he did *10*, so at this point he was a true movie star.) During the recording session—where they were making what was basically Christie's album, *An Innocent Man*, Billy could tell that Dudley was unhappy and did not want to be there, "and I thought," says Billy, "*This is kind of cool—she's got a few guys who are battling over her, and she's digging it.*"

Christie had that kind of impact on men. "When you're that good-looking, it's almost freakish. I call it the Frankenstein complex. You're beautiful now, you're going to be beautiful when you're older, you're going to be beautiful till you kick off. You're just one of those lucky people. And she understood that; she accepted her beauty. She wasn't overly self-conscious about it. I guess I would compare it to when people tell me I'm talented as a musician. I don't dispute it, but I don't dwell on it either. It's all about what you do with it."

Genetically speaking, Billy and Christie didn't know who Alexa was going to take after. Physically she looked more like Billy's family, especially on his mother's side, than Christie's. (Pictures of Billy's grandmother, a pretty young woman, make it evident that Alexa bears a striking resemblance to her.)

When Alexa was a kid, Christie would dye her hair blond; in fact, Alexa thought she really was a blonde until she was older. Over the years and particularly with the rise of the Internet, Alexa endured a lot of mean comments for not resembling her supermodel mom. She eventually had rhinoplasty on her nose, which she'd apparently been uncomfortable with for a while. As her public profile increased, the tabloid press in particular tried to spot more work—all of which she denied. She strove to get a singing career under way, debuting at a small Hoboken club in 2005 and releasing an EP called *Sketches* in 2006 and several singles since, but she has endured fairly steady jibes from the trolls of the blogosphere. "I used to want to go and smack people when I read some of the cruel stuff that was being said by amateur bloggers online," says Billy. "Alexa is a beautiful girl. She enjoys her own exotic blend. She doesn't look like Christie Brinkley, but all that means is that she doesn't look like Christie Brinkley. It doesn't make her any less beautiful."

In 1988 Billy decided to take a brief break from his standard skill set and accepted an offer from Disney to be part of the animated film *Oliver & Company*. It was supposed to be an adaptation of Dickens's *Oliver Twist*, and Billy would be portraying the Artful Dodger—as a dog. It wouldn't pay much, but Billy thought it was cool, as he phrased it, that he was actually going to be an animated character in a Disney movie that his daughter could watch.

On the storyboards, the dog was sketched in as a scrawny, hungry-looking mutt. Later, in the recording studio, while Billy was doing the speaking parts, the animators were watching—and the next time Billy saw a drawing of the dog, he was "a lot huskier and more messed-up looking. They wanted me to be very New York, so I kind of laid on the New York accent pretty thick, like a Lower East Side, Bowery kind of accent," he says. "It was fun. When I brought Alexa to see the movie, she was mad at me at first because I was mean to the little kitten, Oliver. And then when I stopped being mean, she said, 'Daddy, you're a nice dog.' And I was a hero for a while just for playing a Disney character."

Alexa grew up with vivacious parents, with Billy and Christie both known for having a ready sense of humor and larger-than-life personalities. "What I do is kind of crazy—musicians are akin to circus people—and Alexa was raised in that atmosphere," says Billy. The couple always encouraged their daughter to be confident, telling her, "You're not like everybody else—you are *different*. Now go for it."

As wild as their life together seemed at times, Christie kept Billy grounded. And she still habitually called Billy only Joe, as she had when they first met. The guy in the jumpingly rhythmic song "Christie Lee" shares this pet name:

> *They say that Joe became a wino*
> *They say he always drinks alone*
> *They say he stumbles like a blind man*
> *They say he sold his saxophone*
> *Even the band must face the music*
> *That's what the moral is to me*
> *The only time you hit the high note*
> *Is when you play for Christie Lee.*

"It's almost prophecy there, I guess," says Billy. "Because I'm always assuming that things are going to have an unhappy ending."

IT'S ALL OR
NOTHING AT ALL

OVERLEAF: Billy Joel's boxing stance served him well as a youth, and again as seen in this shot from 1989's *Storm Front*. Four years later, in "The Great Wall of China," Billy Joel would paraphrase Marlon Brando's rebuke from *On the Waterfront:* "Charlie, you shoulda looked out for me."

CHAPTER 11

STORM FRONT

As something of a reluctant pilgrim in the music business, by the late 1980s Billy had passed through the limbo of waiting out his Artie Ripp deal and seen a couple circles of suffering in the trade. Now he was about to encounter some deeper ones, including greed, fraud, and treachery. "It's normal for kids," Billy says, "to think that there's no such thing as a completely bad person. Sure, people make mistakes or head down the wrong path sometimes, but in the mind of a kid that doesn't necessarily make them rotten. But as we grow up, some of us confront people who make us believe that there really are people who are just that: rotten through and through."

For Billy, that person was Frank Weber.

Had Billy been paying close heed to Frank's managerial practices, he might have taken a warning from the complicated legal squabble Frank and Elizabeth had gotten into in the wake of the $5.5 million IRS levy notice that had popped up back in 1984. At the time, Frank's gambit was to go after Elizabeth for half of the liability, on the premise that she had received 50 percent of the income generated during that time. Accordingly, Frank had a lien placed on Elizabeth's portion of Billy's copyrights, to theoretically cover her supposed share of the tax bill. Although Frank's machinations quickly entangled brother and sister in lawsuits, Billy accepted Frank's continued assurances then that he was handling the tax hit.

Frank liked casino gambling, and Billy, in hindsight, might have seen that as symptomatic of a larger problem. Frank would often take off for Vegas to play blackjack, roulette, and craps. He bet on horses, too, and even owned a few Thoroughbreds. Meanwhile, in a strategy separate from addressing the existing IRS claim, he had Billy invested in supposed tax shelters—oil, gas, and real estate deals. "And what did I know? I just figured, *Well, he's a businessman. He knows what he's doing,*" says Billy.

Christie was the one who saw the red flags: "I saw things that I don't think Billy saw, because he's a very loyal guy. He doesn't like to think anything bad about people, and he likes to believe that if he is treating people right, then they will treat him right too. So he didn't check to see if Frank was being honest with him. He just blindly believed that this guy would never do anything to hurt him."

Christie has theorized that Billy may have transferred some of his desire for a father figure onto his manager, which not only gave Frank too much power, it closed his eyes to the betrayal—"because who wants to know he can't trust his family, his own father?"

Even as Billy was reluctant to wake up to the situation, Christie was making her feelings known. "I kept seeing little things—'Gosh, Billy, I don't get it. Why is Frank going on a private jet? Isn't it the rock star who's supposed to be on the private jet? We always fly commercial, and he's always on a private jet.'

"If a horse was making money, it was owned by Frank. If a horse broke down, it was owned by Billy. There was a real trail there. When I finally had enough, I said to Billy, 'I don't trust this guy. I don't think he has your best interests at heart, and I notice before he does business with you, he takes you out for drinks.'

"And Billy's first reaction was 'Hey, I've known him a lot longer than I've known you. You don't talk bad about him.'"

About then Billy's troubles with the IRS over the pre-1984 earnings were compounded by the agency's investigation of the tax shelters Frank had set up. "Wait a minute—how the hell did this happen?" Billy remembers asking. "I had all these successful albums. I'm supposed to be pretty solid here. . . . I owe Uncle Sam how many million?" Billy started investigating and learned about the schemes Frank had gotten him into: shady companies, bad investments, scams. "If the guy had just taken the money and put it in the bank, we would've been set. But I don't think he believed in himself enough to leave things alone, let that nest egg grow. He had to prove somehow that he could turn it into real money. I was never like that; I'm not a gambler."

Even as his financial life was in a shambles, Billy was getting some welcome feedback on his professional life, which increased his absorption in his music—possibly at the expense of minding the store. One night in 1988 Christie and Billy went to see Madonna in David Mamet's play *Speed the Plow*. "I'm a big Mamet fan," says Billy. "After all, he's the guy who called show business a 'depraved carnival.' And even though I wasn't so impressed with the play itself, I'll never forget that night.

"Because when the show ended and people started exiting the theater, the great composer and conductor Leonard Bernstein, who was walking up the aisle with his little cape on, stopped right by my seat. He knew who I was."

Billy was floored.

"Billy Joel," he said. Then Leonard—a bit theatrically—put out his hand and added, "You should be writing musicals. Broadway needs you."

Stunned, Billy thought, *Good God, Leonard Bernstein knows my music? The man who wrote* West Side Story *thinks I should be writing Broadway musicals?* He remembers that "Bernstein was dropping these song titles, my song titles—you know, 'New York State of Mind' and 'Just the Way You Are'—and I hadn't realized that he even knew I existed.

"There have been a handful of moments like this in my life, when it suddenly hits me that these monumental musical figures—people like Sinatra, Brian Wilson, Stevie Wonder, Tony Bennett, Paul McCartney—

actually know my stuff. I always try to keep these moments in mind when the criticism stings. I say to myself, *Wait a minute, what's really important? Ray Charles, that's what.* Because when the troubles come, you have to be able to see the big picture."

At that time, unfortunately, Billy's big picture was clouded by the ongoing legal hassles, and as the accompanying financial troubles deepened, Christie Brinkley's mother, known to not be shy with her opinions, lambasted her son-in-law: "How could you let this happen? How could you be so stupid?"

She was harsh, and Billy was already feeling bad enough. "I thought, *I don't need this from my own in-laws, from my own family.* Although we're friends now, Christie might have a selective memory about how grievous all this was to me, what a terrible time in my life that was. I was in the depths of despair."

"He was going through that horrible period, and at some point in that period he grew a beard," Christie remembers. "And he said to me later that that was like a symbol of trying to just push away some of the difficult things that were going on at that time—it was protecting him, in a way."

What made Billy the angriest about the legal wrangling was that he knew he would have to rebuild the fortune that Frank had squandered, which meant month upon month on the road, away from Alexa, who was nearing her fourth birthday in 1989, a tender stage for her developing personality.

As if the revelations about Frank's mismanagement weren't enough, Billy also had to join in an expanding lawsuit levying a related set of accusations against his attorneys, then the most powerful lawyer partnership in the business, Allen Grubman and Arthur Indursky of Grubman Indursky.

With all of this meshuggaas going on, Billy was about to get to work on a new album, *Storm Front.* To complicate life still further, he had to do so while installing new bass player Schuyler Deale, once of the local favorites the Good Rats ("I just thought it was time to work with someone with a different spin on things," Billy told *Newsday*). Even more challenging, he did so while working with new producer Mick Jones. As good as the work with Phil Ramone had been for Billy, with seven hit albums over ten years, it was time to start fresh.

Storm Front, in accord with its downbeat tone, had on the front cover a black-on-red nautical warning flag snapping in the wind, underscoring the ominous title. It was, in hindsight, proof of Billy's prescience that "there's some shit coming, follow me and you'll see.

"Sometimes you really don't know what the gist of an album is going to be until the last song gets written," says Billy. *Storm Front* presented itself as an account of turmoil, in both personal and business relationships: "There was a lot of anger and frustration and bitterness and confusion in my life then, and I was working through that, I guess."

"He got a lot of good songs out of it," says Christie. "I think everything he did after that started with 'I'll prove [Frank] wrong, and I'll earn it back, and I'll make it happen,' and we're all the beneficiaries, with all the great music he's made since then."

Mick Jones was very aware that he'd been brought to make a change, to push Billy in more of a rock direction. Billy told management aide Jeff Schock that he wanted a "roadhouse" recording, vigorous and lively.

Even given a firm mandate, Jones says, "It was a little daunting for me in that I knew Phil's successful history with Billy. And I admired him as one of the leading producer-arrangers who'd been there from early on. He'd worked with Sinatra at one point, which was kind of wild. We had a certain mutual respect. And I just remember that afterward we bumped into each other at the Grammys, where I was up for producer [co-credited with Billy] with that album. And [Phil] said, 'You know, Mick, if it was anybody else, I'd have been really pissed. But you did a great job, and I'm really very happy—and congratulations.' And I thought, *Wow, that's a real gent.*"

The big hit from *Storm Front* was destined to be "We Didn't Start the Fire," which came to Billy as the result of a conversation with Sean Lennon. Sean had been in school in Europe with Billy's stepbrother

Alexander, a credentialed orchestra conductor based in Europe, and his gang of musicians. One day Sean stopped by one of Billy's recording sessions. It was 1989, and Sean, who was coming up on a birthday, was quite depressed about the times, with all the troubles going on in the news—war in Chechnya, the IRA setting off terror bombs in London, Iraq arming itself, tribal war in Africa, Mideast skirmishes. Billy listened to the litany and replied "Oh, man, we all thought that, too, when we were young: *My God, what kind of world have we inherited?*"

Sean's response was "Yeah, but at least when you were a kid, you grew up in the fifties, when nothing happened." Billy's generation, Sean said, hadn't really had scourges like the current generation had—like crack and the AIDS epidemic.

Billy, who had just turned forty, had been thinking of what had transpired in his own lifetime, so he said to Sean, "Are you kidding me? Have you ever heard of the Korean War? You ever hear of Little Rock? You ever hear of the Hungarian Uprising? All kinds of stuff happened."

"Oh, not that I knew of," Sean answered. Immediately Billy thought, *I've got to write about this.* He started with 1949 and then just went on through to 1989. The song was going to be Billy's response to Sean, and to his generation, explaining that these epic struggles had been going on forever and would certainly continue.

"The chain of news events and personalities came easily—mostly they just spilled out of my memory as fast as I could scribble them down," says Billy. "I had a chord progression that originally belonged to a country song I was trying to write, and I sandwiched the words into those chords—'Harry Truman, Doris Day,' okay, so far so good—but then I didn't know what to call the song, and therefore what words to use in the chorus."

Then one night, in the studio at the Hit Factory, *Rolling Stone* publisher Jann Wenner visited Billy. Jann was a friend of Mick Jones's and a motorcycle-riding buddy and neighbor of Billy's in East Hampton. "I was throwing all these ideas out for titles," Billy remembers. "And each time Jann just shook his head. *Dancing Through the Fire?* That sucks.

Waltzing Through the Fire? No from Jann. *We Didn't Start the Fire*? And all of a sudden Jann went, 'Yeah—that's cool.'

"So it's Jann's fault," says Billy. "I'm going to blame it on him. Because some people hate that song." Though the single did ultimately go to the top of the *Billboard* chart, nagging criticism of it would remain. "Even I realized I hated the melody. It was horrendous, as I said at the time; it was like a droning mosquito. What does the song really mean? Is it an apologia for the baby boomers? No, it's not. It's just a song that says the world's a mess. It's always been a mess, it's always going to be a mess. I'm not apologizing for anything. This is what happened."

Having grown up with *Scholastic Weekly* as a schoolboy, Billy was especially glad to hear that the publication used that song as a teaching aid in one of its issues. Now the staccato rush of events and personalities can be found and studied at leisure online, at Wikipedia and in a couple of clever amateur videos, with the dates conveniently posted alongside.

We didn't start the fire
No we didn't light it
But we tried to fight it
Joseph Stalin, Malenkov, Nasser and Prokofiev,
Rockefeller, Campanella, Communist Bloc . . .
Ole Miss, John Glenn, Liston beats Patterson
Pope Paul, Malcolm X, British Politician sex
J.F.K. blown away, what else do I have to say?
We didn't start the fire
It was always burning
Since the world's been turning.

"*Storm Front* was poised a bit uneasily between songs about the wider world and more personal writing," says Billy. "'I Go to Extremes' was clearly the latter. The presumption was that I was addressing Christie, but given my tendency toward mood swings, I was also talking to myself":

Darling I don't know why I go to extremes
Too high or too low there ain't no in-betweens
And if I stand or I fall
It's all or nothing at all
Darling I don't know why I go to extremes.

Even as he contemplated the new material he was working on, Billy realized that his marriage, though stable enough, had drifted a goodly distance from what had begun as a delirious idyll: "I suppose 'State of Grace' is hard to tag as anything other than at least a subconscious attempt to figure out a way back to what Christie and I once had":

I'm never certain that you read me right
Sometimes you don't want to see . . .
Holding you here is so hard to do . . .
I'm losing you.

"When you're facing a personal crisis, a natural instinct is to go to the basic truths in your life," says Billy. Although he'd grown up in a neighborhood that essentially paved over one of Long Island's traditional industries (farming), the time he'd spent dredging oysters and getting to know some of the Island's native-born fisherman taught him to regard the baymen as the surviving heart of an increasingly crowded and industrialized environment. Under pressure from conservationists and sport fisherman, and forced to travel farther out to sea to find their catch, they were under serious threat from the twentieth century, as he all but roars in "The Downeaster *Alexa*":

I was a bayman like my father was before
Can't make a living as a bayman anymore
There ain't much future for a man who works the sea
But there ain't no island left for islanders like me.

"I composed a song that reminded me of an old-time sea chantey, with the pounding cadences of shipboard work—hauling up rope or an anchor chain." In the mix with his full-throated vocal, Billy added his own accordion and a contribution from someone listed in the credits as "World Famous Incognito Violinist"—Itzhak Perlman, an adoptive Islander, who couldn't use his name due to contractual obligations to another label. When it came time to name the boat in the song, Billy chose the Downeaster designation, which began among boat builders as a description of a Maine lobstering boat. And then his daughter's name was a natural choice as one that would look good in black and gold on the fantail.

Jones knew the record had hits on it, but in the late stages, he felt it was shy one last potential winner. "There was a period when we were quite friendly," he says, "spent quite a bit of time together socially too. And toward the end I sat down and listened to what we had, and I couldn't help thinking that if we got one more song, maybe one more single, that the album would go completely over the top. I started to gently try and suggest it to Billy. I suggested once every few days. And then once every day, and then once every few hours. And Billy got almost down on his knees one night and said, 'Mick, what are you doing to me? I can't do this. I'm going to lose my family, I'm going to lose my wife, I'm going to lose—' and I said, 'Come on, you're talking to me. I know what life as a rock star is.'"

And thus they put in the work, and the tenth cut on Billy's eleventh studio album became Billy's solo performance—on piano, synth, and vocal—of "And So It Goes," one of the rare compositions that had survived for some time on his shelf. The song exemplified Billy's practice of turning his love life's reversals into relatable lyrics, as he recaptured the feeling from six years earlier ("And you can have this heart to break . . .") that his romance with Elle Macpherson would probably be a short-lived one.

For a downbeat ballad, the song would make surprising progress up the charts, to number thirty-seven—as a sort of palate cleanser between "We Didn't Start the Fire" and "I Go to Extremes," which went to number six.

THE HITS WOULD come in due course, but at the time when Billy and company finished *Storm Front,* they didn't know quite what they had. The charts were not a primary concern for Billy because he was seriously distracted by the financial and legal mess he was embroiled in. When it was time to hand in the album, the normal procedure would have been to give it to his manager, who would then go to the record company. But given the confusion that was breaking out, as Billy grew more aware of his manager Frank's malfeasance, Billy handed it to the record company personally, saying that he was no longer working with Frank and that there was going to be a lawsuit.

"There was a lot of paranoia at the time," Billy remembers, "because nobody knew how this was all going to work. Even Columbia Records was unclear—can we legally release this album? That's when I hired John Eastman to be my attorney, and he got the label to sign off on the album and put it out."

Storm Front would become further evidence that Billy had reached a commercial plateau from which he'd never really descend. The *Billboard* charts welcomed, to varying degrees, all seven singles that the album spawned between September 1989 and January 1991, as well as the album itself, which knocked Milli Vanilli out of first place for a while.

With Billy's career stakes upped by that very success, John Eastman, in concert with Ed London of Billy's accounting firm, Gelfand, Rennert & Feldman, reviewed the books kept by Billy's former accountants for the previous eight years. In July 1989, John terminated Frank via letter. He hired the seasoned entertainment litigator Leonard Marks, then filed the suit in late September.

The suit cited Frank's risky—though occasionally lucrative, to him and rare other investors—investments in the various tax shelters and addressed how the investments had been financed. According to the complaint: "Weber took more monies from the revenues produced by some of Joel's tours and recordings than Joel himself received." One alleged tax dodge even involved a shell game with Billy's song copyrights.

Frank pushed back against the accusations. At one stage in his long battle over civil suits, in which he was alternately plaintiff and defendant, he wrote a letter to the presiding judge calling certain allegations "outrageous and distorted."

THE FINAL WEEK of September 1989 marked the nadir of an extremely tough period for Billy. *Storm Front* was set to be released in a month, and Billy was going to kick off an extended stretch of touring with a visit to London to promote the European leg. En route to JFK on September 24 to catch the Concorde, he began getting brutal, stabbing pains in his abdomen, and after a quick phone consultation with his doctor, he asked the driver to head straight for the hospital. He was having a kidney stone attack, something that had been dogging him on and off since childhood. He was operated on at NYU Medical Center. (Guns N' Roses singer Axl Rose, yet another in the long line of fans Billy had no idea were among his listeners, sent a get-well card—accompanied by a bottle of Jack Daniel's.)

The next day, as Billy lay in the hospital, the lawsuit against Frank, charging that he had squandered or illegally diverted $30 million of Billy's earnings, was filed. In addition to the compensatory $30 million, it asked for $60 million in punitive damages. Billy's lawyers had it served to Frank around seven A.M. on Weber's birthday, September 25, 1989.

The story made news in the main national dailies and of course in the trade papers. "Billy Joel Sues Former Manager for $90 Million," said the headline of *Variety*'s September 26 story, which cited the charges of "fraud, breach of contract, breach of fiduciary duty, and federal racketeering statute violations." The sums involved were "believed to be the largest judgment a pop star has sought against a former manager."

The story pointed out that Frank's sister was Billy's ex, and that Weber was also the godfather of Joel's four-year-old daughter. It also revealed that the eighty-three-page filing alleged that $2.5 million in loans had been given without Joel's knowledge or authorization to various horse-breeding and real-estate partnerships and other businesses controlled by Weber; that Weber had lost more than $10 million of Joel's money in investments of a highly speculative nature, many of which involved Weber's own companies; that Weber had double-billed Joel for his music videos, cheated him on expenses including travel and accounting fees, and mortgaged Joel's copyrights for $15 million without disclosing it on Joel's financial statements; and that Weber caused phony financial statements to be issued to Joel, which painted an unrealistic picture of his finances.

The *Los Angeles Times* piece expanded on the allegations against other defendants, Grubman and Indursky, quoting the charge that "the Grubman firm 'repeatedly breached' its duties to Joel by failing to inform him of financial irregularities involving Weber." Other claims cited included allegations that the Grubman firm paid kickbacks to Weber-controlled companies and invested hundreds of thousands of dollars in Weber partnerships in the 1980s in return for assurances of retaining Billy's business, which brought more than $750,000 in fees to the firm in 1981. The claim also alleged that "at Weber's behest, the Grubman firm repeatedly sought large advances and interest-free loans instead of higher royalty rates when negotiating Joel's contracts with CBS," adding that CBS subsequently took a lien on the copyrights to Joel's compositions. "Joel also accuses the Grubman firm of failing to inform him that it also represented CBS. Because of that conflict, the suit alleges, the Grubman firm said nothing to Joel when Weber loaned $300,000 of the singer's money to an unnamed CBS executive"—who turned out to be Al Teller, though subsequent to the loan, he'd been bounced in 1988 after conflicts with Yetnikoff—"for an apartment renovation."

Over the course of some thirty depositions Billy would give in a complex series of suits against Frank, Allen Grubman's firm, and various accountants, some truths finally emerged in the knotted dispute.

Curtly and cluelessly, Billy had dismissed Walter Yetnikoff's attempts to warn him over dinner in 1988. "Billy was selling his apartment in New York for about four million dollars," Walter says, "and he was waiting for Sting to buy it. And he said he's got this beast in the East, one of his places in the Hamptons, not that expensive—maybe ten million—with a lot of land and it was on the ocean. And he said, 'Well, I can't really close on that deal until I get Sting to close on this apartment.' I said, 'You need money from Sting to buy a house in the Hamptons? You should have fifty million in cash. What's wrong with you? Do you know how many records you've sold? You shouldn't need Sting. Something is wrong. Get an auditor to come in and check what the story is. You shouldn't be worried about money. If you want to have three houses in the Hamptons, maybe it would be a terrible idea, but you should be able to do it.' And he told me to screw off, that he trusted Frank, and I was pestering him.

"And then I went to Allen Grubman and I said, 'You should take a look at this. Something's wrong here. Why doesn't he have money? Where did it go?'

"He said, 'I can't do that.'

"I said, 'Why?'

"He said, 'I'm only his music lawyer.'

"So I said, 'Don't give me that bullshit. You're his lawyer and you have an obligation.' And he said, 'Well, my client is really Frank, and if I do that then I'll lose a client.'

"I said, 'You might. You might lose a client. But you might also be able to sleep at night.' And he refused.

"After it all came down, I saw Billy at Sal Anthony's on Eighteenth

Street, and he'd just had the kidney stones, and we hadn't seen each other for a while. I said to him, 'You still want me to fuck off, huh?'

"He said, 'No, no, you were right—I'm sorry.'"

"I tend to be trusting," says Billy. "I tend to err on the side of loyalty rather than suspicion. That's just my nature.

"But at this point in my life, I've become very cynical."

CHAPTER 12

THE RIVER OF DREAMS

One day in February 1990, FBI agent Tim Crino was sitting at his desk at 26 Federal Plaza in Manhattan, where the bureau had three of the upper floors. He picked up a phone call from authorities at one of the country-club federal prisons where his investigative targets, generally white-collar criminals, often ended up. Crino, then thirty-two, had been educated upstate at St. Bonaventure, spent a few years as an accountant, and then brought his skills over to the FBI.

He'd apprenticed in the three-man Topeka, Kansas, office before coming east and racking up an enviable track record of convictions exposing many millions of dollars in fraudulent deals. One notable case led to the 1985 conviction of a garment business con man named Irwin Feiner, a genial grifter who also dabbled in suspect if not quite prosecutable racehorse transactions. In this case Feiner was prosecuted by then U.S. attorney Rudolph Giuliani. Crino laid out Feiner's complex invoicing scam—a kind of bookkeeping swindle manipulating the advances banks gave apparel brokers. Feiner was sent away for five years—he'd won a reduced sentence by funneling information about other players in the scam to the feds.

The prison official who called Crino, exploiting the Federal Bureau of Prisons' right to record inmate calls, had by chance heard Billy Joel's name come up in one of Feiner's conversations. The party on the other end, to whom Feiner was trying to sell a Gulfstream jet in order to collect some kickback money, was one Francis X. Weber. Fraudulent elements on the face of the scheme got the agent's attention (given Feiner's proven effectiveness as an informant), but the amusing thing, according to Crino, was that "this guy, Frank, is talking about Billy Joel and saying he has to be careful making the airplane deal—'I got to tread slowly because I don't want to disrupt the golden goose.'"

Crino was assigned as case agent and soon had a young assistant U.S. attorney for the criminal division of the Southern District of New York, James J. McGuire, on board. A Yale grad who had won a Rhodes scholarship, played pro hoops in Europe, and gone to Harvard Law, McGuire was aggressive, impressive, and so feisty that he would later seek to have his own boss, U.S. attorney Otto Obermaier, prosecuted, claiming he'd solicited campaign money from a securities firm in New York on behalf of Senator Alphonse D'Amato. The charges didn't wash, and McGuire, having run afoul of the party machine, would end up working in the private sector.

The case Crino hoped to make for a time overlapped with the ongoing IRS investigation of Frank, and his scrutiny of Frank's dealings would lead him to interview Grubman and Indursky—one of many twists in the case that can be reconstructed from available court documents. But despite the recordings of Frank musing over the plane purchase—Crino theorized that Feiner proposed that Frank would get "an under-the-table sales commission no one had to know about" if he could sell Billy on the deal—Billy says, his reaction then was "What am I going to do with a plane?"

Gradually the case Crino and the IRS hoped to build crumbled over questions of venue and jurisdiction, as much of the alleged fraud by Weber and Feiner was located in the Eastern District of Long Island, and any indictments would be hard to shuttle from the Southern District to the Eastern. "We were looking under every rock," says Crino, "because we knew—we really felt, let me put it that way—that Frank was doing Billy Joel wrong, but we couldn't prove it. At the end of the day, we could not prove any criminal wrongdoing." What Crino was left with was a set of head-smacking water cooler anecdotes and a sense that Weber had the guts of a burglar.

One of the maneuvers by Frank, who had helped Billy prepare a postnuptial agreement with Christie not long after their marriage in 1985—as we have seen, she increasingly mistrusted Frank as she studied his subsequent moves—was to set up a conflict between Billy and Christie as they upgraded their new $2.9 million Hamptons mansion on Further Lane in Amagansett. "Frank started to come up with a plan to cause tension between them to the point they weren't talking," relates Crino. "He felt he had the best chance of not being found out if he could keep those two from putting their heads together. So Christie wanted a certain kind of stone for the front of the house, really expensive, and as they were deciding, Weber told Christie 'that Billy has a lot of money in the bank right now, it's just sitting there, he's in really good shape. Go out and buy [the stone].' In the meantime, he goes to Billy Joel and says, 'Your wife is out of control, I keep telling her you've got money problems right now, you're cash poor but . . .'"

According to Crino's recollection, the stone went in. Frank also made a pitch to Christie that instead of the inexpensive fruit tree saplings she had been eyeing, she should just buy up the mature orchard that a farmer down the road was willing to let go—at, Crino says, "six times the cost." Although the FBI investigation would be joined by an IRS investigation, for which Christie gave her bill of particulars against Frank, and Attorney McGuire would get testimony from Billy to help build a case for fraud and tax evasion, in the end no federal charges were brought.

All the scrutiny by law enforcement, however, did bring considerable heat to bear on Frank as he fought off Billy's lawyers' civil suit, as well as on Grubman and Indursky—they, too, were targeted by Billy's aggressive hired litigator Leonard Marks, a sometime assistant U.S. attorney himself. The Grubman firm's dealings with Weber were still of interest to the federal prosecutors when it was first summoned to

Federal Plaza, and though the firm was never charged, Marks gained considerable fuel for his later civil complaint against it.

The available record of the Grubman-Indursky interview by Crino is in the form of notes Marks made during the meeting, which was billed as an information session, though the interviewees did bring their lawyer. Very soon after it began, the grilling brought out some sweaty palms as Crino slid the paper evidence of correspondence and financial transactions between Weber and the duo onto the table between them. "They tried to downplay it until I started pointing out a lot of checks—'What's this one for?' That's how the game is played in white-collar crime. If you're holding a good hand, you don't have to come on real strong."

In addition to Grubman and Indursky, Crino would interview Sony Music president Tommy Mottola (who reigned over Columbia via Sony's acquisition of the CBS Records label in 1987) in 1992, after Grubman admitted that Mottola had informed him of Frank's scheme to "burn horses"—something Frank has steadily denied. (Mottola was also quoted by Grubman as calling Frank "crazy.") Frank's Silver W Stables, for example, would insure certain horses, which then mysteriously died. One notably was named Vers la Caisse, which might roughly translate as "to the bank"; the other, Raisin Taxes, bore a moniker almost more suspicious. Grubman's firm, in fact, had lent the stable a quarter million dollars in February 1986, which Frank used to buy a horse that, as it happened, died soon afterward. Once Marks directed reporters to the court exhibit containing his notes on Crino's interrogation of the law partners, the *Daily News* ran the headline, "FBI Told Nasty Horse Tale by Billy Joel's Lawyer," and *The Hollywood Reporter* somewhat misleadingly blared, "Plaintiff Joel Calls In the F.B.I."

The defendants in each case had their rebuttals working, of course, and mounted a vigorous series of legal arguments contending that most, if not all, of the moves were designed to help protect Billy from onerous taxes and to further add to his bottom line via investments. Insiders say certain of the ventures, such as Lincoln Road Associates, with its investment in a patch of Miami real estate that was about to greatly increase in value, had positive outcomes. Music business mandarin and Grubman client David Geffen came to Grubman's defense, telling *American Lawyer,* in a March 1999 piece titled "Good Press, Bad Law," that "the idea of blaming Allen for Frank Weber is crazy."

Frank tried to fight back further with legal kidney punches, filing a breach-of-contract suit against Billy in what he presumably thought was a friendlier jurisdiction—Billy got served papers just before he went onstage in Atlanta. Frank also aimed one at Christie, for $12 million, claiming that her malice toward him had led her to "entice" Billy to repudiate him. (The latter was thrown out in 1992, because any such conversations were protected by the state's marital privilege laws.)

One of the rare comical twists that emerged from all the suits was that Allen Grubman was apparently incensed that he hadn't been invited to Billy's wedding to Christie, and he blamed Frank. Whatever blandishments the Grubman firm funneled to Frank, the money flowed the other way as well: in 1986, Grubman Indursky got $450,000 from Frank for helping restructure Billy's deal with CBS.

Finally, in March 1990, Billy saw the beginning of the end. A state court judge ruled that he was entitled, for a start, to $2 million in repayment of bogus loans that Frank had taken out. However, Billy received only about a tenth of that when Frank filed for bankruptcy. In yet another ironic twist, even that payment was drawn from funds that should have been coming in as revenue to Billy.

When it was later discovered that the law firm had also paid Frank something in the substantial six figures for "financial consulting and tax planning," although he had no real expertise in those areas, Billy's attorneys added a malpractice suit, using the term *kickbacks,* in September 1992.

Grubman and Indursky hired veteran law firm Paul, Weiss as well as Bert Fields to fight the two suits, and Billy spent the first week of August 1993 giving depositions in the Weiss offices, at times with an audience of Grubman or Indursky or even Frank, who at one point, farcically unrepentant, whistled a passage from Billy's song "Honesty."

The flood of paperwork, as well as the aggravations of being deposed and testifying and paying lawyer fees, were by now becoming wearying to all parties. Meanwhile, Billy was on a tear, having come off *Storm Front* with considerable momentum that he would bring to his next album, *River of Dreams*. Hoping to continue his success, senior people at the label and in Billy's camp began to share a more pragmatic mindset: Why prolong a fight over past malfeasances by an incorrigible, disenfranchised (and bankrupt) player like Frank Weber when Billy's near future was glowing brightly?

Also, the system that had brought the Grubman firm to unmatched prominence had made it too big to be marginalized. Sony was simply too deeply in business with Grubman—he represented clients in its executive ranks as well as its biggest acts in the music marketplace—to turn on him. Grubman also could make some quite convincing arguments that the label was complicit in his mishandling of Billy's interests. Still, Marks rattled his saber, darkly warning in *American Lawyer* that "if they play out their cards and take this to trial they will destroy Grubman's career."

Abruptly, what had been very quiet, behind-the-scenes negotiations—principally between Billy's attorney John Eastman and Sony Music chairman Mickey Schulhof—brought a settlement (that included an improved label deal for Billy). Eastman issued a purposefully terse statement: "It's done. Full stop. No one is going into any detail. Everyone believes it should remain dead-ass neutral."

Although it was widely perceived that Schulhof had a vested interest in continuing to do business with Grubman's firm, which ran the books for Bruce Springsteen, Michael Jackson, and other valued acts on the label, few in the business even bothered making cynical comments.

But the combative Leonard Marks still had his blood up, especially when Grubman began saying to the media that he had "totally defeated" Billy. In early April 1995, Marks, resenting Grubman's braggadocio, filed an affidavit in New York Supreme Court stating that the $3 million that John Eastman had once insisted Grubman pay to Billy had in fact been quietly funneled through Sony: "Sony's payments were for one purpose only, to get Billy Joel to settle his case against Grubman."

It was a somewhat quixotic move by the feisty Marks, who clearly joined Billy in resenting Grubman's cockiness. Grubman's attorney Bert Fields vigorously denied it—"Grubman did not directly or indirectly pay one dime to Mr. Joel, nor did he funnel any money through Sony"—but Marks cited a check for $2.4 million that went from Sony to Billy on October 22, 1993, the day the lawsuit was dropped. Another coincidence noted by Marks was that on that very day Billy signed a contract with Sony to endorse some of the company's gear in Japan. The fee was $2.4 million. Marks had filed an affidavit pointing out that various settlement drafts with Grubman along the way had been run through the Sony offices.

As Billy now sees it, "I know Sony engineered the settlement so that they wouldn't be implicated, because they had personal relationships—Allen was representing the executives at Sony Music, too. And neither one of them wanted anybody looking too deeply into all these conflicts of interest. Mickey Schulhof knew, 'The Japanese don't want this. They don't want a scandal. Do it quietly.' This was like a big publicity case, which was bad for business for everybody. And it got settled. It wasn't a large amount; it kind of covered my legal fees. I didn't really get any of my money back. And they didn't go after wherever the money went. For all I know, it could be in the Cayman Islands right now, or a Swiss bank account. I have no idea."

One of the more dire examples of pure greed in a notoriously corrupt business would end in a pathetically scattered way. As in the denouement of the film *Treasure of the Sierra Madre*—when the ironically dubbed "noble brotherhood" falls apart, and the gold the main characters lusted over is blown away in the wind—Weber would plead bankruptcy while lieutenant Rick London's finances were a muddle. (Embarrassingly, London's claim to be living on unemployment benefits was contradicted when a 1990 payment of $100,000 from Frank Management was revealed, and London ended up suing to legally detach himself from the

Weber settlement.) Finally, fed up with the whole ordeal, Billy and his lawyers simply walked away, with a motion that the presiding judge approved, to discontinue the suit against London. Billy would eventually forgive Rick London: "I think he just kind of went along, because that's where the powers that be were [leading him] at that time."

What remained for Billy to reckon with, beyond the financial setback he'd have to work in earnest to remedy, was the emotional residue of broken faith, gut-shot friendships, an evaporating marriage, and the prospect of trying to help raise his daughter while urgent necessities forced him onto the tour treadmill. To listen to his statements in various interviews, depositions, and court filings, is to witness a cavalcade of dashed expectations in two marriages and in almost all his business relationships.

THROUGH ALL THE legal and financial drama, Billy's career sustained itself. In 1989, "We Didn't Start the Fire" earned Grammy nominations for Record of the Year, Song of the Year, and Best Pop Vocal Performance, Male. The following year, *Storm Front* was nominated for Best Pop Vocal Performance, Male, and Billy and Mick Jones received nods for Producer of the Year. That same year, Billy was presented with a Living Legend Award at the Grammy ceremony. "Now, I know I've said disparaging things about these kinds of awards, but to get that Living Legend Award along with Johnny Cash and Aretha Franklin felt pretty special," says Billy.

If Billy had the proper share of Mets loyalty that is many a Long Islander's prerogative, he also knew, as he sang in "Zanzibar," that "The Yankees grab the headlines every time." Born just minutes from Yankee Stadium, he had a literal birthright to become part of the lore of the storied venue. He'd even entertained a gaggle of Yankee stars at his home and was the clear choice to perform the first-ever rock concert at the ballpark, playing back-to-back on Friday and Saturday in the next-to-last week of June 1990. "It was 52 years ago," the inveterate history buff informed the Friday night crowd, "on June 22 in this stadium that Joe Louis knocked out Max Schmeling!" Donning a Yankees cap, he threw some acrobatic moves around the piano to perform "Big Shot" (he laid on the piano and tossed in some lines from "Singin' in the Rain" as a freshening downpour arrived during that song the next night).

The *New York Times'* Stephen Holden opined that "right now Mr. Joel is enjoying one of the happiest moments of his career," pointing out that *Storm Front* had already sold three million copies and adding that "Mr. Joel probably comes closer than any other contemporary pop singer and songwriter to being the everyman of the New York metropolitan area."

The twelve songs included on the video release *Billy Joel Live at Yankee Stadium* later that year were shot (by director Jon Small, as always still in touch with his friend) in a rather kaleidoscopic, busy style that may see some revising with a planned recutting of the concert film in the near future.

A much more compact celebration of his place in the local lore came later that year when, in early September 1990, Billy proudly did a benefit performance for the baymen at Long Island's Jones Beach Amphitheater. (He also pledged to the group's fund-raising the royalties from "The Downeaster *Alexa*" sales as a single.) He reminisced for a bit to Diane Ketcham of the *New York Times,* citing the increasingly upscale succession of Long Island towns he had lived in—"Hicksville, Oyster Bay, Dix Hills, Cold Spring Harbor, Cove Neck, Hampton Bays, East Marion, East Hampton"—and also how he first met lifelong friend Billy Zampino: "'When I was about five or six,' Mr. Joel said, 'my mother told me, "Here's a quarter. Go buy some candy and make a friend.". . . It was the best quarter I ever invested.'"

There would be other highlights during this time, including the news that one of Billy's favorite places, a park in his adoptive town, would be named after him: the Billy Joel Cold Spring Harbor Park. "That was kind of a gas for my mom," says Billy. "A choir sang 'The Downeaster *Alexa*,' and they handed my daughter a bouquet during the ceremony."

Then Garth Brooks recorded Billy's song "Shameless"—originally written as an homage to Jimi Hendrix—and made it a number one country hit in late 1991.

During his years with Columbia, when Billy would hit a dry spell between studio albums, the label would exercise its contractual right to put out various compilations or live albums—they would be titled *Greatest Hits, Complete Hits, Essential Hits, 2000 Years: The Millennium Concert*, and the like. Billy could usually be relied upon to mock or even disavow these releases, at one point describing them collectively as the "We Really Mean It This Time" series.

One way to interrupt that process, of course, was to create a new album of fresh material. Billy had been begun, in the summer of 1992, staging a series of recording sessions in a Southampton church that had been outfitted as a temporary studio, while he also cut two Elvis Presley tunes for the sound track to the film *Honeymoon in Vegas*. But he wanted to immerse himself even deeper in the work, so he cast about on Shelter Island, a ferry ride away from Long Island's easternmost tip, and found a lobster shed that once stored traps. Installed there with the core players—Liberty DeVitto, Tommy Byrnes, and Schuyler Deale—he self-produced a half-dozen tracks, one of which, the hard-rocking Cream-style "Shades of Grey," would make it onto the album that eventually emerged.

But Billy felt there was more to get out of the songs, and based on the recommendation of Don Henley, he brought on veteran session guitar man Danny Kortchmar—Kootch, as he was nicknamed—to bring the best out of the material. While Danny admired what Billy had accomplished with Phil Ramone, and Mick Jones's production had made *Storm Front* a success, he knew Billy had hired him because "he wanted a change—everything can't remain static."

A point of pride for Kortchmar is that *River of Dreams* became the album in which Billy shed, rather than revisited, many of his influences. Aside from "Shades of Grey," an inheritance from the lobster shed sessions that hung in to be one of the final album's ten cuts, "there's no tune on there where Billy's flat-out doing someone else. He really sounds like himself. One of the things he told me was: 'You know, all my hits were novelty records—"Tell Her About It" was Motown, "The Longest Time" was doo-wop, "Uptown Girl" was the Four Seasons.'" Kortchmar can't resist adding that the latter song remains "the best Four Seasons song ever written or recorded, by the way. Vastly superior to anything they could ever do."

Billy gave Danny the Shelter Island tracks, and after a listen (with Niko Bolas, who would engineer and mix the work to come), Kortchmar was frank about being unimpressed with what he heard, even though he feared his reaction wouldn't be that welcome: "We're snotty L.A. guys; we think we know everything, right? Got a major chip on our shoulder. It's true. But finally I realize, *Oh my God, we're going to have to tell Billy.* So I called him and I said, 'Well, I listened to the tapes.' He said, 'So what did you think?' I said, 'I loved three guys in that band. I loved the piano player. I loved the singer. And I loved whoever wrote the songs.'"

Though Kortchmar would ultimately welcome Tommy Byrnes in for overdubs on guitar—"a great guy and a really good, versatile player"—he had session men in mind. "Believe me," Kortchmar shares, "I wanted that gig. It wasn't like I wanted to risk everything asking him to try other guys." But first came the meet-up with the existing band. They were slumped in the studio lounge, unenthusiastic to meet him, recalls Kortchmar: "Liberty particularly was kind of defensive in that he was 'Oh, you L.A. guys, I know what you want. You want me to play just like Russ Kunkel, I can do that.' I never said anything, haven't said a word. Yet." In the back of Danny's mind were his intended drummers: "Everybody knows Steve Jordan's one of the most killer funksters ever. He'll cut your throat from across the room with his beat. And Zach Alford is badass."

The band was grudgingly willing to go at a couple of the tracks again. Kortchmar, remembering the band's apathy, seethes about it to this day: "'Okay, you want to hear it again, it goes like this.' No dynamics at all.

"The first thing you learn as a sideman," adds Kortchmar, "and I'd been one for a long time, is you are not James Taylor. You are not Jackson Browne. You are not Billy Joel. They're Billy Joel. And if you don't believe me, go into Madison Square Garden and say, 'Here I am,' see what happens. I've never said, 'I'm so cool, I'm here forever.'"

Relations between Billy and Liberty were strained, and when Billy perceived the same attitude that Kortchmar did, he was willing to make the change. He had watched when Danny asked Liberty to "bring it up," and he had watched when, as Kortchmar recalls, Liberty played the whole song "real quiet." Billy then became resolute about finding new players.

"In that way he's kind of like Keith Richards," says Danny, "who is the sweetest guy you'd ever want to meet—just the loveliest fellow. Right up until you fuck with him."

As the enterprise moved into midtown Manhattan's Hit Factory, Kortchmar's first priority was setting Billy up to bring the most out of what was clearly a heartfelt set of tunes. "Billy is a guy capable of melancholy," he says, "as many great artists are. To be that smart and that talented means you're going to be miserable at least part of the time.

"But he's so lovable, just a lovable guy. And I felt I didn't want to probe into his life, and I also wanted to be very protective. In some ways this is his most personal album. Whatever he was going through, I wanted to make sure that none of us added to it."

"I really wanted to close the door on the whole angst behind the lawsuit stuff," Billy told Tim White in an interview for *Billboard* in December 1994. But exploiting all he'd been through in the legal wrangles was a double-edged sword. Asked if he really wanted to relive it, Billy said he used to make albums, not dispassionately, but reluctantly: "When I had to deliver an album, I would sit down and write. I've reached the point in my life where I'm not gonna write unless I have something to say, and it makes it much more substantial for me to feel that . . . and I did have something to say on this album.

"I think the song 'The River of Dreams' is the critical point," he says. "I keep referring to this character because that's who I was then and not now. When I was writing, I was actually living through these feelings and working things out—a very cathartic album for me in terms of how I was gonna come to grips with the things that were troubling me.

"I didn't realize how pissed off I was until I got halfway through this thing, and I realized what I'd been writing was angry, bitter, mocking, cynical, disappointed, disillusioned. I mean, ever look at the sequence of the songs? The first song was really just 'the whole thing is a cesspool' "—an echo of his father's disturbing sentiment from Billy's boyhood—" 'the whole thing is a crock of shit.' The second song—completely mocking, completely betrayed, wounded. There's a scream at the end of that song, which I don't know if I'll be able to hit that scream again—just this primal thing."

On that cut, "The Great Wall of China," which began with the working title "Frankie My Dear I Don't Give A Damn," Billy vents the rage he had publicly kept bottled up:

> Your role was protective, your soul was too defective . . .
> All the king's men and all the king's horses
> Can't put you together the way you used to be
> We could have gone all the way to the Great Wall of China
> Now all you're going to be is history.

In composing the songs more or less in the sequence they'd follow in the recording process and on the completed album, Billy was returning to his original template—making concept-driven albums, that, in their striving to have a beginning, a middle, and an end, in some ways resembled musicals. "I'm a real album artist," he continues. "I write an album to be an album from beginning to end, and I only write about ten to twelve songs, tops. Then I'm completely exhausted, destroyed at the end of this thing—emotionally, physically, mentally—every which way. I'm empty. It's hell being in the middle of it . . . and there is nothing more satisfying than having written it all."

On an album that was meant to blow the doors off musically even as Billy sorted through some demons, "No Man's Land" was an excellent starting point. He had all the wrath he needed to perform that song as well, he told White: "What's happening is rampant consumerism. . . . We have destroyed a lot of the physical aspects of the country, and the spiritual aspects. It's this ongoing development of suburbia [that] for so many years we're all programmed to think we want, that everybody wants. We'll make a unique manicured place to live out in the sticks, or we'll gentrify the city or all these things that they look nice on the surface. Everything is pretty on the surface, but underneath it's corrupt. The whole thing is built on crap.

"There's a line in the song that says, 'I see children with their boredom and their vacant stares / God help us all if we are to blame for their unanswered prayers.' I may sound like an old rock-and-roll biblical prophet because of the era I come from . . . but I think they're being manipulated by TV, by the fashion industry. I don't think [musicians] are leaders anymore. Rock and roll used to lead the whole thing, and now the tail is wagging the dog."

Kortchmar and Billy struggled at length to find the right setting for the album's title track. "One version was with [vocal group] the Simms Brothers, and that was very doo-woppy," says Kortchmar, "kind of greaseball Arthur Avenue style. Then the Floyd Brothers did a much more gospel-style version. And then [the one with] his own backup singers from the road, led by Crystal Taliefero, was the one Billy wanted."

Says Billy, "What happened when I got to *The River of Dreams* was that I had begun to reaffirm an underlying faith in myself that I had lost. I had questioned my judgment and my faith in mankind . . . lost faith in myself and my ability to discern and my ability to form any kind of judgment about what the hell was going on around me.

"I had always written kind of as an onlooker from a journalistic sense, and then I realized I had been so wrong in my judgment about the people I trusted and held close—how could I have been right about anything else? It kind of just blew me out of the water, and I realized, by the time I got to this song, that I was looking for justice and nobody gets any justice. All you can have is faith. You gotta believe in something or else you're lost—you're in the abyss.

"You can't always reason or know why things are. Some people grasp for religious faith. . . . I just see it as a river where we're caught up in the flow. I say we start in the streams and fall into the ocean. But no matter what, we're just carried along by this thing. So to think we have control is a joke in a way. We're in this thing, and we have to kind of make the best of it."

Billy noted in comments at the time that if he sounds fatalistic, "what really counts is who's standing in the long run, and that's one of the essential elements of that song—who's standing, and why is that? Why do people continue to survive? If someone believes in me, then I guess that I should believe in myself."

"All About Soul" was a fiercely sung studio performance in which Billy's anguished vocal was leavened by harmonies from the vocal group Color Me Badd, as it clearly rummaged through the shards of the relationship:

> This life isn't fair
> It's gonna get dark it's gonna get cold . . .
> It's all about soul
> Who's standing now and who's standing tomorrow.

"Lullabye (Goodnight, My Angel)" had its genesis around this time as a classical piano piece. The words would come to Billy with their own logic, when Alexa asked her father one night what happens when people die.

"Maybe it was my own sensitivity to the difficulties her mother and I were having"—the relationship had been increasingly pockmarked by unpleasant quarrels—"but I read in that question her fears about what was happening within our family," says Billy. "Would we be split apart, with the threesome she'd always known never to be made whole again?"

For all his wish for family solidarity, Billy had also been touring a lot. In 1993 Alexa would turn eight. "That's a terrible time for a father to be away from a child," says Billy. "You have so much to learn about each other. I was just so crazy about her. I just loved having a kid, and of course I didn't want to be away. Christie had put her career on hold and was spending lots of time with her. But during those absences, Christie and I drifted apart. Combined with the toll the lawsuits had taken on us, well, it was a full-time job trying to hold the relationship together.

"You hear in the music of 'Lullabye' a father talking to his daughter," he says, "with alternating major and minor chords. It's almost like a dying man singing to his child. And he's trying to reassure his daughter, which is what the major key is, but he's also hinting at the fact that there will be separation. And that's where the minor key changes come in. Where there's not a minor, there are suspensions—chords that take longer to resolve—so you have the anxiety of the unresolved chord, then the release of tension when it does resolve":

> Goodnight my angel
> Now it's time to dream
> And dream how wonderful your life will be
> Someday your child may cry
> And if you sing this lullabye
> Then in your heart
> There will always be a part of me.

"On the surface it's the father saying it to a child, but beyond that it was me comforting myself. My mother sang a lullaby to me. She would sing, 'The cutest little fella, everybody knows' from the old lullaby

'Mighty Like a Rose.' But she didn't know all the words so she would sing 'lu, lu, lu, lu lu . . .'"

What Billy came to discover during playback of the recording in the studio was, although "I didn't even perceive at the time I was doing this, there's an instrumental segment in the middle and I'm going 'lu, lu, lu . . .' I got all choked up when I realized that I was doing this—I'm passing along that comforting lullaby sound."

Billy didn't really think he and Christie were in imminent danger of breaking up at that point, but their disputes had increased in intensity over the years, to the point of drawing attention around 1990–91 in dubious reports from the *National Enquirer.* Finally one day Christie reportedly did something that shocked him. The two were having an argument, and at some point in the fight, Christie threatened to take Alexa away from Billy. He remembers her saying, in paraphrase, "I can make it so you can't see her."

Billy's overwhelming feeling at that moment was *Don't say that. Call me every name in the book, but don't threaten to take away my daughter.* "It felt like a knife went into my heart," he says. My first thought was *Wait a minute, I didn't have my father. Now you're going to not let me be a father? Are you out of your fuckin' mind?* Remember that scene in *The Godfather* where [Al Pacino's] Michael is fighting with [Diane Keaton's] Kay, and he says, 'You won't take my children!' I could never let that happen. It just kind of popped into my head. You will never do that. I will never not be her father."

Whether Christie was being serious or not, then and there something snapped inside Billy. Although it would be years before the two even started talking about splitting up, things would never be the same.

As the marriage crumbled irreversibly, one priority remained. "I give Christie and myself credit," Billy says, "for eventually uniting, through whatever tempests and accusations, around the ultimate priority of trying to ensure Alexa's happiness. The irony is you love your kid so much that she becomes the very thing that causes your worst conflicts.

"Christie likes to joke that the end of the marriage, which was an emotional fact by late 1993 [and ironically hit the tabloids on their anniversary, March 23, 1994, precisely nine years after their wedding date], spelled the end of my songwriting career. At least I think it's a joke."

On paper, she's not wrong. The song "Famous Last Words" closed Billy's 1993 album *River of Dreams*. "I can still hear the bitterness and disappointment I was feeling at that time, and then a grasping for a renewal of faith that happened on the second side of the album," says Billy. "It's about a guy who goes through a whole period of disenchantment and disillusionment and anger, but who finds his faith being renewed in things like family and children, the things that are important in life. And with that transition, the album feels to me like a cohesive journey."

After all the years of groping for words and chain-smoking and engaging in the unhealthy behavior that can go with songwriting, Billy wrote "The River of Dreams" pretty much in one straight shot. "I almost felt like I was sleepwalking as I wrote it, scribbling lyrics down one morning, and they didn't change much at all from that first draft," he says.

In fact, he actually dreamed the song. "And when I woke up the next morning, my first thought was that it seemed like it was a three-chord song, a one-four-five progression, which has been done a billion times. And I thought, *I can't write that—it's too simple.*

"But then I got in the shower, and I was going, 'Hatch-u-ati-ati, in the middle of the night . . .' over and over, and figuring that if I couldn't shake it, it meant I should write it. So I sat down at the piano and tweaked it just a bit—and pretty soon I was singing, 'In the middle of the night / I go walking in my sleep,' and it just flowed from there":

> *. . . from the mountains of faith to a river so deep*
> *I must be looking for something*
> *Something sacred I lost*
> *But the river is wide*
> *And it's too hard to cross.*

Even as Billy was writing the song, he was thinking to himself, *Why the hell am I doing this? I'm not a preacher; this sounds like a sermon*: "And even though I know the river is wide / I walk down every evening and I stand on the shore . . . So I can finally find out what I've been looking for."

"It's a searching song, because I really was looking for a way to renew my faith in man," says Billy. "I was just so shattered by the betrayal I'd experienced. I'd lost faith in humanity and I was looking for a way to find it again—without getting 'born again.' "

When it was released, *River of Dreams* immediately charted at number one in *Billboard*, and ticket sales for the upcoming tour, which would include six nights at Madison Square Garden, were strong.

Not just the dissolution of his second marriage but the bitter end of Frank Management would reverberate in Billy's seemingly final pop album. It was a rough stretch with agonies both public and private. As a lyric from *River of Dreams* paraphrased the old spiritual, "Nobody knows about the trouble I've seen."

Some fifteen years later Billy pulled up on his motorcycle to a Japanese restaurant in Southampton for some take-out food. There in the parking lot stood Frank, who'd been lunching there. Billy remembers that Frank looked to be in shock—"Maybe wondering if I was going to punch him. I said, 'Hey, Frank.' "

Frank answered "hi" very tentatively, and Billy asked him how he was doing. Then the two shook hands. "To me it was water under the bridge," says Billy. "It's just like the lyric from 'The Great Wall of China' ":

You take a piece of whatever you touch
Too many pieces means you're touching too much
You never win if you can't play it straight
You only beat me if you get me to hate.

"I just wanted to let Frank know, *I'm not walking around hating you, and I hope that part of our lives is over.*"

CHAPTER 13

THE NIGHT IS STILL YOUNG

I t's pretty obvious to anyone who knows Billy's music that it's often about him trying to figure out—"*haplessly* trying to figure out," as he says—his relationships. That's the skeleton key. And perhaps none has been more deeply explored—and fought for—than his relationship with Christie Brinkley. By 1993 the storybook romance had descended into something bitter and all too public.

One of the daggers in the heart of the relationship would be tied to Liberty DeVitto. Billy had gradually been building a casual, chatty friendship with Carolyn Beegan, who worked for a company that catered all of Billy's shows in the New York area. While the two wouldn't, in fact, be linked until after the split with Christie, those backstage at the time relate that Liberty assumed that Billy was having an affair with Carolyn when he discovered that Billy hadn't returned home after his concert on New Year's Eve 1993.

However, Carolyn wasn't actually the reason he was detained. The truth is that Billy had played the Nassau Coliseum that night and fallen off the piano, bashing his face. Since he had a cold to boot, he decided that he wasn't in good enough shape to handle the drive back to East Hampton. Instead, he stayed at the Garden City Hotel nearby, where the band camped out, and Billy had reserved a room just in case. Carolyn was working Janet Jackson's show that night at Madison Square

Garden, and the two had no contact. However, the rumor that the two had had a tryst found its way back to Christie.

Months later the truth would be established, but it seemed the unfounded story not only pushed Christie over the edge, causing her to decide *Screw this, we're done,* but also led Alexa to mistrust Billy's loyalty to the family. (As Billy's inner circle observed, Liberty had ready access to Christie's ear since his wife, Mary, was very close with her. "It was all very *Peyton Place,*" says Billy.)

Christie had been very supportive when Billy was operated on for kidney stones, but by late 1993, as they were effectively separated, she was spending time with the man who would become her next husband, real estate developer Rick Taubman.

Then, on Friday, April 1, 1994, Christie and Rick were heli-skiing 12,800 feet up a mountain outside Telluride, Colorado, when their helicopter crashed in fifty-mile-per-hour winds. Billy was scheduled to play a gig in Dallas, but when he got word of what had happened, he flew to Colorado and found his way to Christie at the hospital near Telluride, where she'd been transported. She had painful but not life-threatening injuries, as did Taubman. Billy took her and Alexa, who had been staying in Colorado as well, back to Long Island. To Billy's aggravation, Christie and her assistant spent a good deal of time in whispered communication. Although Billy and Christie been separated for a while and the two hadn't talked much about what was going on in her life leading up to the heli-skiing crash, technically he was still her husband, and he wanted to lend support. But Billy didn't feel that he could stay home with her—he still had about a month and a half of tour dates that he felt he couldn't cancel. When he returned from the tour, Christie was gone, back to Colorado, and eight-year-old Alexa was with her. He was greeted by a basically empty house, save for some unwanted Sri Lankan lounge chairs and funky-looking tables.

Christie would marry Taubman in December 1994, having divorced Billy in August, and she would divorce Taubman the following year, having given birth in June to their son Jack. At the height of his marriage's unraveling, on April 8, Billy announced plans to take to the road with Elton John on a "Face to Face" tour that would crisscross America in midsummer, playing major outdoor venues. Anticipating that undertaking hardly improved his mood. About a week after the tour announcement (as Billy's longtime friend Billy Zampino would tell Tim White), Billy put an ad lib in his set for a Florida gig. A local writer had assumed that "Movin' Out (Anthony's Song)" was in the set as a reference to Christie; in reaction, Billy cut it and subbed in "Shades of Grey." As an intro, though, he played an excerpt from Samuel Barber's mournful "Adagio for Strings."

Billy was very depressed, all but dysfunctional, during this time, and relations between he and Christie varied between cold and stormy. The lawsuit with Frank had wiped him out financially, and now the road owned him. But at least on tour he could go on autopilot, shuffle through his days, and draw what energy he needed from the crowds each show night.

Despite the stress he was under—not to mention all the temptations that went with being a musician in the 1970s and 1980s—Billy never succumbed to the chronic use of hard drugs that many rockers practiced. Unlike John Lennon, who dropped acid with George Harrison and famously called *Rubber Soul* "the pot album" when he and the Beatles were making it, Billy never experienced drugs as being helpful creatively.

"I'd like to be able to say I tuned in and waxed creative along with my heroes, but in fact, my adventures with acid totaled all of three," says Billy. The first acid trip, in the early 1970s, was a wonderful experience for him. He was living at Sandy and John Gibson's house in Malibu. They were tripping and listening to music when they all realized they were terrifically hungry. So they ordered food from the local deli, the Bagela, which was also their pot connection. The delivery kid arrived with their order and started laughing at them because they were so high. "I was trying to pay for the food, but it was a struggle to write 'William Joel' on a check with rockets screaming through my brain. If that's the acid test, I'm pretty sure I flunked. Then we proceeded to consume massive quantities of pastrami, ham, and coleslaw, Coneheads style, with our hands."

The second trip was also in Malibu, and it was terrible. "I saw Elizabeth's head turn into a skull and a snake and a phantom as I was floating above the room," he remembers. "It took hours of listening to James Taylor and Gordon Lightfoot to mellow out. I just kept saying, 'Oh, God, please, James, help me.'"

Trip number three, with Brian Ruggles, was a short one. It was 1974, and Billy was living in the Hollywood Hills on Mulholland Drive, in a house overlooking the Hollywood Bowl. He had just gotten his first Moog synthesizer and had big Altec Lansing speakers in his garage. He and Brian plugged the synthesizer into the gigantic speakers and tried out different noises. "It sounded like rocket ships taking off—weird, noisy, cosmic space sounds—so Brian and I decided we were going to form a group," says Billy. "We'd call ourselves the Vree-Oo and Bleep-Bleeps Space Band. My job was to write lyrics and sing; his was just to press the buttons. Brian is a funny guy to hang out with no matter what you're doing; he has this great laugh. So we had a nutty trip that lasted three or four hours. We made so much noise, the neighbors must have thought we were blowing the place up. For acid, that was it—I never tripped again."

The most prevalent recreational drug of the era was cocaine. In the 1970s it still carried a certain jazz-era cachet, and its popularity among musicians, though not yet the general public, was growing. By the mid-1970s it was the drug of choice in every corner of the music business. "Everybody was holding and everybody was sharing," says Billy, so if someone ran out of the "Aztec marching powder" (to use P. J. O'Rourke's phrase) or the funds to buy more—cocaine seemed expensive even to Billy, who could easily afford it—there was plenty to go around.

Like those in his circle, Billy might take a toot now and then, but he understood it was a dubious aid for writing or performing. On those few occasions when he did, he regretted it, because his throat would tighten and he would talk too much onstage. One night, after a concert during which he was high, he stood up from his piano and vowed to himself, *That's the end of that.*

In Billy's opinion, problems come when you mix coke into what is supposed to be a serious conversation: "The chatter becomes very righteous—what we used to call 'valid.' You're so *valid,* and everything you have to say is so important and rational and meaningful. But that's a delusion: you're just yapping your head off because your jaw needs to move, as in 'I love you, man.' It's an ego drug. You think everything you have to say is so necessary that no one can miss hearing it, when in fact you're incoherent—also sexually useless. Basically it's one of the dumbest drugs in the world."

Billy experimented with heroin only once, in Holland, on a plane from Amsterdam to Stockholm with his road gang. The song on *The Nylon Curtain* called "Scandinavian Skies"—a kind of latter-day stab at a "Strawberry Fields Forever"—refers to this experience. It was intended as a lark, a random taste of the forbidden for the latter-day Mean Brothers. "We'd been drinking, and there was some Dutch guy who somebody knew, and somebody said, 'It's safe, it's okay,' and I remember it was a new syringe." On the commercial flight, succumbing to nausea, as most first-timers will, he used the airsickness bag, and for a moment the psychological plunge was vertiginous. And then, "even though I was as wrecked as I've ever been in my life, I was also able to understand why people got hung up on the stuff. It was one of the most euphoric highs I've ever had," he says. "You just feel so good that you can't bear not feeling that way all the time, and that's what scared the living hell out of me. I recognized just how dangerous that feeling was, and I guess I had enough self-discipline to avoid it after that—although just looking around at all the junked-out rock stars who littered the scene by then might have been motivation enough."

Shortly after leaving the West Coast and returning to New York, Billy was finished dabbling with pot, too. All it took was a bit of chemically induced paranoia: "I smoked what turned out to be my last joint in the Upper East Side apartment that Elizabeth and I shared, and then I thought I'd stroll down Madison Avenue. But as soon as I walked outside, I panicked. I was convinced beyond any doubt that every single person in New York City, certainly those within eyeshot, could tell I was stoned. And I said to myself, *This sucks.* It brought me back to the day in 1966 when my high school vice principal, seeing my stubble and bloodshot eyes—the result of my playing gigs into the wee hours and then popping out of bed to go to school—called me into his office and said, 'You're stoned on pot, aren't you?' I wasn't. And now it was time to just say nope again."

Alcohol was, for better or worse, Billy's drug of choice—and the one that created a thorny problem for him in terms of drawing the line. "Alcohol was the most relied-upon escape from whatever ailed me, whether it was social, emotional, or psychological in nature," says Billy. "No matter what, alcohol was always there for me.

"Alcohol is so socially acceptable that it amounts to a kind of religion, with dedicated houses of worship spread around the globe—they're called bars. It's part of a lifestyle, especially in the Northeast, where, at a certain socioeconomic level, it's often the center of the community. Ireland is like that, as the U2 boys showed me when we went to Dublin. England has its pub culture; Germany has one too. Even the French have their wine bars. When you go on the road, where do the local big shots want to take you? To their favorite bar. Booze is just an ingrained part of our shared experience, across the globe, and that's doubly true in rock-and-roll circles.

"But if you do go over the line, you have an issue. Some people never believe they have a problem—or maybe they have the problem and don't really recognize it. As a high-profile guy who eventually went to rehab, I have always felt a certain amount of pressure to be some kind of spokesperson about it. But I've never been comfortable with that."

Billy recalls seeing a big billboard in L.A. with David Crosby's picture on it, along with the slogan DON'T DO DRUGS, shortly after Crosby had had a very public reckoning with his own history—right down to a weapons charge and a liver transplant. "So there it was, 'Don't do drugs'—and it's not that I disliked David Crosby, but I got so pissed off looking at that sign. My thought was, *You've had your innings. Who the hell are you to tell other people what they can and can't do? You got wasted and you blew all your money. Well, good luck with that, but it's not the world's problem.*

"I often get all bent out of shape with these temperance spokespeople reminding everyone, *I know better than you*. Sorry, no, you don't; you're no better than me. You were just an idiot, and now it's my turn to be an idiot. So anytime I've been asked to talk about it—sorry, no thanks.

"The truth is, I don't know much about sobriety. I know a hell of a lot about drinking. And there's no point in my talking about that, because everybody has his or her own experience. So I'm not going to be the poster boy for AA. I don't really follow the program. Yet I'm not going to diss it, either, because it works for a lot of people. As I see it, I had my time, I came through it, and that's that."

BILLY HAS ALWAYS been a contradictory mix, sometimes a loner, sometimes almost desperately eager for female companionship. One thing he's seldom done is go for long without a woman in his life. It was obvious to his cadre that after his breakup with Christie, the Carolyn relationship would take root—she had an expansive but also breezily accommodating personality. Carolyn often went on tour with Billy during their time together, to Europe and Asia, and was part of the road gang for the initial 1994 tour with Elton John. Billy even took her to Christie's next wedding, to Peter Cook in September 1996.

All the guys in Billy's circle loved Carolyn, a working-class girl from Queens who was "like the Shirley MacLaine to our Rat Pack," says Billy. "Put her in a gown—like the one she wore at my *Godfather*-themed fiftieth birthday party—and she looked like Rita Hayworth come back to life: tall, angular, all dramatic curves and high cheekbones and a mane of red hair." The latter attribute was never lost on Billy, back to the days of Patti Lee Berridge. "Her sense of humor came directly out of her keen intellect. She knew history, she knew literature, but she used that knowledge without pedantry. And she was always ready to make a night of it. Carolyn was just like one of the boys, but with a hell of a hollow leg: she could drink those boys right under the table."

The road dogs could be something of a tough crowd, even for male newbies. Not everyone can handle being on the road in close quarters and often under duress, a life Billy compared to "running off with pirates." Though stories about touring as a rock band—the groupies, drugs, backstage fighting—are legendary, it has been said that until you've been in the thick of it, you really don't know it. Touring involves much in the way of puerile humor, which, in the context of a rock tour's garrison mentality, can seem a lot funnier when you're there.

A typical example Billy cites was the band trying to crack him up while he whistled the intro to "The Stranger": "They've never been too proud to act like idiots to do it, either, like the time they all blacked out their teeth and grinned at me in unison as I started that supposedly forlorn intro. But payback is always available when you're the bandleader." He owned the floor and the microphone, plus a ready audience, when it came time to taunt his mates.

After adding a new face to the band—master trumpeter and flugelhorn player Carl Fischer, who received his musical graduate degree as part of the great Maynard Ferguson's band—it was Billy's duty to introduce him at concerts, to "let people know he's about to blow them away. So because Carl is at least feasibly Austrian, and he's a big, jolly guy, I began doing ersatz Schwarzenegger impressions—'Yah, da Trumpinator's gunna play for you now . . .' The you-had-to-be-there part is watching how uncomfortable this makes him."

According to Billy, the point to all of the humor was to keep the band loose—to keep them "on the front foot." Sometimes the band couldn't believe where Billy went with these bits. One time in Hong Kong, instead of singing the line "She can ruin your faith with her casual lies" from "She's Always a Woman," Billy sang, "She can ruin your face with her powerful thighs." "Trust me, if you do it straight-faced and sing your heart out, the band cracks up. It's the little things that keep you going when you're on the road," says Billy.

"Sometimes, when I'm singing onstage, my mind wanders—to some buried moment in my own life, or even to *Where's a good steakhouse in this town?*—and suddenly I can't get back. Then I'll shoot a glance at another member of the band, like *I'm losing the lyric, where the hell am I?* And they'll always pretty much know where I am, because they're cue-ing what they play partly based on where I am in the song."

Billy used to shoot this glance to Liberty DeVitto all the time, espe-cially when it came to playing "Just the Way You Are." One night, when he was supposed to be singing, "I couldn't love you any better" (which is followed by the line "I love you just the way you are"), Billy reached "I couldn't love you" and got lost, singing "uh-oh . . . hunnhhh . . . nnn huuuh hnnhnn . . ." Liberty helpfully threw in, "She got the house, she got the car . . ."

Billy understood that people had been coming to his concerts chiefly to see him and couldn't necessarily name the musicians around him, but he always felt that, onstage, you couldn't separate them; it was all about the band dynamic. He believes that you can always tell when musicians are having fun onstage: "If it's a slog for any one of them, the audience will know it. It'll drag the whole arena down. So it was very important to me that the band's morale be way up and stay there; I need them to be kicking this thing as much as they can; I need them to sell it, play it, believe in it as much as I do. Otherwise, it all comes down to me alone."

Mistakes are going to happen with any band, he says: "Someone will miss a change, there'll be a clinker now and again." To Billy these errors are forgivable and forgettable—once the band has properly mocked the culprit after the gig. (He's not immune; after a few miscues he com-mitted vocally and on the piano in a mid-2014 Phoenix, Arizona, show while dogged by allergies, Billy sent the band an e-mail saying, "Sorry for all my clams.") But the one thing he won't excuse onstage is an absence of clear commitment: "Nothing is more important up there than passion—that's what it takes to have a successful performance. And I don't think I've ever lost sight of that. Even if you're not feeling all that hot up there, or you're sick or just not in the mood, you've still got to make that gig work. You've got to give a hundred percent no matter how you're feeling, and that takes its toll, emotionally and physically."

The tough part, he adds, "is when you're not getting a great response from the audience—especially when coming off a few dates of being spoiled in cities where the fans are fervent. Whether you work the audience into a frenzy, or they psych you up into one—it works both ways—the effect is kind of like sex. There's this exchange of energy and enthusiasm: you make them feel great, and so they make noise, and then it's your turn to feel great, and you make noise. By the end of the show, it's just, boom, there's this big orgasm of applause, and everybody's going *Ahhhh.* Then, when it's over"—he laughs at his own analogy as it winds down—"you have a smoke and bathe in the afterglow of your performance.

"That's really what you hope for, anyway. It's what you go for every time. You work it and work it and work it—you're supposed to kill yourself up there. And if you're going to do it right, that's exactly the way to do it."

This exchange across the footlights was exactly what had made the concerts in the Soviet Union in August 1987 so much fun for Billy. The whole experience, especially onstage, was an exercise in subversion. "It was like they had no idea what to expect other than the very worst [disruptive energy], and we kind of liked that: *Oh, we represent danger! For the first time in my life, I'm a threat to something! This is fantastic. What power!* You can literally feel the sense of electricity bouncing back and forth between you and the audience."

By contrast, apathy can unexpectedly rule in certain venues, in certain cities. "When there's no vibe happening, no connection between you and them—then you're like a soothing dose of herbal tea. It's a bit of a downer, and everyone in the band and the road crew can sense it."

Japan is a country where the politeness of audiences can often and notably does override the enthusiasm—the kind of audience that Billy terms "an all-too-respectful oil painting that can border on hostility." But the band has encountered tepid audiences on random nights all over—in Canada, England, and Holland, among other places. "When an audience like that is out there, I'll look over at Wayne Williams, my keyboard technician, and he'll be shrugging his shoulders, as if to say, *What are you going to do?* We dread it," says Billy.

A joking approach can be dangerous, as the band discovered one April Fool's night in Chattanooga, Tennessee. Billy and the band went onstage and played their first song, then, with a few hollered thank-you's and appreciative waves, bounded off the stage as a group.

"Hilarious, right? April Fool, right? And 'Let's make sure it really takes, let's give it a good couple minutes,'" recalls Billy. "Then the crew guys were coming back saying, 'They're getting really kind of pissed off.' We finally came back out. 'Okay, April Fool.' But the rest of the night was a smelly, cold, dead mackerel, just lying there, and we could not save that show no matter how hard we tried."

All over the United States, and in Germany and Mexico, Billy and the band regularly see audiences "go apeshit." "It sometimes makes me want to say to those other crowds, 'Aren't you folks having fun? I'm trying to make you feel good, baby. Let me know *something*. Give me a little feedback.'"

Experience and age have wrung most of the vanity out of Billy: "It's when you lose sight of your role as a court jester and start taking yourself too seriously, like you're the oracle of Delphi or something, that you've got a problem. As dark as my life has felt at times, I've always been able to get onstage and keep sight of the fact that I'm just a clown with bells hanging off his head."

The self-deprecation doesn't mean he can't trace his métier back to some of the classical greats he so admires. "I've read a lot about Beethoven, so I know he resented the great class divide. Everybody who came before him had been hired to write music and perform for dukes and counts and princes and barons. And then Beethoven came along and said, 'I'm not coming in through the kitchen door. I'm coming in through the front door like everybody else; I'm an artist.' I respect that and I relate to it. But I am paid to be an entertainer. So I'm just hoping to get in and get out and put on a good show in between.

"At this point in time, I also have to consider that my core fans, baby boomers, don't go to concerts the way they used to, and they're not as wild when they do. So there's not a whole lot of sexual tension you can feed on when you're up onstage. I wasn't exactly a matinee idol to begin with, and these days, when I'm playing 'Still Rock and Roll to Me' and doing my Elvis thing, flipping the mike stand around and stuff, I often feel like an idiot.

"I mean, I'm having a *great* time making believe this is what Elvis would do, but I've got no hair and I look funny on the screen, and it's almost as if I'm sending up that whole hip-shaking thing, which is not why I'm doing it. I'm actually just forgetting my age. I'm gyrating because I feel, for a couple minutes anyhow, like I'm sixteen years old."

IN THE SUMMER of 1998, Billy didn't feel sixteen. He was exhausted from touring the globe—and the tour wasn't over yet—and he wasn't taking the best care of himself: "It started to feel like I was back on the treadmill that summer as we got ready to perform in the U.K. with a series of dates booked with Elton John." What came to pass in the weeks that followed would mark a low point in relations with the Englishman.

"We did a show in Japan, and Billy blew his voice out really bad," remembers Steve Cohen, who by then had grown into the role of production designer. "We were on our way to Scotland, and he knew on that flight that he was going to have a problem. We landed, and instead of taking four days off and going to bed and taking care of himself, he was with Carolyn Beegan, and we decided to go drinking. We were going to drink in every pub in Scotland—you know, where they make the Scotch.

"We were going to Mecca. It was like a junkie going to the poppy fields in Afghanistan. And I remember looking at him, thinking, *This is going to be bad*, because he had this real I-don't-give-a-fuck attitude—*My voice is gone, and it's just going to go, and there's nothing I can do about it.*

"And I was thinking, *No, Billy, there is something you can do about it.*

"So we did Scotland, we did Ireland, we hung out with the guys in U2, and it just got worse and worse and worse. Every show was tougher and tougher and tougher, but he's so powerful with a head of steam; you're either on the bus or you're off the bus, and I chose to stay on the bus."

A throat specialist in Dublin warned Billy not to stress his voice and to rest as much as he could. But by the time the band got to Glasgow, he was already headed for a bout of sinusitis and general fatigue. Looming just ahead were a pair of early June shows at London's Wembley Stadium, the "Hallowed Turf" of international soccer matches and near the top of the bucket list for the biggest rock acts to play.

"We were doing the concerts with Elton, and I was sort of the go-between between the two camps," says Cohen. "And whenever Billy would fuck up or something would happen, my phone would ring, and it would be Elton saying, 'Listen, we've got to look out for our boy. Tell me what's going on. Is there anything I can do or fucking yell at him for?'

"It was torturous. We were in London, and there were a couple of moves that could've been made that could've saved the tour—namely, to cancel a Manchester show and a Birmingham show. But it turned out that on Elton's previous solo tour, he had thrown a hissy fit in Manchester—he'd walked offstage—so he couldn't cancel two times in a row. He had to play. But if we'd blown off Manchester, we would've had six days off, and Billy would've definitely recovered; we would have played the Wembley shows in London; and we would have done what was going to be a big deal, an HBO special.

"Elton would not cancel, saying 'I don't give a fuck. I don't give a fuck. He's not taking care of himself.' That was his attitude. So Billy just continued. He was getting sicker and sicker. And in the Dorchester Hotel in London, I came into his room, and he and Carolyn were lying in bed. It was, like, five o'clock in the afternoon, and I said, 'How do you feel?'

"And Billy said, 'You know that scene from *Patton* where they ask Patton how he feels after he got fired for the second time?' And then he did this George C. Scott impression from *Patton*. He said, 'God, I feel low.'" Soon afterward he and Carolyn boarded the Concorde, flying home. The illness that developed from there took Billy six months to beat.

The collapse of the co-billed tour dates in the United Kingdom would scatter consequences across the years. Elton would resent Billy's canceling, and Billy would resent Elton proceeding with the dates solo (even throwing in a couple of Billy tunes, including "Piano Man"), dimming future prospects for Billy and Elton touring those cities singly or together.

But a few months later, after Billy had recovered, he received one of the great honors of his career, and it gave him the major lift he badly needed.

THERE'S AN AXIOM that all manner of public figures become respectable if they hang around long enough, and in late 1998 Billy was informed that, having reached the Rock and Roll Hall of Fame's minimum twenty-five-year anniversary of the release of his first record, he was on the short list for induction the following year. Five years prior, he'd attended the Hall's groundbreaking tenth-anniversary ceremony in Cleveland, along with Pete Townshend and Little Richard. He would be there again for its twenty-fifth-anniversary celebration, held at Madison Square Garden in October 2009. But a nomination for admission into the hall isn't a guarantee of being voted in, and in 1999 two of the places were assuredly going to his fellow nominees Paul McCartney and Bruce Springsteen. (Ultimately joining them were performers Curtis Mayfield, Del Shannon, Dusty Springfield, and the Staples Singers.)

In the end Billy was voted in, and that evening, March 15, 1999, felt more significant to him than all the Grammy ceremonies that brought him awards over the years. When he heard that Ray Charles himself would induct him, he was all the more gratified. Ray did not disappoint, winning fervent applause as soon as he appeared onstage. With his wonderfully ragged-but-right style of speechifying, he gave Billy a great introduction, in which feeling, at times, trumped coherence:

I'm here to say something to you that, sincerely from my heart. . . . My friend, Billy Joel, I want you to know, first of all, I genuinely love and respect this man. He's ultratalented—that's number one. Now, some of you are gonna say, "Well, wait a minute, now—where do you come off. . . . Why do you feel like that, Ray?" Well, I'll give you just a little insight into my brain. First of all, if you think about a man who has maybe thirty-seven, thirty-eight huge hits, thirteen of 'em went in the top ten, three of 'em were number one, that gives you what they say, "the proof of the pudding is in the eating."

Billy Joel said, "I want to play my music from my experience," which said to me he wanted to play his music according to the life that he saw around him, what was important to him. Beautiful man. Piano Man, they call him. I like that. "Just the Way You Are," yeah, okay, man, I hear that. And you know—I don't want to bring myself too much into this, but I have to say, to me, he wrote one of the most beautiful songs that we sung together, called "Me and My Baby Grand," you know. And I guess I'll leave you with this thought, because he said it himself. He said, "Yeah, but it's still rock and roll to me." I like that. All right. All right. Did y'all hear and see all of that? I would like to say, ladies and gentlemen, it is truly my privilege to introduce a man, as I said earlier, that I truly love and admire, into the Rock and Roll Hall of Fame: Mr. Billy Joel. You're inducted, Brother. You're inducted now. I got you!

Ray seemed like a tough act to follow, but Billy had prepared some remarks, and he managed a few thank-you's to some of his longtime bandmates and crew members, including Ruggles, Cohen, and production manager Bobby Thrasher. The emotions flooded in as he spoke. "Can you believe this?" he began.

That's the Washington Monument, you know? . . . I've had the most amazing life, and it's mostly because of rock-and-roll music. I love all kinds of music, and I'm right now writing what would be considered romantic mid-nineteenth-century classical music. . . . Music has made such a wonderful life for me. . . .

Now, I grew up in Levittown, okay? Not exactly the epicenter of soul in America, you know? . . . So where were we gonna find soul? Where were we gonna find the soul of America? You know where we got it? We got it from the radio. We got it from rock-and-roll music—that's where we got it from. And I'm not talking about Pat Boone. And I'm not talking about Fabian. And I'm not talking about Frankie Avalon. I'm talking about Ray Charles, and Little Richard, and Chuck Berry, and Fats Domino, and Wilson Pickett, and James Brown, and Otis Redding, and Little Anthony and the Imperials, and Frankie Lymon and the Teenagers—that's where we got it. So I wanna thank those people, 'cause they were the real pioneers. And I know I've been referred to as derivative.

The charge still rankles: "What I said that night was, if being derivative was a reason to exclude a musician from being inducted, then there wouldn't be any white people here at all." He concluded, " I know we're on TV, but we've gotta get some outrageous shit started here, you know what I mean?

Then they got the obligatory jam going, and due both to the elite cadre of musicians present and to the raw emotion that followed Paul McCartney's tribute to his recently deceased wife Linda, the evening would be described by *Rolling Stone* as "the most emotionally moving, musically satisfying night the Hall has ever seen." The stage was crowded with musicians, Billy's peers, and even his idols. He even got to kick off "Let It Be," singing the first verse himself. Then Paul McCartney made his way onstage and took it home.

* * *

BY THE FALL of that year, 1999, Carolyn and Billy were nearing the end of a great run. They had traveled the world together, and she had stood beside him both figuratively, as a boon companion who could handle herself well in any setting, and literally, such as when they stood at the door of his house on his fiftieth birthday greeting his friends and family. But the things she wanted and needed from the relationship—stability, starting a family of her own—just weren't what Billy could offer at that stage.

While Carolyn and Billy never really lived together, she may have been hoping they'd get married someday—although Billy had told her from the start that he didn't want that again. He was still feeling burned from his second failed marriage to Christie, and he was pretty sure it would be a mistake to go for a third. If she wanted a chance at marriage and kids, Billy wasn't going to stand in the way.

The couple finally accepted romantic defeat one night shortly before the end of the year. It was the dawn of the new millennium, and to Billy it seemed like everybody was trying to reprioritize, to do the right thing. He was thinking about Carolyn and himself—how they weren't going anywhere—and it felt to him like a stalled situation. So after a series of very amicable conversations, they decided to go forward as friends, before any bitterness developed. By all accounts, Carolyn seemed to agree, although Billy learned later that she had been seen parked in a driveway not too long afterward, sobbing that it was really over.

Looking back, it might have been naïve for Billy to assume that no matter what happened later in his life, he and Carolyn had built such a strong bond that their friendship could survive anything. But then he started seeing Trish Bergin, who wasn't keen on him maintaining his close friendship with Carolyn. Years later, neither was his future wife Katie Lee. "Nobody wants an old flame around," says Billy. "You're only asking to get burned."

CHAPTER 14

MOVIN' OUT, AGAIN

Part of the reason there's been almost no new pop music from Billy since 1993 is that after eleven albums of thorough self-revelation, he felt a barrier building, preventing him from writing much about his personal life. He'd given a great deal away in his lyrics over the years, revealed a lot emotionally, and he "just plain didn't want to do that anymore."

Early on, his label, his band, and his fans on the street must have been baffled as to why he'd stop at this stage. The title cut from *River of Dreams* came out on the last day of July 1993 and quickly rose to number three on the singles charts. The album followed ten days later and became his first album to enter the charts at number one, in the third week of August. Three more singles charted, though not as impressively.

The reviewers reached deep in their praise, with *Rolling Stone* saying Billy was "diving further into the philosophical abyss of middle age with the fury of a dreamer searching for an answer before time fades away." *Entertainment Weekly* called the album "a popmeister's epiphany, a pensive record that manages to be irresistible." *Billboard* pointed out that this was his fastest-selling album ever and a top-ten hit in many foreign markets. The by-now-familiar Stephen Holden byline in the *New York Times* review of an October 4 Madison Square Garden show said

that both Billy's performance and the success of the new album suggested that "he is one of a handful of pop entertainers who need not fear
middle-aged obsolescence."

But neither the praise nor the avid commercial reception seemed
to induce Billy to make plans for the next album, and his resistance
speaks to the sincerity of his stance, which by now few doubt. His deep
reluctance to further dredge up and churn out his inner self in his music
is evidenced in an experience he had—*almost* writing a song. One night
on his 2008 Australian tour, sitting at a baby grand piano in a nearly
empty nighttime bar in a Melbourne hotel, Billy played a few chords to
a poignant melody he was still hashing out. It was a love song that had
been in his head, and in the bar that evening he got an idea for a lyric.
The visual in his head was of a young woman standing on a hill in a
meadow calling to an older man, "Come on, come with me. Don't stay
mired in the past."

The song, according to Billy, had a bit of an "Innocent Man" feeling,
and it moved into an even more direct beseeching—*Come, trust me. I'm
not those people, I'm not your past. I'm the future, come with me.* "Though
it would probably make for a damn good song," said Billy, he wouldn't
be writing that one. It felt too personal, and at this point Billy claimed
to not enjoy sorting through his romantic history.

But while Billy's decision to stop writing for a pop audience roughly
coincided with the Christie breakup, it wasn't only about that—or Billy's fatigue with the music business. It was largely because he felt he
could continue to express himself musically without having to struggle
to find the right words, and without grinding on as part of the machine
that was engineered to create and distribute pop music.

In a sense, the classical compositions that would make up his next
album, 2001's *Fantasies & Delusions*, forced themselves into being. The
inspiration for these pieces would come somewhat randomly to Billy.
"Waltz No. 1" is subtitled "Nunley's Carousel," after an old carousel,
built around 1912, that is part of Nunley's Amusement Park, the Long

Island family institution that closed in 1995. That waltz would have an added life when it was adopted by classical pianist Jeffrey Biegel, who had grown up riding that same carousel (and had taken piano lessons from a friend of Billy's dad's named Morton Estrin). Biegel assembled a concerto based on "Waltz No. 1" and several of Billy's other *Fantasies* pieces that he called "Symphonic Fantasies for Piano and Orchestra."

Another waltz had been playing in Billy's head for a while, and one day it just started to spill out. He happened to be in midtown Manhattan, near the Steinway showroom where he was well known, so he walked in and asked to use a piano. They offered him the Rachmaninoff Room, which was empty at the time, and he went inside and wrote the piece down, not a little intimidated to be doing so in full view of a mammoth oil painting of Sergei Rachmaninoff himself looming over him. (Not many years later, his own portrait would be hanging very near the master's.)

Over the next few months, Billy finished the waltzes with the help of pianist Richard Joo. He would take Billy's compositions, which mostly existed only in his head, notate them, and undertake the actual piano playing. By April 2000 they had recorded six pieces, with three more in the hopper.

One composition that illustrates how some emotions seem to run deeper than Billy can comfortably express in words is "Soliloquy (On a Separation)." About being apart from Alexa—a scenario he often faced during the time she was in Christie's custody—the song grew out of a kind of internal set of lyrics: "I let the piano give voice to phrases I never would have sung—'We say goodbye' and also 'I watch as you leave and then I slowly return to this quiet house.' As Alexa was being driven away, not only literally but figuratively as well, a sadness would come over me, and the notes would just come—more and more minor key, sadder and more somber. I realized that adding lyrics could not make the piece any more expressive of what I was feeling."

When Billy announced that he actually intended to use this music on an album, the reaction in the music business was: *You're gonna do what? You're gonna do an album of piano pieces in the Romantic era, with no lyrics—and you're not even playing them yourself?*

"That's what I wanted to do," says Billy. "And I absolutely had to have another pianist play them—I'm not nearly good enough to perform those pieces. I can write them, but I can't play them."

While the material worried Sony, it gave Billy a certain freedom. He could continue to express himself musically, and by stepping off the pop music treadmill, he could create music without subjecting himself to his emotional ups and downs. Also, the meanings of the songs would not be scrutinized under the sometimes-blinding spotlight he'd worked under for four decades.

There was no shortage of material, after all, to take on the road. Despite a certain wariness in both camps, in mid-January 2001, after talks between Elton John's longtime agent Howard Rose and Dennis Arfa, the reconciled piano men launched an ambitious series of shows that began in Honolulu, took in the West Coast hoops courts and hockey rinks that hadn't been serviced in recent swings, then hopscotched across the continent to end in Minneapolis in mid-May, having scooped up some $56 million in gate receipts from some 530,000 fans.

ROMANTICALLY SPEAKING, as the millennium arrived, Billy began a new relationship, with Trish Bergin. They had first met in 1995, when the local news personality interviewed him for a Long Island television station called News 12. What was just an acquaintanceship—she was married to her first husband at the time—gradually started to heat up just prior to New Year's Eve 2000, as Billy was getting ready to play a Millennium Concert at Madison Square Garden. Trish arrived to interview Billy again, in a walk-and-talk on the grounds of the house he would soon sell. (It was actually Christie, who knew Trish as well, who pointed out to Billy that Trish was no longer wearing a wedding ring.)

By the spring, Trish and Billy were involved. Insiders said that theirs was the kind of relationship where, when everything was good, it was very, very good, and when it wasn't good, it was awful.

Some of their problems were seemingly superficial. Billy's reasons for leaving the Further Lane house in the Hamptons might very well have begun with Trish and her feelings about it. The house was a sort of French château, and Billy had added a few architectural details to it, such as stone balustrades.

But Trish didn't like it.

The two had a conversation in mid-2000 when they started to get serious. Trish told Billy, "I'm not going to live here," which floored him. "I mean, who wouldn't want to live in that house? Are you kidding me?" says Billy. "But she was adamant about not wanting to live in a house she associated with another woman." Billy had lived in the house for thirteen years all told, first with Christie and then from 1994 to 2002 on his own. "So even though I had mixed feelings about leaving, I decided to sell the place. If Trish wasn't going to be part of the dream, I didn't want the dream."

Billy figured, *Okay, it's a big house; if she doesn't want to live here, I can probably get good money for it. But first, let's see who might buy it.* One day Billy was talking to his actor friend Paul Reiser, who was friends with Jerry Seinfeld. They were part of a group of guys, mostly sometime Long Islanders, who had a yearly New Year's party.

Paul told Billy that Jerry had been looking at his neighborhood, and the prices kept getting jacked up on him—everybody was giving him the runaround. Billy suggested that Jerry take a look at his place. Paul got hold of Jerry, and Jerry visited Billy at his home. It had recently snowed, but despite the soppiness underfoot, Seinfeld spent a good amount of time strolling the sprawling property, then came back into the house with a big smile on his face. Afterward he got his wife, Jessica, to come over and take a look. Then he turned to Billy and asked, "How much?" Billy pulled a number out of thin air: "Thirty-two point five [million]."

To which Jerry said, "Okay." Just like that.

Billy replied, "*Okay* okay?"

Jerry laughed and said, "*Okay* okay." Billy took them out to dinner that night, and it was a done deal, all in the same day. No house had ever sold for that much money in Long Island or, in fact, in all of New York State.

After Jerry purchased the home, which has since accumulated considerably more value, he referred to it as "Versailles," to which Billy replied, "For that much money, call it whatever you want."

Billy and Trish had deeper issues, to be sure. To begin with, Trish reportedly worried that Billy might wander romantically—he had to fight the shadow world of suspicion that is always at hand when you're a popular entertainer—and the resultant jealousies damaged their rapport.

They were portrayed as a happy couple when the *New York Times* visited Billy's sixty-five-foot yacht *The Islander* in August 2000, but a little more than a year later, right after 9/11, they made the decision that they shouldn't get married. Trish was around thirty then and seemed eager to start a family, and as much as the decision was the product of considerable shared doubts, sources say she took it as hard as he did. "To this day I still regret that. I hate hurting anybody," says Billy. "I think a lot of people, after 9/11, reevaluated where their lives were headed. You're confronted with this great tragedy, and it made a lot of people question what was truly important in their lives."

For the Concert for New York City, held on October 20, a grave-faced Billy (with a begrimed fireman's helmet set before him) had the uniformed cops and firefighters in the audience punching the air with his fierce version of "Miami 2017." Throttling strong emotions, he hollered, "We ain't going anywhere," to a heartfelt roar. (If the song saw Manhattan sink "out at sea," the line that hit home this night was "We went right on with the show.") Then he played "New York State of Mind," and as he exited, he picked up a policeman's cap tossed onstage as a tribute.

Interviewed by Charlie Rose in December 2013, he would state that he'd been so "stunned by the inhumanity" of the attack that he was down in the dumps for years. The inspiration of the young Pakistani

Malala Yousafzai, who defied the Taliban and continued to do so after they failed to kill her with a shot in the head, "lifted me out of it."

But the profound despair that settled on him just after 9/11 indeed took its toll, and there was no salvaging the Trish relationship.

Steve Cohen subscribes to the theory that Trish was Billy's Ava Gardner, the woman who stayed just out of reach, but a real note of regret sounds in Billy's reminiscences. Though the roller coaster of the relationship lasted just a couple of years, as opposed to the lengthy, combative Frank-Ava marriage, the analogy is proper in terms of intensity.

"I suppose I've always assumed that if you really want to work things out, you can—because there is nothing like that kind of good when things are going well," says Billy. "But as with many passionate affairs, the end seemed to come very quickly, and that would trigger some of the deepest melancholy I'd ever known.

"Trish today is markedly different from the Trish of those days," says Billy. "She's married to an environmental lawyer, and they have three kids and, by all accounts, a great life." When she ran for a Suffolk County district legislative seat in March 2009, Billy was happy to give her a wholehearted endorsement, which began, "I would vote for Trish Bergin in a heartbeat."

PER ITS LONG-PLANNED release date, *Fantasies & Delusions* came out on October 2, 2001. Somewhat to Billy's amazement, given that it was a somber and stately piece of work that didn't indulge in orchestral fireworks, it went immediately to the top of the classical chart and remained there for twelve weeks.

In the usual music press outlets, there is no natural spot for a rock musician's album of classical music to be reviewed, so it ended up being judged by newspaper critics. In some cases, reviewers found the kinship with Chopin, Schumann, Debussy, and Rachmaninoff to their liking, as in the *Boston Herald-American*: "What is surprising is the depth of understanding of late Romantic-era piano writing in all its varieties that he so deftly demonstrates in these 10 miniatures. Even when he's quoting liberally from [the] masters, there's a sincerity, an underlying devotion to the art that makes Joel's work more homage than pillage." In other papers, notably in Philadelphia and Washington, Billy was raked over the coals for those same similarities. "I don't think the *Washington Post* was tossing me a bouquet when the reviewer described the album as 'a garland of homages,'" says Billy.

During a question-and-answer session between Billy and National Public Radio interviewer Susan Stamberg in December, some gentle probing brought out the hard-to-articulate feelings that had gone into composing these wordless keyboard meditations. "Innamorato," he said, was spurred by the breakup of a love affair. "All my life," he confessed, "I've been writing for women . . . they like it when you write stuff for them."

BILLY WAS STILL getting over the split with Trish when he heard of her engagement. That news and other pressures, including the strains of steady road work, pushed him to an emotional precipice. In mid-March 2002 a Madison Square Garden show with Elton went awry, when a combination of cold medication and the usually mellowing jigger or two in a cup on the piano combined to set off the anger that Billy was still carrying around from 9/11. "That overwhelming tragedy had changed all our lives, and we had an administration that was using it as the proximate cause for what loomed as a long and futile war in Iraq," says Billy.

"I think it was in the beginning of 'River of Dreams,'" recalls Tommy Byrnes, "pretty close to the end of the show. I was standing right next to him." Billy began by rebuking the Garden management. "This is the most expensive room in the world," he said to the audience. "You paid a lot for your tickets, and that sucks." With the anger surfacing— Billy had never understood why some of the 9/11 tribute concerts hadn't featured more of a homegrown lineup—he hollered to his startled audience that he wanted to "throw out a couple things. . . . Bunker Hill!

Antietam! That was a bad one!" He stood for the rest of his recitation, citing the Alamo, San Juan Hill, Argonne Forest, Corregidor, Midway, Guadalcanal, Normandy, Iwo Jima, Chosin Reservoir, Khe Sanh, and finally, perhaps fortunately running out of highly memorable armed conflicts, "Desert fucking Storm!"

He had one question for the loudly murmuring crowd: "Who the hell do they think they're fucking with?"

Around that time U2 was doing a concert tour of the States and expressing a lot of anger over what the terrorists had done, and even the pacifist Bono would cap some shows by proclaiming, "Osama bin Laden can kiss my rosy Irish ass!" Billy's tirade, for all its sincerity, didn't quite work out. "I remember walking over to him and going, 'You all right, boss?'" says Tommy. "And he was like, 'I'm really fucking up, aren't I?' I go, 'No, man, you're fine. Just friggin' get through this song and we're out of here.'" Billy recalls riding away from the gig in a van with Steve Cohen and the guys and asking how the outburst had gone down on a scale of zero to ten. Steve waited half a beat before saying, "Zero." "The audience had been warned that he had a cold," wrote *New York Times* reviewer Kelefa Sanneh. "But Mr. Joel seemed to have ingested something quite a bit stronger than cough syrup."

Shortly after the outburst at the Garden, despite some subtle words of caution from those around him (and the memory of Elton's disapproving scowl onstage that night), Billy was drinking very heavily again. The planned summer dual tour was postponed to September, and Billy told *People* magazine that the delay only worsened his mood: "I then began what I ultimately realized was a prolonged period of overindulgence." And yet in looking back at a disturbing series of events around that time, he says, "I was in a dark place, but in contrast to the rumors and printed speculation at the time, I want to set the record straight about something: none of my infamous traffic accidents were alcohol-related."

The police reports of each accident—albeit based on observation at the scene rather than on analysis of his blood alcohol level—back that up. The first accident occurred in East Hampton on June 12, 2002, the result of a simple, well-intentioned act: a deer ran across the road, and Billy swerved to avoid it, sending the car sliding across a grassy area next to the road and smack into a small but well-rooted standpipe. Someone called in the accident, and when the police arrived at the scene, Billy spoke to them and then simply went home, leaving the car to be towed.

The second accident, six months later, was more serious. It happened on a January night in 2003 as Billy drove home on Route 114 from the American Hotel in Sag Harbor, where he'd had what he recalls as a glass of champagne. He'd entered the bend in the road that some locals call Dead Man's Curve, because so many drivers are thrown off it, and hit a patch of black ice. Luckily he was seat-belted into a very safe car, a bulky Mercedes, but when the passenger-side door slammed into a tree, the impact knocked him unconscious. The car crumpled against the tree and bounced back onto the roadway. To get him out, rescue workers had to use the Jaws of Life, peeling the Mercedes open like a tin can. Thinking he was in bad shape because of the blood pouring from a small cut on his head, as well as a lot of bruising around his eyes (which actually was the result of sinus surgery a few days earlier), the rescue workers loaded him into a rescue chopper, to be airlifted to the Stony Brook University Medical Center. After a night of observation, the hospital released him, and when the papers ran pictures of the car, the crash looked much worse than it was.

The worst part for Billy was Christie's reaction to the news. She was so upset that she made a statement to the press: "The seat Alexa was sitting in only hours before was completely decimated.... I'm worried about Billy, but like any mother would be, I'm alarmed and concerned about my child's safety by this frightening pattern of events.... I hope Billy will honor his promise to use a professional driver when he's with Alexa. It eases my concern for the safety and well-being of both of them."

"Absurd as it was to think that I would ever compromise my daughter's safety, I kept my silence," says Billy.

Then, at about four P.M. on April 25, 2004, after picking up a pizza from one of the local Oyster Bay joints, Billy got into accident number three. He was driving "a dopey little Citroën, a French character car—I think it's made out of papier-mâché," says Billy—and it was raining. When he hit the brakes, the car slipped off the wet road and into a roadside house. It just tapped the foundation, enough to leave a little crack in the facade. Pretty soon the firemen and policemen showed up, but none of them noted any evidence that alcohol had been involved. Someone gave Billy and his cold pizza a ride home from there, and Billy thought that was the end of that.

Then the woman who owned the home was quoted in the local press saying, "He hit my bushes and the wall. He'd better come fix it. I'm sure he has the money." Billy subsequently sent her a check to cover the cost of all repairs. Still, the homeowner wasn't finished: "I'm ninety-four years old and I still drive. I've never had an accident."

The 1967 vintage Citroën, meanwhile, was completely totaled. Billy wrote it off and presumed it would be headed for the scrap heap, but somebody found the car's small plastic grille, which some local disc jockeys then auctioned off for charity. Then came the requisite *Saturday Night Live* skit, in which Horatio Sanz played Billy guzzling out of a bottle while driving some girls around the Hamptons—one of whom was played by Lindsay Lohan. While the sketch didn't exactly help the Billy Joel driving mythology, he admits that he found it funny. (A minor irony is that in August 2011, during a spate of serial public embarrassments, Lohan revealed a newly tattooed Billy quote on her rib cage: "Clear as a crystal, sharp as a knife / I feel I'm in the prime of my life.")

The timing of the next widely publicized event would not help the unwelcome legend, as a couple of days after the first accident, on June 14, 2002, Billy decided to check himself into a rehab center called Silver Hill Hospital, in New Canaan, Connecticut. Although Mariah Carey had been there a year or so before, to little fanfare, Billy's visit triggered a minor press frenzy. He told *People* that his talks with Alexa, then sixteen, had much to do with his decision to check in: "I told my daughter that I recognized I was having a problem, and my gift to her for Father's

Day was going to be cleaning up my act." But all the media attention made the other patients and the staff uncomfortable, even as some of his fellow patients were paying undue attention to the celebrity in their midst, and he left after a few days.

Over the years, Billy has had a problem with the prevalent cure for substance abuse: the tenet that puts it all in the hands of a "higher power." "I mean, no disrespect to anybody who finds sobriety through that path, but I'm an atheist," says Billy. "Also, I'm not one for psychotherapy, and certainly not one for group sessions in which people aim to correct one another's behavior. If you don't go for any of those approaches, you start to run out of traditional treatment options pretty quickly."

The rehab visit is supposed to be an occupational hazard with rock stars. "I call it mental floss," explains Billy. However, he did not want his issues with alcohol to be blamed on the supposed pressures of his career: "Believe me, I'm well aware that my life's a lot easier than most people's. Making a lot of money—what's the problem with that? Being able to get a table in a restaurant anytime you want because they recognize you—what's wrong with that? Being able to meet a beautiful woman and not have to pull out your résumé? I'm not complaining. Anyway, I don't think the rock star life pushed me into drinking. The fact is, I like to drink—sometimes too much.

"I know I have a melancholy streak, and, yeah, I can feel alone sometimes. But I don't mind my own company—I'm comfortable with it. After years of being on the road and living in hotel rooms, you learn to deal with isolation. Sometimes I'll read a book or watch TV back in my hotel room, and sometimes—well, sometimes I'd rather hang out with the band in a bar."

Research proves that alcohol is a depressant and that it aggravates depression. "But if you're drinking by yourself, it's not always about drowning your sorrows," shares Billy. "There have been times in my life when it was just a habit, part of my day. I'd have a glass of wine in the afternoon, and that would lead to another glass of wine later in the day, and by nighttime I'd be in my cups, as the Brits say. I'm not a psychologist, so I don't know how to explain what the calculus is there, what triggers having a few too many. But I'm aware of it. And no matter who you are, I think you have to be aware of what drives you to excess."

Billy eventually gave up hard liquor but will from time to time have a glass of wine with dinner. "When I know I'm heading into a tailspin or feeling depressed, I watch even how much wine I consume—and at times I stop altogether, until I've pulled out of whatever mood I'm in," he says. "It's probably fortunate that by now, anything more than a couple glasses of wine tends to make my body rebel, to guard its own gate—I feel physically ill, nauseous, out of sorts. There's also a psychological component—anything approaching some easy euphoria, and I start to feel dread. So that's where I stand today."

In November, as the troubles of 2002 slowly faded, Billy would have a consoling acquisition. Overlooking the peaceful Oyster Bay Harbor where he once dredged oysters was a fifteen-acre plot of gently sloping land that had been home to various rail and finance barons. In 1996 it was capped by a newly constructed Jacobean-style mansion that was dubbed Middlesea. Billy bought the twenty-thousand-square-foot two-story brick home for $22.5 million. It straddled the world he'd grown up in, sharing a shoreline with humble Oyster Bay's working fishery docks, and yet, on his peninsular Centre Island enclave, also boasting fat-cat neighbors on the order of (later-arriving) Rupert Murdoch. With two guest cottages, an ample garage for motorcycles, and a tennis court that would be replaced by a helipad, it was baronial but unshrouded by shrubbery, affording causal boaters the chance to troll past, peering through binoculars in the hope of catching a glimpse of the island's homegrown rock star at leisure.

ALSO IN THAT early winter of 2002, Billy had what felt like a happy accident: he met Katie Lee. They literally ran into each other in the lobby of the Peninsula Hotel in New York. She was in town from Ohio with some friends from Miami University of Ohio, and when they came face to face, they each took a step back. "Standing in front of me, I saw a woman who looked like a young Ali MacGraw, with a great smile. Even then, I knew it was a turning-point moment," says Billy. "I knew there was going to be more to the story than just that collision."

"I literally bumped right into him," Katie concurs. "I was looking for something in my purse as I walked, and we got to chatting. And he invited me and my girlfriend to dinner, this great place where I had my first truffle, and then he said, 'Hey, I've got a Broadway show—let's go over there.' So we go over, and he jumps onstage, and he sings the last two songs of the show. I thought that that was his job, that he did that every night. I had no idea he was doing it to impress me!

"Then it turned out that the president's daughter, Barbara Bush, was in the audience with a friend, and they wanted to come backstage and meet him. So we all went out, and the Secret Service was with us, and I was thinking, *God, this morning I was in Ohio, and now I'm out with the Secret Service. This is so weird. Boy, New York's fun!*

"I went back to college in Ohio thinking, *What a great New York experience.* I had no idea that I'd ever talk to him again or anything. And he called me about a week later, and we started up a friendship talking over the phone. And I went out and bought the greatest hits album and I was like, *Oh, I know "Still Rock and Roll," I know "My Life"—I love these songs.* So it was pretty funny. But then I ended up over the years knowing every word to every song. And I love his music now. I still listen to it when it comes on the radio. I sing right along."

As Katie and Billy were first getting to know each other, he found something jaded northerners might describe as "hillbilly charm" in her youth and innocence, and something classic in her proper southern manners. "Certainly I could do the math and recognize that the thirty-two-year gap in our ages could make for a challenging leap of faith on both our parts," says Billy.

Billy didn't think Katie was really aware of the extent of his career or of the success he'd had. To her, he was just the guy who wrote "Uptown Girl" and "We Didn't Start the Fire"—those were among a handful of Billy's songs she knew. She was so far removed from the 1970s and 1980s—and even part of the 1990s—that she had completely missed the heart of his career.

"I was actually very comfortable with the fact that she didn't define me at all by my greatest hits," Billy says. Still, he would later realize that there were a lot of things they just didn't have in common: "Aside from classical music, there was an obvious disconnect in terms of cultural touchstones such as TV shows, trends, and politics."

"As we talked on the phone more and more, a few months later he said, 'Why don't you come visit me?'" recalls Katie Lee. "It was in January, and I went up to the Hamptons in a huge snowstorm, and we cooked pasta and watched *The Godfather* and stayed in. And by the end of the weekend, I felt like, you know what, I could really fall in love with this person. And so we started seeing each other more and more."

Katie's visits grew more frequent, and Billy was happy to stay off the road. "Touring has its pleasures, but that hour you spend onstage having fun is not always counterbalanced by the other twenty-three spent riding in planes or vans or limos, and staying in places where you bite the wrappers off the soap and order lukewarm pasta," says Billy. "Instead of that grind, I was once again spending time on Centre Island or in my Sag Harbor place, enjoying the kind of domesticity that feels like a break from the storm."

By the end of 2003, Katie had become part of Billy's life, and part of Alexa's, too. (They were born just four years apart.) The domesticity was becoming ever more natural-seeming, and not to be discounted was Katie Lee's superior touch with comfort food. "Thanksgiving and the holiday season rolled around, and it just seemed natural to be hanging out in the kitchen boiling water and chopping garlic," says Billy. "Katie was starting to feel like family, and I was starting to think we should make that feeling a fact."

CHAPTER 15

A WILD AND RESTLESS MAN

I f Arthur Miller's account of his introduction to Marilyn Monroe—
"The eye sought in vain to find the least fault in the architecture of
her form"—reminded Billy of his first meeting with Christie, Miller's
reaction to the news of Monroe's death could stand in for Billy's eventual feelings about Katie: "I realized that I still, even then, expected to
meet her once more, somewhere, sometime, and talk sensibly about all
the foolishness we had been through—in which case I would probably
have fallen in love with her again."

But back in 2003, Billy's love for Katie was new and all things
seemed possible. Katie herself seemed content that when Billy wasn't on
the road, he was a homebody. "Maybe it was that residual influence of
the *Godfather* saga for me," says Billy. "I can go to the mattresses, and I
don't need a mob war to justify sticking around the house.

True to that mafioso ethic of being at least able to cook a decent meal
when housebound—or in a homey prison kitchen like the wiseguys in
GoodFellas—Billy developed his specialty of pasta with red sauce: "I'll
put mine up against any other amateur's. But as Katie stocked the pan-
try and her cooking skills went into full swing, I began to see her great
knack for putting a new spin on familiar comfort foods." Eventually
her drive to become a celebrity chef would take its toll on their relation-

ship. Early on, though, it felt very natural to Billy to watch her grow in stature.

"The early days of our getting to know each other were marked by quiet times at home—our notion of an ideal evening consisted of cooking a feast together, then picking a movie and watching it while sharing some popcorn," says Billy. "The feeling between us was one of affection and attachment and discovery, something I'd written about nearly twenty years earlier in 'This Is the Time'":

> You've given me the best of you
> But now I need the rest of you.

"But since I'm hard-wired to inject a little pessimism into every song, no matter how buoyant the overall tone, I'd added back then":

> This is the time to remember
> 'Cause it will not last forever.

"At first, when we were dating, my mom was saying, 'A rock star! Has he been tested for STDs?'" jokes Katie.

"I didn't tell any of my friends. I was finishing up my senior year of college, and I didn't want everybody talking about me. I just told my friends I was going home to see my mom every weekend when really I was either going to the Hamptons to see Bill or meeting him out on the road, because he started touring again. And then the weekend before graduation, the *National Enquirer* did a story on us dating. And I still didn't tell anyone it was in there. I thought, *Nobody reads the* Enquirer; *it'll come and go.* But the day before it would have gone off the newsstands, somebody saw it, and every convenience store and grocery store in our town in Ohio sold out of that issue. Everybody I knew in school was talking about it. I just couldn't wait to be out of there and done with it.

"I tried to blow people off when they'd ask me about it. It was when we had just gone to war, and I would say, 'Don't you have anything better to talk about? There's other things in the paper—we're at war. Why are you reading that?'

"And then after I graduated, I moved to the Hamptons, but I told Billy, 'I'm not moving in with you—I'm only coming to stay for the summer. In the fall I'm moving into the city and going to culinary school. This is only temporary.' Well, what do you know—I didn't leave. And we got married about a year and a half later."

IN JUNE 2003, Katie and Billy attended the Tony Awards together. Before sitting down to enjoy the show, though, Billy opened the event by doing "New York State of Mind" live from Times Square. During that performance, he had one of those only-in–New York moments when a tour guide, chattering away on a microphone at the front of a double-decker bus that went gliding by, simply incorporated Billy into his routine—"and there's native New York son Billy Joel, performing his classic 'New York State of Mind.'" "That's what I call a seasoned carny guy—in a few blocks he'd be giving Macy's the same treatment," says Billy.

Billy's bit was followed by a medley from *Movin' Out*—with Twyla Tharp's dancers flinging themselves about expertly to "River of Dreams," "Keepin' the Faith," and "Only the Good Die Young." The potent athleticism of the dancers, the muscular chops of the band, nominee Michael Cavanaugh's deft vocals, and Tharp's inventive choreography brought the crowd (including Philip Seymour Hoffman, seen applauding with a lickerish grin of sheer appreciation) to its feet. From among the show's nine Tony nominations, Tharp's choreography deservedly won, as did Billy and Stuart Malina's orchestration. Afterward Billy handed over his statuette to Tommy Byrnes, the guitar player, "who truly deserved the credit for all that arranging," says Billy. "The players he put together for the show would form the backbone of the reinvigorated band I'd front the next time I went on the road."

Because *Movin' Out* was heading for a national tour soon and a key venue was the Pantages Theatre, on that famed stretch of Hollywood Boulevard known as the Walk of Fame, Billy was given a star of his own. "It looks like I'm always going to be here," he admitted to the crowd. "I have to tell you that I had not considered this when I wrote 'Say Goodbye to Hollywood.'"

Meanwhile, *Movin' Out* was still a hit—it ultimately ran about three years on Broadway, through more than thirteen hundred performances. By then Katie finally knew for sure that Billy's job wasn't performing those last two songs in the show each night.

"He's Billy Joel when he goes onstage," says Katie, "and when he's at home, he's Bill. He's not the one who's the life of the party—he's kind of a little bit more reserved. But put him in front of fifty thousand people, and he just completely comes out of his shell. When he plays in New York, the people go crazy—it's amazing. At Madison Square Garden you can literally feel the room move, because it's built on springs and everyone is up out of their seats. I would go backstage, and I would look at the couch, with the dogs sitting on it, and it would be vibrating. Because everybody is going crazy.

"I don't think he ever really thought of himself as this big rock star. I think that's what keeps him grounded and laid back. His attitude is, *Man, I'm such a lucky guy.* You know, he's still this kid from Levittown who grew up without any money. He wants the big house because it makes him feel good and he didn't have that growing up. So he's thrilled that he is where he is. But I think he pinches himself every day."

OVER TIME, BILLY has discovered that even the feeling of fulfillment a celebrated career brings can take one only so far. "Okay, I recognize that the second I walk on that stage and start performing, it becomes for that moment the most important—in fact, the *only* important—thing in the world," he says. "And good Lord, in terms of scale, there's nothing else in my life that compares to the enormity and intensity of being up there—it feels like the epicenter of some history-making spectacle out of ancient Rome. How many people get to experience that? They can be happily married or otherwise very content with their lives without ever knowing what the roar of the crowd feels like when it's roaring just for you—but then they won't know what the letdown feels like, either. Because after a few hours, it's all over."

Once the crowd and their showers of adulation have vanished, once the stage is vacant, reality comes back quickly, says Billy: "The gladiator leaves the arena; he'll be back to fight and be rewarded another day. But in the meantime, he'll be just another schmuck on the highway."

Sure, there might be a four-motorcycle police escort to lead "the schmuck" down that highway, momentarily preserving the feeling that it's all so special, but for Billy, this would also deepen his painful awareness of what he *didn't* have: "that other person who makes the mansion a home. Because none of those people in that arena screaming your name really know you, and you just need one—*one* person out of millions—to know and accept and love you for being, well, just the way you are. And when you don't have it, man, do you miss it.

"I see old folks walking down the street who look like they've been together fifty years, and there's something very touching about it—that they've lasted so long. I used to wonder: *How come I don't have that?* I can dream about it, think about it, write music and lyrics and sing about it. I can even try to achieve it again, and often have." After some decades of rebooting his emotional life by plunging fairly quickly into one promising and highly publicized romance after another, says Billy, "At some point I had to say to myself, there you are, already fifty-something and single.

"And then you have to do something about it."

Billy did, proposing to Katie in St. Bart's—unforgettably the spot where he first met Christie—in the first week of January 2004.

Katie had some pretty good clues as to what was coming—they had looked at rings in a jewelry store Manhattan some months before that— but Billy was having a hard time working his way up to the proposal.

"We went to St. Bart's, and he was kind of making a big deal out of this trip. I had never been there, and I was really excited," says Katie. "Then one night, it was a full moon, and we went to this restaurant on the water. And he said, 'Why don't we go take a walk down by the boats and around the water?'

"I said, 'No, I'm tired, I want to go to bed.'

"So he said, 'Are you sure?'

"And I said, 'Yeah, I don't feel like it. My feet hurt. I want to go back.' So we go back to the room. We were staying at a place called the Carl Gustaf, which is a beautiful hotel that overlooks the harbor. We had our dog, Fionula, with us, and he said, 'Let's go take Fionula for a walk. It's such a pretty night, she needs to go out.'

"And I said, 'You take her out.' And he's like, *My God! What do I have to do!*

"I can't believe he proposed after I was such a pain in the ass. So he takes the dog out. Then he comes back and says, 'Come sit out on the patio with me; look at the moon.' But I wanted to watch TV.

"Finally he says, 'Will you just come sit outside?' And I'm like, *Well, golly, fine,* you know. So I go out there, and I could see he had, like, the chairs set up, and I thought, *Oh my God, something's happening here.* Before anything else could come out of my mouth, before I could be a bigger pain in the ass, he got down on one knee and proposed."

"Was it some kind of naïveté?" wonders Billy. "Perhaps I was still, unknowingly, coming out of the emotional turmoil that hit so hard in 2001 and for many months after. Maybe it was partly the setting? I mean, there we were in St. Bart's in a nice hotel on a beautiful moonlit night, and I had the ring on me. I asked her to come out onto the balcony of our room so that I could ask her to marry me, and she said yes. I thought to myself, *This is the way it should be,* without even thinking deeply about the fact that I was fifty-three and she was twenty-two. Why would I, when everything was going so well and feeling so right?"

Says Katie, "We were at an event, and we were talking to Demi Moore and Ashton Kutcher, and a photographer came over and said,

'Can we take a picture of the four of you?'" The quartet grinned for the camera: "And Bill's like, 'I can see the caption now—what's wrong with this picture?'"

Katie and Billy found a loft-style apartment for just under $4 million on Hubert Street in Tribeca in September 2004. The good-sized kitchen was a real selling point, as Katie had embarked on her cooking career in earnest. But first there was the not-so-minor detail of actually getting married, which they did on October 2, on the grounds of Billy's Centre Island home. Among the 250 people in attendance were Billy's mom, Christie, Alexa (who served as maid of honor), Jon Small, and some of Billy's friends from the trade, including Howard Stern and Don Henley. Billy's half-brother, Alexander, served as best man. They got lucky when the clouds parted just in time for the four P.M. ceremony.

The newlyweds spent their honeymoon in Europe, and for Billy, something about living out of a suitcase for a few days, remote from the routines and duties of a (multiple) householder's life, helped convince him to think about touring again in the near future.

When Katie and Billy first met, he had been winding down a fairly lengthy tour with Elton John. After they married, Billy was initially determined to stick around the house: "With a new marriage to focus on and a chance finally to pull back and live a normal life after all those years I'd spent as a habitual road dog, I wanted to be home," he remembers. "But then I began to wonder if I needed the road to keep me on some sort of even keel. The elephant that is a tour lurches up onto the circus stool gradually."

Billy and the band knocked off three dates, including what's known as a "private," for a major beer company gathering. A date like that brings in about $1.5 million, and soon afterward Billy was playing shows at several colleges, such as Syracuse University, and at performing arts schools, such as Juilliard.

Katie Lee saw a noticeable difference in Billy when he was performing and when he wasn't. Being on the road had served as a kind of gyroscope, providing a center to his life for so many years. Without that routine, some of the bad old habits pushed their way back in. "I felt like he went through a really hard time. We had only been married four months when he went to rehab."

One day Katie approached Billy and told him, "You're drinking a lot, and I don't think you're aware of it. I also don't think you're aware of how much of a problem this is becoming for our relationship. I love you very much and I hate to see you destroying yourself. And if you love me and you value the relationship, you'll do something about it."

Katie never saw Billy drinking, so when he was sluggish or off a beat, she had thought he was just tired: "I just didn't put two and two together at all. Maybe I was naïve. But then in January 2005—a couple months into being married—we went back to St. Bart's, and I started thinking something was wrong with him. I thought maybe he had a neurological problem—because I was with him all the time, and it wasn't like he was sitting around with a bottle of wine and I was watching it happen."

The imbibing wasn't obvious, but it was quietly happening, unseen. Billy, too, was realizing that there was a problem: "I finally said to myself, *You know what, if my drinking doesn't slow down or these episodes with booze keep happening, I guess I have to consider going to a place like Betty Ford.* Because the first time I went to rehab, I didn't really stick it out. But now I was very much in love with Katie, and I didn't want to damage the relationship. She was cooking a real healthy diet, and I'd agreed to have a trainer come in regularly to work me out."

On the day en route to that difficult moment, he wasn't in a frame of mind to do a training session—lethargy and the residue of the prolonged binge overruled that. He felt "this whirlpool of—helplessness. And I realized, *That's it. I don't want to continue like this.*"

That same morning, Katie recalls, "I got on the phone with Billy's attorney, Lee Eastman [son of John, and grandson of his family's lawyer patriarch], and his business manager, Todd Kamelhar, and said, 'Listen, you better set up something for him because he's either going to rehab today or I'm moving out—one of the two.'

"And they called Max Loubiere, his tour director, who came up from New Orleans. Max got a plane for the next day to take Billy to Betty Ford. When Bill woke up that morning, I didn't want to have to give him an ultimatum like, *You go, or it's me.* I wanted it to be his decision. Luckily he woke up and said, 'I've got a problem. I've got to go somewhere.' And [his intimates] said, 'Well, good thing, because there's a plane coming tomorrow, and your suitcase is packed.' So we got on the plane for Betty Ford the next day. We checked him in, and after we dropped him off, I went to a hotel and slept through the night for the first time in months. I felt like I had just died in that bed, I was so tired."

Billy remembers, "When I talked to Katie that morning, I just said, 'Let's do it.' I was thinking, *I'm going to do it. I'm now going to follow through with the conversations I've had with Katie. I love her, and I'm going to do it.* And I really didn't want to do it. But it was important to me to show her that I was finally going to do this the right way."

When they arrived, they checked Billy in—he would be there for a month. "The trip out felt all too short, because all of a sudden I was there. I was hoping the plane ride would last a hell of a lot longer," he says. "I was probably still hungover on the flight. But there I was, filling out fifteen thousand forms and in a line with everybody, to get my detox meds. Boom—there was no turning back now."

"We couldn't talk on the phone while he was there," Katie recalls. "The only time you could visit was for three hours every Sunday." Every Saturday night she would fly to L.A. and then drive to Palm Springs for a few hours' visit. She'd fly back in the evening.

"I have to give her points for that," says Billy. "She flew all the way from New York to visit with me. It could be for only two or three hours, to have a meal with me, then she would have to leave. There was no physical contact allowed except maybe hand-holding, and they even discouraged that. But it helped me a great deal to see her and realize that she was supporting me in this, and I loved her for that. Just to be able to see her was a great comfort, and it kind of reinforced why I was doing this. *She's why I'm doing this.*"

* * *

ALCOHOLICS ANONYMOUS IS supposed to be just what the title implies—a place for first names only. But in rehab, Billy quickly realized that he could hardly go unrecognized—and he wanted and needed some degree of privacy when he was airing his problems: "When any other guy gets up and says, 'Hi. My name's Bob and I'm an alcoholic,' that's all he is to the other people in the room. But when I get up and say, 'My name's Bill and I'm an alcoholic,' they go, 'Oh, it *is* him.'

"I felt as if the other people in the room were looking at me like, *Well, of course he's an alcoholic—he's a rock star.* And I didn't blame them. I was just another one of *those* people I always used to make fun of. I always used to think, when I heard their stories, *Oh my God, what a jerk. How can you blow a life like that?*"

Billy even had a groupie, a would-be bro, in rehab: "He would want to hang out with me. And the counselors saw that right away and separated us, because everybody in rehab has profound issues, and you're supposed to focus on yourself. They explained to him that I had to work out my deal, so why didn't he concentrate on *his* thing?"

Despite these challenges, Billy went ahead with the treatment. He admitted to the group that he'd probably done a lot of "stupid stuff" and was self-destructive. "I just bought right into the whole spiel; I didn't hold back," he says. "I didn't embrace the entire twelve-step experience, though, especially the 'higher power' thing. Still, I kind of took what I needed out of it to get fixed."

Katie noticed changes in Billy when he returned from Betty Ford. "He was very timid, quiet, even scared," she remembers. "There was this real childlike feeling, where he was on sensory overload just being out in the world. He had been in this safe cocoon, and it was the first time he'd been without alcohol in a long time.

"I've never met anybody more forgiving and soulful. When I say forgiving, I look at how he had a manager who stole tens of millions of dollars from him. And instead of carrying around his dark hate for this person, when he saw him once seven or eight years ago, he said hello. Most people would want to spit on him.

"He doesn't talk bad about people. It's not that he's into yoga and, like, all enlightened. That's just his outlook on life. He has a certain naïveté with that, and trust—it can be his downfall when bad things like that happen. But on the other hand, it's what makes him have this beautiful light around him, that he can still be like that when he's had so many people take advantage of him."

The changes Katie saw in Billy when he left rehab were indeed real. "I felt like a deer caught in the headlights," he says. "Everything felt like an ordeal. I didn't want to see anybody. I didn't want to do anything. I was a different person. I'd gone through something like shock therapy. Even just going out for a meal somewhere took enormous effort; there were so many people around. I was very timid and raw. My nerve endings were exposed, and I felt like I'd been beaten up. It took quite a while for me to come out of that. I would say there was about a three-month period of just recovering from recovery."

Billy never tried to self-diagnose. "I just assumed, this is part of my personality, and I have to deal with it, without the booze," he explains. "I remember reading a book on Lincoln. It was interesting because he was very prone to melancholy, but he also kind of embraced it. It made him much more of an empathetic person, because he was aware of the dark parts and able to integrate them effectively into his political and personal life. If it's there, it's there. I don't know whether I would be considered bipolar or manic-depressive. I just have a tendency to get sad from time to time. And I know that's helped me a great deal as an artist. So sometimes melancholy can be beneficial. As long as you're conscious of it—and not making it worse by drinking—it can be dealt with."

"I remember that for a while after rehab, Billy didn't want to work," shares Katie. "And then I said to him, 'Bill, idle hands are the devil's playground.' That's what I've always said. And I said, 'I think you really need to reconsider.' It was really difficult for him. But I think going back on the road really helped him."

* * *

WHEN IT'S TIME to go on the road, you don't have to tell Dennis Arfa twice. When Billy told him he was ready to tour again, Dennis's notion was to play a row of dates in early 2006, beginning with a couple of shows at Madison Square Garden.

Dennis had been Billy's longtime booking agent and had always been a master at spotting—and even creating—pent-up demand. That's why he used the time-honored tactic of having promoters throw a giant curtain across half an arena and sell just the front part, rather than scatter fans throughout the drafty old hockey rinks. People got used to jumping on tickets while they were available, as Billy and the band built their audiences by degrees in various cities.

Every major rock act has its own primary, secondary, and tertiary towns, and of course no two acts have the same preferences. A welcome complication in Billy's scheduling, since they first went out with Elton John in the summer of 1994, was figuring the difference between a solo tour and one featuring the two-headed beast.

As a duo, Elton and Billy exceeded any previous co-billing as a drawing card, and even with reasonable ticket prices, the 2003 tour grossed $46 million. Says Billy, "That's the industry's way of keeping score. To Dennis Arfa, it's about, *Can we keep getting the fannies in the seats?* To me—and the real key to whether and how long I should keep doing this—it's, *Can we get those fannies up and out of the seats during the show?*"

Touring with Elton was a mixed blessing for Billy. Elton had so many hits that the audience wanted to hear that he almost had to do them all. If Billy was to be part of the team, he felt that he needed to do hits as well. Album tracks just wouldn't cut it.

As they had on previous tours, Billy and his band didn't hang out much with their counterparts down the hallway for shared dates, and also per long habit, the principals didn't see each other backstage much. "I stay in my production office, which looks like the back room of a deli, and Elton's in this setup with racks of clothes, shoes, and sunglasses, like the grandeur that was Rome, everything except—I think except—you know, togas," says Billy. "But he's a very witty, generous guy to be around. And I owe him very personal thanks, especially for the concern he showed some twenty years ago when I was having problems with booze, not taking care of myself, and he said, 'I'm worried about you.'" That would not be the last of that theme in their history.

From time to time, Billy would hear from Dennis how great it would be, with or without Elton, to get back to Madison Square Garden. Billy had performed six closely spaced shows at the Garden in 1993 in support of *River of Dreams.* But he had been absent from the Garden as a solo act during the intervening time, and additionally, he hadn't been on the road on a significant solo tour since a 1998–99 run of sixty-four shows. About a million people had seen those shows. "But history means nothing," said Billy, quoting football coach Bill Parcells.

Perhaps that distance between solo Garden concerts would work in Billy's favor, his team conjectured, because the last time he was onstage in the Garden, with the Face to Face tour in April 2002, was the night of his infamous meltdown.

When the tickets for the first couple of Garden dates went on sale, they were quickly snapped up; and as more concerts were added, the response didn't let up. At first Billy and the band were reluctant to announce ten performances—the record Springsteen had set for consecutive Garden shows—but they plowed past him to twelve. "That seemed like the right place to stop," says Billy, "because even though I'm not superstitious, why land on thirteen if you don't have to?"

Billy had found a real rapport with his new road band, and these Garden gigs would showcase their synergy. Drummer Chuck Burgi, who had been recruited by Tommy Byrnes from the *Movin' Out* pit band, came into his own. According to Billy, "He kept great time and, as they say in the trade, 'moved a lot of air.'" In addition to his forcefulness on the powerful numbers, he had the knack of knowing just how and when to hit a rim shot for a sardonic underpinning to Billy's onstage shtick.

During the twelfth and final concert, radio veteran Bob Buchman—

Billy's colleague in the charity he helped start in 1978, Charity Begins at Home—went onstage and announced that the consecutive Garden concert record had been attained. A banner bearing the name "Joel" and the number twelve then rolled down from the rafters—the first tribute of that kind to go to someone other than an athlete.

When it came time to pick the performances for what became the thirty-two-song double-disk set *12 Gardens Live*, the choices were obvious. Among them, the band tucked in what's called a "deep album track," "The Night Is Still Young," with Crystal Taliefero filling in the higher-pitched part Billy had originally sung on this somewhat obscure number. (Although it had gone to number thirty-five as a single in 1985, the song was basically a throw-in on that year's collection, *Greatest Hits, volumes one and two*.) Says Billy, "Even as I sang it onstage, I realized that the same problems a career can bring to one marriage are likely to crop up in another":

> *I'd like to settle down, get married*
> *And maybe have a child someday*
> *I can see a time coming when*
> *I'm gonna throw my suitcase out*
> *No more separations*
> *Where you have to say goodnight to a telephone*
> *Baby I've decided that ain't what this life is all about.*

Those lyrics now sounded autobiographical twice or even three times over.

CHAPTER 16

GOODNIGHT, SHEA STADIUM

At a 1969 press conference, four years after "Satisfaction" became a hit, Mick Jagger was famously asked if he was any more satisfied with his life. "Financially dissatisfied," he answered, "sexually satisfied, philosophically—trying."

Prior to meeting Katie, Billy's situation was somewhat the obverse, whether he recognized it or not. At that point in his life, he hadn't had to think about money in many years, but somehow the two other categories were bound up together. "In terms of a life partner, I didn't know if I'd run out of time and it would be too late for me," he says. "And then Katie came along. Miracle of miracles, she made everything okay. Despite having folded up the pop songwriting tent some years before, I wanted to do something special for her. So I started composing 'All My Life.' I wasn't thinking about having a hit song or anything like that—I wanted a song specifically from me to her and only her. I just wanted a standard, something that Tony Bennett could have sung, or maybe a saloon song that Sinatra might have done. I think I succeeded in that, and performed a bit of emotional exorcism as well":

All my life
I've hurt the ones who cared

One by one
No loving heart was spared

I've been a wild and restless man
But still a man who needs a wife
That was my dream and now it seems
You've taken all my life.

"I think I always wanted to write a song like that, but never had. It's long and very slow. It's also very emotional and kind of self-deprecating in some ways, as if I'm saying, 'Hey, I did some bad stuff in my life, and I paid for my mistakes.' I probably had to have gotten to this age to be able to write it and sing it with any kind of confidence."

"He wrote 'All My Life' for our [second, in 2006] anniversary," says Katie. "I'd been working in San Francisco for two weeks at that time. He came to visit me, and there was a piano bar in the hotel lobby. He goes, 'I wrote something for you. I want to play this for you.' So we go in, and he starts to sit down—it was very dark—and the woman working there said, 'Excuse me, you can't play the piano in here.' And I thought, *I'm not going to let you ruin this for me.* So I said, 'Um, that's Billy Joel. I don't think anybody's going to care.' She said, 'Oh,' and kind of ran away.

"Then Bill sat down at the piano and started singing this song for me. It was so touching, but the best part was that this couple got up and started dancing. They had no idea that it was him sitting there playing it, and watching them enjoy the romantic song that he wrote for us made it so much better for me, to see how the music can touch other people."

Billy recorded "All My Life" on December 29, 2006, not quite three months after the couple's second anniversary, as a response to Katie's regular requests for him to play the song: "Finally I thought, *Maybe I should just make a recording, and then she can play it whenever she wants instead of my having to sing it all the time*," Billy says.

It was an expensive session. Billy hired a full orchestra and a rhythm section in a big studio and got Phil Ramone to produce the song. "I knew it was an extravagance," he admits, "but it was for my wife.

"I had never expected the sort of thing that happened between Katie and me to happen. I'd thought I was done. It was fantastic: a love song come to life. But sometimes you know that other, much darker verse is waiting, not far away."

HOPING FOR A little R&R in the new year, Billy kicked back for the holidays in late 2006. The label sent out a notice in January 2007 announcing the impending release of "All My Life" (initially on Valentine's Day 2007, on the *People* magazine home page). Midwinter loomed as a fairly relaxing stretch for Billy, with just one duty: a second appearance at a Super Bowl to sing the national anthem. He figured it would be an easy enough gig, as Super Bowl XLI would be in Dolphin Stadium, not far from his Miami home. With a thirty-second commercial going for $2.6 million as the Colts battled the Bears before millions of viewers, it amounted to substantial exposure.

Billy had performed the anthem without a hitch at Super Bowl XXIII in 1989, but in Miami, when he sat down at the piano, it began to drizzle, and thoughts raced through his mind: "Now, one thing you know, going into a Super Bowl national anthem performance, is that a group of military fighter jets is already screaming toward the stadium when you start the song. After that you have about ninety seconds, and then you'd better be done with the last verse."

There were more than ninety-three million people watching, and Billy had refused to do what many singers do and pretape the performance for lip-synching. "All I needed to get it right was a working set of sound monitors, so I could hear myself," he explains. "I was also playing the piano, which means you have to be able to hear your vocal so you know that you're in key with the piano." The band did three rehearsals, during which Billy rested a stopwatch on the piano to time the performance because of that flyover. The time came in at 1:29 all three times—right on the money.

Then, just before the show was about to start, the drizzle turned into a downpour and soaked the piano. But the show had to go on. Says Billy, "They were giving me the hand sign—showing me the fingers, five, four—and I was frantically testing the mike, but there were no monitors. They didn't turn on the goddamn monitors. I couldn't hear a thing."

And then, more fingers. Three . . . two . . . one! "I had to go on, I'm a professional. What am I going to do, say on live TV that I can't sing because I can't hear myself?"

Thinking fast, Billy did a piano intro, hoping to detect the pitch—but he still couldn't hear a thing: "So I started singing, and I had to wait a good several seconds to hear the bounce-back of my vocal from the public address system. Anyone who's ever been to a ballgame knows you can hear the sound echo off the walls of the stadium, but as a performer, you're still not really certain you're on pitch. I was pretty sure I wasn't."

On top of it all, at the press conference before the game, some people thought Billy was being a smartass when he said, in all honesty, that "'The Star-Spangled Banner' is a slog and 'America the Beautiful' is a better song." And in response to a question about what it's like to sing the anthem before the Super Bowl twice, he answered, "I don't know, I haven't done it yet."

Many journalists thought Billy was making fun of them and the whole process. They went after him and his performance with hatchets. They even accused him of using a pitch-correction device called an Auto-Tune. "I have never used one and don't need to—as long as I can hear myself," countered Billy. Following that Super Bowl fiasco, Billy vowed to himself to avoid the traps of ill-managed TV audio set-ups.

If the grand spectacle of the Super Bowl had backfired, an attempt at capturing the public imagination with something more intimate also lacked traction with the broader audience. When "All My Life" was released in early 2007, it received no airplay. That said, Billy was philosophical: "There was nowhere for it to live, which is what I kind of liked about it. That made it even more personal for me, as though the only person who was ever going to hear it was my wife."

Though the song came and went without finding listeners, Dennis Arfa had a herd of more than willing promoters and lined up a sequence of concerts that would take Billy and the band through the whole year. They worked scattered dates throughout the south in midwinter and moved north and into the Midwest in the spring. "Whether it's Albany or St. Paul, the concrete backstage dungeons don't change much, but the crowds all have their own vibe," says Billy.

When "My Life" almost disappeared into static after an equipment glitch in Cleveland, Billy told the audience, "We are not on tape up here! These are real rock-and-roll fuckups!" The crowd belted out part of the song for him, and at one point Billy went back to piano fundamentals and banged out "Heart and Soul," to a disproportionately ecstatic response. In Atlanta, Billy tossed out tributes to Georgia greats by doing two songs by the state's favorite sons—Little Richard's "Good Golly Miss Molly" and Otis Redding's "Sittin' on the Dock of the Bay"—as well as "Georgia on My Mind," which was written by Indianan Hoagy Carmichael but made famous by Georgia-born Ray Charles.

Billy's penchant for local references is an intriguing mix of show business and simple courtesy. As opposed to some performers who toss their gems out listlessly to the audience, Billy engages and, in searching glances around the audience, takes their temperature regularly during shows. The crowd as a whole gets a glimpse at what Billy's seeing when Steve Cohen, toggling between shots from the live-feed video cameras, grabs a panoramic view of the front rows and projects it on the large screens behind the band. The unusually attractive array of happily cavorting young women seen at such moments might fairly be categorized as eye candy.

This arrangement has not gone unnoticed by various fans who comment online. Billy's band and crew will often spot amusing items on the

Web, and during a recent tour, one of the guys in his crew forwarded him a post from a woman named Ann who caught a show in Dallas. "Okay, I'll admit that I'm naïve," Ann wrote on a message board. "But what's up with filling the front section with twenty-something blondes and continually showing them on the screen?"

"We didn't really plan it that way," says Billy. Twenty-five years ago he and his company had stopped selling the front rows the traditional way after they noticed that those choice seats were being snapped up by the well-to-do folks, whether in initial ticket buys or through scalped tickets. "We'd end up looking out there at these rich guys and their blasé girlfriends, sitting on their cans like, *Okay, entertain me, piano man*," he remembers. So production instituted a routine of distributing those tickets to the crew guys, with instructions to go out and circulate where the real fans were, find the people headed for the cheap seats, and make them a gift of these tickets in the front two rows.

"Being guys, they picked out the best-looking girls," says Billy. "Sure, I may have hung up a poster of Nicole Kidman in the production office as a sort of guideline. And sometimes when they were down to just a pair, they would give them to the female half of a double date, a policy they named Dump a Chump. And it all helped the show—it perked the band up, it perked me up. Once Elton learned the trick, there was a kind of counterbalance, because the way his distribution worked, the seats on his side of the stage got filled up with good-looking guys. And it really helped his show a lot, too.

"So, Ann in Dallas," concludes Billy, "guilty as charged."

AFTER A PAUSE for the holidays, and some downtime in warmer climates while New York was freezing—Billy typically tells his friends that he's "practicing to be an old Jew" when he retreats to Florida, for some years in Miami and more recently a swank community about an hour north—he and the band were back on the road in early 2008. They toured California in February, hit Montreal in April, and played Jazz

Fest in New Orleans at the end of that month. They also did ten dates at Mohegan Sun in Connecticut that induced a hundred thousand people to tear themselves away from the slot machines to see them.

But the most memorable moments of 2008 were still ahead. This had been clear since Dennis first hinted to the fans, back in September 2007, that Billy aimed to schedule a performance to coincide with the closing of Shea Stadium in Flushing, Queens: the Last Play at Shea.

Billy was aware that it was going to be a bit of a hullabaloo. He had resolved to never again have a manager since Frank Weber was sent packing, so his business discussions with his team of experts— sometimes a team of rivals—were always personal. From the first mention of him playing Shea, Dennis looked Billy in the eye to be sure he fully understood what he was signing on for. "Bill," he said, not without some savor, "it's going to be the circus."

The Mets had wanted Billy to play the ballpark in '07, but, says Dennis Arfa, "Billy and I were on the same page about wanting to close the stadium, wanting to be the last act in the building. And it was not something that the Mets wanted to do. The Mets wanted McCartney. And I told the Mets, 'You can wait for McCartney and get nothing— but we're ready to go.'"

Paul and Billy were friendly, from years of sharing stature as icons and both having John and Lee Eastman as their attorneys and advisers, and it soon became clear to Billy that Paul felt he couldn't top what the Beatles had done at Shea in 1965—so why even try? With Paul out of contention, Dennis negotiated with the ball club, who would take a goodly percentage of the gate and also bear some of the costs. Although the overhead would run up quickly, to the tune of several million dollars, they wanted to keep the bulk of the tickets at ninety-five dollars each. The club would sell some of their suites and elite box seats at a premium, but most of the fifty-five thousand seats would cost two digits.

Lastly, they wanted to play during the baseball season. In recent years, Bruce and the Stones had played Shea dates in the off-season, but

With Christie and Alexa—whose middle name, Ray, is a tribute to Ray Charles—shortly after Alexa's birth on December 29, 1985.

When Billy recorded "Baby Grand" with Ray in 1987, producer Phil Ramone instructed, "challenge him."

As a road-weary pair of pop culture ambassadors to the Soviet Union in 1987,
Billy and Christie Brinkley (seldom without a video or still camera on the journey,
she doubles here as Lady Liberty), found respite from sometimes
over-adoring crowds when and where they could.

Billy, minus a sneaker, cavorts onstage in
the Soviet Union.

With the Sony brass, from left to right, Walter Yetnikoff, Billy, Tommy Mottola, and then-manager Frank Weber, in June 1988.

"We all end in the ocean / We all start in the streams . . ." For the "The River of Dreams" video in 1993, Billy and the production shot on and around the Connecticut River (from the Mohegan word for "long, tidal river"), which empties into Long Island Sound.

Billy and Elton John began their series of sporadic, record-setting Face to Face concert tours in 1994.

Billy and Carolyn Beegan, as they toured Italy in the late nineties.

Billy and Trish Bergin met when the Long Island TV newswoman was assigned to interview him in 1995; she came back on a second assignment as Y2K approached, and the romance took in spring 2000.

Billy married Katie Lee on the grounds of his Centre Island estate in October 2004, with his daughter, Alexa, as maid of honor and his half-brother, Alex, as best man.

When Billy set a new record for Madison Square Garden by selling out twelve consecutive shows in early 2006, he earned a number in the rafters alongside the arena's various sports heroes.

For the May 2006 Rock for the Rainforest benefit, Billy, seen here with James Taylor, Will Ferrell, and Sting, did his Joe Cocker impression with "A Little Help from My Friends."

Billy helped design a series of boats built for utilitarian purposes; to travel to his Last Play at Shea gigs in July of 2008, he rode on a 57-foot Shelter Island commuter called the *Vendetta*. Here he's seen aboard *Argos*, a 36-foot lobster boat he commissioned from Maine's Ellis Boat company.

Two sold-out Shea Stadium evenings before 55,000 fans each night sealed the legend of a storied ballpark that had seen some of rock's greatest acts, several of whom took the stage with Billy over the two evenings.

Paul McCartney's transatlantic race to arrive at Shea Stadium in time to cap off the concerts' second night was a career highlight for Billy, and they rocked hard on "I Saw Her Standing There."

On a balmy winter's day in Miami in 2011, Billy and Bruce Springsteen shared lunch and a ride across Biscayne Bay in Billy's 28-foot landing craft/utility boat.

Father and daughter at the keyboard, in September of 2013: Alexa Ray did one of her rare performances of dad Billy's work singing "Just the Way You Are" for a Gap ad.

Billy met Alexis Roderick, then a risk analyst for a stock market firm, at a Long Island restaurant not far from his home in 2010, and soon after they were living, and traveling, in tandem.

Billy's motorcycle collection is quartered in downtown Oyster Bay in his Twentieth Century Cycles shop, where Bruce Springsteen once made a pilgrimage to order a custom bike. Here Billy stands on his Centre Island property with a lovingly updated variation (he codesigned) on a 1939 Harley-Davidson "Knucklehead."

The series of Madison Square Garden dates that kicked off in January of 2014 was unprecedented in time span of the residency and the ticket sales generated. A bonus was the intensity of crowd enthusiasm that fed Billy's own enjoyment of the shows.

the stadium hadn't permitted a show during the season since Elton John and Eric Clapton played there in 1991. Its proposed late-July date would leave the team with some home games still to play, and Billy and the band would be setting their stage up in center field facing home plate, so the groundskeepers would have their own set of demands for protecting the playing surface.

"We were going to use the history of Shea Stadium—that the Beatles opened it and that Billy closed it—as a marketing event," says Dennis Arfa. "You have to be here because this is historic. And Billy at one point said to me, 'Do we have to say "historic"?' Then he goes, 'I guess it sells tickets.' My daughter at the time was fifteen, and her friend was at sleep-away camp. And the dad said he felt that he had to bring her home to go to this show, so she could be a part of this history. I heard that and I said, 'Mission accomplished.'"

Finally Billy bought into the plan, and the concert was officially announced during the last week of January 2008, when Dennis bought a full-page ad in the *New York Times* (at about $88,000, a third of a hefty promotional budget that included other newspaper ads and a heavy rotation of ads on the local NBC station).

By that time, Billy had begun reaching out to various guest artists, especially his old label mates, such as James Taylor and even Bob Dylan, as well as Jimmy Buffett, John Fogerty, and Brian Johnson of AC/DC. ("Let's face it, he's one guy who could give my roadie Chainsaw a run for his money on AC/DC's 'Highway to Hell,'" says Billy.)

While a number of them had scheduling conflicts, thanks to their own summer tour dates, an impressive list began to solidify. None of those names were released to the public, but Billy, the band, and his crew could already feel reverberations through the media, simply from the number of friends and cousins they were suddenly hearing from.

Billy also did a press conference on February 7, days before the tickets went on sale. When asked whether he would consider adding a second show, he said it was a possibility, if the demand was that great. But at that stage the Mets weren't interested in a second show, so Billy and his circle all thought it was unlikely.

When the tickets for the July 16 show went on sale in late February, they were surprised by the reaction—the show sold out in forty-eight minutes. Dennis even claimed that if the online orders had been done by the Ticketmaster computers instead of the rather more rudimentary Mets ticketing system, they could have thrown in six more dates and sold those out.

It soon became clear that a substantial number of tickets had actually landed in the hands of scalpers—prices on even the legitimate resale site Stub Hub escalated into five figures—and that the great majority of real fans hadn't even gotten a crack at buying seats. Meanwhile, the Mets, who had been hanging back for their own reasons, offered them the facility for a second night, Friday, July 18. Billy consulted with his brain trust—Dennis, Lee, business manager Todd, crew bosses, and so on—and, after some debate about how the original ticket buyers would react to a second, later show going up for sale, they decided to go ahead and do it. They had enough guest artists lined up to cover the two dates, and Billy would have a night in between to rest his voice. When the tickets for that second, Friday-night show went up for sale, they sold out in two minutes less than the first bunch. The *Daily News* would report some fervent complaints from fans who felt their tickets for the sixteenth had been devalued, but the groaning was stilled when the Mets released a transcript of Billy's February 7 statement affirming that more shows would be possible.

And so on the afternoon of the Friday show, the final concert, Billy found himself standing on the yacht club dock in Oyster Bay looking at one of his favorite things in the world, a black beauty with great curves, an impeccable pedigree, and a name out of a James Bond film, coursing across that flat, glassy surface of the bay at low tide.

Designed to emulate industrialist John Hay Whitney's Aphrodite commuter boats of the 1930s, *Vendetta* was mostly custom-built, down to the hatches, chocks, and cleats. She cost a couple million dollars and guzzled fuel, but Billy couldn't imagine any better way to travel down to Shea: "We planned to dock a stone's throw from where, in 1964, my old band the Hassles came in second in the talent competition at the New York World's Fair." Each time he rode past that decrepit and squat but somehow dignified cylinder that was the New York State Pavilion, he envisioned the calendar pages flipping backward.

According to Billy, the equation goes something like this: "You can grow up poor in a Levittown tract home, but if you keep working at your trade, down the years and decades till your back aches and your hair goes, with a little luck you get to have your Jay Gatsby moment, you get some ownership of the things that you once thought belonged only to the privileged class."

Unlike Gatsby, part of Billy always knew that entering that high-society world when you're not born into it is a sucker's bet—thus the name *Vendetta*. The idea for the name goes back to another set of Fitzgerald's characters, *Tender Is the Night*'s Dick and Nicole Diver, who believed the adage that "living well is the best revenge." "Just what I need revenge for sometimes eludes me," Billy says. "But I can still remember sleeping in Laundromats back when I was inventing who I would become, and that's a memory that sticks with you."

Now here was Billy on the North Shore, in the heart of Long Island's Gold Coast—where Fitzgerald briefly lived and found his inspiration—standing on the weathered but impeccably maintained dock of the Seawanhaka Corinthian Yacht Club, a refuge for white-shoe yachtsmen since the 1800s. Says Billy, "Some years back, the club's good gentlemen even accepted me for membership." (Billy's Centre Island home was a short drive from this dock. When he bought the place, he had planned on traveling to the city from his own beachfront, but environmental regulators refused to allow construction of a dock along the rocky shoreline.)

Captain Gene Pelland was the ace skipper Billy employed for *Ven-*

detta and various other watercraft—all the way up to the eighty-five-foot "expedition ship" *Audacious* that capped the fleet when Billy was deeply invested in boating and boat-building, for a decade or so beginning in 1998. Captain Gene had first suggested the elegantly simple solution for getting Billy to the stadium, though the idea also had a historical precedent.

Even during the Depression that followed the Crash of 1929, John Hay Whitney and some of the other swells from this neighborhood—people with names like Vanderbilt and Pulitzer—had used powerful commuter yachts much like *Vendetta* to zip down to Wall Street, avoiding traffic and the street-bound common folk. Billy had made the same trip to Shea just two days before, and at forty-five knots, it had taken just half an hour to coast out of Oyster Bay Harbor, then round the top of Centre Island, head west through Long Island Sound, and wind south to a channel in Queens that leads to the stadium, just in time for the first concert.

"Now, I'm no major league baseball player. And I certainly don't look like a rock 'god.' Yet all those people who were going to schlep to that place were expecting me to put on a great show," says Billy. The Wednesday event had gone well, though Billy had begun with something of an apology: "After all, that Wednesday night crowd had bought tickets to Last Play at Shea, and there they were watching the Second to Last Play at Shea. When I said into the mike, 'I want to apologize to those of you who bought tickets thinking this was the last show at Shea,' some of those present gave me what you might call a rousing New York welcome or, as one magazine described it, 'a chorus of jeers.' I added, 'I know. I suck. A lot of scalpers got ahold of tickets, and a lot people who wanted to go couldn't get in. They don't enforce the frickin' laws in this state anymore!'"

The upshot was that the Friday show, the last of the last, was indeed pressurized. "If this had been a show at any other arena, I wouldn't have been so concerned. But living up to that tag 'Last Play at Shea'? In many ways I felt unworthy of the whole thing. I've had a great career, but it was mind-boggling to think that I would be the guy who turned off the lights at that stadium. So I was really grateful for the backup."

Billy had persuaded some big names to perform with him that night—Tony Bennett, John Mayer, Roger Daltrey, Garth Brooks—but there was still that one person he had fervently wanted from the beginning: Sir Paul McCartney. "I don't care who you are," Billy says, "as far as I'm concerned, that stadium still belonged to the Beatles. It was still their room."

"Billy had always wanted to have Paul play at this show," says Steve Cohen. "He had asked him before we went on sale, asked him after we went on sale, and the line that we had heard back was he had to respectfully decline because he believed that the Beatles at Shea Stadium was a onetime event and could never be topped.

"But deep down inside we knew what it meant to Billy. No matter what goes on in Billy's life, there's always something more that he wants, there's always something more in his mind that's going to make this thing perfect."

THEIR ARRIVAL AT Shea on Friday went smoothly. Gene nestled *Vendetta* into a small marina, where Billy's tour director, Max, and his security man, Noel Rush, were waiting in a golf cart. Billy hopped into the cart with his physician and pal, Anthony Ardito, who had traveled with him from Centre Island.

It may have been a way of deflecting any brooding about Billy's own responsibilities to this landmark occasion, but for the next several hours, the topic of conversation was all Paul all the time. As Billy made the journey to the stadium, Lee Eastman was in touch by mobile phone to let him know that Paul was willing to try his best to appear, if only he could arrive in time. Paul had told Lee, "Tell Billy, 'I Saw Her Standing There' in the key of E," Eastman recalls. "I said, 'Key of E, right? If I can make it.' So it was this high-wire act for the next few hours or so, where it was unclear if Paul's plane was going to be late." McCartney had boarded a plane at London Heathrow, bound for JFK, but there were no guarantees. He was due to land perilously close to the end of Billy's show, sometime after eleven P.M.

"Friday afternoon, it was about four o'clock, we were in the corridor backstage, and I walked into the production office and there was a bit of a flutter," says Cohen. "Noel looked at me and said, 'Paul's coming.'" The potential flight delays that might have undone the plan had been avoided. "And then I walked right into Billy's dressing room, and the first thing out of his mouth was, 'Paul's coming.' Then I walked out of the dressing room, and [tour director] Max Loubiere came up to me and said, 'Did ya hear that Paul's coming?' So within thirty seconds the inner core of our group knew exactly what was going on."

Whether Paul showed up or not, there were a whole lot of people out there who'd come to see an epic show. Says Billy, "We started, as we tend to, with 'Angry Young Man,' and I was pounding out that intro when I realized just how sweaty I was going to get under those lights on such a steamy night. Then, during 'My Life,' Steve put the lights on the whole house, and I looked out and told the crowd of fifty-five thousand exactly what I was thinking—'Is this cool or what?'" Then Billy mentioned how the place really still belonged to the Beatles, and the impact that band had had on him in 1964, the first year he joined up with a band and started playing rock and roll, a year before the quartet played Shea.

Then suddenly everyone was pulling in the same direction. Billy pounded out his set, with guests, as the road company clustered backstage to begin working the phones, contacting British Airways, U.S. Customs, the Port Authority, the state police, and the city police department—all striving to speed Paul's arrival at Shea.

Sometime in the middle of the concert, Wayne Williams, Billy's piano tech, brought him a fresh towel and let him know that Paul had entered New York air space. It turned out that both Billy's doctor, Anthony Ardito, and his motorcycle-riding buddy, Rob Schneider (who was also his partner in a custom-bike business Billy had started recently) knew a guy in air traffic control. The controller had arranged for Paul's British Airways flight to land well ahead of schedule. Once Paul was on the ground, the police ran out onto the tarmac and escorted him all the way from JFK to Shea—eleven minutes, door to door.

Says Paul McCartney, "I got off the airplane faster than anyone's ever got off a plane before, and they just whisked me through. It was, 'Ah, don't worry about that, you're coming with me!' And customs— 'Just go through!' You know no one's ever had it so good—the best ride ever. I said, 'I wanna travel like this all the time.'"

"Because I was so focused on Paul making it on time, much of the rest of the concert is a blur," says Billy. "But there were definitely some high points for me. Tony Bennett went wonderfully off script on 'New York State of Mind,' and we were joined onstage by some cops and fire-fighters [as the chorus for a stirring treatment of "Goodnight Saigon"]. 'Thank you,' I said to the crowd, 'and thank them!'" The ovation for New York's finest and bravest, as Billy gestured to them, was huge. "Another moment was hearing John Mayer play so sensitively on 'This Is the Time.' He wrung music out of the song that I barely knew was there."

Mayer remembers, "Billy said, 'I have a song I think you'd be really great on.' And I go up there, and I play on the song, and it's magical, because he picked the right song for me to play. He's not thinking about *Well, this is really gonna be great for the profile with the kids.* It's one musician calling up another."

"Sometimes it's almost an out-of-body experience, hearing these songs you sweated through as a kid spilling out to so many people at once," says Billy. "A line like, 'They just found your father in the swimming pool . . .' in 'Captain Jack'—that's entertainment? But when we stuck a bit of 'A Hard Day's Night' into 'River of Dreams,' it was both a tribute to the Beatles and I guess a sort of tease. Would Paul make it? Everyone's having a good time, but the truth is, we were just vamping, stalling for time."

After "You May Be Right," Billy and the band stopped for a first encore. Then they played "Scenes from an Italian Restaurant" and "Only the Good Die Young."

Finally, Wayne put a scribbled note on Billy's piano: "Paul's here."

"Bringing Paul McCartney onstage—at Shea Stadium itself—was truly one of the great moments of my career," says Billy. The band started the intro to "I Saw Her Standing There," and Billy announced, "Ladies and gentlemen, please welcome Paul McCartney," and the crowd went apoplectic. "We had barely rehearsed the song, but Paul gave it his all, hitting the high notes and giving them a good, subtle version of that famous head shake. I couldn't get the grin off my face." Then they played "Piano Man," which they always close their shows with. "As we walked off the stage, I knew we'd do one last encore; I just had no idea what song to perform. What song was worthy of the Last Play at Shea?"

But Paul knew. Backstage he said to Billy, "We should do 'Let It Be.'"

"I said, 'Hey, can I do this? 'Cause I know I'm stealing the top spot—it's your show. I'm just a guest,'" says Paul. "And really, I should've done my thing and then Billy should've finished. But he was very gracious. He said, 'No, you're right—you should finish it.'"

As Billy reflects on the night, "There's really no way to describe what a high point that was—playing 'Let It Be' with Paul McCartney at Shea Stadium. And of course, with all the emotion and the sense of a circle being closed, with this great feeling of my career and my whole life's path coming together at that time, I had a deeper realization on that stage."

It had come to him, almost piercingly, in an off-the-cuff joke he made midway through the show, during "She's Always a Woman." There was a guy near the stage with his date, and Billy's crew had gotten word that he planned to propose to his girlfriend right there.

Seated not far away from the man was Katie Lee Joel, seen fleetingly in the live footage of the concert and also briefly interviewed for the *Last Play* documentary film chronicling the event. The announcement that the couple was splitting up came not quite a year after that evening at Shea.

Billy's piano tech cued him when the big moment came, and Steve Cohen hit the guy with the spotlight as he was quite obviously proposing to her. Billy then tossed out the comment, "Are you gonna marry her?" He raised his arms high with a big grin.

"Yes?" Billy asked. The audience cheered. "Congratulations! Get a prenup!" Billy told him.

There was a big laugh, a roar, from the stands. "That's when it hit me," says Billy. "In this stadium filled with fifty-five thousand exuberant people, I was the only one not enjoying the joke."

CHAPTER 17

ANOTHER DAY COMES TO AN END

Coming off the Last Play at Shea, Billy felt the buzz he needed to commit himself to an extended world tour that would spill right across the rest of 2008 and much of 2009. He would need that energy for the classic twenty-two hours of boredom that give way for a mere couple hours of fun onstage. Touring was also an overwhelmingly male enterprise—often, backstage, the sole female with an ongoing role in mounting the shows was the ever-capable and congenial production assistant Liz Mahon (whose husband tours in John Mellencamp's band)— and Billy hoped Katie would join him along the way.

As the late-autumn start of their swing through Asia and Australia loomed, however, it was becoming clear to Billy that Katie, caught up in her burgeoning career and the new opportunities that came with it, wasn't going to be the kind of wife who enjoyed life on the road. "Let's face it, if you're not getting the onstage buzz, it's a dubious way of life," says Billy. "Even the charter jets and the five-star hotels and the fancy meals and the avalanche of swag and adulation don't really take the grind out of it."

Billy's career had thrown a number of obstacles in front of their marriage, and the signs of strain were multiplying. Insiders say that one emblematic moment presented itself in mid-October, when Billy found himself in a drafty, venerable Manhattan concert hall called the

Hammerstein Ballroom, rehearsing with Bruce Springsteen for a fund-raising benefit for presidential candidate Barack Obama.

Billy had spent a long afternoon in the hall's confines while the Secret Service was at work getting ready to lock the place down for the senator's appearance later that evening. "Bruce and his band were there, and without wanting to sound corny, so was a sense of hope and change," says Billy. "Our bands fell into that easy musicians' camara-derie that's not without an edge of competitiveness to it—but of course that went unspoken."

Midway through the rehearsal, Katie Lee, per Billy's invitation, stopped by with some girlfriends. They were all dressed to the nines—young, pretty, vivacious—and yet there was a feeling in the room that they acted like upper-class debutantes visiting the hired entertainment. "There was something patronizing about it," says one insider. "She had been this girl we thought of almost as a hillbilly. Fresh out of college but still unspoiled, we thought."

The evening itself—billed as "Change Rocks"—was a landmark moment for Billy, given his long-held liberal political side. He felt it was a privilege to play. The bill would include India.Arie and John Legend and even a cameo from Alexa on "Baby Grand." Bruce and Billy had fig-ured out which songs they might trade verses on, and they'd gotten their various band members aligned, but Billy pushed to keep the rehearsals brief. "That was somewhat to Bruce's discomfort," he remembers. "But I just don't like to squeeze the inspiration too thin by overpreparing.

"Bruce is a savvy emcee on a rock stage, and I'm fairly confident in my ability to vamp with whatever's going on, so that evening, as the hall filled up with swells who were willing to pay, in some cases, several thousand bucks per ticket—I'm against inflated prices, but this was an exception—we mingled with the crowd backstage." These attendees included a mix of musicians, politicos, and heavy security under the su-pervision of the Secret Service operatives who were there in number.

At the show's start, Bruce walked into the spotlight and said, "Wel-come to the summit meeting!" He'd take up the same theme in the

spring of 2010, when he and Billy appeared together at the Rock and
Roll Hall of Fame's twenty-fifth-anniversary concert: New Jersey and
Long Island, he theorized, would still be part of a continuous land mass,
had it not been for continental drift. But tonight, for Obama, the two
blended music as well as territory. Thus Bruce ad-libbed on "Tenth Avenue Freeze-Out," "When the change was made uptown and the Piano
Man joined the band . . ." and also "when Jersey and Long Island bust
this city in half!"

"When I didn't know all the changes to his 'Spirit in the Night,'"
recalls Billy, "Bruce called out the chords, and he really invested his
verses in 'New York State of Mind,' 'Allentown,' 'A Matter of Trust,'
and 'River of Dreams' with that Bruce fire and commitment. We had
a heartfelt hug at the end and had raised what turned out to be $8 mil-
lion for Obama's campaign—and perhaps set the stage for some future
collaborations."

For Billy, meeting Obama and his wife, Michelle, more than met his
expectations, and the two men had the chance to discuss the psychol-
ogy of growing up with a single mom, and "how that may set you on a
particular, perhaps hard-striving, path in life," says Billy. "He casually
talked about inviting me and Katie to the White House if all went well,
and naturally I said we'd be honored"—though he was still mulling over
the uncomfortable moment with Katie earlier that day and perhaps realizing the future was going to be hard to predict.

"You register these feelings, and then you try to move on," says Billy.

A month later they were all outbound for the concert tour that
would begin in Hong Kong, hopscotch briefly to Tokyo, then cover all
the major Australian cities. Katie brought her mom, an amiable and
pretty southern lady, and they arrived in Japan and were installed on the
penthouse floor of the lofty Park Hyatt, the hotel that had supplied the
setting for the 2003 film *Lost in Translation*.

The plan was for Billy and Katie to take the several free days between tour legs in Japan and Australia to relax at the Four Seasons in
Bali. Known for its discreet service and for a romantic aura exemplified

by its private bungalows with luxuriously warm plunge pools, the Bali break would be a nice setting for some quality time before the Aussie tour began.

Perhaps she was wary of the line of thunderstorms that was moving across their planned flight path to Indonesia, or perhaps she was thinking about career opportunities that had come up back home, but Katie Lee passed on that experience. After the Japan leg, she and her mom got on a plane to the States, and Billy found himself facing a trip to Bali, amid the impeccable comfort of the luxurious villa of a five-star hotel at Jimbaran Bay—and no one to share it with. The morning of their separate departures, Billy sat alone in a glassed-in anteroom for smokers at the periphery of the Park Hyatt's dining room, working on a cigarette and staring out a wall of glass, across Tokyo to Mount Fuji, wondering what was going to become of his marriage.

A LITTLE TANNER than he had been a few days before, and in some regards more relaxed, Billy arrived in Perth for a November 23 show to kick off his Aussie tour. About as far from the major Australian population centers as you can get, Perth has a slightly rustic air—almost like a frontier town, planted at the edge of a million square miles of western Australia. Billy was somewhat oblivious to his surroundings as he hunkered down with Steve Cohen and Brian Ruggles to concentrate on how best to reintroduce themselves to the audiences in Australia, a country that had always been so welcoming. They would cover the major venues moving from west to east, ending in Sydney before a hop to Auckland, New Zealand, and then head home.

A crucial addition to the set list for most of the Australian shows would be one of only two songs that Billy had written as "pop" compositions, words and all, in many years: "Christmas in Fallujah." The experience of fund-raising for Barack Obama had made Billy's feelings about America's dual wars in Iraq and Afghanistan, as engineered by the outgoing Bush-Cheney administration, all the more bleak. America (and, in a much lesser way, its ally Australia) was now bogged down in a struggle that seemed to offer little chance of successful resolution. The Iraq chapter was fizzling to a close, though with constant violence still cooking, an equally unpromising mission in Afghanistan loomed. "Any thinking person has to sympathize with the soldiers who had to prosecute these conflicts," says Billy.

Not unlike "Goodnight Saigon," "Christmas in Fallujah" was told from the point of view of those troops who, Billy said at the time, "fight in our name, for little thanks." And in this case, for apparently indifferent results:

> It's evening in the desert
> I'm tired and I'm cold
> But I am just a soldier
> I do what I am told
> We came with the crusaders
> To save the holy land
> It's Christmas in Fallujah
> And no one gives a damn . . .
> They say Osama's in the mountains
> Deep in a cave near Pakistan
> But there's a sea of blood in Baghdad
> A sea of oil in the sand
> Between the Tigris and Euphrates
> Another day comes to an end
> It's Christmas in Fallujah
> Peace on earth, goodwill to men.

Billy would perform the song with a fervent rasp onstage, but he hadn't wanted to sing on the recording himself, unwilling to reengage with the music industry and its commercial expectations for anything he might release. Guitarist Tommy Byrnes, who does a good deal of producing between tours, knew a talented young singer named Cass

Dillon, and Billy felt that a younger voice—as young as most of the guys on the ground in the war zone—would be appropriate. Dillon's version would debut as an iTunes single in December and be included there on his EP, with the proceeds earmarked for the Iraq and Afghanistan veterans' charity, Homes for Our Troops, a nonprofit that builds homes for disabled vets.

"Fallujah" was slotted into the Aussie sets as the fourteenth number, between "River of Dreams" and their version of AC/DC's "Highway to Hell." The latter song, number 258 on *Rolling Stone*'s list of the 500 Greatest Songs of All Time, was performed by guitar roadie Ricky LaPointe—better known as Chainsaw (one reviewer said that he was presumably named for the sound of his voice)—a man of impressive rotundity who stalked the stage in baggy shorts, hollering the words that recount the singer's history of paying his dues in a "rockin' band," en route to the promised land. "'Highway to Hell' is a kind of novelty number," says Billy, "though I introduced it in down there [in AC/DC's Aussie homeland] as a spiritual. I suppose if Attila had made the grade, I'd be writing lyrics like that."

Since, in this added part of the set, Billy would already have a guitar strapped on for "Fallujah," he would keep it on to wander about riffing and getting a look at the fans behind the stage. (Steve Cohen, in his wisdom, encouraged Billy to leave the piano stool and roam about a bit—a nod to the days when Billy used to do flips off the piano and climb up into the rigging.) Billy is not vain about what he can do with a Gibson Les Paul. "I can hear my guitar in the monitor," he says, "but I know Brian Ruggles at the sound board doesn't exactly have me cranked up to eleven in the house mix."

Like any touring band, Billy's gang carries something of a lost patrol vibe with them. "Doing those small Aussie cities reacquaints you with the band. I mean, what are you going to do at eleven P.M. in Adelaide?"

But whenever a newer band member gets caught up in what has been a largely self-contained unit—along with Billy and band, the usual core traveling party includes Brian, Steve, Max Loubiere, security man

Noel Rush, and valet Mickey Heyes—the new guy doesn't always know the rules of the road.

For example, in the van to and from the gig, or in the small jets that Billy and his small wolf pack charter to get from city to city, they have what they call the "no-compliment zone." "We actually talked about getting signs made up to enforce that. It's somewhat like the rules for Jerry Seinfeld's show—'no hugging, no learning,'" says Billy.

"They all do their jobs very well; that's why they're here. The deal is, just as I don't walk around and bust people's chops, I also don't hand out compliments. It's just not me."

One day Billy's inner circle was on a charter jet with, unusually, a couple of band members crowded in. Midway through the flight, drummer Chuck Burgi, one of the newer players at a mere eight years, said, "Billy, you're singing like a bird." The old guard—Billy, Steve, Brian, and Max—looked over at Chuck, and the query came in cross-talked disbelief: "What? What did you say?"

Chuck repeated it: "You're singing like a bird."

"Chuck," Billy replied, eyes widening with intense fake sincerity—though the facts were true enough—"you're playing like a *demon*."

Chuck didn't miss the attitude coming his way. "What? What did I say?"

"We had to explain it to him," says Billy, replaying the moment. "As in 'Don't you know this is a no-compliment zone? Get your nose out of my ass. Don't ever compliment me, because it angers the Chinese gods.' Sure enough, the next day I got a cold."

For Billy, on the road, the guys, for better or worse, are his family. The road dogs have aged, and the bonding that used to take place in hotel bars and smoky late-night hotel rooms is now about shared if slightly road-weary professionalism, says Billy, "especially these days, when the snacks table in the production office—which used to be topped with a bottle of Scotch and a few packs of smokes and God knows what else that's bad for you—is now covered in herbal tea and aspirin and glucosamine and saw palmetto and vitamin supplements." Inevitably, as the entire cadre ages with different degrees of grace, some will fall by the wayside—though they are whistling past that notion with very little discussion.

WITH SOME MISGIVINGS that the topic even comes up, the road dogs dutifully inquire after one another's health. In contrast to age-old rock tradition, they discourage bad health habits. Thus when Billy visited his swami in Boston a few years back, determined to kick cigarettes for good, he brought a couple of guys from the road gang: Mike Grizel, who is responsible for getting the band and all their road gear from point A to point B on time and in perfect condition, and even Tommy, "who only looks like he's in perfect condition," says Billy. One evening while Billy's long-standing friend, comic Paul Reiser, was backstage before a gig, Tommy, lean and rakishly handsome and looking stylish in leather, walked in. Reiser said, "You look just the same." Billy, without missing a beat, added emphasis by spitting out a four-letter epithet of the sort only very good friends can use on one another.

The smoking cure actually took for all parties for a while—but by the time of the 2008 Oz tour, not so much. Billy will sporadically state that he plans to go back for a reboot with the swami. Meanwhile, he knows exactly when he fell off the tobacco wagon: "I have to blame Robert Downey, Jr., for that."

The Downey moment happened when Billy was at a party out in the Hamptons at Ron Perelman's estate. "Ron always has a good mix of people—writers, actors, musicians, politicians, authors—at his house. I saw Robert, whose acting I had always admired [and whose troubles with substance abuse had been well publicized], and said, 'How are you, man? How are you doing with everything?'"

Robert knew what Billy meant and said, "Great. I feel terrific. The only vice I have left are these." He took a pack of Camels out of his shirt pocket, shook out a cigarette, and held one out to Billy—a cordial offer. "So, as a joke, after not smoking for seventeen years, I thought,

Oh, sure, why not? I'll show him some solidarity," says Billy. "He lit it for me, and I got stoned out of my mind from sucking on this Camel. Didn't really think anything about it. I was a little bit surprised at how I was able to inhale again after seventeen years. I thought I'd be coughing my lungs out.

"The next day I wanted a cigarette, just to get that nicotine thrill again. I forgot that nicotine is a powerful intoxicant. I lit one up on the patio and got stoned again. Went back in the house with my ears ringing and my eyes glazed. Then, later in the day, I had another one. And then I was hooked. Not too long after that I was smoking a few cigarettes every day. I've since quit again—and then restarted once again."

The reformed Downey would prove a less dangerous acquaintance than the great Downey pal, pre-controversy Mel Gibson. According to Billy, "I ran into Mel once in the eighties in some ritzy hotel in Europe, and—as sometimes happens when people accidentally meet and decide to console each other for being rich and famous and all that—we went on a serious bender." Beyond a certain comradely competition to stay upright and coherent, the precise details have been lost, says Billy: "I just know we crossed paths in the lobby the next day, and a certain look of understanding passed between us, as in *Okay, we're regular guys, but let's be certain never to sit down at the same table again*."

Billy returned home from Australia in late December, not long before the holidays, and spent a lazy couple of weeks, largely in the warmth of his Miami house, with as few obligations as possible. After greeting 2009, he headed out on the road with Elton in the newest incarnation of the Face to Face tour. Although Billy might not have bet on it when they opened at the Hard Rock in Fort Lauderdale on January 2, they'd be out there for almost all of 2009. They traveled from Florida to Vegas and back, tramping through the South and Southwest, over to Anaheim and then up through the Midwest, over to Canada in late spring, then back down for ballparks like Wrigley Field in Chicago and Nationals Park in D.C. Finally, just before the concluding dates in Albany and Buffalo, Billy went down for the count—exhausted, physically and emotionally.

His back was in constant pain, and his gut felt, as he described it, "like a sump of rich road chow and overpriced bottles of red."

Looking back over his touring schedule in 2009, it was pretty obvious to Billy at what stage his marriage to Katie guttered out: "somewhere in between visits to Chicago in May and July," he remembers.

Call it the constant road work, call it the age difference, call it the shift in Katie's aspirations as her career was taking off, call it Billy's moodiness—whatever the calculus, things weren't working. Billy was just as likely to see Katie in a paparazzo photo of a gallery opening or at lunch with the girls as he was to see her on the road. "Turning up for the gig in Fargo wasn't Katie's idea of a good use of time," says Billy.

From mid-2008, the tabloids and gossip sheets started running photos of Katie with Israeli fashion designer Yigal Azrouel, who provided some of the outfits she wore out on the town and for the shots in her cookbook, *The Comfort Table*. At first it was generally presumed he was gay, given the usual stereotypes regarding his trade and his habit of inevitably wearing a scarf piled around his neck "just so." But by the time photos emerged of the two of them dancing at the Delano Hotel in Miami, the leer and the sweat and the one A.M. shadow on his jaw all played into establishing his rep as what one gossip page would describe as a "skirt chaser."

"Those photos looked bad," Katie admits, but adds that they were misleading. "I was dancing with this guy that night at Art Basel in Miami. He was part of our circle of friends—and there were probably ten of us who had gone out. We went to a club—I'd probably gone to three clubs in seven years. And it was about two o'clock in the morning. We're all drinking, having this fun night, and you could have gotten a picture of me with about three other guys, who were gay, doing the same thing. We were all just dancing and having fun. I had my arm around the guy's neck, but it wasn't like anything that should have been incriminating—it was innocent dancing.

"Immediately after that, the person who took [the shot] put it on their blog, and Bill called me and goes, 'Oh, you're on a blog dancing.'

I was like, 'Whatever.' Neither one of us thought anything of it. Then it was April, and I think the *National Enquirer* bought the pictures, printed them. I was upset about it because I never like anybody to be talking about me. But the important thing to me was that Bill and I were okay. But then, two months later, when we split up, that's fresh in the press's mind, like, *Oh, wait, there were these pictures of her dancing with this guy, it must be because of that.* But that had happened six months prior."

The scandal hurt all their friendships. Katie had been friendly with Azrouel for a couple of years—indeed, he had helped debut her first cookbook in June that year at his store on a posh shopping strip in Southampton's Water Mill hamlet. She wore his clothes all the time, and his business partner was one of her best girlfriends—so the controversy made social life difficult for everyone involved.

"If I was having this big affair with him, I probably would have ended up with him."

"The end of my marriage to Katie wasn't about that guy," says Billy. "We just had too many challenges, and maybe she didn't want to be Penelope waiting for Odysseus to come home and slay the suitors."

Despite all these problems, Billy was still holding out hope for the marriage in early May 2009, as his sixtieth birthday approached. As planned, between gigs in Madison, Wisconsin, and Omaha, Nebraska, he and his circle were in Chicago. The party took place at the noted steakhouse Gibson's, where, Billy jokes, "you can wait a long time for a table, unless you're Michael Jordan, Mayor Daley, or our party of eighty-some with the upstairs rented out."

Unlike his fiftieth birthday, which had had a *Godfather* theme—Billy had stood in a chalk-striped suit at the door of a mansion with Carolyn beside him looking like Rita Hayworth—this was an evening of mixed emotions. The afternoon had gone well, as Katie presented him with a hot yellow Ducati 750 Sport motorcycle, a modern take on the low-slung, café-racer style Billy favors. Coming together across the lobby of the Ritz Carlton, Katie stylish as always in a fitted, buttery leather jacket, they looked for a moment like newlyweds who had observed the proper protocols.

Once the celebrants were assembled at Gibson's, what might have been a night of brief roastlike toasts turned into something a bit more like pussyfooting, with many violations of the no-compliments rule, albeit well marbled with profanities. Billy made the mandatory speech of thanks, complete with a hollered aside that "she's not doing the designer"—and then he hit the piano for a cathartic session of pounding out Beatles songs.

Call it the last best time, as the next day Katie was back on a plane to New York, and Billy and the guys were nursing hangovers with the Nebraska gig on the near horizon.

THE DENOUEMENT OF Billy's marriage to Katie would be a scattered and sad one. As the Face to Face tour drifted through the Midwest, bouncing out of Chicago to dutifully play the sometimes-unloved third-tier towns like Fargo, Madison, Omaha, and Indianapolis, Billy took a couple of charter jet flights home for a last try at repairing relations.

He and Katie had talked about taking a trip to Italy when the present tour leg ended. "I wanted to go," says Billy, "and then she wanted to go ahead and get divorced. And the key question she asked was 'Are you happy?' I said, 'No, I'm not, either. I'm not happy with the way things are. It doesn't mean I want to cut the cord. I want to work on it. Let's work on it.'

"I wonder now, should I have just grabbed her hands and said, 'How can I make you happy? What do you need? What should we do to resolve this?' Instead of saying, 'Do you want a divorce?' Because as a guy, I always feel like I'm holding her against her will, unless I give her the option. '*Do* you want to leave?' I think it's a more chivalrous thing to do. 'Are you so unhappy that you want a divorce?' "

The couple were going to speak about reconciling with an intermediary, and Billy remembers, "Katie went off on an [irrelevant tangent] about the furniture. I realized, *It's not going to happen. We're over.* You have to face it.... *Just don't send me messages, don't leave me cute little phone calls, don't tease me, don't fuck with me, just end it.* 'Cause I'm an old man now, a vulnerable man, *Don't do that to an old guy.* What are my chances of getting somebody in their twenties at this point? I don't want somebody in their twenties.

"It was then that I realized that the marriage was finally over," he explains. "The phone calls back and forth with Katie, where we talked, sometimes angrily, sometimes lovingly, about what might be done to keep us together, were yielding no results. It was just about time to hand it over to the lawyers."

"There were lots of days like that in those last few months where I thought, *I can't do it*," Katie recalls. "And then he'd be okay, and I'd see that great Bill, and I'd be like, *Okay then, I love him so much; we can make this work.* Finally I just got to the point where it's like, *I just can't.* And it wasn't even the tougher episodes; it was what comes after that—the mood swings. It affects your character. And finally I just thought, *I can't deal with it.*"

There was a prenup in place, as well as a reasonable fund of good-will, so there would be no hostility, no unseemly wrangling. Instead, what Billy found himself facing was "a mother lode of disappointment and chagrin."

Billy was almost mournfully fixated on how little consolation is to be found in more material evidence of a life well lived: "None of the rest of it means a goddamn thing. You can have all the money in the world, you can have mansions, you can have properties, you can have yachts, you can have limousines, you can have motorcycles. Without the right girl, it doesn't mean a goddamn thing. You take the whole centrality out of it."

He continues: "That's what it's all aimed at—*I want to be your white knight on my white horse, with you riding with your arms around my waist, and I will ride with you into Camelot.* That's what you want. And you've felt like that since you were a little boy. And you take the girl out of the mix, and what have you got? A bunch of *stuff.* And who gives a shit?"

The news came in midsummer:

NEWSDAY - LONG ISLAND, N.Y.
DATE: JUNE 18, 2009
START PAGE: A.12

Billy Joel and wife Katie Lee confirmed yesterday that they are splitting up after nearly five years of marriage.

"This decision is the result of much thought and consideration," the couple said in a joint statement. "Billy and Katie remain caring friends, with admiration and respect for each other."

Rumors have been swirling about Joel and Lee's marriage for months, especially after speculation that Lee had been romantically linked to fashion designer Yigal Azrouel, who had been escorting her to numerous events while Joel was on tour.

Joel's publicist Claire Mercuri denies the speculation, adding that the decision to split only came in the past two weeks. In that time, Joel has been staying at the couple's home in Sag Harbor, while Lee has been living in their Manhattan town house.

The piece went on to misreport that Katie had failed to attend his birthday and included a sidebar:

THE WOMEN IN HIS LIFE

Married manager Elizabeth Weber in September 1973, divorced in July 1982

Married supermodel Christie Brinkley in March 1985, divorced August 1994; one daughter, Alexa Ray Joel, 23

Married TV entertainment correspondent Katie Lee in October 2004, confirmed split yesterday

If Billy's agonies were personal, they were once again anything but private. When the numbers were compiled for Nielsen Syndicated TV Show Ratings for the week ending June 21, 2009, the takeaway was that it was a great week for the daily suppertime showbiz newsmagazines: "Extensive coverage of Billy Joel's divorce from his third wife, Katie Lee, sent *ET* weekend numbers up 20% to 1.8, tops among first run weekly hours."

The Chicago gig, scheduled at the height of his personal turmoil, should have been a fun midsummer one for Billy. As a lifelong baseball fan, he knew the lore of Wrigley Field. That ivy-covered bandbox of a ballpark is so tightly wedged into its typical Chicago neighborhood that much of Billy's usual encampment had to be positioned in the street alongside the stadium.

The crew set Billy up in a camper van under the bleachers. And in those shadowy, unfriendly confines, after hobbling out to the ballpark (accommodating his increasingly sore hips, groin, and back) to do a quick sound check, he sat in the van just letting the despair over his failing marriage have its say. Tommy Byrnes dared to sit in the gloom with Billy, knowing he could be a silent presence and still something of a comforting one. "You know, boss," he ventured, "when we head back east, there are some cities where some of the guys know some chicks who just, you know, are 'dying to meetcha.'"

The "meetcha" was of course a reference to the Rolling Stones' 1978 hit "Miss You" from the *Some Girls* album, which had some less sanguine lyrics as well:

Well I've been stumbling on my feet
Shuffling through the street . . . Lord, I miss you child.

Billy gave Tommy an even look. "Thanks, man," he answered. "But you know what? I'm not thinking that way right now. What I'm thinking is, *You lost her. Call it what you want, call her what you want, but—you lost her.*"

Billy strove to imagine himself getting back into the game, but he was by now mystified as to what age group might be right for him. "I've been a rock-and-roll star all my life, so come on, it's an immature job that's kept me immature. I think the optimal age would be anywhere from midthirties to fifty." Soon afterward he met a charming, intelligent beauty, actress Alex Donnelley, and they were even snapped by the *New York Post* embracing in his backyard in Sag Harbor. "She was very, very nice. I think it was just too soon, right at the rip, at the tear [of the breakup with Katie], and I was just—whoa, I can't deal with this."

A few days after Chicago, Billy had dates scheduled for Buffalo and Albany, but he hadn't slept for days and was exhausted. He was disoriented, too, and could barely walk, eat, think straight, or talk. Attempts to touch base went unanswered. The matrix of physical and emotional pain was rendering him mute and remote. A worried round of calls in his inner circle started up: Max to Steve to Brian to Dennis to Noel and back. Brian eventually visited Billy at his house, took one look at him, and said, "You can't gig, because you can't even walk." Billy told Brian that he couldn't possibly cancel, but Brian answered definitively: "You're not doing the gig."

Billy spent the next couple of days in a local hospital, and then his physicians suggested moving him to a big uptown Manhattan teaching hospital. They knew how torturous the series of his skeletal and muscular ailments had been—his recent history included an operation on two disks in his lower back, as well as the pills and therapies, including a lengthy course of steroids, for the sciatica that was later found to be traceable to congenitally malformed hips, perhaps worsened by his delivery by forceps as a breech baby. Once Billy was in the hospital, they changed his regimen of medication—the steroids weren't really helping—and then talked about the bigger picture: how the tour was affecting him, aging issues, all the different psychological concerns, and the looming divorce.

Billy told the doctors that he was just tired, burnt out—he needed time to grieve, to think, to pull it all back together. Says Billy, "You need time to be with you before you can be with somebody else—you can't just plug in another person. I think after a major jolt, you first need to know who you now are, before you can know what you're looking for next."

Billy decided he wanted to live for a while without being a "rock star" and was finally able to take a few months to rest and recuperate. He got back in steady touch with Alexa and quietly give his counsel on the performing career she'd begun about five years before. Though she had attracted some good notice—"as well she should," says Billy, "because she's got the chops and the personality and a real charm and command of the stage"—she felt a bit stalled.

Compounding that feeling was Alexa's breakup with her sometime bandmate and producer Jimmy Riot, a guy ten years her senior—"okay, no judgment from me there," says Billy—and not necessarily thriving in his own career.

"What could I say to her? Why would you ever hook up with a musician?

"The worse Alexa felt about her situation in general, the less communication we managed, but as always, Christie and I kept tabs, exchanged our insights, and did our best to be a pair of loving, supportive, if divorced parents."

Then one day in mid-December came a disturbing, even heartbreaking call. Alexa, in a search of some sort of refuge—what the cliché typically describes as cry for help—had taken an unlikely but thankfully not life-threatening oversupply of a homeopathic antihistamine called Traumeel. By the time Billy got the call, Christie had already rushed to Alexa's side in a downtown New York hospital. They quickly decided that Billy would stay away, rather than add to what was already threatening to become a circus atmosphere. Alexa and Billy got on the phone and had a brief, painful conversation. "I don't think she was in a frame of mind to feel the understanding I so wanted to give her, and in truth, I wasn't getting much back," says Billy. "But that will be an ongoing project—and the most important one in my life."

Alexa remembers him telling her that he was only a bit younger than she was when he drank the bottle of furniture polish: "I think it's hard to be in your early twenties and not know what you want and how to feel and who you're gonna be. I think he was very troubled in those times, and I think after that incident he had some perspective 'cause he said that he had checked into this psych ward and realized, 'Wow, I'm doing just fine—this is whacked over here. I gotta get out of here and move on with my life and get into music and be positive.'

"When I was on my first tour, I was a mess. I was saying, *What am I doing, this is crazy!* waking up in a different city every day," Alexa recalls. "I had gotten sick before one of the shows, and I was on the phone with him. 'Dad, what do I do?' and to kind of calm me down, he played 'Lullabye' for me on the piano, over the phone. That is really the song that is closest to my heart."

Part of Alexa's gaining more emotional resolve was embracing the fundamental show business ethic Billy taught her: "As it is with many artists, one of his most meaningful relationships has been with his fans, and I really think his most honest relationship has been with them.

"I think it's hard for people who have a job that they love, but it doesn't define them. With my dad, it defines him; like, he is musician, that's who he is."

Billy quietly traveled to the facility where Alexa had been hidden away from the media attention, in upstate New York, and remained at her side for several days. Then it was time, despite the twin distractions of his daughter's woes and his own marital ones, to once more address the tour. "The makeup dates we played upstate, for the postponed shows, really brought me around quite a bit," says Billy. "I have to say, I was enjoying those audiences." He was going to find some psychic handholds wherever he could: "There's always a lot of pretty women up front who are having a good time, and they grab at me. Sorry, I like getting felt up onstage. And that's one of those things I didn't think was still going to happen."

Billy also began planning for the kind of lectures he'd been delivering sporadically over the years: "There's a lot of satisfaction to be had in doing those, usually with a piano ready for a few bits illustrating what I'm discussing, but mostly talking about what I've learned from my career and from all the influences and my own musical heroes, the ones who helped make the career what it is.

"And at least by implication, a lesson I try to bring up is, *Don't be turned around in seeking what you want out of life. Don't be talked out of what you know is right.* Or as I've put it on occasion, *Don't take shit from anybody.*"

AS BILLY WAS musing on his career in 2009, he could hardly have anticipated the career revival that was about three years around the corner. He had real doubts about being an aging rocker.

The "Don't take shit . . . " admonition that had appeared around 1977 would give way to the wisdom of the age, though it was uttered at Madison Square Garden as late as 2012. While he had told Tim White in 1980 that the original meaning was meant to extend to "not giving shit *to* anybody," he eventually felt a little hypocritical saying it: "I wasn't the struggling, fighting, pissed-off angry young man I used to be.

"I'm in my sixties now. I was in a restaurant recently, and I heard 'It's Still Rock and Roll to Me,' and it hit me why people might not like this song. It's very snotty—'What's the matter with'—it's kind of a nyah-nyah-nyah-nyah-nyah song. I think it was Carolyn Beegan who first pointed it out. She said, 'I don't like that song . . . I just don't like the attitude.' And then I realized, *I get it, it's kind of snotty.* I was trying to be sarcastic. I might have overdone it. You can push that a little too far, making fun of being fashionable and hip and taking the piss out of that."

Early in his career, Billy recalls, "I was the struggling indie guy, and they were calling me a punk with my leather jackets and my cigarettes and my snotty attitude. I thought it was par for the course. I don't think you're supposed to be a shy wallflower in rock and roll. You got to get up on stage. You got to have some balls, man.

"And nowadays when I do the stand-up thing on 'Rock and Roll' and throw the mike stand, it feels a little funny. There's a chagrin aspect to it. *What am I doing up here? This should be done, this should be over by now. I should have been put out to—I should have been retired.*"

Certain strategies employed by bands he grew up hearing seemed chancy to Billy. Steely Dan played entire albums, while other contemporaries mixed in a number of "deep cuts" the audience was less familiar with. "Springsteen can go out and do the most obscure song," Billy says, "or Dylan can do that, and the crowd just eats it up. They know the words even to these album tracks. If I do it, the crowd may just sit there looking like a deer in the headlights. *What's that? Why isn't he doing his own stuff?*"

More than a few crowds, depending on just how Billy is feeling on any given night, have heard this aside when the spotlight catches him early on, or his image flashes thirty feet high on the video screens behind the stage: "Billy couldn't be here tonight—I'm Billy's dad."

Of course that's a typically canny move on his part—name the misgiving that otherwise might haunt the show, and in so doing, make it dissolve in laughter—especially for audiences full of fellow baby boomers. Still, despite his best efforts, "that feeling has only been enforced by moments in recent tours when I've been onstage, thinking, *I'm just too old for this stuff. No, you can't do this. Stop it, man.*"

And yet Dennis Arfa continues to come up with ideas. Not all of them draw enthusiasm from Billy: "I'll hear that my music is very popular in China. That it's played in every piano bar, and people have the records via bootleg or something. I don't think we've ever gotten like a legitimate offer to go and play a concert tour of China, which I'm not all that thrilled to do at this point. When I was younger, yeah, it would have been a Marco Polo adventure. But stories I hear about being in China for a while, it doesn't sound all that great. I already did my Russia-Cuba things—I'm not Henry Kissinger."

If diplomacy isn't his aspiration, even his chosen profession has begun showing its limitations: "In a way, I'm starting to kind of burn out on who I'm expected to be as a rock star. It's ironic, it's funny, it's amusing in some ways. But it's sometimes a pain in the ass, and the celebrity aspect of it horrifies me. Especially nowadays, celebrity is such a ridiculous over-the-top business on its own—look at the Kardashian syndrome—and I don't like it. I'm supposed to be this [celebrated] person, and when people meet me, they're so strange—'cause I'm this celebrity, and then I have a hard time breaking through that."

Other factors intrude, like *Forbes* magazine's 2010 estimate of Billy's net worth as $160 million. "It's north of that," he says without particular relish, and in an era where the money in pop music is at the box office even while his royalty payments pile up alongside, it's not likely to shrink anytime soon. David Geffen once said that continuing to earn on top of a large fortune isn't about needing any more, but simply "keeping score," and in that regard, Billy says, "there's an element of that. I trust Dennis that we don't want to fall behind in the box-office-dollar value competition. It's nice as a great payday. And I appreciate it.

"But I'm not doing it because I need that.

"I'm just doing it because—that's what I do."

CHAPTER 18

CARELESS TALK

"Some love," Billy had written in "A Matter of Trust" in the wildly happy days of 1983, "is just a lie of the heart / The cold remains of what began with a passionate start." "But that won't happen to us," he sang to the unnamed loved one, obviously Christie. And yet, the almost inescapable element he calls "the knife" was in there: "So break my heart if you must."

By midsummer of 2009, he was living these lyrics again. Katie was on her own, splitting time between the West Village townhouse that would be part of the divorce settlement and, as a kindness from Billy, the $16.5 million Sagaponack beachfront house he had acquired from actor Roy Scheider—as an indulgence for Katie that she protested—during their marriage. She was nominally out of his life and yet curiously in it, as they kept up a difficult postmarital friendship by phone and e-mail.

One of the worst days of Billy's early summer had come several weeks before, when, during a lonely, uncommunicative stretch that had caused consternation among his best friends, a small group had sought him out at the Centre Island mansion. Sitting down with long faces and considerable nervousness, they urged him to get some help. The session did not go well.

"So [they] came into my house, reading me an essay, and expect me to go, 'Oh, I get it, so I'm going to change my whole way of living.' I said, 'Look, my wife and I split up. I had a rough summer. There were a couple of nights I might have gone overboard. When I was in Scotland, I drank scotch. What else you got? 'Cause I went to rehab once, and I'm not going back again. And I'm not going to AA, and I don't buy into this shit. And I can control my intake, okay? And if I fuck up onstage and I fuck up the show, then you can come to me and tell me, "Look what you did, you fucked up." But I don't do that. I'm professional. A complete professional. I keep my shit together.' And when they buy into an orthodoxy, it bothers the crap out of me."

He had a special greeting for a trained counselor who had come along, a stranger: "There was that one guy sitting there in the chair, I was like, 'Now who the fuck are you? Who the fuck do you think you are?'

"They picked the wrong time. I said, 'I'm down, and I have a right to be down. I broke up with my third wife, and if I'm depressed, it has nothing to do with drugs or pills or booze. It just means I'm fuckin' bummed out. You're going to have to accept that,' I said. 'You would have been better off taking me out to lunch and saying, "Sometimes you're going over the edge, you got to watch it. Just be cool."'"

The entire situation was highly reminiscent of the 1993 B-side of "All About Soul," "You Picked a Real Bad Time":

> Tell me why you're tryin' to give me aggravation
> You picked a real bad time 'cause this man's got the blues.

A bit of a bump in maintaining cordial relations with Katie would occur in July 2011 with the release of *Groundswell*, a novel she would find herself defending as not being derived from the marriage. While the effort was undercut somewhat by the previous year's *New York Times* article "How to Cook Up a Food Celebrity," in which Katie's agent called the book "loosely based on her and Bill," the characters diverged in significant ways.

Still, the event conjured uncomfortable memories of an appearance she and Billy had made on *The Oprah Winfrey Show* when her cookbook came out in April 2008. During Billy's interrogation on the talk show queen's couch, Oprah grilled him about his car accidents, displaying photos along the way, and he sparred with her before elucidating that he wasn't such a bad driver; he had simply had bad luck. Winfrey asked him about his rehab visit to Betty Ford, and about relations with Christie, then leaned in on the couple's age difference. "I would have married her if she was thirty years older," Billy riposted with growing defensiveness, as Oprah moved on to press Katie on her relationship with Alexa. "I'm always impressed by her," Katie offered. Meanwhile, Billy would later recount, he was so obviously miserable being ambushed as he sat on Oprah's couch that Alexa cried watching him.

That turn in the road endeared Katie to neither husband nor stepdaughter. The 2011 novel would have to make its way without him, albeit with the notoriety the divorce had churned up.

Forthrightly designed as a "beach read," it was synopsized by *Kirkus Reviews* as "a novel whose self-important heroine is a famous actor's much younger wife who leaves him (with prenup) when he cheats on her, only to find love true weeks later with her surf instructor."

In the opening pages, Emma, a newly celebrated screenwriter working on a script for Harvey Weinstein, has a key revelation, and after the tale is told in flashbacks, she dumps her unfaithful husband. Soon enough she gets the kiss-off note from him: "You will no longer be able to use my name or to use any of my assets as collateral to arrange loans or credit—except, of course, for your half ownership of the apartment."

As it happens, life and art shared certain elements, as postdivorce Katie Lee would sell, for $11.65 million in February 2011, the Perry Street townhouse that Billy had bought as their Manhattan pied-à-terre for $5.9 million in 2006 and deeded to her when they broke up. It wasn't made publicly clear exactly how the couple's shared assets were divvied up, but insider accounts suggest that she was treated far more generously than the prenup would have mandated.

During the postbreakup summer, she stayed in Sagaponack as

something of a recluse, though she did recount on her Twitter feed her adventure of learning to surf. Friends privately shared the information that she had grown enamored of her surf instructor. This, too, was not made public; it might have undercut the purity of *Groundswell*'s fiction—by the book's late innings, with the actor dispatched, it's Emma's surf guru who is nibbling her earlobes during a "sex for hours" break from the restorative surf lessons.

Billy would get a nod in the acknowledgments as "the best ex-husband a girl could ever ask for," and indeed, the two have remained friendly, despite an early misunderstanding over precisely which artwork and pricey Nate Berkus–chosen furniture would be leaving Billy's possession. One insider account portrayed an assistant (who entered the property after Katie had made a culling) as calling Billy's staff in alarm in the belief that a full-scale burglary had occurred—a six-figure estimate of the items' value was privately tossed about. After a quick redo, the situation was resolved. On September 25, 2009, Katie Lee issued this tweet that was apparently about the scenario: "Drove a 14-foot Uhaul through the Bronx today (don't ask) . . . still recovering."

The amiable connection with her ex continues, although since new girlfriend Alexis Roderick came into Billy's life in October 2009, on a less frequent basis. Billy says, "Everything's cool that way. She's had to take more of a backseat in my life because I have another woman in it. So we speak once in a while, and I e-mail once in a while. She's living her life."

In fact, after befriending young piano-based songwriter Cassandra Kubinski in the aftermath of the Katie Lee breakup, he described his feelings of forgiveness in sufficient detail that Kubinski composed a song, "No Hard Feelings," depicting his take on it all:

You got the house, you got the cash
The furniture and all that trash
The dog's even going with you . . .

But you know, the hardest part
Is when I search deep in my heart
I got no hard feelings, no hard feelings
Because I know you really loved me.

"We still think of ourselves as friends," says Billy. "The great thing about my ex-wives is they all still like me. I've been able to retain friendships with my exes—Christie, Elizabeth I see from time to time, and I enjoy being a good friend to them."

ALMOST AS TRYING as his breakup with Katie was Billy's dispute with former drummer Liberty DeVitto, which kicked off in late May 2009, precisely when relations with Katie were at their marriage-ending worst. At age fifty-eight, Liberty said that since being discharged from the band in 2005, after thirty years with Billy, he'd been working studio gigs and teaching drum students to support himself and his family. He asked for royalties for songs he felt he had contributed to, and his lawyer proposed that they should audit Billy's books as part of their suit.

"Everybody always assumes that you make a lot of money because you worked with Billy Joel," DeVitto told a wire service reporter. "It didn't happen that way." (Billy's longtime associates know that Liberty had made $3 million in Billy's employ.)

DeVitto told the *New York Post* he was bitter over the way he lost his job: "People get fired, they get severance or insurance for a certain period of time. I didn't even get a phone call. It was cold."

Per rock legend, drummers are the volatile ones in most bands (and the most often replaced or, as *Spinal Tap* would have it, lost to bizarre circumstances best left unsolved). And for many years, Liberty DeVitto filled that role in Billy's band—mostly operating as what might be called "good crazy," a vibrant mix of undeniably pummeling chops, flamboyant onstage gesticulations, and such habits as slinging drumsticks into the audience. Beyond keeping a beat, he was Billy's comic foil onstage—a windmilling center of energy while the boss man was usually confined to his piano stool.

He'd been recruited from the very clubs Billy had played, and his band had even shared bills with Billy's Hassles. As Liberty would recall in 2013, when interviewed by the filmmakers on the occasion of the twenty-fifth anniversary of the Russia trip, "I was in a group called New Rock Workshop, and we used to walk past each other and just be like, 'Hey, how ya doin'?'"

When Liberty moved on to form Topper with Russell Javors, Doug Stegmeyer, and Howie Emerson, soon adding Richie Cannata, they drew enough attention to be recruited by Billy for the *Streetlife Serenader* tour. Believing that an artist should stick with one unified band in the studio and on the road, Billy told Doug, "I'm moving back to New York. I want the same guys to play on the record that go on tour with me, and I want a New York–style drummer." And Doug said, "Well, you know the guy."

Before hostilities erupted in 2009, Liberty told his story at some length for a fan site called the Electric Beard: "So Billy came to New York and I played for him, and he loved the new stuff that I played. He was going to do what eventually became *Turnstiles*, and it wasn't until many years later that he found out that Doug had slipped me a tape of the new stuff before I actually went into the audition. So I had that going for me."

With some further encouragement from Doug and Liberty, Billy brought on the Topper guitarists, and the band was set for nearly a quarter-century to come. There was still, however, the glitch in the *Turnstiles* sessions that occurred when Billy's temporary management wanted Elton's band to play. In an interview for *Drummer* magazine, Liberty recalled being plunged into that turnabout: "The funny thing is, when I got the phone call for the Billy audition, I asked, 'What is Billy into?' They said, 'Go buy [Elton's] "Captain Fantastic."' So I learned all of Nigel's licks . . . 'Don't Let the Sun Go Down on Me,' where he rides that cymbal for the longest time. On [Billy's] 'Honesty,' 'Leningrad,' I do the same thing in there."

Over the years, Billy would give Liberty credit for his court jester antics on- and offstage, and he even mentioned some input Liberty had in the studio on certain arrangements. But the slow accumulation of aggravations—what the band noticed as Liberty's lack of enthusiasm, sabotage on songs that had predated him, his suspected role in bringing false rumors to Christie about Billy, and his listless approach to working with Danny Kortchmar on *River of Dreams*—had taken a toll.

The drummer continued on the tack he'd set. Although Liberty didn't write any of the songs and didn't have a recording contract (beyond a particular bonus royalty pledged for a specific set of recordings), and although he had been paid triple scale for the bulk of the sessions he played on, he reportedly sought royalties for claimed creative input. Individuals privy to the back-and-forth in the lawsuit said the parties traded accusations—Liberty claiming that if he hadn't played the drums on *The Stranger*'s "Only the Good Die Young," it would have emerged as a reggae song, while a contrasting anecdote claimed that if Liberty's urgings had been obeyed, the most successful song on the same album, "Just the Way You Are," would have been recorded as a cha-cha. Whatever those differences, Billy had twice taken a stand in favor of retaining DeVitto despite the opinion of prospective producers George Martin and later Jimmy Guercio, each of whom had suggested a change of musicians and then moved on when that request was denied.

Among the contentions Liberty had made in the media was that Doug Stegmeyer's downward spiral to suicide had been worsened by his dismissal from Billy's band. Insiders spoke of a lingering resentment dating to the 70's when Liberty pulled away a chair Billy was about to sit in, possibly causing long-term damage.

When various bandmates felt Liberty was pushing the beat too avidly, leaving the lead singer panting out lines behind him, the change became inevitable. And yet Billy found himself missing the drummer's showmanship: "He *was* very exciting to watch, a show in his own right onstage. People loved watching him. He was a good drummer for many, many years with me. "

Liberty had also been indulged as Billy's team fought off a lawsuit caused by the drummer chucking his drumsticks into the audience. At a time when a certain amount of wanton destruction on the road was any rock band's birthright, DeVitto reportedly did his part. One tour had even been forced to leave the state of Ohio after Liberty crashed a car into a motel lobby, as he described for a podcast program called "Worst Gig Ever": "Next morning the cops are there, they take me away . . . I got bailed out . . . that's when we started to change our names on the room list . . ."

The alienation only increased around the time of Liberty's divorce from his first wife, Mary, as he recounted in an interview for the Electric Beard: "I remember exactly what it was . . . I walked up to [Billy] and I said, 'I'm getting divorced and she's getting it all. So if any crumbs fall off the table, maybe you can sweep them my way.'"

By estranging himself from the Billy camp, DeVitto perhaps missed out on considerably more than crumbs when Billy decided, deep into his 2009 tour schedule, that he would distribute some $13 million in bonuses to his band and crew—an unprecedented outlay in the realm of rock, with the longest-serving members getting six and even seven figures along with advice on tax strategies. Prior to the filing of Liberty's lawsuit, Billy had reportedly planned to dole a goodly portion out to Liberty; the lawsuit, via its settlement, greatly diminished the payment to the ex-drummer.

Not unlike the long-lived resentment attorney Allen Grubman had nursed after not being invited to Billy's wedding to Christie, Liberty had been upset about not getting an invitation to the Katie nuptials in October 2004. As the word had gone out to friends and band members, Liberty had gradually realized he was not included. He further alienated Billy by publicly sharing with the Electric Beard site a doleful, rambling letter he had composed years before, concluding with the thought that he was trying "to rebuild my career. It's tough starting over with nothing at the age of fifty-four."

The letter would have no impact on negotiations as the lawyers for the opposing sides conducted a brief backroom battle that reportedly included Billy taking Liberty to task for the incident with Christie. Then in late April, almost as abruptly as it had begun, the dispute was settled. Billy's legal team released a statement saying, "The case has been amicably resolved." The sums involved, and the punches and counterpunches that had been thrown in meetings, were not disclosed.

Today, Billy has moved on: "I do feel bad that it ended the way it did. I never wanted to get back at him in the press, 'cause I'd been asked about it—'What happened with Liberty? How come you're not working together?' And, 'He said this about you.' I wanted to take the high road there and leave it as it is. I was a little bugged when stuff that he said came out in the press, but you just get over it. And now I don't really have any hard feelings."

IF BILLY'S HISTORY with Liberty was ultimately a tangled one, his history with Elton John, rock's first famous piano man, has been even more complex. Ever since Billy and Elton first hit the road together in 1994, an arrangement brokered by Steve Cohen and Elton's then-manager (and Cohen's very good friend) John Reid, their story has been a saga of alternating camaraderie and competition—two iconic figures on a world stage, sometimes frolicking, sometimes fighting.

When their concerts clicked, fans and critics alike had responded to the juxtaposition of the two rock icons. At the 1994 opening show for about sixty thousand fans, the *New York Times*'s reviewer Neil Strauss had found that "Mr. Joel's piano player [in other words, his onstage persona] comes on like a pint of beer and Mr. John's like a cup of tea." He summed up the approach as "two gifted, idiosyncratic artists [who] exist in the nether world between pop and rock, where Broadway show tunes, classical compositions, ragtime gospel and rock-and-roll mingle freely." However, by 2009—when Billy's marriage to Katie and his relationship with Liberty were at their worst—long-simmering tensions were hiding beneath their planned revival of the Face to Face tour later that year.

While the two had been a modern-day touring money machine—*Billboard* had declared their 2001–2 campaign to be the most successful tour package ever—both felt less sanguine about the gigs this time around. Elton, on the one hand, had never fully forgiven Billy for the Wembley cancellations in 1998. Billy, on the other, continued to feel as he did as late as 2007 in an interview with the *Oakland Tribune*, when he opined that the original Elton tours had been fun, but "after ten years, we were pretty much doing a stock greatest hits show. Elton was the opening act on the tour, he went on first. So we'd be sitting backstage and Elton would be playing hit after hit after hit. We'd be sitting there saying, 'Oh, my God, we have to follow this?' Well, if you try to go up there and do album tracks or obscurities, the crowd is going to go to the bathroom. So we were doing greatest hits for ten years, and that got a little old. As much as I liked working with Elton, we wanted to do other songs."

And yet, after six years of individual tours, 2009–10's ambitious three-leg, twenty-seven-show Face to Face began in Jacksonville in March. Making his Miami home the pivot point for the winter led to some enjoyable moments in the winter sun, but despite an efficient charge across the early part of the tour, Billy and Elton both would be dogged by health problems along the way, with eleven postponements and one cancellation, in Little Rock. Fans in Buffalo perhaps had the worst luck. Billy took ill just prior to the planned December 4 date—the announcement of "flu-like symptoms" came around three P.M., even as fans began descending on the HSBC Arena. That show, and also one scheduled just after in Albany, was rescheduled for March.

Then November saw a raft of rescheduled dates, as Elton contracted a withering *E. coli* virus that knocked him out of his solo Red Piano tour of the U.K. as well as the northwestern wing of the Face to Face tour. As Elton gradually recovered in an English hospital, Billy's agonies with sciatica and hip dysplasia worsened. Betrayed by his very joints, sitting at home stewing over his broken marriage and the anomie of facing boisterous crowds in a state of emotional free fall, Billy had those closest to him worried.

The combined effect of Elton's illness and the need for Billy to get some time off was to push an array of scheduled dates later into winter, as eventually the piano-playing odd couple made up the dates, and wholeheartedly. By the time they got to Salt Lake City, for example, the local reviewer applauded Billy's "lovable crassness that only added authenticity to his story songs" and concluded that he "plays like a gunslinger and gets the job done."

Sometime between that date and the San Jose gig three days before, Elton's agent broke unwelcome news to the Englishman, just before Elton did a press conference from Beverly Hills via satellite, promoting his production of *Billy Eliot the Musical*. No Face to Face dates would be added, the agent relayed—Billy was done for now. "Billy," Elton said, "has decided to take a year off. It doesn't gel with my plans, but he's my friend. And as an artist you have to respect his decision."

Privately, of course, Elton was fuming, and his disapproval found its way into the media. Billy replied in an interview with *Rolling Stone*'s Austin Scaggs that appeared online on February 26, bearing the headline "Billy Joel Dismisses Rumors He Yanked Tour with Elton John." The key quote was the lead: "There was never a tour booked this summer!" Billy continued: "Obviously, this has the smell of a really juicy story: 'Why did they cancel? Did Billy and Elton have a fight? What's going on?' The truth is, there's nothing going on. I had made up my mind a long time ago that I wasn't going to work this year."

The feud then went quiet—for the moment.

Regardless of the seeming détente, the final two upstate New York Face to Face gigs were fraught. But both Albany and Buffalo went without a hitch in early March, earning a heap of warm reviews ("the pair

have power, even majesty," wrote one local reviewer) and drawing enthusiastic audiences. Still, the performances were hardly as buoyant as
they had been when the 2009–10 Face to Face tour had begun. Now it
was history.

Billy's 2009 had been a tough year, as he remembers: "I promised
myself more personal time. I said, *I'm going to Italy, and I'll probably go to
Paris. I'll probably take my boat to New England and hang out on the coast.
I'll ride my motorcycle.*" For the first time in what seemed like ages, he
thought, "I'll just be a bum."

AIN'T IT SWEET
AFTER ALL THESE YEARS

CHAPTER 19

THE IDOL OF MY AGE

Facing the long span that began in the late spring of 2010 with no concerts scheduled, Billy felt genuine relief that each day's biggest decision would be about lunch, and he found other pursuits. By early summer, he was much more interested in spending time in his burgeoning Oyster Bay motorcycle emporium, Twentieth Century Cycles, than in doing anything with music. For several years prior to the current motorcycle fixation, the lure of designing boats, like his beautifully custom-made Shelter Island runabouts, was in the forefront for Billy. To describe his pursuits as hobbies undersells the investment of time, capital, and passion involved.

In 2010–12, as he renovated an expansive storefront space just around the corner from the Oyster Bay town hall, the avocation was almost becoming a full-time job. Hiring veteran bike savant (and sometime racer) Alex Puls to come up from down south and settle in with his family marked a turning point.

"I design bikes, I think, similarly to the way I create music—the notes are mine, the composition is mine, but the execution is done by master craftsmen. The whole process of going from concept to design to finished product has often reminded me of the scene in *Close Encounters of the Third Kind* where Richard Dreyfuss is trying to re-create Devil's Peak.

"At first he doesn't know just what he's doing. But he hangs in, and eventually he lets go and says, 'Just close your eyes and hold your breath and everything will turn real pretty.'

"It's a similar thing with me and motorcycles. I love taking a stock bike and customizing it. It's almost as if there's a reincarnation aspect to it. For some reason I always want to go back to the year of my birth, 1949. Everything I like stylistically comes from that era—the late forties and early fifties—and I feel like I'm always trying to re-create it.

"Some designs at that time were so beautiful and functional, I often wonder why they had to stop. Why did they have to change? Why all this emphasis on new, and cutting-edge, and experimental, and innovative? Why not explore the nuances of what was already there and improve on that?

"I feel the same way about music.

"I love to play around with genres—blues, doo-wop, a waltz—and because of that, I've often been accused of being derivative. You know what? Hell *yes*, I'm derivative. Nobody grows up in a test tube. We're all influenced by what's come before us. But what is it that you're always drawn back to? What is it that speaks to your soul?"

Recognizing the overlap between Billy's taste in music making and motorcycle building, Steve Cohen was unsurprised at his boss's new regime. More than perhaps anyone, he knows the ebb and flow of Billy's interest in music: "Having been there for four decades, I can set my watch to when Billy gets tired of being Billy. And sometimes it's a two-year period, sometimes it's a three-year period. Sometimes it's a six-month period. But there's always a point where after we've done however many shows, after he's strapped on the Billy Joel face night after night, he gets fucking tired of being that guy. He'd rather just be Bill.

"And then after a period of time, whatever it might be, whether it's relationships, whether it be a bilateral hip surgery, whether it would be turning sixty, whether it would be 9/11 for that matter, there's a place in his head where he goes through a couple of different changes."

When Cohen pauses, the hesitation reverberates momentarily; he doesn't need to explain that once or twice such fallow periods have ended in troubles—and just as surely, a spate of musical activity provides a welcome focus. "And then what ends up happening is it suddenly isn't painful or arduous to be that guy again. And I can see him embrace it. Look, we all know that with the advent of the Internet and the fact that he's now got access to all of that stuff, he got really fed up with celebrity for celebrity's sake."

Perhaps his awareness of just how deep underground he was going led to Billy's thorough involvement in the editing of *Last Play at Shea*. He had mandated that he appear only sporadically, as the mostly unseen "shark," as in the film *Jaws*, and Cohen, as a coproducer, leaned in with director Paul Crowder to enforce that strategy. The *New York Times*'s Stephen Holden found it "exhilarating . . . guaranteed to put lumps in the throats of longtime New York residents and suburbanites, especially Long Islanders, this fist-pumping, backslapping film is, first and foremost, an up-close record of Mr. Joel's two Shea Stadium concerts."

As a portrait of "the quintessential smart, streetwise, hardworking guy from a suburban neighborhood in emotional lockstep with his audience over the long haul," Holden found the tunes he heard to comprise "hearty, tough/tender little monuments to growing up in a certain time and place . . . today Mr. Joel, who largely abandoned songwriting in the mid-1990s, sounds more and more like the rock 'n' roll answer to Irving Berlin and George M. Cohan. His blunt, irresistibly tuneful songs, however autobiographical, are also nuggets of American cultural history." His enthusiasm was hardly dimmed by the "almost too good to be true" arrival of Paul McCartney to close the show: "The final number, 'Let It Be,' rings as a sweet valedictory to all the struggle, the teamwork and the glory captured in this wonderful film."

Though *Variety* would snark that "Billy Joel may look like a mob lawyer these days" and compare the work to "90 pounds of film stuffed into a five-pound bag," it also saw Billy as "the supremely down-to-earth, gimlet-eyed charismatic Everyman." Such reviews, along with strong word of mouth, set the film up not so much for its fleeting, token theatrical run in October as for the later DVD release, ultimately to be joined by a more straight-up concert documentary.

MEANWHILE, ANY NOTIONS that Billy was precious about his catalog were put at least partly to rest when he gave the young choristers on the network television hit *Glee* free rein to choose from it for the October 5, 2010, episode, "Grilled Cheesus." The previous year Neil Patrick Harris had covered "Piano Man" for the show. But this time, Billy told *Access Hollywood* (in an unusual nod to the electronic tabloid press, for a man likelier to be watching black-and-white footage of German tanks grinding over rubble), "Yeah, go ahead, use my stuff. I was in a chorus when I was in high school, so why not?"

This new accessibility of Billy Joel—a pop star who previously seemed to occupy his own outlying, if expansive, area in pop culture—had begun with the lovingly sardonic angle taken by the arrival in June 2009 of *The Hangover*, in which Zach Galifianakis's pathetic wannabe Alan is a die-hard Billy fan, down to the *Glass Houses* poster in his room. Perhaps the most perverse use of Billy's work came from Ed Helms's character, migrating down a Thai river in the second of the three films, strumming a guitar as he sings a bawdy, shamefaced variation of "Allentown." Not pleased, Alan stands in for a whole new generation of Joel fans when he says: "You totally butchered that song."

If the *Hangover* films add future iterations, perhaps Alan himself will join the legion of fans (and wedding singers) who themselves have butchered a Billy Joel song. And yet the professionally rendered cover versions are legion, from the Beastie Boys' "Big Shot" (live) to Barbra Streisand's and Tony Bennett's respective versions of "New York State of Mind" to Sinatra's "Just the Way You Are."

One of the better efforts to pop up in recent years came when a British department store appropriated British singer Fyfe Dangerfield's tender yet not sappy cover of "She's Always a Woman" and played it under a clever ninety-second ad showing a girl growing from infancy to old age. The resultant attention would vault Billy's version of the old song, which was number fifty-three in the U.K. in 1986, to number twenty-nine as a reissued single on the May 2010 British charts. Dangerfield would be rewarded with a few opening-act spots on Billy's late-2013 U.K. tour.

Only two weeks after the *Glee* episode aired, *Two and a Half Men* broadcast an episode called "The Immortal Mr. Billy Joel," in which Jon Cryer's character attempts to entice a girl with his cover of "We Didn't Start the Fire." His jittery shtick, as he invokes "the piano man," feels at least partly sincere, and it asks the question fans and critics keep asking about Billy Joel—is he an entertainment deity or that guy whose songs play too often in the drugstore sound system? (It is a grisly irony that the song playing on piped-in music system of the pedestrian mall below the World Trade Center towers minutes after 2 WTC was struck—as heard on the first street-level video from the scene, taken by a Fox News cameraman—was an instrumental version of "She's Always a Woman." For Billy, who was so profoundly disturbed by the events of 9/11 that he would later say they cast a pall over a decade or more for him, it just folded into the unthinkability of the entire cataclysm.)

It happened to be the day after the *Glee* episode aired that Billy acceded to his friend Howard Stern's request and made a "surprise" (to the audience) visit to Stern's satellite radio show to discuss *Last Play at Shea* on the eve of its one-day theater unspooling. An adoring Stern stoked Billy's witty responses, as they chatted about song origins and the never-fulfilled notion of Billy's forming a supergroup with Sting, Stevie Winwood, and Bruce Springsteen. Because Billy made passing mention of the drug experiment that led to "Scandianvian Skies," the lengthy chat was widely distilled by avid media reports down to "Billy Joel Tried Heroin."

In the same week came the announcement that Billy was allowing aspiring musicians to learn his tunes for the video game *Rock Band 3*. Pop culture continued to rummage through his catalog with the mid-February episode of *The Office*, "Threat Level Midnight," named after a film supposedly made by regional manager Michael Scott. Called "outstandingly bad in every way" by one recapper, the film used Billy's "Running on Ice" for a *Karate Kid*–style hockey training montage, and "Pressure" for a gunfight/speed skating scene. (In season nine, in September 2012, *The Office* would deploy "She's Got a Way," for Roy's marriage scene—naturally, given Billy's stature as go-to bard for decades of America's nuptials.)

Further proof that both the public and the media had a renewed appetite for news of Billy came with the release of the *Last Play at Shea* DVD in early February 2011. Per the marketing plan, the release prepared the ground for its late March follow-up *Live at Shea Stadium: The Concert* (directed by old pal Jon Small), with a series of PBS showings of the latter film in the network's *Great Performances* series.

Upon its release, the concert package, stadium package, two CDs, and a DVD shot to number one on *Billboard*'s Top Music DVD/Video chart. Added in with the box office from the 115,000 tickets sold for the shows themselves (a $12.9 million take against some $2 million in production costs), those two July 2008 evenings made for a pretty fair payday.

JUST AS BILLY'S woodshedding period was going peacefully, Elton John gave an interview to *Rolling Stone* for the fortnightly magazine's early February 2011 cover story. The interview, perhaps more than Elton could have calculated, brought a lot more attention to Billy than to its ostensible subject.

Elton, sixty-six, said he was bringing "tough love" to his sometime friend and road partner, insisting Billy wasn't taking care of himself: "At the end of the day, he's coasting. Billy, why can't you write another song? Billy's a conundrum. . . . We've had so many canceled tours because of illnesses and various other things, alcoholism. . . . He's going to hate me for this, but every time he's gone to rehab, they've been rehab light. When I went to rehab, I had to clean the floors. He goes to rehab where they have TVs."

John added, "I love you, Billy. . . . You have your demons and you're not going to get rid of them at rehab light. You've got to be serious. People adore you, they love you and respect you. You should be able to do something better than what you're doing now."

Billy quickly defused the situation: "I've worked with Elton for such a long time and I've enjoyed our relationship too much to let something as random as these comments change my affection for him. . . . Elton is just being Elton."

Still, the attack nettled.

Perhaps the most aggravating slap was that Billy needed to "do something better" with his life. Privately, Billy sent off a palpably angry note, asking, "What gives you the omnipotent moral certainty and authority to justify the public humiliation of anyone—especially of someone to whom you should, at the very least, consider according a modicum of honor?" He closed with a curt, "We are done."

About a week later John appeared on *Today* and updated Matt Lauer: "Billy hates me at the moment. He sent me a message and he's not happy. I understand that. I'm sorry I had to say it, but I'm saying it because I really want Billy to live a long life and be very happy. That's all it came from. I understand why he's mad at me. I'm only trying to help. Maybe I should have done it privately, but I've been so frustrated over the years."

He added that Billy, perhaps metaphorically, wanted to punch him in the face.

That blend of contrition and prickliness brought the following public statement from Billy, who included a reference to a film Elton had been plugging when he appeared on the show:

1. I do not hate Elton John.
2. I do not want to "punch him in the face."

3. If he wants to call me, my number is still the same.

4. Good luck with the movie.

—BILLY JOEL

Time was on the side of reconciliation, especially given Billy's capacity for forgiveness over the years. But even a year later, in another *Today* show appearance, Elton was still troubled and confessed he had not heard from Billy in over a year, apart from the single letter that had never gone public.

"He wrote me a thing, 'You're—you—you shouldn't judge people. Who are you to judge?'" he told Matt Lauer. "And I said it because I thought it might get through. And I can understand him being angry about that. And we haven't really communicated since."

Still, Elton said, "Billy Joel is the kindest, sweetest man, and the most talented songwriter and great, great artist. If he called me tomorrow and said, 'Let's have lunch,' I'd go like a shot. 'Cause I adore him. I only said it as tough love. But he was upset. And I'm sorry I upset him."

By April 2013, although the two had not been in the same room since the 2010 Albany gig, the dance continued with Billy's statement to *Rolling Stone*: "It's absolutely possible I'd play with Elton again. Sometimes he runs off at the mouth. But . . . I would always work with him again. I still love the guy. He's a great guy."

Then two months later, as both attended at the 44th Annual Songwriters Hall of Fame event at a Manhattan hotel, Elton picked up his award and offered, "Mr. Joel, I haven't seen you tonight, but I love you dearly."

Later during the ceremony, Billy took the stage for his award and reciprocated: "Is Elton still here, by the way? We're okay," he said. "Call me."

Finally, capping the diplomatic saga—until, perhaps, negotiations for a different brand of shared tour in the future—Billy attended the October 2013 benefit for the Elton John AIDS Foundation. There, finally, as described by Billy in his April 2014 visit to Howard Stern, came the rapprochement and Billy's *Godfather*-style reminder: "Don't ever talk that way about me." And the historic photo was taken, Billy in a dark suit and shiny scarf, Elton all in black and shiny bloodred sunglasses, with a firm grip on his best-friend-forever's shoulder (or was it his neck?). In any event, they were finally back.

IN CONTRAST TO the ups and downs of his relations with Elton, Billy's relations with Bruce Springsteen have always been easy, and the time off the road gave them a chance to further the friendship with their overlapping enthusiasm for motorcycles.

They were a perfect fit in concert, as they'd proved in 1974 doing "Twist and Shout" at a New Jersey college concert (Billy inviting Bruce up), and again onstage together at the 2008 Obama benefit show, then more recently in 2009 when Bruce, as ad hoc bandleader for the 25th Anniversary Concert of the Rock and Roll Hall of Fame, conspired with Jann Wenner to lure Billy to the show as a surprise guest. The Jerseyan and the Long Islander had combined on "You May Be Right," "Only the Good Die Young," and "New York State of Mind," and they'd capped it all with "Born to Run," Billy's reading of his verses informed, as always, by his spot-on Bruce mimicry.

The two had been trying for a casual get-together for a while when, one brilliantly sunny midwinter 2011 day in Miami, Bruce drove down to visit Billy, pulling through the tall iron gate of his La Gorce Island manse in a man-of-the-people's aging and faded SUV. After a mellow summit meeting over an Italian meal, they boarded the craft Billy sometimes preferred for jaunts across the bay, a battleship-gray re-creation of a World War II landing craft.

They discussed what kind of bike Billy's motorcycle shop might one day build for Bruce. It would turn out to be a Sacred Cow "bobber"—in other words, a custom rebuild of a Kawasaki W650, a relatively stripped brute with a single seat, the front fender removed, and the back reduced or "bobbed." It would emerge as a handsome, low-slung thing that might have looked all business before the black frame was topped with a metal-flake-gold gas tank.

This taste of the good life and conversation about bikes then evolved into a brief discussion of how very lucky they felt to have thrived at a time when their kind of rock-and-roll artistry lined up with a ready audience of album buyers. There was no need to mention that those days were gone forever, and given the track record each had, no need to moan about it, either.

Another man of the people who's made his liking for Billy abundantly clear is country king Garth Brooks. Born in Oklahoma in 1962, Brooks emerged in 1989 to lead the infusion of rock music into country, bringing on his stature as the best-selling album artist in the nation in the Sound Scan era (i.e., since that rigorous tallying system became *Billboard*'s standard in 1991; Billy ranks sixth by its count). His cover of Billy's "Shameless" was a number one hit in 1991, and his appearance singing it in *Last Play at Shea* marked a key surfacing in the period during which he largely stayed out of the spotlight, from 2001 to 2009. As Brooks said in an interview on show day for the documentary, to a baseball nut/Billy Joel worshipper, it was irresistible: "I will forever love him for inspiring me to go do things that make my life better . . . time is a friend to all things good."

A curious aspect of Billy's relative isolation during the months spanning 2011 and 2012 was that he frequently seemed to leave his house to meet with, and assist, friends like Springsteen and Brooks, who have sold, well, tens of millions of albums. (The trend had started when Billy returned McCartney's favor for *Last Play at Shea* and helped Paul inaugurate the renamed facility, Citi Field, in July 2009.) Then in October 2011, when Sting gave a birthday party for himself (the proceeds went to an antipoverty charity), Billy guested on "Every Little Thing She Does Is Magic" and "Don't Stand So Close to Me," hitting the high notes (but afterward clutching his throat theatrically).

More often in recent decades, though, Billy has taken time during breaks in his touring schedule to help young musicians—those with much less experience than his famous friends—gain a truer sense of songwriting and the music business than he had when he began. Over time he's appeared everywhere from Harvard to the Oxford Union to less posh state schools and also some institutions with younger audiences. (He was even a mute but appreciative audience member for a Long Island elementary school's spring 2014 concert, "The River of Dreams: A Billy Joel Tribute.")

In some of the 2012 events, typically billed as question-and-answer sessions interspersed with "a little music," Billy seemed to be building confidence for a return to the arenas. At the University of Connecticut in November, he pointed out that success is the product first of all of hard work: "Look at me, do I look like a rock star? No, I look like a guy who makes pizza."

Several days later he turned up at Cornell University's Bailey Hall for a similar session. No doubt the deans and human resources types had mixed reactions to his response when asked if he'd tried to write hits—"I was usually trying to get a girl into bed," he explained. He then moved to the piano to play through snippets of Mozart, Bach, and Beethoven, breaking in to insist, "Beethoven got smoldery! He's so deep! So troubled!" He politely declined one girl's request to accompany her to her sorority's formal party.

Billy pointed out that even his more celebratory songs usually had an element that was emotionally a bit dissonant. "Sometimes your limitations become your greatest gifts," he said. "I just don't believe too much in sugar and sweetness—there's always that knife in it, and that's what makes it real."

"His best performance of the night, undeniably, was his 'Vienna,'" a student journalist wrote. "The song, he said, is for his father, who died last year. The audience, completely silent, watched Joel's passionate delivery. His scatting, which he'd added to other songs during the night to make up for lack of instrumental breakdowns, was anything but corny."

A week later Billy was in Manhattan, at the city's temple to the piano and its masters, attending the unveiling of his Steinway Hall portrait at the flagship store of Steinway & Sons on Fifty-seventh Street. A drape was pulled off a large canvas to show artist Paul Wyse's lifelike portrait of a reflective Joel with arms folded across a leather jacket. Predictably self-deprecating, Joel explained that he'd bought the jacket in Miami without female supervision and only later did a girlfriend remind him that the members-only look "went out in the eighties." Still, he said, "I'm really honored to be hung," waiting a beat for the startled laugh from those assembled, then closing with an anecdote about his younger, shaggy-haired self accosting—and scaring away—Vladimir Horowitz in a chance encounter on the street nearby.

During a Florida college tour he visited Boca Raton's Lynn University and was asked about "Lullabye." He pointed out daughter Alexa in the audience and spoke of writing it for her when she was age seven, to explain death, no less—but he declined to sing it because it was "personal." (And as he knew, it often brought her to tears.) A man in the audience waving a cane asked, "Can I shake your hand?" Years before, he had fallen six stories and broken his back, but was visited in the hospital by Billy, a stranger to him. A standing ovation followed their handshake. A few days later he was at another school doing an amused version of Weird Al Yankovic's 1980 parody song "It's Still Billy Joel to Me." By this time a blogger named Will Stegemann, who started his "A Year of Billy Joel" Web log hoping to understand why Joel fans were so avid and widespread, had gone from skeptic to unabashed fan. Next thing he knew, he was personally in touch with an amused Billy, and soon thereafter would be welcomed into backstage hospitality suites.

BACK ON HIS home turf, in search of what another Long Island summer might bring, Billy made the rounds, with the hope that, as he wrote in "The Night Is Still Young," "I'm young enough to see the passionate boy I used to be." Sure enough, his fortuitous chance meeting with Alexis Roderick happened in mid-2010, at a bar-restaurant in Huntington, not far from his Centre Island home. "I was with friends waiting for a table. Here was this attractive woman at the bar, and we just started talking." He persuaded Alexis to give him a ride home when his friends wanted to leave earlier than he did: "It's a bit of a schlep to Centre Island, a dozen miles, and I was laying it on thick. And I remember going back to my house, and if you've seen the movie *The Seven Year Itch* with Tom Ewell and Marilyn Monroe, he's got a cigarette holder and a silk cravat and a dressing gown and he's playing Rachmaninoff, trying to impress Marilyn Monroe, who lives upstairs, while his wife is away." Though it quickly became apparent that Alexis didn't really buy the act, she did entrust him with her contact info and they stayed in touch.

At that stage she was still working as a senior risk analyst in the Garden City office of Morgan Stanley brokerage, he approaching sixty-one and she, twenty-nine. Some months after they began dating, the relationship hit a bump—only scanty details emanated, but the speculation was that she wanted to solidify the relationship.

Perhaps not coincidentally, Billy was anticipating, then undergoing, double hip replacement surgery—doing both hips because, as still-supportive ex Christie Brinkley told *Radar Online*, he had said, "If I do it one at a time, I know I'll never go in for the other." When he had visited Howard Stern's Sirius radio broadcast in mid-November, he utilized twin walking sticks and looked all but infirm to those who saw him there. But the day after the November 20, 2010, procedure in a Long Island hospital, he was on his feet and on the mend with Alexis at his side.

By the time he was reinstalled at home, Billy and Alexis were ready for something of a formal coming-out. The couple decided to go public on December 9, and she spared a thought for the *Daily News*, noting, "We were friends for a while before we started dating."

By the summer of 2012, Billy's renewed contentment would be summarized rather endearingly in a late July post on his website, showing their newly adopted pug, Rosie, hanging out with Alexis and Billy in their barn-scale Centre Island kitchen. Rescued from a puppy mill by the North Shore Animal League America (the charity of choice for Howard Stern's wife Beth Ostrovsky and later a beneficiary of the take from Billy's May 9, 2014, Garden show), the compact pooch joined the much-loved pug Sabrina, age eight. The new pug sits on Alexis's lap staring at Billy in what looks like outrage, but as Alexis explained, "She is in love with him!"

The quiet domesticity that the couple, and their pugs, were enjoying as the months passed would be interrupted by the approach of Superstorm Sandy in late October. Forming around Kingston, Jamaica, it would span eleven hundred miles and become the largest Atlantic hurricane on record before being downgraded to a (nonetheless ferociously destructive) storm that affected twenty-four states. When the time came to sign on for the benefit concert to relieve Sandy victims, Billy was quick to join up.

As he told an interviewer in a promo for the concert, he watched his patch of the harbor with shock as the storm hit with "traumatic" effect: "I saw boats being torn off moorings, crashing onto the shore . . . houses being flooded, it was scary. It hurts to see all the lives that were disrupted. People were stranded—people died. I'm a Long Islander, and to see something like this happen, it's devastating. A way of life has been disrupted." Centre Island, perched on its hill, was largely spared, though as he said to friends with rueful irony, it flooded his helipad. He didn't mention the giant munch it took out of the shoreline near his white elephant of a Sagaponack house, a washout that was later remedied by fresh truckloads of sand.

The eventual charitable effort to cure some of Sandy's ills with a benefit concert not quite two months later would join up with, and serve to highlight, changes that were arriving on a parallel track for Billy's public persona.

His quietly expanding fan base would understand and appreciate his revival in 2012 before it was really discussed in the media. But the world of pop culture that had been sliding away from beneath the feet of most of his musical peers had somehow come to a halt immediately beneath Billy's body of work. The culture was clearly having a positive rethink about a performer who had once divided it into lovers and haters.

CHAPTER 20

I'VE LOVED THESE DAYS

When in mid-November the invocatory media tom-toms announced "12.12.12 The Concert for Sandy Relief," the initial concert lineup hewed to a kind of geographical billing, with hard-hit New Jersey's Jon Bon Jovi on top and Long Island's Billy named next. But it also included Alicia Keys, Paul McCartney, Bruce Springsteen and the E Street Band, Roger Waters, Kanye West, and the Who, along with other world-class artists (the Rolling Stones and Eric Clapton) yet to be announced.

"When we did 12.12.12," recalls Steve Cohen, "Billy was really nervous, because he didn't know whether he was going to be good enough. And he said, 'I'm not going to do this if I can't be as good as we used to be.'"

When the night arrived, Billy readied himself much as he would for any other gig, with a major difference in the cameo players. Owner of the dressing room closest to the stage, Billy mostly stayed within the cinder-block retreat, *Godfather*-style, while politicians (Governors Andrew Cuomo and Chris Christie), actors (Jake Gyllenhaal), comics (Chris Rock), and of course musicians either looked in or greeted him at the doorway or briefly inside. A sweaty Pete Townshend, traipsing back from the Who's set, gave him a slow, comradely smile and an enveloping, slack-limbed hug. Paul McCartney all but skipped by with his band (on the run, as it happened), singing, "Hey, hey we're the Monkees" in unison en route to the stage.

"It was a lot of fun," Billy recalls. "A lot of kibitzing backstage, and everybody else doing everybody else's material. Keith Richards comes over, and he starts—[singing in a gravelly south-of-London drawl], 'You may be right, ah may beyah crazy . . .'"

But the case of nerves Steve Cohen noticed was only amplified by the surrounding star power. "When you stand to lose something, that's when you really got to deliver the goods," Billy was thinking. "I wanted I see how it feels."

According to Billy, the tightness of the set list was a product of necessity: "It came about by the producers saying, 'Here's how much time you've got.' I think it was twenty-five or thirty minutes. And we said, 'This is going to run late, and we're probably going to have to chop something.' So we rehearsed six or seven songs, knowing that we'd probably have to edit the list. That dictated that the set had to be power-packed—'cause it's the Garden, and we were near the end."

Kanye West's grinding set half-emptied the hall, which was unfortunate given how generally old, white, and school-of-rock the rest of the lineup was. Says Billy, "McCartney was going to go on after us, and we followed Kanye, who had a lot of people leaving. And I'm just watching this going, *Oh, shit, thanks a lot. I'm going to play a half a house.* And I went onstage, and we saw people coming back in, roaring in."

Six powerfully delivered songs later, the exultant crowd's standing ovation left little doubt who owned the evening. Beginning with an appropriately updated "Miami 2017 (Seen the Lights Go Out on Broadway)" and moving through the classics "Movin' Out (Anthony's Song)," "New York State of Mind," "The River of Dreams," and "You May Be Right," to finish off with "Only the Good Die Young," Billy galvanized the arena and reminded all watching of the seasoned command he has onstage. Afterward, Paul, before he went on, passed Billy's dressing room and stuck his head in, saying, "Thanks for bringing 'em back, Bill."

As they clambered into a van near the Garden's vehicle exit, Billy remembers that he, Cohen, and Brian Ruggles shared a look, thinking: "What's the big deal? We did six songs. This is nothing. This is like a sissy set. And everybody's raving about it. I said, 'I guess we must be pretty good.' 'Cause I do have doubts about how good I am anymore."

At long last, the critical establishment, almost unanimously, didn't join him in that doubt. "And who won the evening?" mused the *New Yorker*'s Sasha Frere-Jones. "... The Yanks—along with Bruce and Kanye, Billy Joel sounded fantastic. We know the rap sheet. Joel hasn't lived clean, and yet there he was, his voice appearing to have aged only about a week since 1987, and his piano playing fluid and strong. The mood relaxed, as if someone who really knew how to play a stadium was in charge, and the crowd really wanted to hear him. 'Movin' Out' and 'New York State of Mind'? Perfect."

Opined *Rolling Stone*, "Billy Joel hasn't lost a step. Joel was the only performer of the night who has been out of the public eye for a few years. The time off seems to have treated him well. He may look more than a bit like Brian Dennehy these days, but his voice is absolutely unreal. If you closed your eyes you'd think you were listening to *Songs in the Attic*. It's impossible to pick one highlight from his six-song set. Backed by his longtime touring band, Joel ... almost blew every other performer off the stage."

Entertainment Weekly admired Billy's sure-handed touch in delivering appropriate, heartening sentiment: "Following a guy like West can be difficult, but Billy Joel was up to the task. The veteran piano rocker put forth the evening's most thematically consistent and aesthetically pleasing performances: 'Miami 2017' featured all the lyrical modifications he made when he played it at the last Sandy telethon a few weeks back, and the inclusion of 'River of Dreams' was a nice nod to Sandy-affected Connecticut."

As a *Rolling Stone* interviewer would assert while interviewing him some weeks later, "It may finally be cool to like Billy Joel."

Perhaps the most cogent essay on this would be by *Grantland*'s

Steven Hyden in April 2013. Citing the Sandy show triumph as "kind of a big deal," he set the context: "Outside of a stray appearance here and there, including cameos at Paul McCartney's Yankee Stadium concerts in 2011, Joel had not commanded the public's attention on a big, important stage in many years."

The gaggle of rock critics assessing the show on Twitter, with "catty comments about the overwhelmingly geriatric bill," had piled up a widely negative, "all-out classic-rock turkey shoot—except for Joel. The sea of snark miraculously parted for him. Here is a guy whom music scribes have historically gone out of their way to slag . . . and yet this wretched hive of cynics and grumps was stumping on behalf of the Piano Man with unbridled enthusiasm."

Noting that Billy's look—"an Atlantic City pit boss"—was a logical acceptance of his age, he applauded that Billy *acted* his age: "He merely sat behind his keyboard and played some very old songs very, very well." Hyden even seemed to like the "characteristic prissiness" of Billy's reply to *Rolling Stone* about whether it's cool to like him: "I suppose after a long enough time as the Antichrist, it has its perks. 'Cause I don't give a shit."

Hyden clearly framed how the attitude shift that evened the playing field for the Boss and the Piano Man had taken place: "Twenty years ago, Springsteen and Joel represented opposing sides in a debate—'authenticity' vs. 'artifice'—that formed the crux of nearly every conversation about popular music. Today, this dialogue has been marginalized to the point of virtual silence. Hating Billy Joel is no longer a meaningful act; at best, it suggests that you're the sort of person who's actively annoyed by things that most people tend to like or at least tolerate."

In fact, he added, "Joel's strengths—his accessibility, his knack for romantic balladry, his understated versatility in adapting to different songwriting and production styles—are no longer held against him. As far as Billy Joel's legacy is concerned, staying put has been the next best thing to dying."

* * *

POST 12.12.12, BILLY kicked off the New Year with a January visit to Vanderbilt University. There, taking audience questions midway through his appearance, he called on a young man, Michael Pollack, who had played piano with sometime Billy band regular Richie Cannata and now asked to join Billy onstage. Billy waited the merest beat: "Okay."

Pollack wanted to play "New York State of Mind," and when Billy asked him, "What key do you do it in?" the reply came, "What key do you want it in?" In earlier times, Billy actually kept a gong onstage at such events in case he felt the need to ring an inept player off. But from the opening notes, Pollack showed an assured aptitude, and though Billy did some business donning sunglasses and threw in some light-hearted impersonations as Pollack began accompanying him, he soon shifted into a nicely committed vocal that drew sustained applause and eventually went viral online. "The kid had chutzpah," was Billy's summation, "and chops."

It was nearly time to test his own. As his booker Dennis Arfa tantalized him with possibilities for the coming touring season, he was spurred to, in effect, open out of town, with an upcoming live gig in Australia, closely followed by a return to Jazz Fest. He had told *Rolling Stone* that even a return to touring with Elton was feasible—that in sum, he had no immediate intent to retire and that ultimately, "I just love the game too much to not play it well."

At Jazz Fest, he lived up to a vow to pay tribute to the city with a surprise—during "Scenes from an Italian Restaurant," as he sang the lyric "drop a dime in the box, play the song about New Orleans," the Preservation Hall Jazz Band horns, plus bass drum, strutted onstage. "Pure joy coursed through the set" was the *Rolling Stone* précis, further noting he "held tens of thousands of visitors to the New Orleans Jazz & Heritage Festival in the palm of his hand."

In May, as Carole King was awarded the prestigious Library of Congress Gershwin Prize for Popular Song—Billy would be the recipient the following year—he was among the guests paying tribute to her in the East Room of the White House, performing "The Loco-Motion" in a fashion that captured both the song's propulsive playfulness and a certain gospel fervor. The president and first lady boogied discreetly in their seats alongside Carole and Joe Biden, before Billy ended with a throttled Ray Charles exclamation. He somehow brought out the nobility in the supposed novelty dance tune, then sang a duet with James Taylor on "Crying in the Rain."

A less happy duty for Billy was the mid-May memorial for Phil Ramone, who had passed away on March 30. "Working with Ramone completely changed my life," Joel told the mourners. "I am not just talking about fame and fortune, but also about joy and enrichment." Phil had told him, when they made *The Nylon Curtain*, "This album needs an epilogue," so he wrote, "Where's the Orchestra?"—"which has been running through my head ever since Phil passed away."

The mid-June ceremony at the Songwriters Hall of Fame that gave Billy and Elton a chance to start patching relations also renewed Billy's friendship with sometime neighbor and producer Mick Jones, whom he inducted into the Hall along with fellow Foreigner Lou Gramm. Jones and Billy had been out of touch until, not long before, they'd run into each other in a Miami restaurant. "I hadn't seen him for at least two or three years," recalls Jones, "and we just picked it up as if it were yesterday. I had just been informed that we were going to be inducted. I couldn't think of anybody better that I would love to have [to deliver Jones's induction speech] . . . and I kind of popped the question at him. I was really nervous. I was building it up for like two or three hours. I don't think he realized, but it was monumental for me. And he said, sure, no problem."

The out-of-town performances would continue, as gigs in Dublin, London, and Manchester were booked for October and November, and in an April interview with *Rolling Stone*'s Andy Greene, he described plans for a return to the road. "I'm putting my toe back into the water to see how performing feels," he said, predicting "more songs that weren't hits" played in some large cities beginning with Philadelphia. Even as he revealed his boredom with the hits, he cited a Led Zeppelin concert of deep tracks that disappointed him, and he recalled a 2006 Florida gig when songs like "All for Leyna" didn't play well.

Then in May came an interview in the *New York Times Magazine* that located him at his Sag Harbor house: "He is seemingly never alone, spending his time in the company of his two pugs or his live-in girlfriend of three years, Alexis Roderick, a former Morgan Stanley risk officer (who he probably wishes had been alongside him in the 1970s to assess his first record deal)."

Billy and his interviewer agreed that Elton, otherwise at least partly forgiven, looked like a mom. Reminded that he once would rip up bad reviews onstage, he admitted, "Maybe it was a Long Island thing. We had a chip on our shoulder." He also depicted the cancellation of his autobiography for fear it was being steered to "more of the sex and wives and girlfriends and drinking and divorce and the depression"—topics the interview then pursued. He told of his agonies at the hands of Oprah—"I did the show because Katie had a book coming out." He relived his history of being duped by the music business. Then he described just how far he would go into being an oldies act: "If I don't think I'm any good . . . I'm going to stop doing it. It has to be fun. You have to feel good about it."

Finally, under steady pressure from Dennis Arfa and not a few asides from the circle of friends and road dogs whose livelihoods—and in many cases, sense of identity—depended on Billy being on the road, the optimistic noises began. Both for himself and for his band and crew, Billy was finding that the money had its say: "I'm from Levittown. They come at you with these huge offers. First I say no, and they think I'm negotiating. And they come back with twice as much. There's only so much of that kind of money you can turn down. But I have to want to do it—I'm wondering, will I want to go out at sixty-five, okay, here's my swan song? I don't think I've ever done my farewell tour. I don't know if I believe in those things."

Even as Billy and company began preparations for something much more elaborate, they suddenly announced on October 15 that the next day, Billy would play a one-off concert at a classic old venue, the Paramount Theater in Huntington. It would be his first show on Long Island in twelve years. The proceeds would go to a favored charity, Long Island Cares—The Harry Chapin Food Bank. The rush for tickets was over almost before it started. Some side deals that Billy's people could do nothing to forestall had seats in the 1,555-capacity hall going for $800 or more.

"It's been a long time since he's played a room anywhere near as tiny as the Paramount," wrote *Rolling Stone*, "and Billy soaked in every bit of love from the screaming fans, who had absolutely no idea they'd be seeing Billy Joel in concert when they woke up the previous morning."

"Long Island, long time no see," said Billy as he began. "This is harder than it used to be." In accordance with the new ethos that had spread among the reviewers, the raves came in. "He was clearly in good spirits," wrote *Newsday*, "breaking out in a wide grin at the ovation he got for 'River of Dreams,' as well as being in fine voice. His recent hip surgeries seem to have done the trick as he swiveled his hips during the encore 'It's Still Rock and Roll to Me.'"

He had introduced "Blonde Over Blue" by noting, "I don't think we've ever played this one before—it could be a car wreck," but after a "huge ovation," he said, "I like that one. We're going to keep it." He closed with, "Maybe we'll see you again soon," setting off Internet rumors of shows to come.

Within days the dominoes started to fall. A gig at an arena in Sunrise, Florida, was announced for January, and on October 31 came the announcement that Billy would play New Year's Eve at the eighteen-thousand-seat Barclays Center in Brooklyn. "When we opened Barclays Center thirteen months ago," said Barclays CEO Brett Yomark, "Billy was one of the must-have artists for our building."

Still, in metropolitan New York and perhaps the entire world, there is only one arena that is agreed to rule them all, and that's Madison Square Garden. In early November came the news that Billy would establish an unprecedented (except by sports teams) "franchise" at the Garden. Health permitting, he would do a monthly gig, as he said himself in his usual straightforward way at a press conference, as long as, he boldly promised, "there is demand."

"We welcome Billy home," said the Garden's executive chairman James Dolan, "and look forward to many unforgettable nights of music at the Garden." Governor Andrew Cuomo, Billy's fellow motorcycle enthusiast and increasingly a friend and dinner companion, added, "It is particularly fitting that these two great icons are coming together to make entertainment history right here in New York City." He offered congratulations to both Billy and "the millions of fans worldwide who will benefit from this collaboration for years to come." Cuomo and Billy had ridden motorcycles side by side in September for a 9/11 memorial trip from a midtown firehouse to the World Trade Center Ground Zero site, and days after the Garden press conference, Billy would be the star guest at a Cuomo fund-raiser where tickets went for as much as $50,000. As the crowd at the Roseland Ballroom roared with laughter, Billy put new words to the tune of "Honesty": "Find a bunch of millionaires with lots of cash to burn / And be sure all your sex tapes hide your face."

The initial Garden shows had sold out as quickly as the technology would permit, with tickets at a relatively restrained range from $64.50 to $124.50. Of course, these tickets were in many cases resold for as much as three times their face value, and a Forbes.com article predicted that the "demand" could continue for perhaps forty shows or so before beginning to lose steam.

If the Garden residency was a coup that very few other artists—perhaps only Springsteen—could even contemplate attempting, the news that came in mid-September 2013 was more significant yet to Billy. In early December of that year, he would stand alongside Carlos

Santana, Herbie Hancock, and opera singer Martina Arroyo to accept what for any American popular artist was the nation's most coveted recognition: a Kennedy Center Honor.

At the ceremony, President Obama called him "an artist whose songs are sung around the world but are thoroughly, wonderfully American."

"Billy Joel is so much more than a piano man," said his friend Tony Bennett, noting that Billy had added much to the American songbook. "He's our poet and our pal."

Then Don Henley's sandpapery voice proved to be the right vehicle for a stripped-down "She's Got a Way," and Garth Brooks brought out the country in "Only the Good Die Young" and added sturdy renditions of "Allentown" and "Goodnight Saigon," backed by a gospel choir and, later in the song, U.S. Armed Forces veterans. The latter moment brought forth a standing ovation and, for many present, tears. Rufus Wainwright brought a disciplined theatricality to "New York State of Mind," then led the crowd in a sing-along of "Piano Man." And Brendon Urie of emo band Panic! at the Disco delivered a dramatic version of "Big Shot."

As Billy would sum up the day for *Billboard*, "That was a really moving experience. You just sat there and one thing after another is happening. The State Department gives you the award, you meet with the President and First Lady, and they're saying all these nice, effusive words about you. People come up shaking your hand, I didn't have to do nothin'. I didn't have to do a speech, I just sat there. There's Tony Bennett talking about me. It's funny, I go to places and people say, 'You were great at the Kennedy Center Honors,' and I say, 'But I didn't do anything. I just sat there.' So it was an easy job."

In mid-2014 came word that Billy had won the prestigious Gershwin Prize.

The inaugural show of the Garden residency had its share of sardonic Billy moments. At one point he looked at the huge video screen and noted, "I didn't think I was going to look like this. I look just like my dad. I thought I was going to look like Cary Grant."

The performance was dogged by equipment glitches that caused some patchy sound and, most conspicuously, robbed the audience of part of Carl Fischer's hot solo on "Zanzibar," but it was greeted rapturously, and the press had admiring things to say. "From the ovations here, Joel seems well on his way toward morphing from musician to New York institution," said the *Daily News*, while *Billboard* found him to be "playing at championship level," and *Rolling Stone* pointed out, "No other rock star has ever attempted anything like this: a gig a month as long as he wants, on his home turf, in the white-hot spotlight of the world's most famous rock arena ... and every minute of last night's show was a reminder why Billy Joel can keep these monthly blowouts going as long as he's willing to show up."

"Clearly," Steve Cohen would say, as another couple of highly praised shows were turned in, "what we're dealing with now is no mystery. There's no record coming out. There's no new product coming out. He's been touring with no new product for twenty years. So how do you make that unique and interesting? Well, it comes from his perspective sitting at that piano wanting to do what he does.

"We were just catching up backstage at a gig one day—he was in his dressing room by himself, and I was just hanging out. He was talking about next year, about what he might want to do. And then, he does that thing where he looks at me and shrugs and he goes, 'What else am I going to do?'

"So, I think that that's a little disingenuous, but really, at the end of the day, that's what it is. And I think this is just another cycle. . . . It will reach its conclusion when he has gotten what he wanted out of this particular run emotionally and creatively. When it stops being fun, he stops wanting to do it. So our role in all of this, meaning all of the guys in the family, is to try and make it so that the set and the show all feels good—so he walks offstage and he's stoked. I've had conversations with him after every one of these shows where we just kind of giggle and think, *Wow, we're still good*. Remember, he had said, 'I'm not going to do this if I can't be as good as we used to be.' And I think we're better. I think we're better than we've ever been."

CODA

The concert dates that Billy scheduled monthly through 2014 for Madison Square Garden quickly became destination events—a reason, if you could find a ticket, for a trip to New York City from anywhere on the globe. The scattered additional shows around North America looked almost random, though largely they were nods to various arenas that were overdue for a visit.

But the trio of shows booked for the Los Angeles area on May 17, 22, and 27 were special on several levels. While Billy had played at a variety of local venues over the years, from the Executive Room to the Staples Center—and, most recently, the Honda Center in Anaheim five years before—he had never played the true, globally revered classic, the Hollywood Bowl. Built in 1921 to showcase the Los Angeles Philharmonic Orchestra, it had hosted Aaron Copland, Arthur Rubenstein, Sergei Rachmaninoff, Van Cliburn, the Beatles, the Doors, and countless others—but not Billy.

True to his way of shrinking a sprawling arena down to the intimacy of a club, Billy drew the crowd into his own reflections after opening the middle show of his L.A. stand with a bravura (if geographically non-topical) "Miami 2017 (Seen the Lights Go Out on Broadway)." "I didn't know I was gonna do this when I started out at the Troubadour," he said as he gazed about appreciatively from his piano stool, motioning toward a scrubby hilltop that loomed in the background. "I used to live right over the hill, at 6800 Mulholland," he noted, and indeed, the house where he lived briefly in 1974 was but half a mile from the Hollywood Bowl Overlook that commands a view of the entire city sprawling to the west.

He would invoke memories of his Angeleno days each evening at the Bowl, mocking the idea that he and Elizabeth thought they were big shots staying at the down-market Tropicana. (But at the adjoining Duke's coffee shop, he added with a gesture, "You could get a sandwich like *this* for a dollar fifty!") Backstage after his sound check on the first night, he indulged in a smoke and some casual touristic memories. But the easeful reflections tapered off as the sprawling tarmac of the load-in area became a logjam of local industry types and, more imposingly, actual family—Elizabeth Weber herself was seated restively on a folding chair near the loading dock alongside her son Sean Weber Small, as well as Sean's wife and young daughters.

There was a reunion of sorts, as Billy and Elizabeth shared an awkward embrace and some talk of Sean's kids. Sean, now based in L.A. and running a small production company, would attend two shows and also make the ninety-minute drive north to the rented Santa Barbara house where Billy was lodged, to visit the man he refers to as his stepfather. The chats they had there were not superficial: "I think Sean is trying to put together the jigsaw puzzle of what his life was," says Billy pensively, "and I can understand that."

Billy's commute to the show each night was by helicopter, to the roof of an office tower on Wilshire Boulevard. No one recalls better than him, though, that playing L.A. wasn't always helicopter lifts and people eating pricey catered dinners at twilight. Some decades ago, when he stood a good chance of being dropped by Columbia (until Walter Yetnikoff was lured to a show and opened the label money spout to help the band establish itself), none of the present-day success may have seemed likely. Now it's for Billy himself to say when enough will be enough: "Yes, I can do it, I can tour, I can get an audience to come. I can make money. I can continue to generate income for everybody else.

But is that the right thing to do? I tend to think not. Why did DiMaggio step away from the game? Why did Mantle leave? Why did these great athletes step away? 'Cause they loved the game too much to not play it well. And I know eventually I'm going to run out of the physical ability."

One song that seems to have a lifetime guarantee of being included in every full set list is "It's Still Rock and Roll to Me," with its demanding drum major routine of Billy twirling the microphone stand. The song was a significant hit, a number one in the summer of 1980, and despite a subsection of the audience who cordially loathe it, and his own admission that he can see why, Billy sticks by it.

He likewise doesn't repudiate what he and his forebears and peers once created: "It's an admirable format, the pop format. It's very hard to do, almost a miniature, and it's very hard to cram all this meaning and feeling into three minutes. And people might go, *Why don't you just challenge yourself to expand the song genre into your music writing?* But in a way it feels like kind of painting a moustache on my own original painting. I should be able to convey what I want with the music alone. That's what the great composers all did.

"I think there's a song cycle in every songwriter that eventually kind of runs out. There is an arc to creativity, especially with songs, that eventually peaks and then diminishes. And I'm not afraid to admit to that. Maybe the 'river of dreams' dried up. Because there's a line in the song—and I was always trying to figure out, why did I write that?—'So I can finally find out what I've been looking for.' That's a metaphor, I think, for how I always wanted to be better, to write better songs. And I got to a point where I said, *I can't be any better than this.* And I've tried. I tried and I tried, and I beat myself up and went through all kinds of emotional angst because of that. I'm not going to be any better than I am in that genre. I've done it."

RESOLVED AS BILLY may be on the topic, he would make time, during the mellow backstage hours prior to his L.A. shows, for a trio of meetings that may usher in another musical avenue. In meeting on back-to-back nights with two of the top five or so electronic dance music (EDM) deejays in the world, David Guetta and Avicii, he was on a path, should he decide to follow it, for sharing pop music's ascendant territory. The meetings came at the behest of the younger artists. Of Guetta, a Paris-based deejay ("no one has done more to make EDM part of the pop universe," says *Rolling Stone*) in his midforties, Billy remarks, "They say he's the biggest deejay in the world, which is a weird kind of category, like, 'most jumbo shrimp.'"

Yet Billy saw a possible avenue to work with him: "What he had to suggest is that you both go in the studio and you just try putting things together the way we do when I do my [traditional] thing—which is you take sounds and rhythms, and they get a beat and a pulse, and then they kind of flesh it out." After meeting with Avicii, a Stockholm-based deejay in his midtwenties whose "Wake Me Up" was a massive 2013 hit, Billy said, "He seems like a really bright guy too. And he's at that age where he wants to create, create, create, create. He was very enthusiastic about me writing something with him. Maybe it'll create some sparks. I said, 'There's nothing wrong with that. That's good.' So I'm going to give it a shot."

Yet another backstage meeting was with Universal Pictures executives who want to involve Billy in some forthcoming sound tracks, not just for the onscreen song uses called syncs, but as a composer. Though such assignments would interlock nicely with his new Universal Music publishing deal, he's staying open to offers from other studios: "There's talk about a remake of *The Magnificent Seven*, with some big-name guys. And the minute I saw that, I went, 'Yeah, I always wanted to write that sound track.' Because 'The Ballad of Billy the Kid' is kind of an homage to that Elmer Bernstein score."

All this activity was welcome news to Steve Cohen, who is sought after by the film as well as the music industry and would factor into any new planks Billy establishes. "If Billy were to decide to author something fresh again, I'd be really interested, because I think there are so many more layers to him. I think he is all the more an incredible artist now because of life experience. I think the craftsman that he is could probably sit down and pick up a new set of paints and just come up with something incredible."

"I think people have this idea," says Billy, "that Billy Joel is set in concrete. They either like my stuff or they don't like my stuff. They either like me or they don't like me. I don't think they really know a lot about what I can do. Maybe I don't even know anymore what we can do, what we can't do. But I suspect there's a lot more that I can do."

DURING HIS LOS ANGELES stand, Billy was spending his days in Santa Barbara in a house overlooking a long curve of shoreline. It offered ready access to hill-climbing two-lane roads, the kind ideally suited to the small gaggle of motorcycles his road crew had ferried across the country and loaded into his garage. Alexis gamely rode along with Billy on an expedition into the hills, her underpowered Vespa gruntingly trying to outpace the barreling delivery trucks that came up fast behind the pair. As Billy mused on the relationship, in comparison to the lost love with Katie Lee, he was reflective but upbeat: "She's exactly the same age as Katie [who was born in 1981], but she's from Long Island, not too far from Hicksville, so we have a lot more in common right off the bat."

A goodly part of the unusually comfortable philosophical resolve Billy seems to have found of late clearly comes from the fulfilling relationship he and Alexis have built from this foundation. He sums things up this way: "We've been together more than three years now, and she left her job. She went from Morgan Stanley over to Merrill Lynch and was having to schlep into the city, do the Wall Street commute, and was working well into the night. She took on a lot of work with the new job and would come back just stressed out. I said, 'Stop—life's too short.' I see how Wall Street firms, they chew people up, they just spit 'em out. Yeah, there are big bonuses handed out. But she was hitting her head against the glass ceiling. I said, 'Just hang out for a while. Take some time off. Live my lifestyle for a while. I'll cover you.' And it's been like that for a while now. And I like it. It's nice."

"Alexis made her own money. She has her own house. But she's decided she likes to live with me. We live together, and we get along really, really well. And she enjoys my cooking. I'm the housewife. She would come back from work, and I'd have dinner ready, and I'd clean up. 'How was your day, honey?' I'm a homey guy, so I kind of enjoy that. Things are very good. She's intelligent. Except we can't watch TV shows together. She likes *Seinfeld* and *Friends* and *Golden Girls.* And I'm watching the History Channel and MSNBC, and I'm always yelling at those sons of bitches—Rachel Maddow, she gets my blood going, she's so smart."

As a matter of fact, Alexis is a few degrees to the right of the multi-millionaire socialist Billy (a contradiction he jokingly asserts and embraces), and yet in another proof of love, that doesn't bother him much. "She's very good to me. Really very patient and kind and thoughtful, a lot of good things. As for the future growth of the relationship, I'm not closing any doors."

ANY ROMANCE UNDERTAKEN as late in life as Billy's—he celebrated his sixty-fifth birthday in May 2014 with eighteen thousand fans at the Garden—has to take account of the end game; ideally, you find a boon companion for the declining years, for which he's beginning to prepare. He says, "I've got to start setting that up, because decrepitude isn't that far off, and before I get too old to do the traveling and the schlepping and the organizing of it, maybe I should just get ready. It's a fun project. When I go, I'm going to go big time and do it right. Katie didn't get it. 'Why are you talking about death? It's so morbid.' I said, 'It's actually part of life, and I don't want to end up being caught short.' I've seen people who have these catastrophic illnesses when they're old, and then they're screwed, and they're stuck in a hospital room with a big, nasty old nurse. I want my nurses all picked out beforehand, from college. Send them to nursing school—I'll pay for it. I'll even pick out the outfits."

Billy has said that when he dies—and as a committed atheist, he's not anticipating any postmortem surprises, positive or negative—he'd like to buried in Bloomingdale's department store, "so my wives will come visit me." He also has at times had his eye on a small graveyard, a "burying ground" since the 1960s at a peaceful backroads intersection in Sagaponack, not far from his house on Gibson Lane there: "Recently my lawyer had me go over various documents, a will and a living will— after you're sixty or so, you'd better have that ready to go. So I thought about where I'd like to be interred. It would either be in that little grave- yard in Sagaponack or in Sag Harbor."

Of the former, he says, "I don't know if you're allowed to inter peo- ple there anymore. They could be maxed out, and it's not like calling the maître d' at a restaurant to get in. I don't think I'd like to be cremated— although it might have been kind of appropriate to have the ashes scat- tered in the water, since I'm such a water guy. But nope, I think I want my spot—just bury my ass in a nice little graveyard. I like real estate. I can't give up on the real estate. You can't take it with you, but maybe [the soil he lies in] can take me with it. There's something about it that's strangely comforting to know—I'm not going to be just another head- stone in one of these mass places; give me a nice little spot, and maybe have my family think of me as they drive by and throw a flower down once in a blue moon, maybe think about me.

"As much as I feel that I'm a lifelong native of Oyster Bay, I feel actually more of a kinship to Sag Harbor and the east end, because that really looks like the Long Island of my childhood, the greener, small- village feel things used to have when I was a kid. I think people are so conscious now about preserving what *is* left that this area may stay pretty much like this, not get developed like the rest of the island did and lose its soul. I'd like to be a son of Sag Harbor when I go."

As to any observances, he hasn't really thought about that in detail. "But," he says, "I don't want a religious ceremony. I don't want some priest or rabbi, waving their hands around. You keep those guys away from me. Music—I'm sure they'll probably play something of mine that's appropriate, maybe the Elegy, which is called 'The Great Peconic,' that would be nice. Or 'And So It Goes,' or 'Lullabye.' Alexa will probably pick out some kind of apt piece, and there are classical pieces I would find really emotionally appropriate, like Barber's 'Adagio' or a Beethoven piece. It would be nice if it was a simple local ceremony, and I do like churches. The old whaling church in Sag Harbor would be nice. Or however big they want to go with it, that's their call—hell, do it at the Cathedral of St. John the Divine. It should be more of a celebration than a dirge."

These days Alexa is never far from his thoughts. He naturally roots for her in her career and agonizes when, in her vulnerability, she has a setback of some sort, as in the late 2009 Traumeel incident, or in May 2014 when she collapsed onstage—though she was quickly revived without any aftereffects—during a Hotel Carlyle performing stint. Sometimes he wishes she had more skepticism about people and would put up more of a protective barrier between herself and an often hurtful world: "She likes to believe the best of people, will always give somebody the benefit of the doubt and doesn't have a shard of mistrust. And I'm trying to tell her, 'Yeah, you're Pinocchio,' just like sometimes I'm Pinocchio. That's where she gets it from."

Their shared, trusting nature reminds him of a scenario he's had in his head for a while—one he wishes he could figure out what to do about: "What would it be like if, when you were that eighteen-year-old idealistic, naïve, sweet kid, you met yourself at an advanced age?

"When I was eighteen, I was almost a socialist, and a liberal and an idealist and naïve. I trusted everybody and believed in the greatness of humanity and the kindness of strangers. And here I am, the sixty-plus-year-old—it would be an interesting meeting. What would I say to that eighteen-year-old and what would that eighteen-year-old say to me? Would he be disappointed in how I turned out, or would I think he was a young idiot and a fool?"

While Billy's innocence has been tempered by the betrayals that have dotted his personal and professional lives, the same forgiveness he has granted his transgressors like Frank Weber extends to a sometimes hostile universe: "Out of disasters and catastrophes, somehow or another, it all made everything possible. It's a good way of looking at things, I think. The management thing, if that disaster hadn't happened, I might have just stopped doing what I was doing. I was ready to kind of stop it all by the time of the *Bridge* album. I was getting tired of the treadmill then. But because I had to make back the money, and I was going to be recording more albums, that kind of lit a fire. You can go all the way back—if it hadn't been for the Nazis I never would have been here."

As Billy passes the Medicare age, sixty-five, the question remains—just where is "here"? At the simplest level, it's in his Centre Island house, a literal stone's throw from the oyster-strewn inlet where he worked long, chilly hours as kid. "Here" for now is also the road, or even the nearby confines of Madison Square Garden. If sports teams call their home arenas "our house," Billy, more than any other artist, and in fact by official proclamation as a franchise, can call the Garden home.

For Billy, his residency there comes down to a simple ethic: "I'm a working man. It's still a job. And I work very hard when I work." It reminds him of a discussion he and Bruce Springsteen had on a balmy day in Florida, looking back over their times and unlikely careers. "There's an element of luck and timing—absolutely, we caught the wave. We were at the right place the right time doing the right thing.

"But aside from the luck and the timing, there's a lot of dedication involved. You have to be completely committed, and it's not about being famous, and it's not about being a star. If I wasn't as big a star as somebody else at a certain time in my career, it wasn't an issue for me.

"It's your dedication to your craft that really separates the men from the boys."

AT SOME STAGE even a life lived in public must be recaptured, made one's own. Billy's life has never been an unexamined one: "I sometimes wonder, what if I had never lived at all, or what if my life had been cut short when I was young? You get what you get. Why are we being greedy and expecting more after that? Anything else is all made up. Mark Twain wrote a book about it called *The Mysterious Stranger*. The thesis is, because we have the power to reason, we came up with this whole afterlife thing. I've said since I was a kid—I don't believe in an afterlife. I think you're lucky to get what you get—so make sure that you live it well. And when you get to the end of things, you go, *Boy, did I do that right, or not?*

"While you're living it, you hope to ensure that you can ultimately say, *I did it as well as I could.* And then you got to learn to let go. In *Network*, sometime after admitting he's 'run out of bullshit,' Howard Beale says, 'This is not a psychotic breakdown, this is a cleansing moment of clarity.' I'm at that point in my life—I can see the end of things. And how am I going to come to grips with that? Dying is part of living. But you try to squeeze as much out of life as you can.

"I do have this theory that the person who steers us in the right direction is somewhere between the eighteen-year-old and the twenty-one-year-old, when you're at the height of your idealism. You get to middle age, and you'll know what the smart thing to do is, you'll know what the good business move is, the diplomatic or the accepted thing to do, but that eighteen- or twenty-one-year-old is the one that's telling you that's the right thing to do. And you can't fool that guy, and you're going to wrestle with him your whole life. He's a pain in the ass and he won't go away.

"I recognize him in myself. I hope I haven't compromised him too much because I have a lot of respect for that guy, even though he was naïve and he was foolish about a lot of things. It turned out he was wrong and self-destructive in some ways and was reckless and maybe inconsiderate, maybe self-absorbed, but he was full of idealism and always knew that the right thing to do was to be true to these ideals.

"I look back on the younger guy—who the hell was he? He was so ambitious, and he worked so hard, and he accomplished a lot. I almost don't recognize who that is at this point. What was your problem? Were you overcompensating, overachieving? What are you doing? Like almost listening to the words from 'Vienna'—'Slow down, you crazy child.' Like how about living your life a little bit? But this has been my life for a long time.

"Nobody's immortal, of course, and as much as I believe that someone like Beethoven will live as long as people listen to music, I don't know that my work has that kind of staying power. But I am glad that the music I've created over the past four-plus decades is an important part of a lot of people's lives. And I hope it lasts at least another four.

"I'm assuming some of my music will survive, either as I recorded it or in some other form. I don't look to that as a consolation, though. For me, I see it as a justification for my having existed in the first place. You've created something, you've had an impact on your time.

"I don't know why that is so important to me, but it is."

Billy Joel outside the family home on Meeting Lane in Hicksville, about to leave for a gig with his first band, The Echoes, in the summer of 1964. Once shy, the fifteen-year-old Billy was realizing, "I could make my piano talk for me." The career was underway.

AFTERWORD

Just after four p.m. on an overcast Minneapolis afternoon in mid-May of 2015, a state police cruiser rounds a corner of the Target Center and flies halfway down the block toward the metal door buck that is slowly grinding open. The cruiser swerves to a stop at a protective angle off the flank of the van it's been escorting, keeping watch as it disappears beyond the closing barrier.

The front passenger door of the van opens as the man who will be in the spotlight in four-plus hours disembarks from his usual front passenger seat, already the focus of all eyes. His cadre—what lighting man and show designer Steve Cohen calls a "light attack team"—scatters in several directions. From here on out, it's rock tour *Groundhog Day* for the crew and the local support teams of riggers, security, and hall workers. This is what Billy Joel does now—he visits the arenas of the nation, bearing a stature somewhere between a legend and a working stiff. As has been true since his earliest days traveling the highways in an overstuffed, wheezing station wagon, he wouldn't want it any other way.

The members of the van's small core-squad, who landed not long ago in a private charter jet from New York, individually make their way toward the hall's typical array of cinderblock retreats—offices large and small and locker rooms converted into dressing rooms. The black curtain at the back of the stage coughs out a few test blasts of the theatrical "smoke" that will subtly play into the lighting scheme later.

The mood is purposeful but light—very few live show-business events carry as strong a guarantee of success with the audience as a Billy Joel show does. Since his Madison Square residency began in January 2014, he's enjoyed a string of sold-out dates (the slated July 1, 2015, concert would soon break Elton John's record for any one act's appearances at the venue: sixty-five). In August, the native Long Islander will play the final show ever at the landmark arena that opened in 1972 just as his career began: the Nassau Coliseum. He's also been knocking off an additional one to three shows per month around the nation, including a headlining appearance at Bonnaroo in June. "I'll be supplying the dad rock," he japes, but the offer to headline at the summer's largest music festival, where the bulk of the acts are described by *Rolling Stone* as "thoroughly now," is further testimony to his surprisingly expanding demographic reach into the youth market. (*Entertainment Weekly* would later say that his live-streamed set before tens of thousands exhibited "a palpable joy that seemed to reach festival goers of all ages.")

The mood backstage is upbeat, Steve Cohen assures before heading to his mid-arena control center for sound check: "It's reconvening with the people we love and have spent so many years with. And the opportunity to live our lives and work on a schedule like this is a blessing—you don't generally have that in this business. And after all these years, to be able to do this—c'mon." He punctuates his point by fishing out one of the not-inexpensive cigars that are almost like a totem of the vices this road company once indulged in. Combine the principal performer's thirty-odd hits with the entire rolling circus's age, experience, and road wisdom, and there's a near certainty that there will be no untoward incidents with this gang these days.

The demands of treating audiences to a solid helping of those familiar hits means that the ongoing challenge is to find new ways to "interest up the set." It's a mission Joel devotedly oversees before each show.

Tonight in Minneapolis he and Cohen sit with the proposed set list before them, Cohen's urgings meeting amiably with Billy's veto power. The sound-check run-through with the band had produced some amusing oddities, including such evocatively Minnesotan songs as Prince's "Purple Rain," "1999," and "Raspberry Beret" (retitled by Joel as they worked on it to "Asbury Bidet," "Pillsbury Ballet"—a possible reference to what he called his current uncomfortable level of "girth"?—and "Robert Goulet") as well as Bob Dylan's "Mr. Tambourine Man" and "Like A Rolling Stone." The latter song would end up as a snippet in the show, though fortunately, as Joel led out of it into "Piano Man," he dialed back the quicksand-voiced Dylan mimicry he had deployed during sound check.

Joel sets comprise about twenty-four songs these days, and the audience usually gets to vote at least twice on proffered choices. "I'm always looking for obscurities," says Joel. "They don't always work, but I realize I have an entire well of hits that we can just put the dipper into. I thought if I put one next to another, I'd find out which ones work, which is why we started the whole audience participation."

Cohen acts as gatekeeper. Knowing that Joel squirmed during a recent set where he did "Just the Way You Are" next to "New York State of Mind " (the singer felt it was "a kind of mushy, middle-of-the-road part of the set"), Cohen now strolls up from the rear of the hall during the sound check to rule on a change: "Watch out for the two ballads in a row."

Just afterwards, Cohen notes, "My biggest concern is pace. . . . I come up and say, hey, let's not let it go too far off the rails." Cohen noticed recently that "Say Goodbye to Hollywood," with its quick pumping rhythm and uplifting tone, "was a good little pearl we found." His discussion with Joel tonight has them brooding over whether the ice fishermen of Minnesota could relate to the saltwater anglers of "The Downeaster Alexa." Cohen proposes setting it against "The Stranger"—a choice he admits just might be a "sandbag." (Indeed, the crowd roar would later handily elect "Downeaster.") Cohen says there's no point to the entire enterprise if the key man isn't having fun: "I just want him to be comfortable—to get the response he's looking for that feeds the show."

Both men seem rather proud of the set's almost Houdini-like big dare, in which Joel warns the crowd that he may not be able to hit the high notes in "An Innocent Man." That he does it sitting down enhances the stunt, Cohen says: "Is he gonna make it? It's not just a falsetto, it's a powered falsetto." Says Joel, "I thought I said goodbye to that note when I did that album in my thirties," referring to the Christie-Brinkley-inspired *An Innocent Man*. Cohen quickly notes, "That's a good line to use." Later, Joel repeats the story onstage: "I wrote the song when I was thirty-four; I'm sixty-six—anyway, it didn't work out, but I got a song out of it."

With the set as snugged down as planning can make it, and opener Gavin DeGraw onstage and faintly audible in the background, Joel leans back with his familiar popcorn supply handy and reflects on how well it's all going—especially since he recently learned (as the world would several months later) that his girlfriend of nearly six years' duration, Alexis Roderick, is pregnant with a daughter who's due to arrive in mid-August.

Observers, both public and private, have inveighed against the late-in-life fatherhood, but he's not buying it. "I have people going, 'What, are ya crazy? You're in your sixties, you'll never even gonna live to see the kid graduate from high school.'

"Look," he says evenly, "I've got longevity in my family—my dad lived to eighty-nine and my mom to ninety-three. I don't intend to check out anytime soon, and I'm living my life in such a way that I'm gonna have nothing but time with this child. And the limited amount of time I have with her will be longer than most fathers get to see their kids anyway. It's kinda weird, 'cause my mom passed away in July of 2014, and then [Alexis] started talking about having a kid—which I didn't think I would do. I had to kinda be convinced somewhat, and I thought, why not? May the circle be unbroken . . ."

He's mindful that his row of monthly Madison Square Garden concerts, combined with various other gigs, have made him one of music's top earners for the past couple of years, and shows no inclination at this stage to stop. "I'm flush. I've got good financials set up; I've got great places for a kid to grow up. . . . " Recently, Joel acquired a large estate and mansion near Palm Beach, Florida, bolstering his domestic comforts with "A-Rod." "I have nothing but time, and with Alexis—this is a good lady. She's the right one."

He confirms that there was some persuasion involved: "Yeah, she's at the prime of childbearing age [thirty-three]. They all want kids; they've all got that thing, and I don't want to deny her that. You can't always meet the exact right person at the exact right time to have the exact right family—some families are different. There must be another reason. It's as if it is written somewhere that 'you may have a child at this point in your life,' because everything is just hunky-dory. So why shouldn't another little creature enjoy some of the fruits I'm gonna leave her? Yeah, I'm older than Alexis, but she's very mature. She's the right one. She's gonna be a great mom, and it's gonna be a great situation.

"I'm still active," he says, as an assistant pulls his tie into a tight knot. (He'll loosen it later when he has to lead the vocal charge on the deeply harmonized "The Longest Time"). He slips on his black shoes in the casual sort of way he would after climbing barefoot onto his watercraft from the shoreline, more or less kicking them on. ("This is how you put on Prada's," he informs.) "I'm not this old, beat-up, tired guy sitting on a porch rocking in a chair. At sixty-six—" he gives a querulous sideways look as if the thought just occurred to him, "I'm almost peaking in my career right now."

Outside, the swelling strains of Randy Newman's soundtrack to *The Natural* are filling the hall, and the crowd is making a correspondingly eager noise, eighteen thousand strong. This time Joel's grin is more frank than bemused: "What else am I gonna do? Watch TV all my life? Try to find a good book to read?"

Joel's band is gathered around him in the overlit hallway as DeGraw and his bandmates traipse past. The younger artist is showing some sweat and his usual ebullient grin. (Much later that night, they'd be pounding out a Beatles medley together on a hotel piano.) "Thanks," DeGraw says, referring to logging yet another night's work, then, referring to the upcoming birth, "and congrats!" "Thanks," Joel says back, and offers a sidelong smile. In a fashion that's almost free of braggadocio, and more like a musical sensei offering his protégé some dutiful feedback, he tosses a comment over his shoulder as he turns for the stage: "Still got the mojo."

NOTE ON SOURCES

This book is the result of research and interviews dating back to mid-2008, commencing around the time of Billy Joel's landmark Shea Stadium concerts. Additional updates have been constantly added through the midsummer of 2014. All quotes from Billy, except where specifically otherwise attributed (including a pair of quotations from our 1985 interview for the *New York Daily News*), are from these approximately one hundred hours of interviews.

Beyond the interview sessions, I spent a significant amount of time in Billy's company, at various homes and on the road, as he toured North America, Japan, Australia, England, and Ireland. In hotel rooms and lobbies, in cars, vans, buses, trains, and aircraft large and small, Billy was patient with the myriad queries and thoughtful in his answers.

At least another hundred hours of interviewing has included his friends, family, relationship partners, bandmates, crew, and close colleagues of all stripes. Some of these speakers have been with him for many years (more than forty in at least three instances), some for just a few months. These intimates have been forthcoming, articulate, and of enormous help in recounting their shared history and entrusting their insights to this effort.

Another great asset has been the opening of the Joel archive for research. The archive's director, Jeff Schock, has been an invaluable resource. Beyond his indispensable firsthand recall from decades of working in close concert with Billy Joel, Jeff has freely shared the physical resources of a sizable collection of unique items. Along with its countless photos, illustrative materials, and transcripts, the archive is a rich trove of filmed and audio recordings of Billy Joel's doings and those of his bandmates, colleagues, and peers. Along with the actual footage of the various films and the videos of concerts, highly informative master classes, and press conferences, the outtakes from various documentary histories of his career have been crucial in telling the story.

A great deal of what was once called ink has been devoted to Billy Joel since the first reviews and features emerged forty-some years ago, and the often-impressive insights and observations of various writers have been credited as they appear. The reliably informed work of sometime colleagues at *Rolling Stone*, early and late, has been a particularly helpful resource. The Long Island newspaper of record, *Newsday*, especially in the person of pop music writer Glenn Gamboa, has been a steadily informative asset. I would also like to mention earlier biographies by Mark Bego, Hank Bordowitz, and Bill Smith. No such book of any heft is easy to write. Each effort inevitably adds context to a broader and hopefully deeper tale.

Special note should be made of the inclusion of some especially revealing and involving quotes Billy gave to the late Timothy White, a friend and colleague of mine at *Crawdaddy!* and *Rolling Stone*. Tim wrote the first cover stories on Joel in each magazine (over resistance in each case), tracked Billy's career through the years as he edited *Billboard* magazine, and contributed the liner notes for the sprawlingly comprehensive *My Lives* collection. Through the graciousness of his widow, Judy Garlan White, I was given access to his thorough and unparalleled trove of interviews and articles, including some material coming to light for the first time.

Also deserving of special mention is the United States Holocaust Memorial Museum, notably Ron Coleman of the museum's resource center. Not only did his help in exploring the archive's deep documentation confirm time lines and events of the Joel family's perils within and escape from Nazi Germany, his added historical information and context enhanced the account at both a highly personal level and a more universal one. (Through that research, Billy Joel would learn for the first time of a Holocaust survivor, cousin to his father Howard, who made it to America and is buried near Billy's present home.) The museum's work is a vital link to the past and could not have been more helpful to this particular effort.

Very much of a piece with the museum's important work is that of distinguished film and theater director filmmaker Beate Thalberg, whose 2001 documentary *The Joel Files* was key to this book's effort to capture both the factual and the spiritual implications of what Billy Joel's forebears endured in the Holocaust. Like Alexander Joel, Billy's half-brother whose life story led Thalberg into the larger story told in the film, she has been a friend to this project.

PHOTO CREDITS

ACKNOWLEDGMENTS

Thanks must first go to Billy Joel himself, for his music, which has intertwined with his life as he has written and performed it over the past few decades.

With the help and understanding of various members of Billy's support team, and with the guidance of my agent David Vigliano, arrangements were made with New York–based Crown Archetype, an imprint of Penguin Random House, to write this book based on extensive interviews and research.

From the outset, the team at Crown, including my editor, Matt Inman, never missed a beat. Perhaps no writer should confess how very vital was the role Matt played in ways large and small. He was indefatigable, impeccably attuned to both the orderly and creative aspects of the effort, and had his eye on every comma while never losing sight of the larger picture. Willing and expert help from his editorial colleague's Julia Elliott and Jenni Zellner and the copy, art, and production departments has meant that any flaws are mine, but the ultimate result owes many thanks to them. Also, many thanks to the publicity and marketing teams at Crown, including Ellen Folan, Tammy Blake, and Julie Cepler.

The team around Billy Joel is an exceptionally able and amiable one.

I'm grateful for the help of his longstanding creative touchstones, Steve Cohen and Brian Ruggles, and to tour director Max Loubiere, tour manager Mike Grizel, assistant road manager Bill Zampino, security man Noel Rush, assistant tour manager Mickey Heyes, personal assistant Keri Aylward, production manager Bobby Thrasher, deputy Liz Mahon, piano tech and all-around problem solver Wayne Williams, and guitar tech Ricky "Chainsaw" LaPointe.

The crackerjack band that's been traveling with Billy for the past several years includes Dave Rosenthal on a variety of keyboards, who's achieved a kind of concert master stature in his three decades with Billy; Mark Rivera on sax, vocals, guitar, flute, and even a little cowbell and other percussion touches, perhaps matched in his versatility and showmanship only by Crystal Taliefero on percussion, guitar, saxophone, and vocals; Andy Cichon on bass and vocals; Chuck Burgi on drums (including many a strategic rim shot); and Carl Fischer, much lauded for his trumpet and flugelhorn solos. Guitarist Tommy Byrnes brings great chops and stage presence. Utility player Mike DelGuidice has also become an essential addition.

Key help has come from folks at his label, Columbia, and other support staff. Booking agent Dennis Arfa has been a savvy guide since very near the beginning, and publicist Claire Mercuri brings her expertise and has been a steady confidante and protective presence for Billy for many years. Archivist Jeff Schock's assistance and insight have been crucial in completing this book. Lance Freed and Rondor Music lent crucial help. Motorcycle savant Alex Puls and Gene Pelland, skipper to Billy's small fleet of boats, bring their own unique skills.

To the many willing folks who were interviewed and who appear in these pages, sincere appreciation. Jann Wenner of *Rolling Stone* shared his archives and his insight. I was immeasurably buoyed along the way by my brain trust of Jason Fine, Roger Director, Dave Hirshey, Doug Lane, Guy Martin, Gil Schwartz, Michael Solomon, Bob Wallace, and James Webster. Thanks to Gil Schwartz and Laura Svienty, Richard and Kristina Ford, and to Tripp and Holly Frieldler for warm hospitality along the way.

Going back many years to the generous support of the Labor, Industry and Commerce Organization of Students, especially founder Stephen McWilliams, I offer everlasting thanks.

You too, Hoods!

To my beloved wife, Kate, and my son, Ridley, all my love and gratitude for hanging in, time and again and always, while I was on the road or deeply enmeshed in the work.

My ultimate thanks go to the readers of this book.

INDEX